GEORGE OPPEN
MAN AND POET

MLA

THE MAN AND POET SERIES

Louis Zukofsky: Man and Poet
Edited by Carroll F. Terrell, 1979

Basil Bunting: Man and Poet
Edited by Carroll F. Terrell, 1980

George Oppen: Man and Poet
Edited by Burton Hatlen, 1981

In Process

May Sarton: Woman and Poet
Edited by Constance Hunting, 1982

William Carlos Williams: Man and Poet
Edited by Carroll F. Terrell, 1983

Charles Reznikoff: Man and Poet
Edited by Milton Hindus, 1984

Charles Olson: Man and Poet

TO
GEORGE AND MARY OPPEN

GEORGE OPPEN

NATIONAL
POETRY
FOUNDATION, INC.
UNIVERSITY OF MAINE AT ORONO

Man and Poet

Edited
with an introduction by
Burton Hatlen

Published by

The National Poetry Foundation
University of Maine at Orono
Orono, Maine 04469

Printed by

The University of Maine at Orono
Printing Office

The National Poetry Foundation
University of Maine at Orono
Orono, Maine 04469

Library of Congress No. 81-83386
ISBN 0-915032-53-8

PREFACE

When Oppen's *Collected Poems* was published in 1975, Hugh Kenner noted with some trepidation the prospect that Oppen might soon become a candidate for admission to the academic literary canon: "All those years, academe (alas) is about to discover, an *Oeuvre* has been growing." Indeed, academe has been slow to discover Oppen: one dissertation, a half dozen extended articles of criticism, a dozen or so important reviews—until 1980 these were the only critical writings on Oppen that a serious student would feel compelled to consult. The very existence of the present book demonstrates, however, that academe is beginning to discover Oppen. And the sheer bulk of this book, as contrasted with Oppen's own abstemiously lean *oeuvre*, may tempt some readers to echo Kenner's "alas." But Kenner himself, in his review, almost immediately (and to his credit, for after all he is himself an academic) retracts, or at least qualifies, his "alas": "Alas, but why not? Academe is what takes care of Poetry for us, and we may as well not begrudge it something substantial." Kenner is here, I think, right. For better or for worse, academe has assumed responsibility for the care of poetry, and the present volume demonstrates that the list of poets that academe cares about (and for) now includes George Oppen. And if literary critics are beginning to discover Oppen, it is not because we feel a self-serving need to create a new academic "industry," or because we have a perverse desire to supplant the lean elegance of Oppen's poetic discourse with the more turgid discourse of academic literary criticism. Rather it is because his poetry does offer us something, in Kenner's word, "substantial"—something which we sense to be new and important. His poetry opens up new possibilities of language. Both his poetry and his life (with Mary, always—we cannot imagine them *not* together) define a certain way of being in the world which many of us feel we must understand, if we are to know how to live our own lives. In writing about Oppen, then, we are (most of us at least) struggling to articulate to ourselves precisely what is new and important about the example that Oppen offers us. Thus the present volume of writing *about* Oppen, no less than the collection of personal tributes offered *to* Oppen in the recent special issue of *Paideuma*, constitutes an act of homage, and I hope it will be accepted as such.

In preparing this volume, I am indebted first of all to George and Mary Oppen themselves, who have assisted in a variety of ways throughout this project.

My second major debt is to Carroll F. Terrell, who conceived the "Man and Poet" series (soon to include some "Woman and Poet" volumes as well), who himself edited the first two volumes in the series (*Louis Zukofsky: Man and Poet*, published in 1979, and *Basil Bunting: Man and Poet*, published in 1980), and who provided general editorial guidance and day-to-day advice, assistance, and support throughout my work on this book. Terry has established the pattern for the books in this series: the Zukofsky and Bunting books were "benchmark" volumes, designed to serve as a starting point for future scholarly and critical work on the poet to whom the volume is dedicated. Both these volumes were given over to essays on a poet whose work had not previously received the attention it deserves, and the books were designed, not to be "definitive," but rather to make information about a neglected poet available to a wide audience, and to serve as a stimulus for further work. In all these respects this volume seeks to follow the pattern of its predecessors. (The same will also be true of subsequent volumes in this series, which will be issued at a rate of approximately one volume a year. Volumes on May Sarton, H.D., and William Carlos Williams are currently in preparation.)

I have many other miscellaneous debts: to Michael Alpert, who first introduced me to Oppen's work, and whose own life and art display an integrity worthy of Oppen himself; to Marie Alpert, who typeset most of the book, patiently correcting my errors along the way; to Sharon Stover, who, no less patiently, typeset the rest of the book; to Julie Courant, my research assistant for a year, who assumed charge of many matters bibliographic and editorial, who not only helped write but who typed a good portion of the manuscript of the Annotated Bibliography, and who amid all this managed to preserve her own love for the words of George Oppen; to Marilyn Emerick, who typed many portions of the manuscript; to Cathleen Bauschatz, the most meticulous and patient of proof-readers, who also prepared, with the help of Paul Vatallaro, the Index to this volume; to David McAleavey, whose diligent work alone made the

"Testament" section possible; to the members of the Interlibrary Loan department of the University of Maine library, who patiently searched out for me essays from the most obscure of journals; to the University of Maine Faculty Research Fund, which provided support during my work on this project; to my colleagues in the University of Maine Department of English, especially my fellow Oppenite Harvey Kail, for their advice and support; to my wife Barbara and my children Julie and Inger, for tolerating my often distracted behavior during the preparation of this volume; and above all to the contributors to the volume itself, who seldom violated my deadlines, and who without exception responded promptly and graciously to my editorial queries and suggestions.

This volume is not, repeat NOT, a reprint of the special issue of *Paideuma* devoted to George Oppen. Rather, the contents of this volume consists almost entirely of new work, never before published. The only exceptions are as follows: In Part One, ("The Milieu") some portions of the essay by Rachel Blau DuPlessis appeared previously in her essay "Oppen and Pound" (*Paideuma*, 10, 1 [Spring 1981], 59-83). And Part Three, "The Canon," reprints William Carlos Williams' classic 1934 review of *Discrete Series* (from *Poetry*, 44, 4 [July 1934], 220-5), together with four valuable discussions of Oppen's recent work: the essays of Donald Davie (From *Grosseteste Review*, 6, 1-4 (1973), 233-9), Michael Hamburger (from *Art as Second Nature* [Manchester: Carcanet Press, 1975], pp. 153-6) and Michael Heller (from the *American Poetry Review*, 4, 22 [March/April 1975], 1-4) on *Seascape: Needle's Eye*, and Ted Enslin's essay on *Primitive* (from *American Book Review*, January, 1979). The Williams's essay is reprinted with the permission of the Williams's estate; the essays by Davie, Heller, Hamburger, and Enslin are reprinted with the permission of the authors.

B.H.
Orono, Maine
August, 1981

TABLE OF CONTENTS

THE METHOD

THE CANON

Discrete Series

Middle Period

Recent Work

THE TESTAMENT

BURTON HATLEN

INTRODUCTION

George stood a few steps up the stairs to the second floor dining room (Does the house have a ground floor? I never found out) of their Polk Street house in San Francisco (rows of two-storey stucco houses, mostly pastel, curlicues of wood on the cornices), to greet us: three academics, Marjorie Perloff, Carroll Terrell, me, all of us feeling a little presumptuous, in town for the MLA Convention, come to talk about a book on his life and work—*this* book in fact. Smiling, a little diffident, apologetic even (Mary has gone out, she'll be back in a few minutes), but facing us squarely, giving nothing away, but open (the half-pun on his name seems irresistible) to anything, and truly glad to see us. Just like an Oppen poem, I thought. Then up the stairs—and to our delight, Charles Tomlinson too, also in town for the MLA Convention. And a few minutes later, Mary, with Mrs. Tomlinson. Mary, energetic, cagey, sizing us up. George and Mary turning upon a single, unseen center, always more attuned to each other (no words needed, after all these years) than to anyone else in the room. And an hour of talk into the tape recorder: of Pound and Zukofsky, poetry and politics. (But afterward the tape turned out to be unuseable: George's voice so soft as to be inaudible, though Mary's voice came through rich and clear.) Then off, back to the downtown convention hotel. And Marjorie Perloff in the taxi afterward: "Maybe I'm giving away my vintage, but when I hear someone talking about Communism I get very nervous. But the poetry...." Ah, the poetry.

Oppen's presence, no less than his poems, radiates (to me, anyway) a constant integrity that both shames and inspires. He writes slower than anyone, he told us. Each word weighed—*not* because he insists that every word be heavy, but because he wants every word to have exactly the *right* weight. "To" and "and" have their own weight, however slight, and he wants to respect that weight absolutely. On the other end of the scale, the weight of "humanity" is vastly greater than we can bear, although we must try. Here is a writer who *means* every word he says. By contrast, his example forces us to recognize how many light, loose words the rest of us allow to slip from our tongues, or our typewriters. An anecdote may serve to illustrate the poetic integrity of George Oppen. While I was preparing this book, I wrote to the Oppens asking permission to gather together and print the poems which he had published in one place or another, but which he had excluded from the *Collected Poems*. "I realize you had your reasons for leaving these poems out," I wrote. "But sooner or later your readers will want to find these poems, so why not make life simpler for them?" The answer came back: a firm, polite "No." I was disappointed, but as I thought about this response I soon realized that in this matter Oppen not only had the right, but also *was* right. The excluded poems, in his eyes, fall short. He wants them forgotten. That they *won't* be forgotten is no business of his. He has made his decision, and he will stick with it. What we see here is a man with no interest whatever in playing the game called "literary oneupmanship." There's only one game (may the spirit of Wittgenstein here hover over this word!) he is interested in playing, and that game is called Truth. And if the world doesn't care to join in, that's the world's problem. In the face of such rigorous integrity, almost all of us (for most of us are playing games called "careers," or "success") must feel a little ashamed. Yet Oppen does not offer himself to us as a unique "genius." He has no interest in ego games either, no impulse to display for us his brilliance; and he neither seeks nor needs our applause. Rather he wants to write the unwritten poem of humanity, and of necessity he must write his poem as Everyman. Thus his poems reveal to us not so much his own achievements in clear sight, rigorous thought, and forthright action as our own such potentialities, yet largely unrealized. While his example is chastening, then, it is also inspiring. And this is, I think, the reason why this poet who has refused to bend to the world, now finds the world (as the very existence of this present book attests) bending to him.[1]

---

1. Zukofsky, Reznikoff, Niedecker, Bunting, Rakosi—all the major Objectivists display a similar kind of integrity. All were willing to work patiently away for years in total obscurity, concerned only with the work to be done, the task at hand. The exception may be Zukofsky, who did seem to crave success, and who sometimes voiced bitterness at the failure of "the world" to recognize his achievements. Yet even Zukofsky

Oppen has always opened himself to the world. Therefore it seems appropriate that the first section of this volume should be given over to writings which in one way or another help us to recover and to understand the milieu in which he has lived. This section of the book begins with some words by George Oppen himself, first as orchestrated by Harvey Shapiro and then as recorded in a four-way conversation among George and Mary Oppen, Tom Mandel, and me. In the third piece in the "Milieu" section, we hear, too briefly, the voice of Mary Oppen, George's inseparable companion for over fifty years now, speaking of an important part of their world: the Maine coast where they spent their summers for many years. There follows a group of six essays, each of which attempts to place Oppen in one or another philosophic, poetic, or political context. John Peck explores Oppen's relationship to a tradition of systematic thought on the nature of the *polis*; Randy Chilton seeks to establish his relationship to the tradition of metaphysical thought that Heidegger sought to maintain; Paul Lake places Oppen within an essentially religious tradition; Rachel DuPlessis examines Oppen's transmutation of the heritage of poetic modernism by focussing on his relationship to his principal poetic "father," Ezra Pound, while Edward Hirsch further elaborates this theme through a discussion of Oppen's relationship to one of his poetic "sons"—or nephew at least—Charles Tomlinson; and Eric Mottram and Eric Homberger both attempt to define Oppen's relationship to the socialist/communist political tradition.

The essays in the second section of this book focus on his poetic method. (I wanted to title this section "The Poetic," but the phrase seemed a little ambiguous: thus I have called the section simply "The Method.") Again this section begins with some words of Oppen himself: a group of fascinating "outtakes" from Dembo's famous 1969 interview with the poet. In these previously unpublished portions of this interview, Oppen discusses in depth some specific poems. In the ensuing group of

---

(and on this point I think Oppen is wrong—cf. his comments on Zukofsky in the interview below, pp. 23-50) never allowed his desire for fame to corrode his absolute fidelity to his craft. How many examples of this sort of integrity can we find among more recent poets? Olson popularized an alternative model: the poet as supreme showman, the resourceful entrepreneur. And the poets of the Black Mountain generation have generally followed the example of Olson, rather than the example of Zukofsky. There are exceptions—but an Eigner, for example, seems like an isolated "case," rather than a representative of a school. Is the fading of the kind of integrity I have here described related in some way to the consolidation of the academic monopoly, which offered poets (the "counter-culture" poets no less than the "academic" poets) an opportunity for "careers," i.e., money and power—but at what a price?

essays, Marjorie Perloff looks carefully at Oppen's prosody; Michael André Bernstein articulates his sense of the distinctive honesty and integrity that radiates from Oppen's poetry. Abby Shapiro analyzes the "cubist" qualities of Oppen's poetry; and Hugh Seidman and Harvey Kail both explicate in detail specific poems by Oppen.

In the longest section of the book, "the Canon," I have gathered a series of essays which collectively offer a systematic examination of Oppen's poetic *oeuvre*. First come three essays on *Discrete Series*: William Carlos Williams's 1934 review of the book, and two thorough explications by Tom Sharp and Harold Schimmel. A second sub-section, "The Middle Period," includes an essay by me on *The Materials*, an essay by Norman Finkelstein on *This In Which*, and two essays one short and one long—on *Of Being Numerous*, by Henry Weinfield and David McAleavey. The third sub-section, "Recent Work," includes essays by Donald Davie, Michael Hamburger, and Michael Heller on *Seascape: Needle's Eye*, and essays by Norman Finkelstein and Ted Enslin on *Primitive*.

This volume, following the pattern established by the previous volumes in this series, concludes with a bibliography of critical materials on Oppen's poetry. This bibliographic section ("The Testament") is in two parts. First comes a listing alphabetical by authors, of essays, reviews, etc. on Oppen's work, prepared by David McAleavey. This is followed by an annotated chronological bibliography which offers summaries (and sometimes extensive extracts) of all significant reviews, essays, dissertations, etc. on Oppen's work to date. The chronological structure of this bibliography allows the reader to re-trace th the dialogue that has occurred among literary critics as they have sought to come to terms with Oppen's poetry, and to watch the graduale emergence of a consensus among the critics that Oppen is one of the major poets of our time. (Two final notes: 1) The reader who wants a complete bibliography of Oppen's own writings should consult the special issue of *Paideuma* devoted to Oppen's work. 2) For bibliographic purposes, we have treated interviews with Oppen as works by him, rather than about him. Thus such interviews do not appear in the bibliographies in this volume; instead these interviews are listed in the bibliography of Oppen's work which David McAleavey prepared for the *Paideuma* special.)

All the contributors to this volume worked independently of one another. As a consequence, the attentive reader will discover some overlaps in the essays that follow. I take heart from these overlaps: when two minds arrive independently at the same conclusion, there seems to be good reason for accepting this conclusion itself as valid. On the other hand, the careful reader will also discover some disagreements among the critics who have contributed to this volume. In particular, the "apolitical" critics (Lake, McAleavey, perhaps Peck) seem to line up in opposition to the more "political" critics (Finkelstein, DuPlessis, Mottram—and me). I have made no attempt to resolve these differences of opinion. If criticism is (as I believe) a dialectical mode of discourse, then disagreements such as those which appear in this volume should be welcomed as openings to further critical work. In any case, my goal here has been to let a hundred voices sing, rather than to promulgate a single, putatively "correct" reading of George Oppen's life and work.

In summary, this book is not intended as a definitive statement of any kind. It is intended to perform a simple function: to introduce the poet and his work to those readers for whom George Oppen has heretofore been little more than a name. I have been directed by a desire to answer all the first questions of such readers and to direct them where to go to find out more.

So much for the menu. The feast follows.

THE MILIEU

George & Linda Oppen. Photograph 1958, courtesy of Mary Oppen.

HARVEY SHAPIRO

BROOKLYN/SAN FRANCISCO

In that small apartment,
tenement rooms really,
on the other side of Atlantic Avenue,
windows braced with clear plastic
against the wind off the east river.
The words slow, the jumps between the words,
as in the poetry.

"We walk. We walked up Tamalpais —
the final peak, which is almost
a steeple. Wonderful   So high
the ocean curved I thought
and pieces of fog went below us

Occurrences — events   the heavy events ——
and down or someplace to the toys
of everyday, small self-interest,
the wings of the wasp

I think of you reading
the three old Jews who look down.
Well —— the three old Jews including Freud
look down, and cluck their tongues,
they always did, they've always been there,
I've heard them clucking —— they sure
clucked over me as a G.I., and
they're clucking now
like crickets in a summer evening

I think the new poems are good
sparse but they move
and yet I wanted them to move elsewhere
Toward greater self-satisfaction?
I guess that's it. Greater complacency.
Drift and drift and drift: the image
everywhere is the sea and its horizon.
Everywhere in my mind too

For all my metaphors of the sea,
  they think our feet ain't wet   in moments
of anger they suspect
we aren't drowning
                and they're wrong,
they're wrong, but I see the point
Brilliant and beautiful young people

There comes to me
a variation of that parable
about the note found outside an orphan asylum,
adjusted to the poet:
'To Whoever Understands This: I love you.'

However: the walks!   and just places
cafes   stores   I think we haven't
felt such excitement together
since we were first in Paris
on the great venture"

Note: the words within the quotation marks were selected from letters
George Oppen sent to me. [H.S.]

BURTON HATLEN and TOM MANDEL

POETRY AND POLITICS:
A CONVERSATION WITH GEORGE AND MARY OPPEN

NOTE: The following is a transcription of a conversation recorded in the dining room of George and Mary Oppen's house in San Francisco, in late June, 1980. The Oppens and Tom Mandel reviewed the transcription and suggested some minor changes. I then edited the transcription to exclude several anecdotes which had already appeared in print, either in Mary's *Meaning A Life* or in one or another of the published interviews with George or with George and Mary. In editing the transcription, however, I have attempted to preserve the flavor of an actual conversation, and therefore I have left in a certain amount of repetition and plain banter.

Before we went to the Oppens' house, Tom Mandel and I had agreed that we would try to keep the conversation focussed on the relationship between George's poetry and the political concerns that largely shaped the lives of the Oppens from the mid-1930s to the late 1950s. Our attempt to control the focus of the conversation was (perhaps fortunately) not entirely successful. Yet we believe that the unique value of this conversation is the new perspective which it offers on the long hiatus in George Oppen's poetic career during the years in which he and Mary lived chiefly within the orbit of the Communist Party.

Dramatis Personae

GO	George Oppen
MO	Mary Oppen
BH	Burton Hatlen
TM	Tom Mandel

† † † † †

BH—One of the reasons I'm interested in your work is that the modernist tradition in America, the one that is officially approved within the academic establishment, tends to be politically very conservative: Eliot, Pound, etc. And it seems to me that your work represents some sort of alternative to that. Yet the fact that you stopped writing poetry when you became politically active also suggests to me that you make in your mind some sort of division between the two, and then that the return to poetry in some ways represented a giving up of political activism.

GO—At that time, the time of the Second World War, poetry was not the most important thing in the world.

MO—Or in the 30s.

GO—Or in the 30s.

BH—But some writers, Tom McGrath, for instance, went into the Communist Party, or were at least close to it, yet continued to write, whereas you did not.

TM—Is it true, George, that you stopped writing altogether, or is it more accurate to say you stopped publishing and being active as a poet?

MO—He stopped writing.

GO—I stopped writing, yes.

MO—The political action became imperative and we looked around and there wasn't any way to continue in the style of life which we had been leading and meet these very urgent political problems that faced us when we came home from France where we had been working at publishing. George had a book ready for the Objectivist Press right at that moment and we went ahead and published. I don't think George even looked at the book, nor did he read the reviews. We looked at them later as people presented them to us.

TM—The book you're referring to is *Discrete Series*?

MO—Yes.

GO—That poetry was not the most important thing in the world at that time or saying, in brief, it took 25 years to write the next poem means. . . .

MO—. . . when we came home it was imperative to do something about the things we saw on the streets and we looked around for some way to be active and we found that the left was. . . .

GO—It means we knew we didn't know enough from the poetry that was being written; from the poetry that we had written. And when the crisis occurred we knew we didn't know what the world was and we knew we had to find out so it was a poetic exploration at the same time that it was an action of conscience, of feeling that one was worth something or other. And I thought most of the poets didn't know about the world as a life—so that I fairly easily gave up a great many poetic friends. (*Laughter*)

TM—But that does cast a different light on your decision to stop writing. It wasn't that politics and poetry were alternatives but that you realized that you didn't know enough to continue writing poetry, that you had to know more about the world.

GO—Right.

MO—I'd put it this way: there wasn't enough in that poetry for the politics. But by the time we finished with the politics there was plenty for the poetry.

GO—That's what I meant. I think that's well said.

BH—So you do feel there is a relationship between your political concerns and the poetry, at least at the other end of the process.

GO—Sure, sure.

BH—Would you try to say how you perceive that relationship? I mean, you're not writing political poetry in any sense of poetry as a weapon. . . .

GO—I think I said before I write about the world. Which could be understood metaphysically, too. And I wanted to know a great deal about it and I thought most of the poetry was utterly inadequate.

TM—What were you thinking of . . . what poetry were you thinking of?

GO—Well, this skips and really partly changes the subject but there were some other bad blows, Pound—the position that he took. Williams was a populist, but he really didn't know what he was talking about. Ah, Eliot, Yeats.

TM—Wouldn't it be fair to say that part of your decision to stop writing came not just from the way the world looked to you, and which you described very vividly, Mary, in your book, coming back from Europe and seeing the state of things—but also the reaction to what you saw in the world of poetry or you saw among poets?

GO—We were disappointed.

TM—I would take issue with the idea that the tradition of Modernism is itself a right wing tradition. Yet it is true that it did become institutionalized in America in a very right wing position and there really wasn't anything to do about it at that point in the 30s. There really wasn't any way to retain a modernist stance in writing and fight that hegemony of the dons, of Eliot, the Church of England, and of agrarianism.

GO—Yes. It took 25 years to write the next poem. And it was a difficult poem to write for the reasons you're saying.

MO—There was also Brecht, and there were other trends in political writing, but I think that that came in at a slightly different time in the United States. If you think of East German poetry which has been written since the Second World War, it's certainly political poetry.

BH—Well, in some ways the American example seems to me a sort of anomaly because modernism in Latin America, for example, is decidedly a politically conscious kind of movement—and in France for that matter. What about a writer like Pound? It's clear that as a writer, let's say, before you made this break, he was very important to you and how do you see him now? That is, can you see him as an important writer despite the politics or. . . .

GO—We wept on each other in the New Directions office, that's what happened.

MO—In 1969.

GO—And I don't know how sincere he was or wasn't. That was when Pound visited the U.S. and Jay Laughlin had arranged small groups to talk to Pound. Everyone was somewhat afraid that. . . .

MO—We met in Jay's office. . . .

GO—We met in Jay's office—that was our little group—he wanted to keep the groups small so that the news shouldn't break out that Pound was roaming around free or anything of that sort that might make waves. And we were waiting for Pound to come in and ah, making chatter and finally Pound arrived with Olga and sat absolutely dead silent and everybody became nervous and started chattering and Jay had a moment of inspiration and said, "Ezra, show George your new book." And Pound in a sepulchral voice

said, "How do I know he wants it?" You understand well enough
what that means. So I stood up and walked over to him and held
my hand out and said, "I want it"—a very dramatic thing—and
Pound stood up and once he stood he was very close to me. We
were in fact touching, and Pound began to weep so I wept. So we
went home. Neither of us could speak so we went home, and it's
impossible to understand. . . .

MO—That book?

GO—No, to understand Pound.

MO—But that book also had the blacked out phrases and so on
that Jay would not print—the unspeakable and anti-semitic. . . .

GO—I think Pound in fact was caught in the idea of being "macho"
though the word didn't exist at that time. He was going to be the
pounding poet, the masculine poet.

TM—I think, to me the most striking example is in the *Objectivist
Anthology* when Zukofsky asked for a contribution from Pound
and Pound sent him this stinking fish, you know, this incredible
anti-semitic, anti-black ballad which Zukofsky proceeded to print!

MO—What piece is that?

TM—I no longer remember the title if it has one. It starts "Gentle
Jheezus sleek and wild" and is full of imprecise Yiddish and black
dialect. The piece is supposed to be "jazzy," jazz being another of
the many subjects upon which Pound expounded without the
restrictions of any real acquaintance let alone understanding.

MO—Was it two sides to Pound? This is such an old discussion by
now.

GO—Yes.

TM—Maybe we should talk rather more about what prompted the
decison to begin writing poetry again. Was it a conscious decision
or. . . .

MO—You have a wonderful story about that dream in Mexico in
which you were driving along the street. I was going to a psychiatrist. I was very upset about coming back to the United States.
I'd been full of courage going to Mexico, taking the family there
and so that for me, the fear really hit when we were about to
come back to the United States and I was truly upset and very
very depressed and I went to a psychiatrist and in fact he was the
first psychiatrist in Mexico. He was American-trained. He turned
out to be an extremely fine young man. And wanted to see our
daughter and he wanted to see George so George went to see him

once or twice and had a dream. And in this dream—this is how I remember it—you dreamed that your father, that you and your sister were going through your father's papers after he died and in a drawer marked miscellaneous was a. . . .

GO—A pamphlet titled "How To Prevent Rot, Rust, in Copper." It was one of those dreams in which you fool yourself. I woke up laughing hilariously and saying to myself I'm unfair to my father even in my dreams—and I told this to the psychiatrist still laughing and of course that I was laughing outrageously was duck soup to the psychiatrist who said, "You dreamt that you're not going to rot." And I said thank you and went home.

MO—And bought your paper and pencil on the way home.

GO—Right. I'm sorry for you guys cause I've told everything to everybody whether they asked or didn't ask and whether I knew them or not. (*Laughter*)

BH—Well, I have a few more questions here.

GO—Might as well go on and do it.

BH—Is Marx as a writer important in your thinking and your work?

MO—Both of us refer to Marx as something basic from which to proceed. I don't know any other economist that I would look to for information on which to base my ideas.

BH—Were there others that seemed to you a key to . . . key thinkers to help you understand the world better, social or political thinkers?

GO—I think we were rather isolated people and that we wanted out of that situation, and I think we wanted to see a poetry that embraced more than poetry was embracing at that time.

BH—In a sense there are two ways of being "left"—you can sit in a university and write about Marxism or you can go out and do something. My sense is that the latter was the direction in which you went—that is, you weren't interested in an academic sort of radicalism. But when you say you needed to understand more. . . .

GO—Yes. I think that's very important.

BH—There were two sides to it, too. There was action as a means of understanding and vice-versa.

GO—Yes. I think it was very important. Reznikoff also wanted to know exactly what was going on out there which I think is a line by me. I think I wrote that and he wrote *Testimony*. The first little volume labeled *Testimony* is a wonderful piece of work. After that Rezy made a mistake. He came to the conclusion, because he had a certain amount of background as a lawyer, that what was said in court was the absolute truth, because this has been said and so on. And that was a very obvious mistake. As a matter of fact it's doubtful if anything that is true is ever said in court under the rules of testimony and so on. It was certainly a mistake. The first book was beautiful. I'm just telling this story to show you that a mistake can be made and Reznikoff certainly made a mistake there. He also wanted to know what was really going on out there and made the mistake of turning to the damn law courts.

MO—Where his poetry really is what's happening on the streets.

GO—Yes. His poetry is marvelous.

MO—And I think that both of us feel that it's rather sad that in Britain and here the books *Testimony* are the ones which are being noted and being commented upon and are more popular in the book stores and the poetry is, I don't know, being overlooked somewhat, though Black Sparrow I think has done a good job of getting it all in print. I don't see it in the book stores . . . and *Testimony* is in the book stores.

TM—Maybe because it's the most recent of the big publications.

MO—That's possible.

TM—But in the case of Reznikoff, he felt that the continuation of his craft was a way to get the world into poetry, was a way to write poetry. Whereas at a certain point that was not your decision. I mean quite consciously and fairly abruptly it seemed to you that you could not write poetry. I take it that you could not write poetry that really took in the world or understood the world with the stance that you had, with the information and experience that you had.

GO—Quoting Rezy, too, "We wanted to be ourselves among the rubble" which held us half in and half out of political doings. And that line to me is one of the most powerful lines in poetry.

MO—"The girder . . . "

GO—"The girder still itself among the rubble" and we recite that line over and over to ourselves—and we meant to be ourselves among the rubble—and it was rubble or it was very close to rubble. It was very close to catastrophe, you know, not only close but was catastrophe because a world war is catastrophe, after all.

MO—If you think of the life that we had been leading it was certainly very isolated. We were in France; we were very young; we were 22, something like that.

GO—And maybe in all this we should have said exactly that to begin with: we knew we were too isolated. Therefore the poetry and therefore also the other thing.

TM—But you don't, as you look back at the first book, at *Discrete Series*, you don't disown it or anything like that?

GO—I think it's great!

MO—And the seeds of all of the ideas in the metaphysics are all there in the *Discrete Series* which later developed into the other poetry.

BH—But you wrote *Discrete Series* very rapidly, didn't you? Over a relatively short period?

GO—I would say several years.

MO—It was, what, 1934 when it was printed?

GO—Yes.

MO—And by that time . . . George was born in 1908 . . . and had been writing for some time. . . .

GO—I write extremely slowly. More than anyone I know of.

BH—Do you feel that the cutting short of your formal education . . . in a sense you had one year of college . . .

GO—Yes.

BH—was a . . .

MO—One semester!

TM—You know, less is more. (*Laughter*)

BH—Was this ah, an advantage in the long run, do you think?

GO—Dropping out of college?

BH—Yes.

GO—Since we had some money, it was. Otherwise, I don't know.

BH—There was still a kind of college in the streets at that time, I think.

MO—I think we pursued our education but I don't think at that time college had any appeal to us nor any necessity for us at all. I never felt that it did. But I wouldn't recommend it for other people. They have to go to college. That's what we tell people. And I think it's still true. You may quit after one semester as we did but you've got to go to college.

BH—It's the way you get away from home!

MO—Right, right!

GO—Also we wanted to know if we were any good out there. . . .

MO—(*In unison with George*) . . . any good out there . . . Yes, as Sherwood Anderson said.

GO—We thought a lot about Sherwood Anderson, as a matter of fact. It broke on us before we knew that there was that kind of poetry being written, however badly.

BH—This is in a sense back to a question I was raising earlier but when you did set out to know what was going on out there did that mean a systematic self-education program, too?

GO—We wouldn't have called it that. We'd have, yes, we wanted to know, we wanted to see, we wanted to be free of our different backgrounds.

TM—You wanted to make yourself or be yourself.

GO—Yes.

TM—Which is certainly a modernist project, I mean there's a lot of continuity, the same impulse would have led you to break out of the world of poets which seemed inadequate, to the history of the moment. Was that not the same impulse that led you to break out of your social class, your family backgrounds?

MO—That's right.

GO—That's exactly right.

BH—But in so far as you were involved with the C.P, there was a very tightly organized kind of world you were also entering.

MO—Indeed, and we had no idea at the time of how many years it was going to entail.

TM—Yeah, well, you didn't stop writing and join the C.P. on the same day. (*Laughter*) That would have been too much.

GO—Each of our interlocuters would have objected to what we were doing.

BH—It seems to me a sort of . . . classic moment.

MO—They had a hard time accepting us and digesting us.

GO—Yes.

TM—Oh, I can imagine.

MO—They tried hard.

GO—Yes.

MO—No, it was a period if you remember the history of that moment, the minute we walked in was just after the Seventh

World Congress Reports on the Dimitroff trial, after the Dimitroff trial and the strategy of the United Front was being put forward and we entered exactly in that spirit.

TM—Un-huh.

MO—The people who we met, who are still our friends, who we met in that first group that entered the party . . . we all were exactly that . . . it wasn't even a mixed group. It was artists, writers, us, I don't know who else, but a small group of intellectuals is what they were. Many of the others didn't give up their arts nor their writing careers or whatever it was. They continued them. But we were in this other position of having a little money and we could support ourselves and we could just switch over and go into the political activities. There were some very strange things. The very first thing they asked us to do . . . it was a sort of trial, I think . . . to see if they could trust us. The party people found us extremely strange. They were still leather-jacketed and very much in the East European/Russian model of who was a communist and we walked in—I still had Parisian clothes, our other friends were intellectuals. They were giving us some sort of test and they asked us to join a Coughlinite group in Green Point. We'd never been to Green Point and we went down there and joined the group and observed. There were all kinds of groups going at that time. Everyone knew that something had gone terribly wrong, and they were looking for an answer. When we were organizing we'd start at one end of the street and knock on every door, and by the time we got to the end of the street, we'd have a group organized and ready to act. They were exciting times. There was a kind of poetry there, being with people in the streets.

BH—The dilemma of the modernist in poetry—when I read Sandburg say, today, I feel there's a poet who compromised an awful lot in order to have a mass audience, an audience of people in the streets.

GO—Yes.

BH—And you weren't willing to make that compromise either, that is, in a sense it seems like what's most rigorous about your work is its demand to have it both ways—to be as hard and precise and challenging as possible on the poetic level, but also to take the people seriously as a presence. Is that . . . I guess this ought to be a question rather than a lecture . . . is that your sense of what you were doing? That you wanted to be as rigorous in your art as possible, but also, again, not to write off the masses with contempt the way an Eliot did?

MO—I tell you I think we did a tremendous lot of talking, maybe a year's talking before we came home to the U.S., and from the time we came home in March until either September or October when we finally walked into the Communist Party headquarters, we did nothing but analyse, read the left-wing journals and publications, anything we could lay our hands on. A friend of Zukofsky's who was quite politically active, we met him and he took us on a sort of tour. We went to visit as many different political groups as we could visit to find out what they were doing right now. We had no particular leanings toward the Communist Party—we were looking for someone who was active and who was doing something right now, and was something we could join. But we looked at the poets, we looked at the writers and we did not think that was any kind of art. Neither the paintings, the things that I was doing or— George can speak for himself—but we couldn't enter into that sort of artistic world. It was propaganda art. We weren't interested in. . . .

TM—You weren't interested in going ahead and taking over the practice of art as a skill and putting that at the service of political organization. You were interested in changing your lives to meet what you saw as the demands of history.

MO—Yes, I think that's all true . . . in a way. Don't you?

BH—So at this point, let's say in the mid-30s, the poetry and politics—I wrote this down so I'll have to read it—seem to represent to you two alternative ways of acting in the world, and you wouldn't compromise one for the other. You would not put your poetry in the service of politics in the sense of making it a weapon in the class struggle or whatever . . . on the other hand, you also did not want to simply act out your political concerns by writing poetry. That is, the political concerns demanded knocking on doors, not. . . .

GO—It's a narrow public for poetry. It always will be. We didn't dream of addressing the crowds with poetry. And we distinguished, as I said, between poetry and politics.

TM—Or perhaps the political action was more properly your course as a poet at that moment, not simply to continue to write poetry from the same base or subject that you had been working from to that point.

MO—It was for us. We weren't making any generalizations. We were trying to find . . .

GO—. . . the thing to do . . .

MO—. . . for us, the next step.

BH—But then, when you did go back to poetry, it was also with all that experience as something that was now to enter into the poetry. You weren't writing off those years and saying, "Now I'm going back to poetry." Instead, it was a kind of new organic development.

GO—Rome had recently burned, so there was no reason not to fiddle.

TM—But you first of all went into the Army.

GO—Yes, well, I was coming to that. I was thinking about that. And that was a mistake. That was unnecessary and wrong.

BH—To go into the Army?

GO—Yes, I still feel guilty about it. It was essentially at Mary's expense, or partly at Mary's. And the Army didn't want me. They wished to hell I wasn't there most of the time.

MO—Well, that was because you were 37 and the kids were 18.

GO—And the officers were slightly embarrassed—and you know, they really didn't particularly want me. I was a very fancy driver, that was about the only thing they valued.

TM—And a translator?

GO—No—oh, yes, it's true—awfully bad French, but that's what we had. Oh, boy, what a translator!

MO—The people in George's outfit called him Fader Oppen.

BH—Un, I would like to get into questions about other sorts of intellectual influences—simply out of curiosity on my part—but there are references to Hegel, Heidegger in the poetry and Maritain. Do you read a lot of philosophy, and/or theology, or have you at various times?

GO—I was reading quite a bit—Mary was too—the people you mentioned.

BH—Is Heidegger particularly important to you?

GO—He was. I don't know now what I'd say, now. He was very important at the time.

TM—I've seen—within the last 6 or 8 months—I've seen a book of Heidegger open on your table, so you must still be reading Heidegger.

GO—Yes. We were influenced. And Maritain, too.

BH—*Being and Time* in particular?

GO—Yes, in particular.

MO—Maritain was very important to us. We discovered that while we were still in Mexico. And it's necessary to make it clear that we lived many years within the Communist Party. There was a very proscribed reading list and one couldn't keep the wrong kind of published books in your house and you couldn't be seen reading them and be in good standing and there was a very great deal of writing and thought that we didn't look at over a period of many years. And it just happened, I suppose, I don't remember exactly how it happened that we got hold of Maritain's *Creative Intuition in Art and Poetry*. George read it and was very taken with it and I read it too. It was very important to us. But when Maritain writes really for the Church I'm not interested. I haven't seen any such writings of his that impressed me very much, but that book was valuable to us.

BH—Hegel, too?

GO—Ooooh, of course Hegel's . . . it's rather difficult . . . we're talking back an awful lot of years.

MO—I think that those were ideas that were digested. I don't think we look at . . . Heidegger somehow isn't there anymore. We seem to have taken it. We look at it again and somehow it doesn't have that freshness or that discovery that it did have.

GO—Yes. Your mentioning Sandburg is interesting because that was what we set out on. I think I told you that.

BH—He was really the first poet you were sort of galvanized by. . . .

GO—. . .that we recognized as a modern poet. We had rather thought that poetry had ended a trifle before our birth or something like that.

MO—But when we went up to college, there was this young professor, Jack Lyons, who was entirely immersed in poetry and who read with great enthusiasm. He was passionately interested in poetry. He came up from the University of California. And he read from that Aiken anthology, and he read well. But he snared a little group of us and that was how we found out that there was poetry now and some idea of how to look about and off we went.

BH—You got an education there.

GO—. . . from him. I had thought I was a poet from a very early age—I don't know what age—There was a scene my younger sister tells of my father and mother coming to the boarding school I was in, for a drive and a talk and to ask what was I going to be?

And I said I was going to be a writer. And my step-mother thought a moment and she said, "Oh, like uh, like James." And my sister remembers with amusement the intensity with which I said, "Not like James Barrie."

BH—You were right.

GO—And I never did.

MO—He's still holding up.

GO—Yep, still holding up.

BH—Most of the people of your generation did start by writing a little early Keats and things like that. Did you also?

GO—Keats, of course—and Shelley.

BH—There are some sonnets way, way back then?

GO—Yes, there were some sonnets.

TM—Is there any of that still around?

GO—I think of that as a long time ago. I was walking across somewhere in boarding school carrying a book and the book was *The Way of All Flesh* and one of the instructors found me with this book—whipped it out of my hands, tore it up. I didn't even know what he thought it was. It took me a long time to realize what he thought I was reading.

BH—One of the rare books where the title sounds more obscene than anything in it.

GO—Oh, it's been a difficult life.

TM—Poor George!

GO—Are you sure this is a literary conversation?

BH—More and more so. . . . Well, was your family at all religious?

GO—No, not at all.

BH—So you didn't have any kind of . . . .

GO—Back to my grandparents. They were non-religious.

BH—Before I came here, I just went through the *Collected Poems* and picked up allusions because it seemed to me that these were in some ways kind of a clue. One is from Robert Heinlein. Do you read science fiction?

GO—We did at one time quite a lot. That also is political, isn't it?

MO—Just last week I reread—I stored a lot of books away in the basement and came upon some science fiction and reread Heinlein's *A Man from Mars*, 1951 or 2—something like that—a most remarkable book.

GO—Yes.

MO—A complete understanding of these cults.

GO—I thought they were brilliant, the science fiction writers.

TM—Have you kept up at all on recent science fiction?

MO—No, not at all.

TM—You don't, ah, you haven't gone to *Star Wars* or any of the movies?

MO—Oh, yes, but not reading. It seems to me that the state of affairs has pretty much caught up with them . . . it's very hard for them to . . . visualize.

TM—Hard to keep ahead.

MO—Yes, and they *were* just incredible!

GO—Yes, they were marvelous.

TM—Do you maintain an interest in movies? Do you go to the movies?

MO—Oh, we go to loads of movies.

GO—We walk out of them.

MO—We walk out of an awful lot of them, but we do go to the movies.

GO—One of our nieces as we left a movie said, walked along silently, finally she said, "it's kind of hard to know what to say when you've just seen half of two movies." (*Laughter*) We're a bit brusque it seems as babysitters. Yes, we were very fascinated by them and during the McCarthy era, there was very little one could read. The best things going on were in the women's magazines which managed to be very political for people who had any sense of politics, and the science fiction writers.

MO—And *Pogo*.

GO—And *Pogo*, yes *Pogo* was absolutely great.

†††††

BH—I'm curious about your sense of syntax. In many of your poems you seem to be engaged in a deliberate disruption of syntax, breaking sentences down into detached phrases or even isolated words. I wonder how conscious you are of syntax in your poetry. Are these disruptions of syntax the result of a consciously thought-out set of poetic principles?

GO—Yes, definitely. All along I've had a sense that the structure of the sentence closes off the little words. That's where the mysteries are, in the little words. "The" and "and" are the greatest mysteries of all.

MO—Well, also, George almost never uses punctuation or he uses it very sparingly, and this use of the line and the way one is directed to read because of the use of the line accomplishes, much more powerfully it seems to me, than the use of punctuation. . . .

GO—Yes, I use space.

MO—Well that can be compared almost to the spaces in sculpture, which sometimes accomplish as much as the solid stone itself.

BH—Was a musical analogy important too, the silence as a kind of defining of the form, or do you think of it more in visual terms?

GO—The music is very important to me, extremely important, but it's the music of a poem not the music of something else.

TM—You mean the music of a poem as in Pound's Melopoeia? The sound of it, or do you mean the music of the thought in some way. . . .

GO—I mean the progression of the thought which is music.

TM—Yes, so I'm looking at this poem, "From A Phrase of Simone Weil's and Some Words of Hegel" which starts with syntax, declares itself as starting with syntax as subject matter, and fragmentary syntax and then the thought develops and you know "aflame in the world or else poor people hide yourselves together place place where desire lust of the eyes the pride of life etc"—to me that's a good example of the way the syntax moves from line to line as if the same word moves from line to line—it's not so much the word's repeated, as it is that you get this sense of the word dancing, dancing into place.

GO—Yes, what was it you quoted?

TM—It's "From a Phrase of Simone Weil's and Some Words of Hegel."

MO—Give it to George and have him read it.

TM—Yes, sure.

GO—(*reading*)

> in the sandspit wind this ether this other this element all
> It is I or I believe
> We are the beaks of the ragged birds
> Tune of the ragged bird's beaks

> In the tune of the winds
> Ob via   the obvious
> Like a fire of straws. . . .

It's entirely a discussion of syntax.

TM—Beautiful poem.

GO—. . . "In   back   deep" . . . it's not just this on the page but the whole history behind such a thing and . . . "Pride in the sandspit wind this ether this other" . . . which is not ourselves, it's something that we have, this element which is essential, all it is element or . . . "we are the beaks of the ragged birds" . . . which is ah, can be understood in a lot of ways, it's quite . . . and the language . . . "like a fire of straws" . . . I think it's very good.

TM—Yeah, thank you.

BH—Glad you wrote it.

GO—I congratulate you.

BH—Ah, I've been running some experiments with some of my own students. I've given them the "Anniversary Poem." It's totally unfamiliar to them so that I've just asked them to read it, describe what happens to them as they read, and I have been very, for one thing, very pleased how powerfully moved they are by this poem, that it does communicate to an awful lot of people. It's not a very esoteric kind of poem although when I read it and when I do not find a kind of orderly movement of syntax, I say that's hard, you know, I have to grasp it, whereas most of these students that have been reading it don't react that way.

TM—In a funny way people of their generation have the advantage and the disadvantage of never knowing any grammar or syntax . . . they have no expectations because actually they have no. . . .

MO—They haven't been taught any.

TM—Yes, they haven't, it's not a violation for them. Sentence as fragment is really the form of language that they have come to, rightly, I mean, . . . there's nothing the matter with it. . . .

BH—One of them said it looks to me like someone has erased half of the words and it's my job to find out what goes in the missing spaces. I wonder would that strike you as a good way of responding to or seeing the poem?

GO—Yes, that's good, sure.

TM—Un-huh. George do you work from notebooks? Say, like Coleridge kept a constant notebook and then in a sense the poem would be written out of the notebook.

GO—I write down a word, or something like that and usually forget them. No, I don't think exactly a notebook. I have at times.

BH—But when do you go to the typewriter? Right away? Or. . . .

GO—No.

BH—Or do you work from a handwritten. . . .

GO—I usually ask Mary to type it.

MO—But you have a fairly clear copy . . . and pasting and so on . . . George taught me this method too, and it makes an untidy manuscript but it's a very easy way to work, with neither of us a typist.

TM—Oh, so you cut and paste?

MO—Yes.

TM—It saves both time and it really, it offers you the chance to see things in many different ways.

GO—Frankly I paste without cutting. What I actually do is every correction I just paste on top of the poem as it was, and I paste it loosely so I can tear it out, try another route. Are these things really interesting?

TM—Yes. That's just beautiful, fascinating.

BH—Really this is the area of your work I don't think has been fully perceived. When I read what people have written about you I see only a very faint sense really of how radical what's happening in the relationships between individual words really is.

TM—And parts of the poem, too, not just in individual words— blocks of the poem the way the thought proceeds, and from poem to poem. How do you conceive of a book? I mean the most natural way and sometimes almost unavoidable way to conceive of a book is that like a balance, you get enough pieces of paper over there and it tips the balance and you say now that's the book. And that's one way and pretty much the way poetry has proceeded, that is, the poem is the form, and a book is a collection of poems. On the other hand, within your work and other peoples work there are both serial poems and books that in themselves are just a single work beside just being the collection of poems . . . how is that . . . is that something that is important for you?

MO—You've often said that you had an idea of the books before you wrote them. That you were going to write a certain number of books.

GO—Yes, they occur that way. I was very careful about the *Collected Poems*—where I placed the poems and so on, which I think is what you were saying . . . I arrange the poems very carefully.

BH—I once went through *The Materials* and started circling words, individual words, and I noticed patterns. For instance, stone appears in a large number of poems, or sea, and . . . is this something that happened more or less organically or did you have a notion in your mind that you were going to do "stone poems" or. . . .

GO—No, I don't think so. I'm not exactly sure what the question was.

BH—Well, it seemed to me that I see the title, *The Materials*, and then certain kinds of materials such as stone seem to be recurrent kinds of presences within the poems. That suggested to me that the book had a kind of overall cohesion. . . .

GO—Well, I put it together very carefully which means I spent a long time moving them around.

MO—But George, they're separate books and they're printed in there as books and you did print them, you wrote them it seemed to me with a central idea—*The Materials* out of which to write the things that were central to you and then the problem of the singular or the numerous is certainly the key in that book of that title.

BH—I don't think I have as much of a sense of the individual books when I read in the *Collected Poems* . . . that is that each book is an integral unit. . . .

MO—Well, *Discrete Series* suffered terribly in the way this was printed. Jay Laughlin just got a little bit too Scotch and wouldn't give a whole page to each poem and the way they've been reprinted makes some people think that if there are three little bits on a page, that's one poem, whereas that wasn't the way the *Discrete Series* was printed.

TM—It was poem by poem by poem. I have a tough question for you . . . I think that every poet must, without wanting to, think about history and the judgment of history on one's work and I wonder whether you think about that. What you feel, what you would want . . . what would you want of say, another poet, somebody else or any other reader? What would you want them to come down on in your work? What would you feel that there was really for the younger poets to learn?

GO—Very hard to answer that question. One does various things. No, to tell you the truth, I think it's all fairly clear here. "But the mind rises into happiness rising to what is there I know of no other happiness." It seems to me I'm just saying steadily what I started to say.

BH—Is Wallace Stevens of interest to you? I was just reading around in his *Collected Poems* today and. . . .

GO—Yes . . . it's very lovely to read certainly.

BH—In some ways his philosophic concerns seem to merge with yours.

GO—You know what he lacks that I've got? I'll read what I've got . . . "parked in the fields all night so many years ago we saw a lake . . . " Stevens is very lovely, but there's sort of a narrow tone there.

MO—Bronk of course is very close to Stevens, and we had this new book of Bronk's and because of that we got out a lot of Bronk, and were rereading him and in his early works there are some lines which could be Stevens, later on not so much.

TM—Yes. Again, I don't know anything about Bronk's biography as a writer, but really, as you start out you must work with the landscape that you see around you, and Stevens was high and mighty therein, whereas really you didn't see George or Louis Zukofsky or Charles Reznikoff. You just didn't see them, they weren't there, weren't in print, hell.

MO—Yes.

BH—On the syntax question again. Were you talking with Williams and Zukofsky and Reznikoff and so on in the early 30's about these things?

GO—Rezy never talked about poetry.

> *(Laughter)*

MO—He talked about his father's factory.

> *(Laughter)*

BH—And he writes in sentences.

> *(Laughter)*

GO—Yes he does.

MO—With Zukofsky, I think that was an extremely intimate and almost endless conversation. Far into the night, night after night after night.

GO—And very valuable to me, very very valuable.

TM—Did you feel personally close to him? Aside from the fact that he was obviously brilliant and a comrade in a pursuit. . . .

MO—I think he was perhaps the closest friend in that sort of relationship that was possible to have. It was a very tight little friendship as friendships are when you're 22 years old. Louis was 24, a little bit older than we are, 26 maybe, something like that. We were 20 I think.

GO—But the point is that I learned a tremendous amount from Louis. Yes, I did.

MO—I'd say we were fairly inseparable during that period.

TM—You ate dinner together a lot, and went to the movies. . . .

MO—We were living in Columbia Heights, which doesn't exist anymore—it's a park. But Louis lived over a couple of blocks on Willow Street and ah, I would usually get sleepy and go to bed, and George and Louis would go on talking, and then Louis would have to go teach the next morning so they'd go home and George would walk him over and they would have to have coffee, and then Louis would walk George back home and they would go on and on and on. This was a very very close friendship, I think, the way very young people can conduct it. There are no rules and no meals that have to be had at certain times.

BH—But Reznikoff was part of this too? But not these late night debates?

MO—He's much older you see.

GO—Much older.

MO—He was 14 years older—made quite a difference at our age. George gave him a manuscript, an early manuscript of *Discrete Series* which later John Martin found in Charles' papers and sent us a Xerox. It's not exactly the way *Discrete Series* was finally published, but when George went to see Charles after that, Charles got out the manuscript and said to George, pointed to this one line of "oh city ladies". . . .?

GO—I forget which.

MO—. . . of ah, "oh city ladies" which is I think a Ben Jonson quote?

GO—Yes, its Ben Jonson.

MO—And he said "George this is the only line that sings." It was so comic, I think it's marvelous, I think George was very proud!

GO—Yes, I was very pleased. And then the line about the girder was with me all through that war and every time I thought of it I wept and wept, I don't know what about, just that it was so beautiful.

BH—What I sense as a kind of common bond between you and Reznikoff is the sense of how much is being left unsaid, the sense of the resonance behind the words. Does that seem similar to your feelings about the poetry?

GO—Hard to discuss. Again what I told you. Piling up pieces of paper to find the words.

BH—I had a graduate student who started to write a thesis about Reznikoff and came to me and said, "There's nothing to say."

GO—That's right.

MO—That's what George has been saying right along . . . that there isn't going to be any academic work because it's just perfect.

TM—Yes, he says what he means.

GO—The first *Testimony* is an extraordinary thing, just that ending of it, going along on this testimony from the courts and then those last lines, "ships, harbors, rivers." Just things, just things there, and it's amazing what they do.

TM—It is funny that the insistence of the entire work *Testimony*, most reminds me of Lautréamont. It's a catalog of horror.

GO—Yes, it is.

TM—And it's odd, I mean, it's odd the really continuing fascination with it. I mean, it's kind of an underside to his nature, really.

MO—And to the other city poetry of the streets, and the subways and the moon, and the lanterns, and the leaf blowing giving a message. . . .

TM—Yes.

GO—Later on it was wrong but that first one where it just goes out by rivers and the things that are out there, just keeps going out. . . .

MO—I don't know why the continuation of the horror, but it's certain what George says I think is true, that in the later years Charles wanted to go on writing and this was what he *could* do.

TM—And although it's not his intention the accretion of horror is something very different from the nature of Reznikoff, as it is testified to by his friends, and by much of his work. I mean really that it's very bitter, *Testimony* as a whole, is a very bitter, negative, violent, frightening work. *The Manner Music*, too, sounds this in his nature. Also nightmarish, it is more akin to Raymond Chandler than to much else that comes to mind now.

GO—Yes, yes.

MO—It is. It's very hard to put together again.

GO—Then those dark rivers . . . that just go out there. . . .

MO—I suppose there are two sides of the man, and we don't . . . we know very little about this because he did not talk.

GO—No, he didn't.

MO—We spent a very great deal of time with him, and we walked with him, he worked near where we lived, and we'd meet him after work. We walked with him but the conversation was as we recorded, and he treated us like children.

GO—I learned an awful lot from Zukofsky. . . .

BH—Do you think that, have you gone back now that *A*'s altogether there and looked at the whole thing, and do you see it as a major work?

GO—What broke our friendship was when Louis demanded to know if I preferred my work to his. And then wanted to know exactly what my reservations were about his writing. And, under quite a bit of pressure, I said I thought he used obscurity in the writing as a tactic—which was not a very nice thing to say—but that was the end of our friendship.

MO—But then he said something to you, maybe at another time, I don't remember, about "*they* don't care, it doesn't matter."

GO—Yes, I was struck, as I told you, I had these great heaps of correction and correction and correction—I forgot how this came up—very frank thing on Louis' part—he said, "George, they don't care."

TM—They don't care how hard you work?

GO—They don't care if it's. . . .

MO—Clear.

GO—If it's clear or not.

BH—Do you think that's something that happened in his later works?

GO—I think that cynicism and that tactic were there from the beginning.

TM—Do you feel that that remark really represents him, or was it a remark of someone in a bitter mood, or. . . .

GO—I think he meant it, but I don't think it represents him. It's not the best remark he ever made. But he did do that. It was a tactic.

BH—The work . . . ah . . . I can read through A-12 and not feel that there's any kind of obscurantism going on.

TM—Oh, a lot of it isn't particularly obscure.

GO—Yes. A great deal of it is very clear to me, especially about the son.

TM—Yes, and a lot of it has come clear, which in some sense at least validates the claim of difficulty, which is that it will come clear.

GO—This is rather narrow and unnecessary talk but there are things I happen to *know* . . . incidents that happened when we were together and I know the meaning of that poem and what caused it and so on, and also know that nobody but me will ever know, possibly know . . . "Hi Ku" is an example of that. We hit a cow in our automobile. Nobody's gonna know that except now you. *(Laughter)* "Hi ku," that was the name of it—a pun—it was written like a haiku—It goes on from the cow. Nobody else is going to know except now you. He meant it. It's not just carelessness.

TM—And, I mean, that's something he got from Pound.

GO—Yes. He didn't want to be lumped with the whole gaggle of poets.

TM—Certainly the early parts of *A* are really under Pound's thumb. I mean, as a poetic enterprise, *A* was quite derivative of Pound. Some of the early parts are really affecting, you know, have lyric virtues that Pound actually never had, but pretty much began as a Poundian enterprise. Pound and Joyce. Not that it ended up that way.

GO— It's true enough.

BH—You didn't know Whittaker Chambers I take it?

GO—No.

MO—No. It was a weird thing for Louis to be in on. Scared him to death later.

BH—There's a story that Chambers took him to a meeting, a C.P. meeting, and they told him that he should join an East side branch of the party. . . .

MO—Oh! Hester Street, I suppose.

TM—Why, they didn't want him over there?

BH—He was too much of a dandy, too concerned with clothes and appearance and so on.

MO—Oh, he was very much the man about town. He was an extreme elegante.

TM—He was?

MO—Extreme. I had no idea he would eventually become the Louis who married Celia and live the way he lived. It was very different, the life he was living. He was elegant.

TM—And what were, was he, what were his interests? Was he a man about town?

MO—Music. But he did a lot of things with us. We went to Coney Island. Really did a lot of just kiddish funny things.

GO—Well, the Ricky poem was very touching.

BH—Well, I exhausted all of my questions here.

TM—I hope you got some answers.

BH—I certainly did, yes! . . . Maybe we should think about going?

TM—Sure enough! Thanks for the two beers!

BH—Thanks for all the answers!

Appendix

In the months after we interviewed George and Mary Oppen, Tom Mandel and I exchanged several letters in which we discussed the editing of the interview and other matters. In one of these letters I commented briefly on Tom's own recent book of poems, *EncY*. "Thank you for your book," I wrote. "It seems to me a uniquely pure example of its kind, but I'm still struggling to come to terms with that 'kind' itself: i.e. (as I conceive it) a poetry that aspires to the condition of pure language. Silliman has sent me some explanatory pieces, including *Talks*. I have found them helpful." In reply to this letter, Tom offered some ideas on his own work and on George's work that seem to me worth preserving. Thus I include his letter here as an appendix to our interview [B.H.].

10/22/80

Dear Burt,

I'm a little late getting this typescript back. Hope this hasn't made for problems. We've moved to an old house in Bernal Hts (hill above the Mission), and the displacement has kept me from my desk for some time.

I have made some small changes, including adding a couple of remarks that were in my mind to make at the time of the conversation, but which just didn't get out in time: let me know if these additions maintain the spirit of the interview, and tell me if it seems wrong to add them at this later point.

Reading over the interview I remember how much I enjoyed doing it—thanks for the opportunity.

Neither my poetry nor Ron's [i.e., Ron Silliman's], nor indeed any of what is, unfortunately for what I'm about to say, called "language-centered writing" (a phrase invented to the end of recognition by someone, I guess, a literal handle and under criticism since its first usage), aspires to the condition of pure language, in your phrase, a phrase imbedded in a sentence indicating *interest*—and therefore let me stop you from trying to extend that interest along the false line of resolving the work into its linguistic context. Obviously, language is the means and matter of poetry, of writing, and *EncY* uses those means in new ways. Briefly, invented language, construction within the word (at a level below the word's sacrosanctity), collage, fragmentation, are at work in *EncY* to *create meaning*, meaning(s), matters you and I would agree in, an understanding, but which may not be reached through previous uses of these means and matters. *EncY* is quite concretely critique, breaking down codes toward comprehension of an instituted power in language, the language, specifically, of empire as it surveys its reduction to its meaning (to meaning it) of the entire body of knowledge (*in situ*, viz, the Enc. Britt onzieme edition in its Preface). Just looking at subject matter alphabetization of the world, would that be "aspiring to a condition of pure language"? Rather, it's an act extending the powers of a culture through the matter of its language. Language effects actual meanings current in any of our worlds and is integral to these. This *work* of language (labor theory of meaning) is what makes writing possible, and what makes writing literature possible too. To imagine the possibility of resolving any poem to a level of "pure language" (making a poet akin to say Carnap) commits the same intellectual slip that once erected the idea of "pure meaning": it's idealism, in other words. Language works on meaning, every time; can't hold back from it. That is, we all hum Monk tunes in our heads (MESSAGE MOMENT coming up), the task of Steve Lacy, though, is what can I wring from this instrument by way of its complete extension into musical meaning: I guess I'll keep at it and find out.

I guess I'll keep at it and find out. You do have to. A certain suspicion attaches to George, a suspicion on the part of another generation of poets quite screwed down to what they're spending their lives doing, for having given up the task during 25 years. This is why, in the interview we did, I hoped he would out with having written just not published during those years; just because it seems a questionable move when someone abandons the art as not holding enough for him, "not the most important thing in the world," as if, *a seeker*, one would go only to that "most important thing." But wouldn't that be just the poet's task, to make it important? It may easily seem to another poet that not much good poetry would get written on the basis of such impulses as this of George's. Nor does Kenner's "in short it took 25 years to write the next poem" help at all, since that's *not* what happened but rather a metaphor enabling one to look away from what happened.

Thus, if you will, another poet might see more virtues in Zukofsky's mole-millenia of digging through and casting aside slough (say *"A"-8*, to keep within the sphere of politics/poetry) toward the resplendent poetics of *"A"-22/3*. No matter that one *leaves* the world in the effort, poetry being written at some remove (that is, such is our history as poets: it need not be so written. ((?)) Not-writing moves it no closer of course).

All this is by way of documentation of a literary situation (a lot of writers in my generation *do not* read George's work), the first few poems of *The Materials*—to my ear—announcing a convincing return quite in consideration of effort spent, wasting if not wasted. And to address obliquely George's own opposition of himself to Zukofsky in the charge that Zukofsky used "obscurity" as a tactic: more than one form of disappearance may be at stake in the *ethics* of poetry. In any case, the careers of poets Oppen, Reznikoff, Zukofsky—during the years of their *obscurity*— will come to be seen in the light of a culture that suppressed certain of its impulses in favor of others. Not to mention the puffed ascendancy of the right wing dons of modernism in the 30s & 40s, was it not around 1950 that the *Partisan Review*, in a bizarre inversion of McCarthyism, undertook to investigate (the other sense of course) the "Americanism" of Jewish writers?

I'm far afield from the corrected typescript enclosed (or not). Hope the issue of *Paideuma* looks good to you. Here's to the more reading of Oppen it the more may inspire.

Best,

Tom

MARY OPPEN

RE: MAINE

our boat makes a way for us
a free passage
on a sea of glass
or held in the surges
our words move toward
each other

I

The anchor flukes strike down through ooze to rock. This island can be entered up a bank of drifted wood and worn round stones on a path as small as a deer's trail, but it is made by humans. The firs and spruce stand thick, occasional birch, maple and oak bring light and movement into dense shade in August, on the forest floor. We walk on moss, and ancient stones flat as masonry, make steps. We climb beside trunks of trees, and through branches we see our boat below, the water smooth, glassy, clear. Stones below us enter water, green stones, great rocks of an upheaval more recent than the ancient stones of the steps up the cliff.

A chick-a-dee infant discovers us, he comes chirping down branches, hops from tree to tree—comes close, flutters his wings, asking for food. His parent calls—mouth full of bugs, calls and flies from branch to branch, baby follows, follows for food, hops near us again to see.

A cairn to mark the turn. Probably the piles of rocks mark the path to be cleared anew each spring, rocks stacked make precarious sculptures, sharp angled slabs and shards of the most ancient stones. The cairns are lichen-covered, stained with circles, colors spread and grow on the rock surfaces. Soil is made of fallen spruce needles, birch-leaves, rotting stone; tree's roots are covered with moss, inches deep and various in kinds of moss and shades of green, the pile of this carpet is close-grown, or clustered stars, resilient where the foot falls: we leave no mark. A plank shaped by a carpenter for some other use at some other time, found on the beach, is now a bridge, and nailed to a large root, it makes a firm crossing. Berries and leaves of Bunch-berry are red on each side of the path where we come out of the forest to stand on a narrow, high end of the island above the water; nearly silent water in no wind, water surface is glassy, it swells and recedes—it does not break, it soughs—hsssss—hwww. We stand quiet, we hear it rise and recede.

The path divides and we climb high; steps cut in rich mold, held in place by cedar roots: cedar trees, trunks smooth with fans of cedar branches hang quiet, ferns grow up through the moss. We climb into the sun. Above the tree-tops steps are cut in the rock, we feel beneath our feet the back-bone of the island, back-bone thrust up from the ocean floor deep in Penobscot Bay. Great Spruce Head, from whose top we can see the islands of the bay: Eagle Island in the distance, across from us Dirigo and Bear, and off to the south North Haven Island, but between them all are the rocks, spits of sand and pebbles, Scrag Island is a crag with two trees and piles of stones like slag, where a fisherman has a snug all-year house with storm-windows still up in August and a complex television mast stayed to stand in the winds. The sea still lies glassy, but in the center of the small islands we see on the water that the wind is coming. Southwest wind is turning the water dark blue and streaks of darker blue riffle and sweep in some logic they find among the islands. To the north, east, and west, the mountains rise blue, Blue Hill, the Camden Hills, and off to the east Cadillac Mountain, purple because its rock is rosy-gray granite. Now it is a deeper blue than the other mountains, it shows its sixty miles' distance from us here. We retrace our steps. Back-bone, cairn to cairn. Maine forests are impenetrable without a man-made path. We've tried to walk or climb into forests here in Maine, but exhausted, confused, assailed by black-flies and mosquitoes, we've been lost in dense forest growth pervading as jungle and as fast growing. At the feet of spruce are spruce trees one inch high, up through the moss the new trees start from seed, next year they grow first branches, rise in height, with lichens and dead branches in the lower levels of the forest where light is scarce, their roots in gloom, their branches are nearly black, their green is so dark against the sky. Two ospreys build their nest in the top of a tall, old, broken spruce. They find a current of air and lie against the sky above the cliff to watch over their fierce young one who sits like a phoenix in the nest: he fixes their gaze, whistles his piercing cry: they answer. We find a long black feather

—a raven's feather; nearby are shells, a perfect large sea-snail shell, clam-shells and mussel-shells lying with both halves open, emptied and cast beside the path or scattered on the moss, far above the beaches. We've seen ten different mushrooms, and a yellow and brown velvet lichen like a velvet hat left lying on the ground beside an old tree-trunk. Flowers grow in the moss and ferns, faces turned down, petals thrust face down to the moss—Pippsissewa, used by the Indians as a medicine.

We near our beach, retrace our path over the plank-bridge to our orange, inflated canoe. We carry it to the water's edge, step in and float on water. We are beside the island, no way is now visible to penetrate it.

II

We flew kites that year, kites that flew high and steady. An engineer and his family visited us that summer and we all made kites. I put them in the barn when the engineer left and Marge and her little brother Samuel came in the afternoons, put the baby in the shade and flew one kite or another in the field beside the house. Marge caused more anxiety to her parents than all the other children. She would go to Boston, she would go to Washington D.C. They drove her there, but she beat them home both times; couldn't deal with the big world she was unaccustomed to. She made friends and then fell in love with a Black Portuguese boy who took her home to his mother. They married and she tried to live with him in his mother's house in a Boston slum. "I got up when he was sleeping, I slept when he was awake. When we walked I was a few steps behind him—he never heard a word I said and I didn't understand their speech. He played cards or practiced his music with other young men. He played the drums, and he shipped out in the Merchant Marine to earn money, and was seldom at home."

"Why did you love him, Marge, what was it about him?"

"He looked like Belafonte," she said in her low, slow, reluctant speech. She came home. Still almost a child herself, she now has a child, a child half-Black, half-Portuguese Black, a glowingly beautiful dark child on these islands of descendants of Scotch-Irish pale people.

"I mean," said Marge, clapping her hands for the baby to dance with her first steps, "she has *Africa* in her veins!"

Marge walked with me that summer, took me to her favorite haunts—where Mumma shot the deer. We walked on a logging-road fast disappearing in the fir forest that grows fast and thick.

She says, "Over there is an old silver mine that someone tried to work." She showed me a miniature graveyard. "Samuel and I made it for all the pets." In a circle of trees in deep forest, small blocks of native granite marking graves. "My bird, our dog"—with a stone, *Dutchess* scratched on the polished fragment of granite, "Duchess went deaf and was run over on the highway."

She and Samuel, the youngest boy, felt close and intimate that summer. Marge tried to talk to us that summer, tried and the effort failed. She tried hard. She came from such shy and quiet people who talk little of what is important to their lives. They keep secret how they feel, how they feel toward each other, what they want in their lives.

Our friend Steve was visiting us and we were talking of Russian Roulette when Marge and the baby came to visit. Steve explained the game to her. . . . She sat, silent as usual, but I heard her murmur, "I could play Russian Roulette and not lose." She is a little wandering spirit—when we first met her she said, "I will get to Peru."

Now in another summer she is married to an insistent suitor, she has a second child, but she lives a strange life. The children reflect her strong, strange adventurous spirit. Not a strange spirit to someone out there adventuring, but she is an adventurer who must live at home. But where Marge is life is not ordinary. One year she couldn't bear to be in the same house with her husband. She took the children and moved into a cabin in deep woods—in Maine, in winter! But it is her country, and they survived. Her husband worried about her, begged her to return. Perhaps she is his spirit of adventure. He bought her a car, made her kitchen modern and shining, but she stays outside, works all the land anyone offers her, plants gardens that grow. Even in a year of drouth Marge's gardens grow. She is dear to her husband and very much trouble. The children are bright. "Little devils," their grandmother says. "I would rather have all my other grandchildren in the house at once than Marge's two." The little girl is in school now, the outstanding child in her class, and the teacher loves her. She is a different child to the teacher than she is to her grandmother, or to her mother's husband. Her own father loves her too, calls her on her birthday, and on Christmas. This year, her third at school, a child called her *Dirty Nigger*. Neither of the children knew what the words meant, but Marge comes to us for comfort and to plan her strategy for protecting this wonderful child, for in the future there will be more, more name-calling, and here in the islands the child may suffer. "Beautiful, she is so beautiful, with a father who calls her on her birthday. He loves her too, even though," Marge says, "he couldn't take care of us down there in Boston, so I came home."

III

Captain Frank sits out in front, almost sightless, nearly deaf, smoking the little corn-cob pipe that George brought him at the beginning of summer. From my bicycle, I shout, "Hello, Captain Frank." He raises his arm in greeting, peering to find someone to connect with my voice. Captain Frank came to Eleanor's birthday party, everyone was there, everyone she still remembers. (Everyone, that is, who is still alive.) Captain Frank stands in the doorway, leans there until he has the attention of the roomful of people, shouts, "Eleanor, another eighty years and maybe you'll be all growed up!"

She came one summer from upstate New York, a girl—Hudson River-Dutch. A tall, lank woman on an island of short, wide women, she married that first summer, a son of a farmer on the island. He had come to meet the steamer that brought Eleanor to Maine. She had sailed down the Hudson on her father's boat, a working boat, the last of the sailing-barges on the Hudson River, from New York to Boston by steamer, on a smaller steamer to Portland, and smaller still, the boat from Portland to Rockland, and then to the Penobscot by one of the many little steamers that were the means of transportation for the islands. A dirt covered promontory of jagged granite blocks made the landing, where every summer a hundred people came for their summer vacations. They came, each to a favorite spot, "a camp," or a rented room in a house opened to summer visitors, or to their own houses. A summer population that was lively, vacationers who brought employment to the islanders to augment their income from fishing or from lumbering, or from shipping out on lumber-schooners or as captain or as crew on the yachts of the rich. The island young people met the steamer at the landing, walking or coming by horse-carriage to meet and to view the new arrivals, and to escort them to their summer homes. Young people greeted friends from past summers, they flirted with boys and girls who arrived with these families. Some families even brought their own horses and carriages in order to have their own transportation on the island. Summertime is the busy time in the islands, summertime means work for those who live year round on the islands, for the women as well as for the men. For the young people it means also the return of the dances that are held in a great barn, a boat builder's barn, used for their dances during the summer; picnics, swimming at ponds warm enough to allow swimming; or trips to places of particular beauty.

Eleanor married into an old island family, and her young husband took her to live in a small house near his family's large farm-house whose acres stretched down to the bay—but Eleanor had no children. She knew, at last, that she would have no children of her own, all her young friends had their first baby, then a second, even a third and she had none. She was barren and desolate. A sister back in New York State died suddenly, leaving three boys. Her sisters were willing to take one boy each, but Eleanor wanted all three. She asked her husband if he was willing to take the boys. "We're too young to take on all that responsibility, Eleanor," he said. "They aren't ours." But Eleanor was persistent, it was her chance to have children, and they were her own sister's children, close to her by blood. She was persistent, she tells. "When I baked, I'd say, 'Isn't it a shame the three boys can't have some of this?' Or when we went sleigh-riding or skating or picnicking, I'd say, 'How the three boys would enjoy this.'" Until one day her husband said, "Eleanor, you'd better send for the boys."

Her husband is long dead, now, and her loyal "boys" visit her in the summers where she now lives again in the little house near the water's edge, the old farm-house and most of the acres sold long ago to summer-people.

IV

In thick fog by the time we passed the bell-buoy, we noted the time, measured the distance on the chart, took a compass-reading on our heading, guessed at our speed and the speed of the current, and waited for Sylvester's Cove to show up out of the fog: vaguely it appeared, but we were almost on it before we saw it. I chose to return on a reverse course, and to wait for the fog to lift. We waited at our mooring until two o'clock when the fog lifted suddenly and we set out again, but with an adverse tide. Visitors, headed for the 4th of July picnic on our island, waved to us from the mail-boat. We were near the bell-buoy for an hour, held by the current and the tide, but the day was fine and we were glad to be in the boat, on the water. The wind freshened and we sailed to Stonington, anchored near the old granite-polishing site under the quarry-derrick, and went in search of a room and a meal. After dark we walked to the main street to watch the fireworks, but the fog returned. The little street was jammed with people and with cars.

Next morning after breakfast we sailed down Stonington

Reach past West Mark, and past Scraggy Ledge, past the big red bell out in the middle of the crossing in open seas to Vinalhaven. We tacked back and forth with a southwest wind; on the ocean-ward tack heading out to the great granite tower which marks the entrance to Penobscot Bay, tacking back to Vinalhaven Island where we were becalmed as we approached land. On every tack we were stopped, although we could see the wind dancing on the water. The tide was sweeping us south where we wanted to go, but when we approached land we were stopped, we couldn't move—a sea of glue. I put up our big, new, light jib and we worked out to sea to sail fast, but each time we returned to land—the sea of glue. In Vinalhaven at last, we anchored in front of our acquaintance's house. He came out in his little sail-boat to advise us on our moor-ing, and offered his pier for our landing. We left our canoe on Mr. Moyer's pier and stayed for a drink. I asked him how old he had been when he played his first concert, "I must have been eleven years old, it was in San Francisco, three weeks before the great earthquake." He played for us on his little spinnet.

In the night I awoke, thinking about the sea of glue, and realized that an upward pressure had made the water dance and that the landward breeze lifting over the high island had left a vacuum, creating the dancing waves.

In the morning in a ten-mile wind, after a swift get-a-way like a runaway horse (we nearly ran down a moored boat that was hidden from our view by our sail)—we were in Vinal Reach with a beam-wind favoring us through islands: narrow passages, won-drously beautiful water with birds, islands, trees, vistas.

Sailing day after day, the first sensations of sailing each year merge with other trips: the foggy day into Stonington on the 4th of July mingles in memory with the 4th of July when we had ar-rived in Stonington in thunder and lightning, in downpour, and the grocery-store lady, Mrs. Bartlett, found us a room. I awoke, in still another summer, not having slept soundly, in a room in Mrs. Robinson's guest-house in Camden. The wind had blown hard all night. It was four-thirty in the morning, and there was some visi-bility. "Would you like to sail home now?" I asked George. The weather report had predicted heavy fog for two days, and it seemed to me to be not yet impenetrably thick. We left the har-bor at five, wind still south to southwest, a favorable wind for home; the tide until eight would be in-coming. We sailed fast in a ten-mile wind for Job's Crossing. We decided on compensation of 20° for safety's sake. Fog became dense, we sailed fast, and sud-denly there was an islet, low in the water on our right hand and a wooded island on our left! I am the navigator, and in such moments I must decide in a split second—hold off or continue, port or starboard—decide, fast, fast—remember which island is low in the water, which island has a long sand-spit out from it, which island has that bent tree? "We are down-wind from La Selle's Island. Haul in the sails and hold up for Job's Crossing!"

George called out, "There's a bell—on our right—"

"Quick, George, quick! Hold up, hold up! This is Job's Crossing and we are too far down wind, we can't cross the bar so close to the sand-spit, we have to be at the five foot spot." The current had been even stronger than we had calculated, or I had not held a true course when I had been steering. (The second time that summer I had allowed that to happen.) The egg-shell we sail in, the little Day-Sailer held up valiantly, we swept through the opening and held our course for home. Fog cleared suddenly, and as we neared Northhaven Island we could see clearly: Channel Rock, Fling Island, Eagle, and even Hard-head beyond Eagle and both Porcupines—and there was Robert Quinn, our friend, out hauling his lobster-pots. He hailed us with an arm uplifted from his work, and we were home.

V

We wake to the raucous clatter and din of a hundred eider-ducks, crows and gulls. The beach is theirs at dawn and by the time I have watched the sun come up behind Hard-head, and have set foot on the beach, I can see who has walked here before me since the last tide erased all marks. I like to say that my feet make the first marks, but mine have never been the first. This morning a large deer's tracks pointed up the beach with each step out of the water, to disappear into the trees: probably a buck to add to the does we counted in the early morning in the field below our windows, or in the dusk last evening, when they did not yet know we were here. This first morning a deer's face appeared at our bed-room window, gazing in. On the beach bird-tracks and bird-noises are still loud, but the birds quickly move out, onto the water. Eider-ducks with flotillas of ducklings are quack-quacking in an interminable conversation between mamma and babies. They sit on the floating seaweed and dive below the surface for their food, the mother anxiously trying to keep her little ones close. If danger threatens the ducklings climb aboard mamma. Gulls attack them, seals attack them, sea-crows and cormorants too. If a mother duck brings two or three to adolescence from a hatching of twelve or fourteen, she is a good mother.

To line the nest with eider-down, the mother duck plucks

down from her own breast, and as this is also a time of moulting for all the adults, while the babies are helpless, they too cannot fly.

From the top of the island which is flat and cleared of spruce and pine, the maples, the oaks, and the birch and alder growth, I look out, turn slowly, survey the bay in a 360° uninterrupted view: after many summers here I can identify and name all the islands I can see. Into the far distance islands lie spread out in silvery water. Far away dark shapes are scattered across an expanse of Penobscot Bay as wide as one's eye, reaching the limit of vision—islands forever, too many to count. I see Isle au Haute, pronounced here Isle "Oh Holt," and there is even a small brown lump of a rock named Colby Pup, a reminder to me that my family sprang up here long ago during the great migrations from England. At the end of Merchants Row, a clear almost straight course for sailing east or west, the wind is abeam, and I can see on any day both sail- and motor-boats of summer visitors making their way homeward toward Portland and Boston, or sailing east to a summer-world that's heaven. I look to the mainland and can make out the prominent peaks. The further distant are the mountains near Bar Harbor: Mount Desert, Cadillac Mountain. To the west are the Camden Hills.

Almost as accurate as looking at the calendar, fog tells us it is July, fog makes an enclosed world, no one hurries and it is a good time to talk. Helene comes to vist, to tell us of her life in the months we have been away. Fog encloses us, no one looks on and we talk, while our eyes are searching, searching, looking, seeing as far as vision permits: the sea, the wind, the fog are present in our vision and in our minds. As I write this, remembering, I return to that white light of fog and that deep, almost dreaming, almost unconscious state of being.

On the mainland land surrounds us, land—peopled, busy. On our small island we are surrounded by sea until our opinions, even our prejudices seem altered, perhaps because the sea comes first, second things are touched and altered as are the ways of the sea in its tides: if not this tide, then the next will surely come again in a rhythm that requires my rhythms to change in some way too, a slower and surer order in my mind.

We sailed to the island at the end of one summer to ask if a place could be found for us. Yes, the camp that was called "Two Bits." We will put it together as three bits. Three 8'x8' cedar rooms left behind many years ago by a summer visitor who could no longer come to the island. The three-room miniature camp was put together with aluminum foil insulation on the inner ceiling, and with bright green fibre-glass roofing that can be seen, a landmark for the mail-boat or other passing boats; a fine old wood, coal, and canned gas stove, a gas refrigerator and electricity, two water tanks, one on each side of the end of the building, to provide water—when there is rain enough, or we carry water from a fine spring on the Light-house beach. Light-house beach, where at one end at low tide we could see the pilings of the light-house pier, from the days when the light-house had been inhabited. The family had been provided for many years with good anthracite coal, unloaded in baskets and carried from the boat up the hill in baskets. In rough weather and with accidents a great deal of coal must have spilled into the sea, for on any day we can gather a bushel or so of coal, enough to keep our fire overnight when it is cold. George and I glean wood from the beach, from the forest, and with a sharp little Finnish saw we cut wood, trying to keep ahead of our daily needs.

Our camp is an acre or two of Maine in dense fir and spruce woods, growing so thickly that we can be lost when we step a few yards into them. We have tied pieces of white cloth to the trees to mark a path to the landing. In the old farm clearing, of which only the foundations of the earlier buildings can now be made out by depressions in the center of the field, eighty-year-old apple trees still bloom, and in a tangle of raspberry vines and tiger-lilies, we make out the garden of the old homestead. In the severe winters of Maine, a house that is not lived in and cared for disappears as rapidly as a house in the tropics. Nothing of the house and barn of this farm remain. The row of seven magnificent locust trees stands, and sprouts spring up each spring everywhere, and must be cut back if they are not to become forest again in a very short time. We built soil of seaweed and mulch from the floor of the forest, where there was no soil, only stones, and in the first year grew vegetables that helped to feed us and our few summer visitors. I have lived most of my life in cities, but in my early childhood I had a garden and when I can have a garden it is a return, it awakens memories I did not know I had.

In the fog of July, George and I have been transplanting flowers and plants, a clump of Evening Primrose. (The moths like them because they stay open at night.) We took the most beautiful path on the island yesterday: the path to the lighthouse, where we dug a clump of Monk's-hood for Joy Stewart. Later I washed them and separated the roots, put them in a mail-bag, and sent them off on the mail-boat. They will be beautiful near Pumpkin Island lighthouse.

One fine evening, sailing from Swan's Island into a fiery

sunset, we sailed on as the full moon rose, sailing toward the blinking light which we saw all the long, almost windless night, flashing SOS—SOS, until at dawn we anchored in the little harbor of Pumpkin Island.

Just to say "Island" brings to my mind the feeling that I love, cut off from the mainland, water on all sides, view unbroken in any direction. Sailing to strange islands we make acquaintances, who in subsequent visits become friends. The people in the outer islands in Maine have a sweetness—I use the word not in its present cliché, but to mean an attitude that prevails. On the islands in conversations we find this sweetness. Sometimes we anchor because fog has made it impossible to know where we are. The fog encloses us and we go ashore in an isolation as total as though we are visitors from another planet, and if we meet a citizen of this unknown place we talk in a privacy that makes conversation somehow without risk. I think that people who live their lives on islands, especially on small islands, live in a meditation, thinking about the world out there. The miracle of being here envelops them and makes for the sweetness I feel in them.

George has written a poem called "Ballad":

> She took it that we came—
> I don't know how to say, she said—
>
> Not for anything we did, she said
> Mildly, 'from God'. She said
>
> What I like more than anything
> Is to visit other islands. . .

JOHN PECK

GEORGE OPPEN AND THE WORLD IN COMMON: A DESCRIPTIVE POLEMIC

If George Oppen, exemplar of necessary feeling, has openly addressed truthfulness in his poems, that must be because he has had to—because his subjects required him to do so, but also (and his readers feel this in one way or another) because too few of the rest of us exercise the same degree of integrity.[1] Yet those subjects are distinguished by being *ours*; that is, they represent our shared situation, to a degree that sets his work apart. The strictnesses, compressions, and reticences of his style have their place not, as some might have it, among the features of an aesthetic formalism. They respond to, among other things, a destructive absence, a vacuum in the space of our common world.

My focus falls on that concern because Oppen's poems, with each rereading, strongly fortify my hunch that American poetry, and not only that poetry, would find its situation much illuminated by the political thinking of Hannah Arendt. "The common world" is her phrase also, construed in a way I shall try to paraphrase. It is not commonly applied by writers to their concerns. "Apply" she most certainly does.

To sketch something of the Greek position on politics which Arendt recovers in *The Human Condition* and also, notably, in her essay on Lessing in *Men in Dark Times*, one might say that precisely where human difference can be moved into discourse and sustained, there "the political" comes into being, a public space or common world which differentiates even as it convenes

---

1. My themes get woven around poems from *The Materials* (1962), *This In Which* (1965), and *Of Being Numerous* (1968), and a few poems from *Seascape: Needle's Eye* (1973) and *Primitive* (1978). I shall quote from the text of the *Collected Poems* (1976), with all references incorporated into my text. I shall also incorporate into my text references to Oppen's two published interviews, the first in *Contemporary Literature* 10:2 (1969), 159-172, and the second in *Ironwood* 5 (1975), 21-24. His essay "The Mind's Own Place" in *Kulchur*, 1963, I take from the reprinting in *Montemora* 1 (1975), 132-137.

us. That very function defines our humanity; and mass culture frustrates or defeats that function. Humanity and its common world are neither the private, the fraternally committed, nor the Christianly charitable, all of whom in this basic political sense are worldless. To put it somewhat differently: the variety of our speech about what-is frames the possibility of the political; the shared speaking of it is the practice of humanity, and the space made by that speech is the world in common. The world that we now inhabit almost always inhibits or shuts off that common world.

II

Let my starting point be literally instrumental. How do labor and the tools of labor reveal truth about the diminished common world actual to us? The question is not quite Heideggerean, being more restricted, but still its answers are not so obvious as they might seem.

First, a digression. The Olivetti Corporation of America recently employed Hans Namuth to photograph old American hand-tools for a "promotional" volume. Namuth's portraits set these tools against rich gray folds of contextlessness. A society pledged to rapid technical and financial mutation, to manipulation first and last, to the systematically profitable irrelevance which Oppen's poems call "extravagance" and "an art *de luxe*," will of course produce such an ornament. It will, without irony, nostalgically convert old tools into the sumptuous gawkery of prestige. The dysfunction of labor under a plutocratic oligarchy has its chastely pornographic symptom in this "book."

Oppen's "Antique" in *The Materials* holds up one of these tools, an immigrant's, against the prospect of distant office buildings. The poem reveals both the construction of the New World and the difficulty with which the builders survive in it:

> Against the glass
> Towers, the elaborate
> Horned handle of a saw
> Dates back
>
> Beyond small harbors
> Facing Europe. Ship's hawser
> On the iron bollard at the land's edge mooring
> Continents of workmen
>
> Where we built
> Grand Central's hollow masonry, veined
> In bolted rails in shabby
> City limits daylight and the back yard

> Homes. In which some show of flowers
> And of kitchen water holds survival's
> Thin, thin radiance.
>
> (*CP*, p. 51)

Show perfectly acknowledges the several braveries, both of spirit and beauty, in life thinned by adversity, and with them the fine tool deliberately held up in line of sight. Both kinds of contrast are deeply affecting in part because their objects are somewhat . . . out of place: for that is the condition of their showing or standing forth. That is, the saw handle not only manifests craftsmanly pride, and the sink water and flowers an immigrant family's tenacious hope and dignity; both also speak of a peripheral existence against the not-so-grand but very central odds, both revealing that aspect of a political truth. Disclosure, within the common world that we have in fact built, begins with that aspect of truth.

Oppen's choice of the horn-handled saw also seems a better revealer of such things than Ezra Pound's example of a craftsman's pride, the signed Romanesque column in the crypt of San Zeno in Verona. While Pound's political targets are the portable, the extravagant, and the exploitative, his measure here, as it was also a political measure for Ruskin, is the artist. Oppen does not subscribe to the same honorable confusion between political and artistic orders of construction and disclosure, and for that we are in his debt. The fine 27th section of *Of Being Numerous*, on poetry itself, interiorizes the forms of labor and construction, but neither as a "basis" for poetry nor as a metaphor of its art; it suggests that their difficult relation is deeper and less schematic than that.

To put my earlier question differently: does labor itself reveal something about our common world through its construction? If we study some of those spaces which give rise to unavoidable impersonal encounters, we get our primary indications not only of the "mass situation" but also of a self-entrapping fate for labor. Oppen finds these together within a subway setting in "Vulcan," also from *The Materials*, where he gives that role to labor and even more pointedly telescopes the New World's settlement with its consequences:

> The householder issuing to the street
> Is adrift a moment in that ice stiff
> Exterior. 'Peninsula
> Low lying in the bay
> And wooded—' Native now
> Are the welder and the welder's arc
> In the subway's iron circuits:
> We have not escaped each other,

Not in the forest, not here. The crippled girl hobbles
Painfully in the new depths
Of the subway, and painfully
We shift our eyes. The bare rails
And black walls contain
Labor before her birth, her twisted
Precarious birth and the men
Laborious, burly—She sits
Quiet, her eyes still. Slowly,
Deliberately she sees
An anchor's blunt fluke sink
Thru coins and coin machines,
The ancient iron and the voltage
In the iron beneath us in the child's deep
Harbors into harbor sand.

                                          (*CP*, p. 46)

One of the settlers' motives, escape into the singular, failed
even in the wilderness, those depths that were also once new. (The
quoted phrase I assume comes from one of the explorers who first
conned the landfalls of Long Island.) The newer depths of the subway contain labor, which sets darkly fixed forms around the meeting that cannot be escaped. These depths also contain three unset-
tling doublings. First, the encounter with the crippled girl, painful
because her injury lies exposed within a confined situation of
anonymity, deepens the sense of disorientation with which Oppen
begins the poem, in his householder's entrance into a common
space. Second, the crippled girl pathetically duplicates the laborer
himself, as lamed Vulcan among the materials of his craft, "the
ancient iron and the voltage." Of course, she is first of all a vulnerable daughter and abandoned inheritor; therefore all the more
strikingly is she the bearer of Vulcan's aspect here. Her incorpora-
tion of Vulcan's defect represents something about labor which
a burly ironfitter does not in himself suggest: the precarious and
lamed status of labor within the house that it has been asked to
build. Oppen makes it her birth-house; and she herself gives birth
to a powerful image. And so finally, the fantasy which Oppen
gives to the girl repeats the moment when the island entered
Western history; and that imagining, also with iron, destroys the
labor of the iron tunnel. She has interiorized the entire cycle,
and short-circuited it. Precarious though her life is, her imagining
turns the moment of historical violation against the condition
which traps her. And, not so curiously, as an impulse of escape,
the fantasy duplicates the original attempt of New World settlement to escape "each other."

Oppen's last three lines, with their deliberate prepositions,
drive into, complete, and accept a great weight of feeling. Because

of the child? Surely, and there is more to say about that. But also because the poem follows a path from involuntary disorientation, to an involuntary flinching away, to an imagining which may come involuntarily but which Oppen has her firmly will, "slowly and deliberately." That development, from unwilled to willed response within the depths of entrapment in the actual common, telescopes an archaeology of our social response. The girl is the lamed result of labor, she is in birth, and she herself gives birth to an image of origination. But she embodies the collective and ongoing construction of escape, a process that maims but continues. That her fantasy would destroy and then repeat the cycle only confirms the fates that have been enacted, and enacted within her body and her mind.

III

Passage from labor to image, as Oppen's girl moves, is one of those deep inflections of the mind that shows us more than we can explain. Taking the same route among Oppen's poems, I pass from "Vulcan" to a poem in *Seascape: Needle's Eye*, in which he addresses some potent collective images of the city while also addressing one of their passionate custodians, Pound as the erring master of their meaning. "Of Hours" suggests with its title a vigil, and goes on to study sentinels. It moves me to imagine the insistent seeing in Oppen's work spaced among levels of figures: the walker or sailor whose eye works as intensely as the eye of the car-crash survivor in "Route," while below them in the subway crouches the girl before her vision, and above them walks the sentinel or lookout. This three-story world hardly maps Oppen's terrain, but it does suggest the urgency of his observations.

Since either Wordsworth or Baudelaire, poetry has had its observor of the mass, a shocked wanderer or an alert *flâneur*. In the London books of *The Prelude*, during his processional entry of the teeming capital, Wordsworth suffers an inward stunning. That entrance still may define the way one registers the unreal aspects of our common world. But Wordsworth's entry, actual and mappable, its impact anticipating even Eliot's, takes only the preliminary step: one enters the common space to find the common world missing, and implodes into the vacuum. The next and harder step is to locate the access-route along which meetings might take place which would constitute a public world in the original sense of that term. That route, more than any literal penetration of a city's space, is speech. All of our neo-epics— Pound's, Williams's, Olson's—didactically point to that passage.

Oppen, seasoned watcher of streets, lodges an etymology in the
first poem of *Seascape: Needle's Eye* which poses the whole knot:
"ob via   obvious." What we can see in the street, or encounter
there (*ob via*, in-the-way-of-a-meeting), seems obvious enough in
a way, but in other ways remains hidden, as an emptied common
world insures that it will. With deepening consistency Oppen's
work perceives those streets, hears the frustration of speech in
them, and suffers the further degree of isolation that comes from
the perception. The first step in the history I have characterized
has never been taken more completely than by Oppen; and Oppen's
way of indicating the second step in his work, however frustrated
its end may have to be, fully warrants him to address Pound, unnamed in "Of Hours" but unmistakable, as a lookout who has
twisted some of the warnings he has spoken over the common
precincts.

The poem opens by echoing Simone Weil in *Attente de
Dieu*—through her most commanding metaphor, which trans-
fixes her Greek sense of the cosmos with the crucifixion's iron
implement. Her subject is the more-than-suffering of affliction,
which she conceives as "a nail whose point is applied at the very
center of the soul, whose head is all necessity spreading throughout space and time."[2] The afflictions against which Oppen himself fought, "Burying my dogtag with H/For Hebrew in the rubble
of Alsace" (*CP*, p. 211), were somehow not seen by Pound, or by
Parisian culture either: "why did I weep/Meeting that poet again
what was that rage/Before Leger's art poster/In war time Paris"
(*CP*, p. 211). Art, which should be a seeing, dishonoured by its
default, compels Oppen to test all of our communal sentinels
with the stroke of evil: the cop on his beat, his antecedent the
lookout on battlements, and the poet walking the city:

> '. . . as if a nail whose wide head
> were time and space. .'
>
> at the nail's point the hammer-blow
> undiminished
>
> Holes   pitfalls open
> in the cop's accoutrement
>
> Crevasse
>
> The destitute metal
>
> Jail metal

---

2. Simone Weil, *Waiting For God*, trans. Emma Craufurd (New York: Putnam, 1951),
pp. 134-135.

Impoverished   Intimate
As a Father did you know that

Old friend   old poet
Tho you'd walked

Familiar streets
And glittered with change the circle

Destroyed its content
Persists   the common

Place   image
The initial light   Walk on the walls

The walls of the fortress   the countryside
Broad in the night light the sap rises

Out of obscurities the sap rises
The sap not exhausted   Movement
Of the stone   Music
Of the tenement

(CP, p. 210)

The blow not only shatters an ineffectual guardian, it also telescopes syntax: "did you know that" (the shattering effect) but also "that . . . the circle destroyed its content" (the city-mandala turned self-devouring), but also "its content persists." Yet what persists—the commonplace image of first light—also gets shivered into its parts: the common world, then place itself, and then the image of origination in that world, none of them of course assured. The image which Oppen then takes up indeed stands initial with the city's fate; does not Aeschylus open the *Agamemnon* with a watchman on the palace roof looking for the beacon flares that signaled Troy's fall? "Walk on the walls," Oppen bids Pound, who had long done just that, making civic achievements and justice his focus, and making the stone trees of Venice, and Amphion's legendary feat of raising Theban walls with lyre-sound, his poem's own images of civic origination. Oppen acknowledges that, but he also takes these myths back from Pound, into a despised common place, the loud tenement. His bold reclamation of these images stands in contrast not only to Pound's style but also to the resurgence of these potent myths in the period diagnostic for Pound and his teachers: the Renaissance which poured such images in bronze (an unattributed medal of Filippo Casoli carries on its reverse an Italian fortress-city whose walls are stridden by a gigantic viol-player).

By this point the poem has brought into one sweep things that we indeed should learn to feel as one: it has struck resonance from persistent civic images, and assessed their mishandling, and acknowledged the sadly actual, and felt the great shaking blow over all. Oppen's continuing acknowledgment that Pound in exile "Fought ice/Fought shifting stones/Beyond the battlement" gainsays nothing of his charge that Pound invalidated some of his own valorizations of civic order through a failure to see. "Old friend old poet/If you did not look/What is it you 'loved'/Twisting your voice your walk" (*CP*, pp. 211-212). The ending walks this figure homeward along his chosen Italian hill-roads, a self-professed teacher who became "Unteachable." The compressions of Oppen's later poems, seldom easy, work here to draw the force of a blow down through icons of the city, and out into a sorrowing judgment of their watchers. Its tone is authoritative.

IV

The relation of poetry's tone and voice to civic images, perhaps because each element in the relation works to fulfil its own kind of power, will make the poet who cares for a common world take thought.

Oppen proposes the counsel of restraint. In section 10 of "Route," as another consequence of a poetry *ob via* devoted to what "comes by the road," there comes a reflection on that poetry's voice. "Not the symbol but the scene," Oppen begins, and then embraces the integrity of such an art's limits:

> If having come so far we shall have
> Song
>
> Let it be small enough.
>   (*CP*, p. 192)

He speaks directly to those of his readers who, grateful for his passion and clarity, nonetheless wish that sometimes he would raise his voice. A touchy issue, surely—but in lines such as these Oppen implicitly acknowledges it. It is not that Oppen is afraid to raise his voice; rather, he will not.

Many are the reasons for that, but beyond those of a style attuned to its materials lie those of power itself. A poem from *This In Which* that segregates art from domination takes Virgil's celebrated messianic fourth Eclogue as its occasion. "From Virgil" quietly opposes with some of Virgil's own lines the claims made by that eclogue for song's relation to prophetic power and state power. Virgil sets any prospective work of his about the child's future deed beyond even the song of Orpheus or Pan. Complimentary convention though this may be, it typifies its song and enunciates the functions of state poetry. Oppen countermands that statement:

> I, says the buzzard,
> I—
>
> Mind
>
> Has evolved
> Too long
>
> If 'life is a search
> For advantage.'
>
> 'At whose behest
>
> Does the mind think?' Art
> Also is not good
>
> For us
> Unless like the fool
>
> Persisting
> In his folly
>
> It may rescue us
> As only the true
>
> Might rescue us, gathered
> In the smallest corners
>
> Of man's triumph. *Parve puer.* . . 'Begin,
>
> O small boy,
> To be born;
>
> On whom his parents have not smiled
>
> No god thinks worthy of his table,
> No goddess of her bed'
>
> (*CP*, p. 84)

The beginning rejects the economic and biological egotisms bequeathed us by the 19th century; the end gathers both us and the saving power into vulnerable byways. The poem was anticipated by the first poem in *The Materials*, "Eclogue:" "O small ones,/To be born!" (*CP*, p. 17). And it seems to claim a descendant in the "Populist" of *Primitive*, whose "magic infants" have something of the same role. Oppen's final lines also conclude the fourth Eclogue. But the Virgil who does not appear in Oppen's poem is significant by virtue of his absence—the prophet whose fulsome intonation culminates the Cumaean Sybil's own prophecy of a new age, Gold finally supplanting Iron.

Set in the tumultuous years preceding 40 B.C., Virgil's poem speaks not of the corners of man's triumph, but about one of its great turns or pivots (a crisis in the literal sense) and the triumphs hoped for from it. With Julius recently assassinated, and Anthony and Octavian violently jockeying for dominion, the Empire awaited the outcome with dread. When a pact was forged at Brundisium, the widespread surge of relief gave rise to an anxious spate of prophecies, some of which were pressed into state service. As Sir Ronald Syme dryly notes in *The Roman Revolution*, "already coins of the year 43 B.C. bear symbols of power, fertility and the Golden Age."[3] Virgil's poem, cast in this mold, remarkably pegs the messianic turn to the consulship of Pollio, Antony's own legate and one of the architects of the pact struck at Brundisium: *te consule, inibit,/Pollio . . . te duce.* Considering the much-disputed identity of the child to be born, Sir Ronald plausibly anchors it to the poem's address to a political crisis. Its final lines, the same ones which Oppen incorporates, nominate actual Roman parents rather than celestial ones, annex the crucial concordat to their marriage, and anticipate, with reasonable hopes for good auspices, the birth of a political heir to Antony and Octavia. Virgil prophesies in a notably loud voice—*maiora cannamus*—the fulfilment of a political consolidation and the pacification of empire.

His vaunt of the power of this theme to lend progressively greater resonance to the poetry which it sponsors, though wrapped in the convention of string-sweeping and therefore usually passed over, poses a challenge to reflection. The child's identity, a bone worried for two millenia, should not obscure this conventional boast, for at issue, in its own terms, is the voicing of prophetic truth and poetic power at the instigation of crisis. The voicing of course serves to compliment and ornament power, and Virgil's terms are the ones usually embraced: crisis calls poetry to speak truth, even prophecy, in a high register, and in attunement if that can be managed. The fourth Eclogue, whatever its mysteries, declares the role of the state poet and calibrates the resonance of state poetry.

It is as if, born of Roman messianism (and captured later by Christian messianism), the poem erected a monument to rectifying Advent within the squares of the imperial common. Benign as this figure may be, nonetheless as a monument to the *next* Reich, the perennially better Reich, it should give us pause.

Very attractive, then, is Oppen's appropriation of the child.

---

3. Ronald Syme, *The Roman Revolution* (Oxford: Oxford Univ. Press, 1939), p. 218.

The little figure does not reinaugurate the state. The power he represents, rather than being co-optable by the imperial mint and addressable to Asinius Pollio, is weak and epicentral. The nurture and sponsorship which this child needs are nowhere to be found near the Princeps. And most pointedly, the poem which invokes this power will not speak of poetry's augmented resonance with respect to it. A truthfulness foolish in the eyes of advantage, and savingly tiny in the eyes of buzzards, will not long survive enlargement, even as enlarged resonance.

Maiora cannamus can be intoned only in a common space believed by its citizens to be favored by fate. The myth of Trojan origins, and later the deification of emperors, set the imperial common apart from the Greek one over which fate worked evenhandedly. The fourth Eclogue may confidently be chanted in the Roman space of the chosen, while elsewhere the unchosen are reduced to silence. This other, deprived common world anticipates that of the mass situation, with this strange qualification: speech anomalously survives in our mass common as the anaesthetizing formulas of luck—vestiges of favoring fate. Oppen takes note of those same myths in *Of Being Numerous*, and everywhere he writes of a light in which perception can recover the openness twisted by an imperial common's sense of fate or otherwise silenced. That his spare style has great evocative power is added testimony to the import these matters bear for us. The whole of that power condenses into single phrases, such as this in "Blood from the Stone"—"the inherited lit streets" (*CP*, p. 31)—a phrase that gives us actual space and its long history in their narrowed light, while making us feel another light in another common space that might have been.

V

Richard Pevear has already written about Oppen with Hannah Arendt's terms:

> The profound and unexpected originality of Oppen's poetry lies in its construing of the relationships between perception ("virtue of the mind") and the opening of a public realm, a *polis*, a place for humanity, in which humanity transcends mass isolation. For, contrary to the views of most politicians, and perhaps most political thinkers, the public thing is not grounded in opinion, in consensus, in theory, in state power or institutions, but in "the right construction of what-is" . . . . Before it is speech, poetry is a space prepared for speech.[4]

4. Richard Pevear, "A Poetry and Worldlessness," *The Hudson Review*, 19:2 (Summer 1976), 318.

Pevear has also translated Alain, Simone Weil's teacher, whose chapter on legend in *Les Dieux* can suggest to an American how remote are his communal occasions from their prototypes. "This kind of storytelling is open and public. The hero's praises are sung on a customary day, at the foot of his purified statue. Commemoration, in which architect, poet and rhapsode invest their own genius, even their own immortality, carries still further the pious labor of embellishment which is so natural to filial piety. And the listeners are all guardians of the legend, as the word itself says, for legend means what must be spoken."[5] Our anonymous bronze veterans in public parks, our impoverished legionary rhetoric on Memorial Day, speak almost nothing that must be said. And beyond memorial rites, Alain's construction of the etymology lets us better sense the public thing that we travesty. A necessary speaking attaches not only to its occasion but also the spaces which frame it, to monuments and even to the streets which lead to them. That we want to prepare such spaces while not knowing how to do so, or while living at cross-purposes with respect to them, defines us in a hundred ways. Visiting Philadelphia in 1904, Henry James stumbled on a culture-stuffed parlor along a street of "immeasurable bourgeois blankness" and asked himself, "What could have testified less, on the face of it, than the candour of the street's significance?—a pair of huge parted lips protesting almost to pathos their innocence of anything to say: which was exactly, none the less, where appetite had broken out and was feeding itself to satiety."[6]

Oppen registers the pathos more deeply. Lines from every part of his work converge upon it; *Of Being Numerous* forms its definitive *legenda*, recasting "A Language of New York"—"the walled avenues/In which one cannot speak" (*CP*, p. 96). Even before they show the frustration of speech, the poems show how the space for it is at issue. A poem like "Sunnyside Child" is exemplary here. Our labor constructs a habitation only to find it partially concealed. Disclosure cannot easily be spoken and debated in such a world, for it must somehow be remembered without ever having been wholly seen. Oppen's writing offers an instrument at just this point; it sees how to see in that way. Approaching the Red Hook section of Brooklyn in "Tourist Eye," he states our canonical equilibration of possibility with travesty:

5. Alain, *The Gods*, trans. Richard Pevear (New York: New Directions, 1974), p. 116.
6. Henry James, *The American Scene* (Bloomington: Indiana University Press, 1968), p. 298.

> This is a sense of order
> And of threat. The essential city,
> The necessary city
> Among these harbor streets still visible.
>
> (*CP*, p. 45)

Our diminished public world of course stands forth first as a physical thing, which then prompts recognition of political absences, inadequate constructions of what is. If we follow Oppen's eye from European monuments to American ones, we can trace the arc of diminishment. That progression is literal in "Philai te kou Philai," where a Gotham dawn lifts the eye back along the entire westward drift:

> the unbearable impact
> Of conviction and the beds of the defeated,
>
> Children waking in the beds of the defeated
> As the day breaks on the million
>
> Windows and the grimed sills
> Of a ruined ethic
>
> Bursting with ourselves, and the myths
> Have been murderous,
>
> Most murderous, stake
> And faggot. Where can it end? Loved, Loved
>
> And Hated,
> Rococo boulevards
>
> Backed by the Roman
> Whose fluted pillars
>
> Blossoming antique acanthus
>
> Stand on other coasts
> Lifting their tremendous cornices.
>
> (*CP*, p. 76)

To observe that these capitals degenerate to Sullivanesque ornament on urban towers (as Oppen does in "Ozymandias": "The absurd stone trimming of the building tops/Rectangular in dawn, the shopper's/Thin morning monument" [*CP*, p. 38]) is not to see exclusively as a Marxist; it is with open eyes to take stock of the goods in a brutal democracy of trade. And even after one has recanted a Marxist tenet, as Oppen does in "Pro Nobis," that does not qualify one's sense of how domination, through its monuments, attempts to turn even time against a public world. "Public silence indeed is nothing," begins "Monument," "So we confront

the fact with stage craft/And the available poses/Of greatness"
(*CP*, p. 127). That poem moves from a Norman chapel wall "Of
the armed man/At the root of the thing," to Oppen's New York
mercantile ancestry, and chooses the sea itself, "Contrary of
monuments/And illiberal."

This illiberality can pay homage at certain monuments, however, if they bear witness to love for a human future. And so the
fine "Eros," whose subject is that sort of legend, that variety of
what must be said, moves from an act of filial piety set at
memorials to both the massacred Parisian Communards and to
members of the Resistance, into the civic space of Paris itself.
This enlarging movement enacts what I take to be the fullest implications of legend; and in this case the expansion outward
reveals a European paradigm for something now general, the
deformation rather than fulfillment of a public world, a dead
weight that also registers, by inversion and by what is absent from
it, the needfulness of "what must be said" and of preparing a
space in which to say it:

> Maze
>
> And wealth
> Of heavy ancestry and the foreign rooms
>
> Of structures
>
> Closed by their roofs
> And complete, a culture
>
> Mined
> From the ground . . .
>
> As tho the powerful gift
> Of their presence
> And the great squares void
> Of their dead
>
> Were the human tongue
> That will speak.
>
> (*CP*, p. 103)

A more primitive, naively upbeat thought about some of
these matters was set down by Whitman for the Centennial of the
republic, but then shelved. With European monuments in mind,
he declared that "we have *more* than those to build, and far more
greatly to build. (I am not sure but the day for conventional
monuments, statues, memorials, &c., has pass'd away—and that
they are henceforth superfluous and vulgar.) An enlarged general

superior humanity . . . we are to build."[7]

The testing of an idea of humanity that can survive as a value became Oppen's inquiry in *Of Being Numerous*, and a dialogue with Whitman emerges from the poem, unavoidably one might say. Oppen closes the poem with part of a letter of 1864 from Whitman to his mother; Oppen weaves several kinds of light through the poem, including daybreak, but his choice of Whitman's words ends things with a civic sundown:

> Whitman: 'April 19, 1864
>
> The capital grows upon one in time, especially as they have got the great figure on top of it now, and you can see it very well. It is a great bronze figure, the Genius of Liberty I suppose. It looks wonderful toward sundown. I love to go and look at it. The sun when it is nearly down shines on the headpiece and it dazzles and glistens like a big star; it looks quite
>
> curious . . .'
>
> (*CP*, p. 101)

That last word, Oppen says in his first interview, expresses his own guarded affirmation. By setting it apart, he writes playfully; but he also heightens the word's estranging effect: we see this still-European monument to freedom, raised over our civic focus, glinting in *Abendland*, an ominous Hesperus of evening rather than morning. Curious indeed that the monument's inaugural, over an inaugural people, should impress most at sunset.

Curious is also the key adjective, quietly and cumulatively estranging, in Whitman's "Crossing Brooklyn Ferry" when he, too, tests an idea of humanity-through-time:

> Crowds of men and women attired in the usual costumes,
>   how curious you are to me!
> On the ferry boats the hundreds and hundreds that cross,
>   returning home, are more curious than
>   you suppose,
> And you that shall cross from shore to shore years hence,
>   are more to me, and more in my meditations,
>   than you might suppose.

The humanity which Whitman's later prose note proposes to build in preference to monuments, he already begins to build in these shore-crossings. Hart Crane's attempt to extend Whitman's idea by reifying that crossing into a bridge, and then unsuccessfully straining to reconvert that bridge into an idea, seems after the fact unfortunately to have been pre-ordained. *Of Being Numerous* blue-pencils that very bequest of Whitman's. Section 5, fixing

7. Walt Whitman, "Notes Left Over," in *The Complete Poetry and Prose* (New York: McLeod, 1948), II, 345.

upon a detail of the Brooklyn Bridge (I am guessing this to be so
from the date), shows the chilling effect which our own *monu-
menta inscriptata* can have within their own world. Crane's
flinging-out his curveships of God darkly responds to that effect
and that world:

> The great stone
> Above the river
> In the pylon of the bridge
>
> '1875'
>
> Frozen in the moonlight
> In the frozen air over the footpath, consciousness
>
> Which has nothing to gain, which awaits nothing,
> Which loves itself
> > > > (*CP*, p. 150)

At such a point Oppen's eye isolates a shortfall common to both
worlds—our actual one, and its proposed transcendental compensation. What drops through the gap between them is the *res pub-
lica* itself. All of this we may sense when hearing the language
which our monuments and inscriptions do manage to speak.

It is not Hart Crane but George Oppen who has advanced
the conversation with Whitman, and with populism, by testing its
terms while living committedly. The commitment lends weight to
the reservations. "Myself I Sing" in *The Materials* sets comradeship and encounter in Crusoe's world; the shipwreck is collective.
Section 6 in *Of Being Numerous* again uses Crusoe to represent
our mass isolation; and daybreak for the poem's value emerges
only from "the bright light of shipwreck" (*CP*, p. 152). Section
14 sets Oppen's own war years of comradeship (Whitman's own
key experience) against the emptying of the term "the People"
by life in the mass. Much later in *Primitive*, "Populist" looks back
on Oppen's own commitment, and on Whitman's language for it,
to find the accounts still unsettlingly open and the "birth-light"
of our landscape still isolating and primal. (Its closing imagery
almost exactly duplicates the imagery of section 28 in *Of Being
Numerous*.) And the whole of the long poem itself checks the
enthusiastic surge of *Democratic Vistas* one hundred years earlier,
although it is also true that we are not reading the book that
Whitman wrote if we overlook its barely suppressed rage and
disappointment at "the piled embroider'd shoddy gaud and fraud"
over a hollow-hearted materialism. But Whitman's best hope—a
last reliance "upon humanity itself" without which "the entire
scheme of things is aimless, a cheat, a crash"—is precisely the idea

and value that Oppen sets out to weigh and if possible to establish. What he finds will not sustain the idea of humanity are exactly those twin supports on which Whitman and many liberals rest their faith: individuality and fraternity.

Oppen's assessment crucially resets any such basis for a common world. What Whitman had called "idiocrasy," or more grandly "the single self . . . on permanent grounds," is that very individualism which Oppen, calling it "the singular," identifies as the source of shipwreck. Whitman would not have invested so much in his other principle, comradeship, had he not already observed in the functions of the single self considerable possibilities for evil; therefore the hopes he entrusted to "adhesive" love or fraternity were correspondingly great and even anxiously insistent. "The safety of these States" hinged upon it, and this kind of love had for him "the deepest relations to general politics." American progressive thought seldom gets beyond the same hopes and sentiments. But Whitman's great counterpart to the singular will not work either, Oppen finds; like the singular, "the numerous" and its corrolaries do not suffice to instill faith in a common world through time. Section 35 locates humanity "beyond rescue of the impoverished" (*CP*, p. 175)—and so it must, for, as Oppen says in the first interview, neither struggles for happiness, nor searches for an altruistic morality, nor reliances upon the poor to confer value, can give man the life which is peculiarly his, the awe before existence which lets him go on. "Neither ambition nor solidarity nor altruism," he writes in "The Mind's Own Place," "is capable of establishing values."

Oppen's paring-away of both the singular and the numerous from a faith in the common does no violence to our daily recognitions. Rather, it sharpens them. Nicola Chiaromonte, writing about urban encounters in "The Mass Situation and Noble Values," has us recognize their typical quality by observing, first, that our situation strictly compels any one of us "to think and act *as if* he were simply one element of the great number," and then also to recognize that, anyway, there is no sanctuary for any of us from that situation. And yet were there nothing for us beyond these realities, Marxist tenets about them would be the only ones that we could possibly hold. And that, Oppen finds, will not account for the faith that we can in fact hold. The conditions of our shared life threaten to reduce even that faith to another feature of mass, to number in the disintegrative sense; but it need not happen.

Oppen has won through to this perception by addressing not only Whitman but also the entire misconception of the common

world bequeathed to us. Rousseau and then the revolutionaries of
1789 equate full humanity with fraternity; Whitman inherits their
view; but its continuing life responds to humiliation and affliction,
and that durable oppression becomes, by virtue of our resistance
to it, an enemy who blinds us. Hannah Arendt's Lessing address
is our best guide here. Only since the era of revolutions have compassion and humanitarian feeling been political bonds, serving as
the basis for political solidarity; before that, in classical political
thought, though of course natural, they were held to be irrelevant
to the real bases of political justice. If this shocks us, that is because the political space between us has been so compressed by
indiscriminate forces that we do not recognize its absent original.
Brotherly warmth in such times, whether it be revolutionary
fraternity or Whitman's adhesive love, becomes what Arendt calls
"the pariahs' substitute for light," and it

> exerts a great fascination upon all those who are so ashamed of
> the world as it is that they would like to take refuge in invisibi-
> lity. And in invisibility, in that obscurity in which a man who is
> himself hidden need no longer see the visible world either, only
> the warmth and fraternity of closely packed human beings can
> compensate for the weird irreality that human relationships as-
> sume wherever they develop in absolute worldlessness, unrelated
> to a world common to all people. In such a state of worldlessness
> and irreality it is easy to conclude that the element common to
> all men is not the world, but "human nature" of such and such a
> type.[8]

It is both surprising and grievous that a world-needy compassion
establishes the politically common world no more than does its
world-withdrawn predecessor, the Christian bond of charity.
"What makes mass society so difficult to bear," writes Arendt
in *The Human Condition*, "is not the number of people involved,
or at least not primarily, but the fact that the world between them
has lost its power to gather them together, to relate and to separate them."[9]

Section 26 in *Of Being Numerous* puts it much the same way,
confronted with the suicides of young writers.

> They have lost the metaphysical sense
> Of the future, they feel themselves
> The end of a chain
>
> Of lives, single lives
> And we know that lives
> Are single

8. Hannah Arendt, "On Humanity in Park Times: Thoughts About Lessing," in *Men in
Park Times* (New York: Harcourt, Brace, 1968), p. 16.
9. Hannah Arendt, *The Human Condition* (New York: Doubleday, 1959), p. 48.

> And cannot defend
> The metaphysic
> On which rest
>
> The boundaries
> Of our distances.
> We want to say
>
> 'Common sense'
> And cannot.
> (*CP*, p. 165)

To relate and separate: "speech" should do both, but cannot in our circumstances. It is in this sense that Oppen writes in section 10, "But I will listen to a man, I will listen to a man, and when I speak I will speak, tho he will fail and I will fail. But I will listen to him speak. The shuffling of a crowd is nothing—well, nothing but the many that we are, but nothing" (*CP*, p. 153). In the same sense, in the poems of *Primitive*, he says that "we have hardly begun to speak," and that it is "to each other we will speak." All of this within a situation from which there is no escape, as he wrote in "A Narrative" in *This In Which*: "What breath there is/ In the rib cage we must draw/From the dimensions/Surrounding, whether or not we are lost/And choke on words" (*CP*, p. 137).

It is Oppen's virtue to have acknowledged in his work that any clear-sightedness about all of this only increases one's isolation. He does not take solace with Whitman in brotherhood, in feelings of affinity which are valued because they are thought to supply the civic bond, but which do not and in fact cannot have "the deepest relations to general politics." The nobility of Oppen's view derives from his seeing all of this clearly and then also saying that there is no separate peace to write, no sanctuary even for the isolating insight. His example here might prompt us to acknowledge our commonest ignoble assumption, that even if the larger fabric collapses from rot or rending, we can wrap a small piece of it around ourselves and escape. But no. We should remember Pindar in his fragment on the possible calamaties portended for Thebes by a solar eclipse: "*olophuromai ouden ho ti panton meta peisomai*"—"But I shall not complain against what I must suffer with others."

Oppen's insistence on clear-sightedness has the *political* quality, in Arendt's sense, of holding to the virtues of light over the consolations of fraternal warmth. For, in the common world of the spoken-because-seen, the world that actually gathers while still separating us, the warmth even of solidarity is no substitute for that light. The recent poems of *Primitive* are shot through with a piercing light which not only shines out a personal valediction but also speaks of the hauntingly ambivalent radiance of the world, both the physical world and the human world in their different forms of continuance. In this, Oppen's recent poems extend and intensify the light, "clarity as transparence, not explanation," in *Of Being Numerous.*

If we are ready to feel how the light in that poem indicates a common world we lack, then we are also prepared to see something of such political meaning unfold through the poem's light.

Its initial aspect is "the bright light of shipwreck" in section 9, a harsh singularity which ascends to menace near the poem's midpoint in section 19. There that light is reified as both trapped fly and threatening helicopter, presiding from great height over madnesses of the actual city. This is the first of two liftings-up in the poem. It corresponds to other elevations of perspective in Oppen's work: the predatory domination in "From Virgil," or the blindness which begins "World, World"—"Failure, worse failure, nothing seen/From prominence,/Too much seen in the ditch" (*CP*, p. 143).

But shortly after this menacing turn the other light seeps through, with section 22's "clarity as transparence." After a vivid glimpse of the unreal in section 26 under the mineral glow of streetlamps on parked cars, and after the suicides abandon the humanity for which one might choose to live, this clarity springs up in the movement of water over stones. In the 27th and 28th sections on poetry, this light from the world and from perception moves into the intense but liminal function of art, "the isolation of the actual," where the interiorized forms of labor shed their own light; but it can only anticipate the daylight of a common world. The light of art, therefore, arrives as the "narrow, frightening light/Before a sunrise" (*CP*, p. 169). In the 29th section light enters the cycles of parentage and posterity, an eros for history rather than a fear of it. From seeing the world as it is, to seeing the real but liminal power of art, to seeing and choosing a human history, light has moved away from the shipwreck of singularity. And so after the 33rd section the "truthfulness/Which illumines speech" can declare itself ready to die within "the wild glare/Of the world" (*CP*, p. 173). What emerges with this illumination of speech is no sentimentalism of either poetry or brotherhood; it begins to constitute a common world founded neither on fear nor in disdain of those facts which challenge its survival. In its 17th section the poem recognizes our diminished public world in the dimmed roots of words driven underground, the ads in subways, whose tunnels rumble with a "ferocious mumbling, in public/Of rootless speech" (*CP*, p. 159). In its last four sections the poem

turns, with speech now lending light to a possible common, to test
that light. And Oppen's test lifts something other than a monument over the focus of a renewed common world.

The 37th section emends the first poem in Oppen's first
book, which studied boredom's power to reveal reality (taken up
with the same window view in section 3 of "Route," and related
to Heidegger in Oppen's first interview). He finds, with moted
sunlight, an image for the peculiarly suspended reality of history.
In "Blood from the Stone" he had written, "we were lucky—
strangest word" (*CP*, p. 33). And now such words, rootless because floating in the myths that shield us from perception and
guilt, swim in the light.

> What have we argued about? what have we done?
>
> Thickening the air?
>
> Air so thick with myth the words *unlucky*
> And *good luck*
>
> Float in it . . .
>
> To 'see' them?
>
> No.
>
> Or sees motes, an iron mesh, links
>
> Of consequence
>
> Still, at the mind's end
> Relevant
>
> (*CP*, p. 177)

With that last word Oppen performs the poem's second lifting-up:
relevare, to raise into sight. What he discloses is the reality of the
secondary, the formulas we attach to history. This secondary
reality is not to be seen as either the world itself or the common
world are to be seen. But even so the motes of it, our self-protective conversions of systematic wrong into the accidents of
chance and luck, can still lock into an image of the determining
and entrapping system, relevant to any pursuit of value.

These two degrees of reality reflect Oppen's constant preference for the substantive thing to anything added to it. In the first
interview he illustrates this with a favorite quote from Hegel—
" 'Disagreement marks where the subject-matter ends. It is what
the subject-matter is not' "—and then adds shortly thereafter: "*Of
Being Numerous* asks the question whether or not we can deal
with humanity as something which actually does exist." The passage

from Hegel is part of the preface to *The Phenomenology of Mind*.[10]
To paraphrase Hegel: the truth of subject-matter abides inexhaus-
tibly in its concretion, but not in the knowledge of a history of
comments about it. And to requote Oppen: "clarity as transparence, not explanation." Hegel's subject-matter, *Sache*, embraces both a thing itself and its function as a concern, much as
our own "object" does. And in section 37 of the poem, the
poem's inquest into the status of its object, the idea of humanity
or the truth of the common world, distinguishes that object from
the haze of explanations and shibboleths, many misleading or
pernicious, suspended through its light by history. The image,
winnowing chaff from its great and problematic substantive, lifts
up the approach to it and holds that suspended.

The remaining three sections swiftly compress the poem's
themes. Seeing and witnessing, finding unknown with known,
knowing persons but caring for "man" beyond one's own death—
these hover over two glimpses of the anonymous death of an old
man with only a hospital nurse to attend him. The death of someone nearly abandoned, and the care given him by a stranger, punc-
tuate Oppen's inquest into an idea that we cannot manage to live
without. This death, too, is a mote in the light, but lifted up this
time to be seen, as an alien power which the common world must
make human, an event otherwise "Occuring 'neither for self/Nor
for truth' "(*CP*, p. 179). This death also ushers in the dying sunlight of the final section, the passage from Whitman's letter about
the Capitol. The end of the poem stages, at the focus of official
public space, the innocent seeing of a monumental mote lifted
up, a bronze figure of liberty in the iron mesh of consequence;
and that vision discloses, though not to its designated witness,
the dying of both light and the common world. Yet this conclusion may complete the poem's testing of humanity as a value
indispensable to us, because another light already has appeared
and survived within the poem to disclose it. The common world,
turned in that light toward both speech and mortality, but lifting
no relevant bronze allegory atop a dome, dispenses with monuments.

Oppen's first interview includes observations about the limits
and even the passing-away to which an ethic may submit, even
altruism. Some of these observations should be set next to Simone
Weil's reflections upon idolatries of the singular and the collective
in her notes on "The Great Beast" in *Gravity and Grace*. Both
have their way of referring beyond themselves to an absolute

10. J. W. G. Hegel, *The Phenomenology of Mind*, trans. J. B. Baillie (New York: Macmillan, 1931), p. 64.

measure. The poems do this with light, and should we dull its edge by unthinkingly flattening the actual, there stands one figure in the poems, an anti-monument of this absolute quality, ready to correct us: the Archangel of the tide in "The Translucent Mechanics," "brimming/in the moon-streak . . ./in whose absence /earth crumbles" (*CP*, p. 222).

VI

A strong but mute contention runs among the work of those few American poets concerned to define an authentically common world. Two senses of the common mark the work of Olson and Oppen, and the debate should be opened.

Both men honor Whitehead; the 12th section in *Of Being Numerous* begins with a passage of Whitehead's on the objectively "actual world." Whitehead's thinking in the twenties and thirties made the actuality of a common world its cornerstone for some of the same reasons that writers embraced the Marxist rejection of individualism. In "The Mind's Own Place" Oppen looks back on the populist aesthetic chosen by his generation with mixed judgments, but holds fast to the tests of truth and perception fostered by "the sense of the poet's self among things." The value of Whitehead to both Oppen and Olson has much to do with that sense of reality; his was a citizenly metaphysic.

And both Oppen and Olson oppose modern writing's addictions to the easier varieties of personality and psychologism. Oppen bracingly insists in "World, World—" that they are attempts "To lose oneself in the self./The self is no mystery, the mystery is/That there is something for us to stand on" (*CP*, p. 143). In *Letters for Origin* Olson proposed that one way of restoring "man as common," although it demanded new handlings of sequence and juxtaposition, was to remove proper names while retaining "the force of the common by not falling for realism, or the false particularism of the 'autobiographical.' "[11] But Olson's objectively common world, while polemically fastened to the polis, turned into an archetypal world, which further grounded the common in what he had called the proprioceptive sense, the body's sphere of awareness. Oppen's objectively common world remains faithful to a political ethic, and to a value beyond that ethic, as well as to a sense of "the common world" in line with Hannah Arendt's Greek understanding of speech and action. His retrospective tone in "Two Romance Poems" from *Myth of the Blaze* contributes the final evidence:

11. Charles Olson, *Letters for Origin* 1950-1956, ed. Albert Glover (New York: Cape Goliard, 1970), p. 82.

                              What one would tell
            would be the scene   Again!!   power

            of the scene I said the small paved area,
            ordinary ground except that it is high above
            the city, the people standing at a little distance
            from each other, or in small groups

            would be the poem

            If one wrote it   No heroics, obviously, but
            the sadness takes on another look

            as tho it mattered, in a way
            'smoke drifts from our hills'
                                        (*CP*, p. 255)

Whitehead himself placed brackets around a proprioceptive sense of the common: "the body . . . is only a peculiarly intimate bit of the world"[12] Oppen's expressed preference for Olson's shorter poems over the Maximus series is no surprise in view of the deeply differentiated senses of the common in their work. But these two senses still meet in a concern for the construction of political space; and that means that the divisions between an archetypal and a traditionally political sense of the common (and by tradition I mean Arendt's "Greek" understanding) remain fertile. Surely a dialectic exists between these two senses of the common, whose articulation would benefit anyone awake to the mess we face. What other question in American poetry (not poetics) promises as much from attention to it as this one?

     The classical polis of course was nothing like a modern city. And neither did that polis resemble the humorless architecture of our political theory. It was, to paraphrase Nietzsche, a hothouse of fierce rivalries and contentions, which turned the arenas for gymnastic and musical competition into the essential civic space. The passion to be best probably consumed more of the same fuel that later energized the blatant *philotimia* of the Roman Empire than historians have allowd. That can serve as one caveat. Another comes with the recognition, which many will struggle to resist, that the place in poetry of the political, "the city," is nothing that one can take for granted, even after Pound, Williams, Olson, Cavafy, Roy Fisher, and others. For one thing, our own poetry has no genuine public (an academic-and-APR audience is not a public). For another, the recognition of different orders of experience (the phrase in section 27, *Of Being Numerous*) entails potentially enormous consequences, which neither committed living nor poetic vocation can by itself address. The recognition represented

---

12. Alfred North Whitehead, *Process and Reality* (New York: MacMillan, 1929), p. 126.

by Oppen's long interim of silence points to the issue, a recognition weightier than Auden's comparable argument with himself in the 1939 elegy for Yeats. But none of this is to say that the polis stands off-limits to a poet. The polis, after all, was for the Greeks not only the order of communal life but also the form of the soul. That analogy, tremendously active even when buried, *is* our tradition. It rests so deeply imbedded that we cannot get rid of it. And that is why the contention between Olson and Oppen's senses of a common world seems fit item for an ongoing agenda. It rephrases that inalienable analogy in terms that it will not be easy for us to escape.

RANDOLPH CHILTON

THE PLACE OF BEING IN THE POETRY OF GEORGE OPPEN

In his introduction to *Discrete Series* in 1934, Ezra Pound de-
fended George Oppen against the charge of resembling William
Carlos Williams. Paradoxically, Pound's defense tied Oppen to
Williams, and it has, says Oppen, "always haunted" him, since he
feels his attitudes are "opposite to those of Williams."[1] But
Pound suggests a useful critical strategy just the same: in inviting
us to consider how Oppen appears to be like Williams, his comparison can also help us understand how Oppen is truly unlike
Williams—that is, how he is truly himself. Certain similarities between the two poets do exist—a sparseness of style, for example,
and a concern with the elemental materials of art and life, and
perhaps a common interest in the relationship of abstract to concrete. But at every point of comparison, Oppen's poetry distinguishes itself from Williams's. More than any other objectivist
poet, Oppen confronts difficult questions of ontology, a result in
part of the admitted influence of Martin Heidegger. Heidegger
played the same role for Oppen that Alfred North Whitehead did
for Williams, and the philosophers' fundamental differences parallel a central difference in the poets. For Whitehead and Williams,
things exist before thought. Thus, they by-pass Heidegger's fundamental philosophical question: why do things exist at all? Oppen,
though, never forgets it. His poetry uniquely blends Heideggerian
and objectivist concerns—concerns with objects of perception,
with modes of perception, and with the intellectual context in
which those objects and modes must be placed.

Oppen reminds us most obviously of Williams through his
sparse presentation of "things." He frankly concentrates in his

1. Interview with George Oppen in "The 'Objectivist' Poet: Four Interviews," *Contemporary Literature*, 10 (1969), 168. Hereafter referred to as *CL* and cited in the text.
Concerning Pound's statement, Williams said that for his part, he did not understand
why it was necessary to deny something that did not exist.

poetry on the noun—the elemental level of language as he understands it. He concentrates so intensely, in fact, that he admits
having difficulty with connections between nouns—with syntax—
in his early work (*CL*, p. 161); but it is precisely through this difficulty, of course, that his poetry engages us in the typical objectivist project of questioning the relationships of things to things
(and to ourselves) at the same time that it makes us scrutinize
what seems most accessible to understanding: the concrete from
which we move to the abstract, the "little nouns," the "absolutely
unitary" (*CL*, pp. 163, 162). For facts which must be dealt with—
"That which one cannot/Not see," Oppen says[2] —are not only
irrefutable evidence of a world beyond the subjective; confrontation with them (as in Louis Zukofsky's "thinking with the
things as they exist") is a central part of the objectivist process
of perception, and one way in which that perception validates
itself.

Oppen emphasizes that "It is . . . a principle with me, of
more than poetry, to notice, to state, to lay down the substantive
for its own sake" (*CL*, p. 161). Within his poetry, this principle
results in at least one stylistic peculiarity common to Pound and
Zukofsky—their use of what Herbert Schneidau has identified
as language "beyond metaphor."[3] In a rather obvious example,
Oppen writes in "Route" of

> The sources
> and the crude bone
>
> —we say
>
> *Took place*
>
> Like the mass of the hills.
>   (*CP*, p. 184)

Or in a much more textured passage from "Population," he describes

> A crowd, a population, those
> Born, those not yet dead, the moment's

---

2. George Oppen, *The Collected Poems of George Oppen* (New York: New Directions,
1975), p. 176. Hereafter referred to as *CP* and cited in the text.
3. Schneidau develops the point in what I feel to be a very provocative article, "Wisdom
Past Metaphor: Another View of Pound, Fenollosa, and Objective Verse," *Paideuma*, 5
(1976), 15-29. Pound himself provides perhaps the best example of this kind of language
when he relates that he "once saw a child go to an electric light and say, 'Mamma, can I
open the light?' . . . It was a sort of a metaphor, but she was not using it as ornamenta-
tion" (*Gaudier-Brzeska: A Memoir* [1916; rpt. New York: New Directions, 1970]),
p. 84.

> Populace, sea-borne and violent, finding
> Incredibly under the sense the rough deck
> Inhabited, and what it always was.
>
> (*CP*, p. 22)

Here "sea-borne" can mean both "carried by the sea" and "born of the sea," and beyond such punning, the use of "under" is highly ambiguous. We might read it in the sense of "under scrutiny," or in the sense of "beneath" (i.e., beneath the sensual level—"insensible"—a reading consistent with understanding "incredibly" as a modifier of the prepositional phrase "under the sense" rather than "finding"), or simply in the spatial sense of being at our feet. But these elaborations reduce the import of Oppen's language. Its power lies in its literal sense; Oppen continually relates images as directly as he can (which is to say arbitrarily) to their referents. He notes that "It is possible to find a metaphor for anything, an analogue: but the image is encountered, not found; it is an account of the poet's perception, of the act of perception. . . ."[4] An "account," like the nominalistic "neat and simple notation," effaces metaphorical complexity, presumes instead the direct (*because* arbitrary) attachment of language to its referent. Inevitably, of course, it also places a great strain on conventional linguistic structures, since perceptions are not "encountered" in those forms.

It generates, that is, a fragmented, disjointed, and at times ungrammatical style—a style that Williams, like Oppen, used in order to return through poetry to the fundamental materials of existence. In "It Is A Living Coral," for example, Williams fragments the scene he describes into its elements in order to make us become aware of their existence as elements and of their historical coherence as a "living coral." Alternately, in "At the Faucet of June" (identified by Zukofsky as an objectivist poem as it appeared in *Spring and All*), Williams borders on surrealism (describing "sunlight in a/yellow plaque" on the floor, "full of a song/inflated to/fifty pounds pressure") in order to dramatize the final, concrete image of elemental reality:

> Impossible
>
> to say, impossible
> to underestimate—
> wind, earthquakes in
>
> Manchuria, a
> partridge
> from dry leaves.[5]

---

4. George Oppen, "The Mind's Own Place," *Kulchur*, 3, No. 10 (1963), 4.

5. William Carlos Williams, *The Collected Earlier Poems* (New York: New Directions, 1951), pp. 251-52. Hereafter referred to as *CEP* and cited in the text.

Mere juxtaposition, always one of Williams's primary tools, carries the weight here of that unarticulated, unifying entity, the thing "impossible//to say," behind the poem.

Oppen uses a very similar strategy in the following poem from *Discrete Series*:

> Bolt
> In the frame
> Of the building—
> A ship
> Grounds
> Her immense keel
> Chips
> A stone
> Under fifteen feet
> Of harbor
> Water—
> The fiber of this tree
> Is live wood
> Running into the
> Branches and leaves
> In the air.
>
> (*CP*, p. 10)

Oppen's careful juxtaposition, just as Williams's, invites us to consider some larger, perhaps ineffable sense of unity. Yet the juxtaposition of bolt, keel, and tree has a substantially different quality from that of wind, earthquakes, and partridge. Williams emerges as the more romantic of the two, Oppen the more opaque. Perhaps we can provisionally note the elements he names as real but hidden parts of our environment; still, that perception does not satisfy in the way Williams's aesthetic sensibility does. We leave the poem questioning it.

Again, as in his poems of juxtaposed images, Oppen often fractures his single images more radically than Williams. What is now the second poem in *Discrete Series* (Oppen's single contribution to *An 'Objectivists' Anthology*) seems at first hardly readable. In the anthology, it is entitled "1930'S":

> White. From the
> Under arm of T
>
> The red globe.
>
> Up
> Down. Round
> Shiny fixed
> Alternatives
>
> From the quiet
>
> Stone floor ...   (*CP*, p. 3)

In the context of Oppen's first book as a whole, this poem becomes only slightly more understandable. He follows it with these lines:

> Thus
> Hides the
>
> Parts—the prudery
> Of Frigidaire, of
> Soda-jerking—
>
> Thus
>
> Above the
>
> Plane of lunch, of wives
> Removes itself
> (As soda-jerking from
> the private act
>
> Of
> Cracking eggs);
>
> big-Business
>
> (*CP*, p. 4)

If, as I understand the poem, the subject of "Hides" and "Removes" is "big-Business" (withheld, for emphasis, until the last line), Oppen's style here dramatizes the distance between the abstract concerns of business (including the roles business determines, such as "soda-jerking") and the private concerns of the people business serves. Also, to perceive "the prudery/Of Frigidaire" suggests some sense in the strategy of describing what is probably a machine as "White. From the/Under arm of T//The red globe." A strange, inanimate false modesty seems to carry over. And the separation of this image from the underlying "quiet//Stone floor" implies as well a divorce of the machine from elemental concerns.

Significantly, we can only provisionally identify the referent of the first poem from the text. Charles Tomlinson sees it as an elevator.[6] For the uninitiated, it may seem equally likely to refer to a light fixture or even a milk-dispensing machine. The real question may be whether or not we need to identify it. As with the second poem of the series, we come away not convinced of the importance of the commonplace, but unsettled regarding our relation to it—questioning that relation, probing it. Fragmentation,

---

6. Charles Tomlinson, "An Introductory Note on the Poetry of George Oppen," *Grosseteste Review*, 6 (1973), 241. I have since had this confirmed by Mr. Thomas Sharp, who obtained the information from Mr. Oppen himself. Evidently, many elevators in New York in the thirties had a device in the shape of a "T" with moving red balls to indicate movement up and down.

then, only superficially ties Oppen to Williams; the fragmented image of "1930'S" works in a significantly different way than do the fragmented images in, say, "It Is A Living Coral." There, fragmentation is a strategy to make us conceive of a historical unity in a new way. In Oppen's poem, the fragmented image seems instead to reflect a truly fragmented society; although it does not wholly deny some unity behind it, its fragmentation means that we must think of unity in terms of a question. We have no more than "discrete" fragments—acceptable in themselves, perhaps, but perceivable as parts of a whole only in a very tenuous manner.

With this contrast, a fundamental limit of Oppen's and Williams's similarities appear. Williams is not unaware that the true nature of the existence of things is often obscured (by society and even language, for example), but his poetry for the most part attempts to return us to the perception of true essences (in the concrete, of course). Truth is accessible to perception; we have the ability to perceive it. Oppen's poetry, although it seems similar in the assumption of a realm of truth not ordinarily perceived, relates to that truth in a significantly different manner. In fact, it continually places that truth in question. Oppen calls objectivist poetry, for example, a "test of truth," carefully pointing out at the same time that "truth" itself is a challengeable term (*CL*, p. 161). The content of that truth cannot then concern Oppen as it concerns Williams, who perceives, after all, ideas in things. It is rather the question of the existence of truth itself that becomes Oppen's focus, paradoxically (it would seem) by his being sensitive to the strong possibility of its non-existence.

From this point on, the more fundamental contrasts between Oppen and Williams begin to emerge. Williams, with his interest in Gertrude Stein's aesthetic, understood the value of abstract design to be a means towards the renewal of perceptual intensity.[7] When he conceived of the elemental, he tended to think in terms of artistic materials—words as words, paint as paint—and an aestheticism in his poetry often results. Traces of it appear in at least two of his poems considered objectivist: the construction worker in "Down-Town" "with a rose/under/the lintel of his cap" and a "rose-petal//smile"; the "whitish moonlight" in *Spring and All* XXIII (identified by Zukofsky as an objectivist poem in his article "American Poetry 1920-1930") that "tearfully//assumes the attitudes/of afternoon" (*CEP*, p. 278). Outside his objectivist pieces, of course, numerous examples occur.[8]

---

7. William Carlos Williams, *Selected Essays* (New York: New Directions, 1954), pp. 118-19.
8. In "Winter Quiet," Williams writes, "Limb to limb, mouth to mouth/With bleached

Williams makes the familiar strange—he defamiliarizes our world in the precise formalist sense of the term. Oppen, on the other hand, seems just as liable to treat the familiar as a significant condition in its own right. He sees poetry, for example, in

> The edge of the ocean,
> The shore: here
> Somebody's lawn,
> By the water.
>
> (*CP*, p. 9)

His work intensifies rather than transforms our sense of familiarity. In a poem on his lover, he seems to find beauty in her very ordinariness:

> No interval of manner
> Your body in the sun.
> You? A solid, this that the dress
>   insisted
> Your face unaccented, your mouth a mouth?
>   Practical knees:
> It is you who truly
> Excel the vegetable,
> The fitting of grasses—more bare than
>   that.
> Pointedly bent, your elbow on a car-edge
> Incognito as summer
> Among mechanics.
>
> (*CP*, p. 12)

For Oppen, the highest praise dwells not on manner or accent, but on the practicality and bareness of the unobtrusive. The care with which he approaches this kind of perception becomes particularly apparent here in the use of the interrogative. His poetry rarely asserts; more characteristically, it questions, and nearly always, in its sparseness and radically condensed quality, it makes us question how meaning can be present in the perceptions it expresses. Hugh Kenner notes more than once that Oppen's poetry seems barely to have come into existence.[9] Rather than making the ordinary strange, poetry such as this makes it fragile, and suggests the fragility of our perception of it.

Oppen's sensitivity to the "incognito" in "No interval of manner" suggests another point of contrast to Williams. Williams assumes that the "very existence" of the material of which the world is made "is law," "the greatest one of all . . . and is the

---

grass/Silver mist lies upon the back yards" (*CEP*, p. 141). Even in *Spring and All*, he gives us the streaming "reddish/purplish forked upstanding twiggy/stuff of bushes and small trees" (*CEP*, p. 241).

9. Hugh Kenner, *A Homemade World: the American Modernist Writers* (New York: Knopf, 1975), p. 171, and review of Oppen's *Collected Poems, The New York Times Book Review*, 19 October 1975, p. 5.

endless mystery of life."[10] That material provides the starting
point for his poetry and the basic element out of which he builds
a poetic statement. Furthermore, Williams makes the perception
of it and of the laws it expresses always available to the reader
through "things." For Oppen, though, the "mystery" of existence is hidden as often as it is revealed; the particulars of our environment interfere with our clear perception of their own basis
—with an unmediated sense of their true being.

A simple example of one object treated by both poets clarifies this point. When Williams uses the image of the automobile,
he does so uncritically, associating it often, in fact, with poetic
insight. In "The Young Housewife," for example, the poet compares the housewife to a fallen leaf, but then writes that

> The noiseless wheels of my car
> rush with a crackling sound over
> dried leaves as I bow and pass smiling.
>
> *(CEP*, p. 136)

In "The Term," a piece of brown paper "about the length//and
apparent bulk/of a man" rolls down the street in the wind, when,
we are told, "a car" "crushed it to//the ground" (*CEP*, p. 409).
The poem concludes:

> unlike
> a man it rose
> again rolling
>
> with the wind over
> and over to be
> as it was before.

In neither of these poems does Williams see the car itself nega-
tively; instead, he simply uses it to dramatize how a housewife is
like and unlike a leaf, how a wind-blown paper is like and unlike
a man. The automobile is a disruptive image, but of neutral value
at worst. More surprisingly, in "To Elsie" (*CEP*, pp. 270-72),
where "The pure products of America/go crazy," Williams does
not reject all of those products, or the system that produces them,
out of hand. The poem ends:

> It is only in isolate flecks that
> something
> is given off
>
> no one
> to witness
> and adjust, no one to drive the car.

---

10. William Carlos Williams, *The Embodiment of Knowledge*, ed. Ron Loewinsohn (New York: New Directions, 1974), p. 168. Hereafter referred to as *EK* and cited in the text.

Although inextricable from the American system of production, the car is not indicted here—only its lack of a driver; thereby Williams blurs, it seems to me, an important social criticism.

Oppen, though, focuses sharply on it. He writes that "Nothing can equal in polish and obscured/origin that dark instrument/A car" (*CP*, p. 4). Later, he deepens his treatment of the image considerably:

> Closed car—closed in glass——
> At the curb,
> Unapplied and empty:
> A thing among others
> Over which clouds pass and the
>   alteration of lighting,
> An overstatement
> Hardly an exterior.
> Moving in traffic
> This thing is less strange—
> Tho the face, still within it,
> Between glasses—place, over which
>   time passes—a false light.
>   (*CP*, p. 6)

In these statements, Oppen places into question the very quality of existence manifest in the car—its status as an object. In the 1968 interview, he points out that his judgment of the car arose from his "sense . . . of the greater reality of certain kinds of objects than of others." The car, he felt, was "somehow . . . unreal and I said so—the light inside that car" (*CL*, p. 167). As an object of "obscured origin" containing a "false light," the car interferes with clear perception rather than facilitating it; as a token of modern civilization, it puts the sense of reality Oppen speaks of into question. In contrast to Williams, Oppen deliberately makes it seem less than real.

Testing the reality of perceptions—placing into question the reality of what we see—also distinguishes Oppen's treatment of numerosity from Williams's of pluralism. Both poets grapple with the relation of part to whole, particular to general, but again for Williams, the terms of the relation and finally the relation itself are not in doubt. As he asserts in an early essay.

> Manners that differ, customs, worships that differ show that no language, no custom, no worship is the truth but that the truth is a formless thing which lies in them as within a suit of clothes, in part. (*EK*, p. 182)

And later, he writes that "by . . . pluralism of effort in each several locality, a 'reality' is kept; in plural—and so verified" (*EK*, p. 150). For him the particular thing has value in its own right precisely because it "verifies" a larger truth or reality of which it is a part;

"The universality of things" is always there "to discover" (*CEP*, p. 256). Thus, abstract, "impalpable" laws (such as "Beauty" and "Truth") can have a meaningful existence for Williams; the phenomenal world provides the proof—the only proof he needs—of that fact.[11]

For Oppen, the existence of those abstract entities is possible, but it is no more than possible; he continually questions their *actual* existence, in the fullest sense of that word. For example, he proposes that *"Of Being Numerous* asks the question whether or not we can deal with humanity as something which actually does exist"; furthermore, he conceives of the book as a "test of images [which] can be a test of whether one's thought is valid, whether one can establish in a series of images, of experiences... whether or not one will consider the concept of humanity to be valid, something that is, or else have to regard it as being simply a word" (*CL*, p. 162).

He seems to come to different conclusions regarding this question at different times. In "Pro Nobis" (*CP*, p. 141; included in *This in Which* [1965]), he writes in reference to his early poetic and political work:

> I had hoped to arrive
> At an actuality
> In the mere number of us
> And record now
> That I did not.
>
> Therefore pray for us
> In the hour of our death indeed.

Of Being Numerous (1968) qualifies that despair, though, by affirming in the title poem our sense of collective existence:

> Crusoe
>
> We say was
> 'Rescued'.
> So we have chosen
>   (*CP*, p. 150)

—"chosen," he says later, "the meaning/Of being numerous" (*CP*, p. 151). Crusoe is rescued *from* solitude *to* society, in other words, and simply by calling it a rescue, we make a social commitment. Oppen's sense of isolation does not disappear—the "bright light" of the "shipwreck of the singular," as he calls it later, continues to occupy him—but this enhances rather than diminishes the "meaning/Of being numerous." Numerosity and singularity give each other meaning. We need a sense of collective existence to provide

---

11. See especially Williams's essay "Beauty and Truth" (*EK*, pp. 159-69).

the context for a sense of our own reality. However, "humanity" comprises neither a sum nor any definable abstraction—it is, perhaps, mere numerosity, which stops short of the "truth" or "reality" Williams's pluralism "verifies."

"Myself I Sing" clarifies Oppen's notion of the relationship between the individual and humanity. The poem begins:

> Me! he says, hand on his chest.
> Actually, his shirt.
>   And there, perhaps,
>   The question
>   (*CP*, p. 35)

—the question, that is, of what *can* constitute a proper self-concept. In a halting inner dialogue, Oppen in the first half of the poem severely questions the simplistic, assertive egotism that takes for granted the complex relation of the self to its surroundings, and ends with a final, hesitant declaration: "I think myself/Is what I've seen and not myself." We cannot define ourselves as easily as the naive, assertive "Me!" of the first line attempts to do. Rather, in a manner wholly consonant with objectivist assumptions, Oppen believes that the process of self-definition takes place only through the careful consideration of one's encounters with an outside world. He expands upon this principle in the following lines:

> A man marooned
> No longer looks for ships, imagines
> Anything on the horizon. On the beach
> The ocean ends in water. Finds a dune
> And on the beach sits near it. Two.
> He finds himself by two.

Again, the "shipwreck of the singular" shows the inevitable failure of man to place himself in solitude; he must imagine "Anything on the horizon," must posit some reference point whether or not it "really" exists, and, ultimately, he only "finds himself" (spatially and psychologically) "by two," by a multiple (not a singular), by something outside himself. "In that a man needs a measure," Oppen says in commenting on this poem, "He defines himself by two."[12]

"Two" might refer to a number of things in the poem—to the marooned man and the dune, to the dune and the ocean, to the speaker and the earlier trailer owner—but the final section (which immediately follows these lines) seems to start from the possibility that it refers simply to another person:

12. Kevin Power, "Conversation with George and Mary Oppen, May 25, 1975," *Texas Quarterly*, 21 (1978), 48.

> He finds himself by two.
>   Or more.
> 'Incapable of contact
> Save in incidents'
>   And yet at night
> Their weight is part of mine.

The quotation refers us to an earlier poem which may also explain Oppen's reference to "Their weight." "Party on Shipboard" (*CP*, p. 8) describes a ship's passengers, who are

> Like the sea incapable of contact
> Save in incidents (the sea is not
>   water)
> . . . .
> The sea is a constant weight
> In its bed.

The apparent substance that makes up the sea (water) does not reveal its true quality (weight); the apparent substance of what we perceive as humanity (that is, human beings) also does not reveal its underlying quality of coherence (again, "weight," but in a metaphorical sense). "Myself I Sing" perhaps makes possible, though, a sense of that quality (with which, again, we come in contact only "in incidents"). The last lines read:

> For we are all housed now, all in our apartments,
> The world untended to, unwatched.
> And there is nothing left out there
> As night falls, but the rocks
>   (*CP*, p. 36)

Beyond individual apartments, beyond any assertive "Me!", beyond consciousness itself lie the rocks, emblems of pure existence, which in the absence of all else ties us together. Moreover, the rocks suggest another bond among us—the bare fact of the enduring common environment in which we find ourselves. Finally, this poem does not assert any strictly defined concepts of the self or humanity; it tries only to establish the context in which those concepts might exist.

In contrast to Williams, Oppen also carefully avoids any movement beyond the particular here. There must be something outside the single perceiver in order for us to exist, Oppen believes, but we can know little more. He does not accede to that impulse, very much like an impulse towards symbolism, which causes Williams to be attracted by "The universality of things." Rather, he appreciates their absolute impenetrability (which he often suggests, as in "Myself I Sing," through reference to rocks or the "mineral fact" of the world). Not surprisingly, then, as L.S. Dembo has pointed out, for Oppen, "What matters is the 'sense of the poet's self among things.' "[13] Instead of saying "No ideas but in things," Oppen declares "things explain each other,/Not themselves" (*CP*, p. 134). For Williams, pluralistic diversity verifies *a* common, multi-leveled and meaningful "reality"; Oppen's numerosity merely allows us to consider the possibility of meaning in a complex world. Numerosity "means," perhaps, simply that we are here—objects, in a sense, among the objects of the world.

Oppen's stylistic peculiarities, especially his concentration on the noun, signal his effort to maintain contact with our selves and our world. He has said that "All the little nouns are the ones that I like most" (*CL*, p. 163)—nouns such as "tree," "hill," "sun," etc.—because "they remain attached to the object."[14] In using such words he intends partly to return us to his own perception of the elemental. At the same time, though, he reveals a provocative insight into the way language can claim to do that, and in a larger context into his own philosophical sympathies. In the 1968 interview, he goes on to say:

> At any given time the explanation of something will be the name of something unknown. We have a kind of feeling—I described doubts about it—but we have a kind of feeling that the absolutely unitary is somehow absolute, that, at any rate, it really exists. It's been the feeling always that that which is absolutely single really does exist—the atom for example. That particle of matter, when you get to it, is absolutely impenetrable, absolutely inexplicable. If it's not, we'll call it something else which is inexplicable. (*CL*, p. 163)

Oppen understands that the relation of the "small noun" to its referent is arbitrary—we might say that it is simply arbitrary. It does not matter what we name the atom, only that we name it. Interestingly, this contrasts directly with Louis Zukofsky's objectivist notion of "sincere" language in which "shapes appear concomitants of word combinations," but it does not negate Zukofsky's larger project: to find a language connecting us to an "absolute" (in Oppen's word), not apart from the world, but in it. Furthermore, the connection Oppen makes between the absolute, the "unitary," the sense of "real" existence, and the "inexplicable," in light of the arbitrary relation of the noun to its referent, means that, as L.S. Dembo has said, ". . . the poet demonstrates his *faith* [in the world outside the self, in the noun's power to evoke that world] by uttering nouns, forms of speech that signify the existence of the object but provide no knowledge about

---

13. L.S. Dembo, "Individuality and Numerosity," review of *Of Being Numerous*, by George Oppen, *The Nation*, 24 November 1969, p. 574. He is quoting Oppen in "The Mind's Own Place," p. 4.
14. Power, p. 49.

it."[15] Oppen himself explicitly takes the existence of what the small nouns refer to on faith, faith "That it's there, that it's true, the whole implication of these nouns" (*CL*, p. 163). Together, these ideas form the central rationale for his poetic practice, and reveal not only its affinity with existential philosophy, but more specifically, its generative source in the ideas of Martin Heidegger.

L.S. Dembo has already explained at length the ways Oppen's poetry manifests existential thought in the two basic responses of "Aesthetic joy or intellectual depression" in confrontation with "bare reality," and the poet's sense of "estrangement" or aliena-tion from the world, from fellow human beings, and even from himself.[16] We might also connect Oppen's concern with the "ab-solutely unitary" and the inexplicable—the place before and be-yond meaning—to the notion that true existence is, for him, prior to essence. By itself, this may not distinguish him from Williams, who can be said to pursue "true existence" just as strongly, per-haps, in his manipulation of "words as words," or "art as art." But Oppen's attitude toward the world does distinguish him from Williams, in a way that suggests Martin Heidegger as Oppen's source of this kind of thinking:

> . . . I set myself again and again . . . just to record the fact, to saying that I enjoy life very much and defining my feeling by the word "curious" or, as at the end of "The Narrative," "joy," joy in the fact that one confronts a thing so large, that one is part of it. The sense of awe, I suppose, is all I manage to talk about. (*CL*, pp. 172-73)

Awe in the face of the real and a willingness merely to confront the pure, absolute, inexplicable sense of realized existence without moving beyond to any philosophical conception of its meaning tie Oppen directly to the Heidegger who pursues *Dasein*. And of course Oppen himself in an epigraph to *This in Which* quotes Heidegger, and he has also admitted Heidegger's influence in much of his thinking.

In light of this influence, it is not surprising that while William Carlos Williams's responses to the world resonate with Oppen's, they are nevertheless fundamentally different. The ex-pression of these responses, for example, takes two basic forms in *The Embodiment of Knowledge*. On the one hand, Williams is confident that accurate perception leads to knowledge. If there is faith, it is beyond faith in mere existence; it is rather faith in the power of his own ability to know. Upon discovering the existence

---

15. L.S. Dembo, "The Existential World of George Oppen," *Iowa Review*, 3 (1972), 81, emphasis added.
16. Ibid., p. 20, p. 73.

of a "law," he says (speaking to himself),

> "If you have been able to provide against one law by knowledge
> and also against many laws you will be able to provide against all
> even against that last one which is death, for there is no tyranny
> but ignorance." It is faith sprung out of experience! Faith which
> inquiry not destroys but deepens. . . . Let me have knowledge, all
> of it, always more and more. (*EK*, p. 156)

On the other hand, mere knowledge is not enough; Williams is
sensitive not only to the existence of what he sees, but to its
beauty, and in his appreciation feels compelled to express that
beauty. That expression has a peculiar motive: "I will go out,"
says Williams, "I will not only see this beauty, find it, but I will
make it mine. Mine, mine, as if I can possess anything. Further
than that, I will give, I will give the beauty to the world in my expression" (*EK*, p. 161). Williams, as I have already mentioned,
may understand that "the very existence of this material"—material of which art and the world is made—"is the endless mystery of
life" (*EK*, p. 168). But in his impulse to internalize, "to win more
and more to myself" (*EK*, p. 164), as in his impulse to gain knowledge, he seems to assume (though not to take for granted) awareness of being; ontological questions do not concern him.[17]

His position compares quite closely to Alfred North Whitehead's, and his differences with Oppen fundamentally reflect the
differences between Whitehead and Heidegger. Whitehead at-
temps to give "the outline of what I consider to be the essentials
of an objectivist philosophy. . . ."[18] He never considers ontological concerns of the type Heidegger treats, partly because his rationality can never put existence or being into question, but must
always assume their qualities (and their presence) without question. The result is an attitude that seems naive in relation to
Heidegger's; on the other hand, Heidegger's thought itself might
occupy only a small corner of Whitehead's concerns. Whitehead's
expression finds its roots in a systematic method of thought
whose basis he describes in this manner:

> I hold that philosophy is the critic of abstractions. Its function
> is the double one, first of harmonizing them by assigning to them
> their right relative status as abstractions, and secondly of com-
> pleting them by direct comparison with more concrete intuitions

---

17. Admittedly, the relationship of these statements to Williams's entire corpus is problematic. I refer to *The Embodiment of Knowledge*, though, because it contains key expressions of Williams's thinking before 1930 (a formative period for him) on the relationships of things to ideas, particulars to general concepts. Then again, the project he
describes in these quotations may find its mature form in *Paterson* itself.
18. Alfred North Whitehead, *Science and the Modern World* (Cambridge, England; Cambridge University Press, 1926), p. 129. Hereafter referred to as *SMW* and cited in the
text.

of the universe, and thereby promoting the formation of more
complete schemes of thought. (*SMW*, p. 126)

He values intuitive perception, then, insofar as it allows us to
know abstractions as they are realized in the concrete. Here, it
seems to me, Whitehead's assumptions are most relevant to Williams, himself always concerned with the significance of concrete
things and experiences, and with the ideas they embody.

Martin Heidegger, in contrast, implicitly criticizes all philosophies not concerned primarily with ontology when he posits "the
first of all questions, though not in a chronological sense": "Why
are there essents rather than nothing?"[19] With this question as a
provisional point of reference, Heidegger's self-reflexive procedure
continually scrutinizes its own assumptions, or, as he might also
say, its own manner of being. It must do so because the process
of inquiry itself becomes a central aspect of his philosophy; engaging in that process, more than any goal in supreme knowledge
or philosophical wisdom, opens his mind to what he perceives as
the end of all inquiry—the apprehension of pure being. In his intense scrutiny of his own question, for example, he points out that
"*If* this question is asked and if the act of questioning is really
carried out, the content and the object of the question react
inevitably on the act of questioning. . . . This question and all the
questions immediately rooted in it, the questions in which this one
question unfolds—this question 'why' is incommensurable with
any other. It encounters the search for its own why" (*IM*, p. 5).
In such questioning, he says, "we find out that this privileged
question 'why' has its ground in a leap through which man thrusts
away all the previous security, whether real or imagined, of his
life. The question is asked only in this leap, *it is* the leap; without
it there is no asking" (*IM*, pp. 5-6). Finally, and of most importance, "the leap in this questioning opens up its own sources
—with this leap the question arrives at its own ground. . . . We call
such a leap, which opens up its own source, the original source or
origin ⟨Ur-sprung⟩, the finding of one's own ground"(*IM*, p. 6).
Through the act of questioning, then, we move towards Heidegger's *Seiend*—the "what-is," the pure manifestation of being.

In the context of this study, the relevant differences between Heidegger and Whitehead are not difficult to see, I think.
Whitehead, though he may have accepted the significance of
an awareness of and confrontation with true being, did not put

---

19. Martin Heidegger, *An Introduction to Metaphysics*, trans. Ralph Manheim (New
Haven, Conn.: Yale University Press, 1959), p. 1. The book, originally printed in German
in 1953, is based on lectures presented at the University of Freiburg in Breisgau in 1935,
according to Heidegger's preface. Hereafter referred to as *IM* and cited in the text.

such emphasis on its difficult accessibility. Intuition, "naive experience," made it always available, and the business of philosophy was really to go on from there. Moreover, Whitehead, as I have quoted him earlier, believed philosophy to be "the critic of abstractions" whose end was in "completing [abstractions] by direct comparison with more concrete intuitions of the universe, and thereby promoting the formation of more complete schemes of thought" (*SMW*, p. 126). Heidegger's philosophy, on the other hand, "opens up the paths and perspectives . . . of knowledge." The verbs express the essential contrast—one "completes," the other "opens up." As for Williams, although he certainly was interested in renewing our ability to see things in their essentiality, like Whitehead he did not see the necessity of moving toward his goal through such a seemingly self-centered, self-reflexive questioning procedure. The nature of the existence of things was not in question for him, even if our ability to see it at times was.

For a study of Oppen, though, Heidegger can help a great deal. As we have seen, Heidegger approaches ontological concerns—which are privileged concerns for him, fundamental and primary—through a radical process of putting one's own existence in question by assenting to the process of questioning. For Oppen, the search for meaning or truth involves an analogous process.[20] Oppen has described the basis of objectivist poetry as the "imagist intensity of vision" which includes "moments of conviction" in which "you believe something to be true." But meaning in a poem exists on a different level: ". . . you construct a meaning from these moments of conviction" (*CL*, p. 161). Such a construction does not precisely embody meaning (or for that matter truth or knowledge), though, because Oppen regards poetry as a "test of truth," or even more hesitantly as a "test of sincerity" (*CL*, p. 161). In other words, he regards it essentially as a questioning process. Implicitly, poetry viewed this way questions itself—questions the ability of language to convey meaning; in one poem, Oppen calls words "enemies" or "Ghosts" (*CP*, p. 97). Thus, even though he explicitly professes his faith in "small nouns" and their referent, the elemental world outside the individual perceiver, he also always qualifies that faith by his awareness of the limits of language. Even though "there is something to mean," Oppen notes that "There are words that mean nothing" (*CP*, p. 131). His "test of sincerity"—his putting words constantly into question—is directed toward detecting them.

---

20. Let me be clear about wanting to explore a relationship here, not to assert a simple, direct correspondence. It is not my intention to transform Oppen into a philosopher, but rather to look at the ways in which philosophy helps to explain his poetry.

He might rephrase Heidegger's question, then, "Why is there meaning rather than nothing?" And as Heidegger, in his awareness of being, is also continually aware of the nothing that coexists with being, so is Oppen continually aware of the possibility of meaninglessness that coexists with meaning. We come into contact with it in his poetry partly in our struggle to extract meaning from a disjointed elliptical style; but the style, as we have seen in "1930'S" and "Thus/Hides the//Parts," also expresses a genuinely alienated attitude Oppen holds not only towards language, but also towards a fragmented modern society. Meaning, and the related concepts of truth and what is truly real, are always in question for him because connections among things and the relations of things to their sources are always obscured.

In *Discrete Series*, for example, Oppen renders, as we have noted, a car as a "dark instrument" of "obscured origin"; it is "somehow unreal." He also understands the difficulty with which we conceive of the relationships among objects and the difficulty of discovering a meaning in our modern environment. A central poem in *Discrete Series* provides an early, important statement of this difficulty:

> Who comes is occupied
> Toward the chest (in the crowd moving
>   opposite
> Grasp of me)
>   In firm overalls
> The middle-aged man sliding
> Levers in the steam-shovel cab,—
> Lift (running cable) and swung, back
> Remotely respond to the gesture before last
> Of his arms fingers continually—
> Turned with the cab. But if I (how goes
>   it?)—
>   The asphalt edge
> Loose on the plateau,
> Horse's classic height cartless
> See electric flash of streetcar,
> The fall is falling from electric burst.

(CP, p. 7)

There are some identifiable images in this poem, and we can be fairly sure that the speaker is viewing a city street scene—but the poem resists strongly any attempt to see it as a coherent whole.

Two thoughtful explanations of it have been written. David McAleavey believes that Oppen "reaches for freshness" here by "aiming . . . for a disjunctive style which points toward a primordial source."[21] L.S. Dembo states that the vision of the horse

---

21. David McAleavey, "If to Know Is Noble: The Poetry of George Oppen," Diss. Cornell 1975, p. 107.

juxtaposed to an urban landscape expresses (is "rendered coherent" by) a particular kind of poetic sensibility:

> The prairie and horse, though imagined, exist as "presences" no less tangible to the perceiver than a steamshovel or a streetcar. To call them presences, however, is not to put them in the category of fantasies. Or better their origin is natural, not supernatural, psychological not psychic. To Oppen, primitive reality is, if anything, more substantial than the realities of civilization.[22]

Both critics agree on the significance of the final, visionary image. In it, Oppen pierces the distractions of a modern technological society and confronts a "primordial source" or a "primitive reality"; he approaches, that is, that level of perception which seems to apprehend the true reality of things—the elemental qualities of existence.

If Oppen were following Williams, such perception should be analogous to Williams's "sight in its intensity [which] has given us . . . joy" (*EK*, p. 184), sight attracted by "The universality of things" or the "classic."[23] But Oppen's image of the classic is divorced from, not present in, the particulars that surround it. Furthermore, the difficulty of that climactic image seems only intensified, not resolved, by the final line, "The fall is falling from electric burst." Significantly, the critics do not seem to agree upon the function of this line, or of the first two images in the poem: Mr. McAleavey believes they work in a disjunctive manner; Mr. Dembo sees them as "presences," different in degree but not kind from the final imagined vision. The critics' disagreement marks an important limit for interpretive thought regarding the poem, and it suggests at the same time Oppen's real theme. (Oppen himself paraphrased Hegel appreciatively in noting that "Disagreement marks where the subject-matter ends. It is what the subject-matter is not" [*CL*, p. 162].) The subject becomes the relation among the images, a relation that in its "looseness" puts the quality of modern existence itself into question. In a much later poem, Oppen provides an illuminating, related analogy. A member of modern society, he suggests, finds a parallel in the "steel worker on the girder" who has forgotten not to look down: "We look back," he says, "Three hundred years and see bare land./And suffer vertigo" (*CP*, p. 131). In "Who comes is occupied," we experience, perhaps, that "vertigo," the peculiar sense of "falling" associated with unwished-for insight when our modern assumptions

---

22. Dembo, "Existential World," p. 68.
23. Williams uses this term most clearly in his review of *An 'Objectivists' Anthology, Symposium*, 4 (1933), 115.

of value are put painfully into question. I am claiming for the poem, then, not a reference to meaning, but to meaninglessness.

Such a claim, though, only regenerates the question to which it is directed: in what sense does meaning exist in Oppen's poetry? We can approach the answer most fruitfully as Heidegger approached his—with the willingness to open oneself to, as Heidegger would have phrased it, the "totality of what-is." Oppen was interested in a larger process of perception he included under the rubric "the life of the mind." This he defines briefly as a "lyric reaction to the world," but it is also "awareness" in general, involving "a sense of awe, simply to feel that the thing is there and that it's quite something to see" (*CL*, p. 164). It is expressed in a curious way in the first poem of *Discrete Series*, an anomaly in his work as a flowing, fourteen line poem comprising only one complete sentence. Here is the independent clause the poem is built upon:

> The knowledge not of sorrow, you were
> saying, but of boredom
> Is . . .
> . . . .
> Of the world, weather-swept, with which
> one shares the century.
>
> (*CP*, p. 3)

The word "boredom" obtrudes more than any other in this declaration, and Oppen himself has made it clear that he and Heidegger are using this word in the same way. The poem, Oppen says,

> means, in effect, that the knowledge of the mood of boredom is the knowledge of what *is*, "of the world, weather-swept." But these phrases I use here to paraphrase the poem are phrases from Heidegger's Acceptance Speech [of the Chair of Philosophy at Freiburg] made in 1929, the year I was writing the poem. And the words "boredom" and "knowledge" are, in their German equivalents, the words he used. (*CL*, p. 169)

Heidegger had said this:

> Real boredom is still far off when this book or that play, this activity or that stretch of idleness merely bores us. Real boredom comes when "one is bored." This profound boredom, drifting hither and thither in the abysses of existence like a mute fog, draws all things, all men and oneself along with them, together in a queer kind of indifference. This boredom reveals what-is in totality.[24]

Oppen followed Heidegger's gist, then, but he gives the state of awareness a slightly different shading in the full poem:

---

24. The speech is entitled "What Is Metaphysics?" in *Existence and Being*, trans. R.F.C. Hull and Alan Crick (Chicago: Henry Regnery Co., 1949), p. 364.

> The knowledge not of sorrow, you were
>   saying, but of boredom
> Is—aside from reading speaking
>   smoking—
> Of what, Maude Blessingbourne it was,
>   wished to know when, having risen,
> "approached the window as if to see
>   what really was going on";
> And saw rain falling, in the distance
>   more slowly,
> The road clear from her past the window-
>   glass—
> Of the world, weather-swept, with which
>   one shares the century.

Oppen, in consonance with Heidegger, differentiates between "boredom" and the commonplace tedium of "reading speaking/ smoking"; instead of a "mute fog," though, it involves a clarity, an almost Jamesian intensity that generates an awareness not only of the emptiness that pervades the real world, but of the possibilities for meaning in it. In fact, Oppen has superimposed James and Heidegger in this poem, with the odd result of mixing desire and indifference.[25] L.S. Dembo notes that "For Oppen, the attempt to acquire knowledge about 'what is really going on' can only end in ennui, for nothing is going on that is reducible to meaning"— reducible, that is, to articulated meaning.[26] Importantly, though, Heidegger shows us that confrontation with nothingness leads to the most meaningful—or perhaps we can only say the most important—experience one can have. For meaning exists only in a special sense with this kind of awareness. James, in his turn, always suggests connections among things, but seldom completes them. With reference to James and Heidegger, then, Oppen affirms only the possibility that meaning exists; what that meaning consists of, though, is not the real subject of much of his poetry.

He uses a number of strategies to create that sense of possibility, but especially in his ideas of place and of the way we locate ourselves as objects in a world of objects does he reflect the influence of Heidegger. In "The knowledge not of sorrow . . . ," for example, the number of perceivers suggests a context within which meaning can arise, but only in a special sense. Hugh Kenner has noted that simply in the first and last lines, ". . . we're aware of three persons, the speaker, 'you,' and 'one,' to which cast of characters the elided middle section adds a fourth, Maude Blessingbourne

---

25. Maude Blessingbourne has been identified by L.S. Dembo as a character in Henry James's "The Story In It." Oppen has said in private, undated correspondence to Mr. Dembo that "I wanted James in the book [*Discrete Series*] —secretely, superstitiously, I carved his initials on that sapling book. . . ."
26. Dembo, "Existential World," p. 70.

. . . and even a fifth, whoever spoke the words, carefully attributed by quotation marks, that say how Maude moved having arisen."[27] He makes the point that Oppen has subtly, and with great economy, created "A populous, complex, difficult world." We might add that in its complexity—a complexity that increases exponentially with the number of perceivers—such a world must implicitly be shared, must be dealt *with*, not consumed or assaulted, and that the individual (represented here by the poet) becomes both limited and self-defined (if we can use that word) by an awareness of the perspectives brought to bear upon it. Simultaneously, the speaking voice virtually disappears into the final, impersonal "one," and with it, meaning (or "knowledge" here) can only reappear in Maude Blessingbourne's "world, weather-swept." In other words, the complex of perspectives provides a framework in which to perceive the phenomenal world; the phenomenal world reciprocally provides the only place where Oppen can attempt to see " 'what really was going on,' " or more simply, what is. This is a truism, of course—if a perceiver perceives, he must perceive something. But the relationship occupies a privileged place in Oppen's thought, as it should for a reader of Heidegger, because it validates his faith in the phenomenal world even while he puts his subjective perceptions of that world into question.

Elsewhere, Oppen opens up the perceived world by demonstrating the way in which our minds work upon the material of perception. "Town, a town" presents details of a small town viewed as if from a train, "Inhabited partly by those/Who have been born here," with "people everywhere, time and the work/pauseless" amidst "houses," "lamp-posts," and "roads." Most important, the town appears passively as a "location/Over which the sun as it comes to it." Oppen has built, as he says of another poem, a "tremendous structure" of small nouns—a structure opposing native and transient, moving and static, changing and permanent. Within that structure,

> One moves between reading and re-reading,
> The shape is a moment.
> From a crowd a white powered face,
> Eyes and a mouth making three—
> Awaited—locally—a date.

> (*CP*, p. 11)

The poem shows us the manner in which the phenomenal world allows us to perceive: within its constancy and endurance, we move "between reading and re-reading" (since, if we are moving

---

27. Hugh Kenner, "Zukofsky, Oppen, and the Poem as Lens," paper presented at the University of Alabama, October, 1978, p. 2.

and the work is "pauseless," there can be no definitive reading); when understanding comes, it can come only as a momentary shape. The town, in other words, provides the location in which perception can take place. In the final image, Oppen makes a comment on the nature of that location. The woman who awaits "a date" (a time or a meeting) parallels the landscape "over which the sun as it comes to it"; the poet, though, abstracts her face to the status of a number. He seems to suggest that location comprises an abstract field inhering in the concrete, a place, perhaps, within which individual moments and objects of our lives can exist.

This sense of abstraction becomes more evocative of Heideggerian thinking in one of Oppen's best known poems, "Psalm" (*CP*, p. 78). The poem centers on the image of "wild deer bedding down" "In the small beauty of the forest." I have already quoted L.S. Dembo's point that the "poet demonstrates his faith [in the world beyond the self] by uttering nouns."[28] Oppen himself writes in the last stanza in "Psalm" of the "small nouns/Crying faith/In this in which the wild deer/Startle, and stare out." Clearly, language (and perception) at its most substantive level interests him here—the "small teeth" of the deer, the "small beauty of the forest," the "small nouns." But, equally important, the forest itself, the "this in which" that sets that smallness off, concerns him. Oppen re-emphasized in the 1968 interview that his "little nouns are crying . . . faith" not simply in their referents, but "in 'this in which' the wild deer stare out," and that he constructs "a pretty emotional poem out of those few little words isolating the deer" (*CL*, p. 163). The emotion in the poem concentrates in the exclamation, "That they are there!" In the first three stanzas, Oppen regards the "wild deer" themselves, awestruck, if anything, at their mere existence. In the last two stanzas, though, he dissolves that emotion into what surrounds them:

> Their paths
> Nibbled thru the fields, the leaves that shade them
> Hang in the distances
> Of sun
>
> The small nouns
> Crying faith
> In this in which the wild deer
> Startle, and stare out.

(*CP*, p. 78)

In part, this poem evokes the sense of "context" Zukofsky mentions in his early statements on objectivist poetics. In part, though,

---

28. Dembo, "Existential World," p. 81.

as well, Oppen's movement out from the particulars of his perception to what surrounds them strongly suggests the Heideggerian
movement towards perceiving the "what-is in totality." Heidegger's phrase is a coined term, of course, necessitated by the difficulties of his self-questioning process of thought; significantly,
Oppen's phrase, "this in which," the phrase that stands for his
book itself, echoes it. It names without naming, implying both the
reciprocal relation between the deer and what surrounds them,
and the problematic, unspecific nature of the place "in which"
the deer and every object, every noun, exist.

In this way, Oppen's language deals with the same difficulties Heidegger confronts in trying to render the problematic concept of true existence. Coincidentally, he deals with a central
objectivist concern—the concern with context. Zukofsky, from
his earliest statements on objectivist poetics, sought in language, he
said, "inextricably the direction of historic and contemporary
particulars"; he suggested later this compared to "A desire to
place everything—everything aptly, perfectly, belonging within,
one with, a context."[29] Oppen responds to the same impulse
Zukofsky felt, but not by trying to construct a web of relations
—social or historical—that somehow holds the particulars of the
world together. Instead, he evokes the space between those particulars that allows them to exist as discrete entities. His context emerges from the "Nothing" Heidegger alludes to that appears whenever we wish most to speak of something; it is the place
where "what-is" can emerge. In Oppen's "this in which"—the
place where all of his poetry exists—we can contemplate both the
limits and the depths of language, thought, and our own being.

---

29. Louis Zukofsky, "An Objective," *Prepositions* (London: Rapp and Carroll, 1967),
p. 23.

PAUL LAKE

THE ARCHETYPAL GESTURE: MYTH AND HISTORY
IN THE POETRY OF
GEORGE OPPEN

"Blake is more important to me than Williams," George Oppen once declared,[1] and it is time that we begin to take him at his word. For far from being a poet merely of the arresting "image" and the acute "perception," as he has too often been portrayed, Oppen offers us a poetic "vision" in a much wider sense. Throughout a career that spans over fifty years, he has spoken with an uncommon directness and sincerity, made truth the object of his art, and with a remarkable consistency, encompassed within a single line of poetic development all of the major subjects the century has offered: world war, economic depression, the expansion of American power, and the threat of nuclear extinction, to name but a few. We, in our turn, have chosen to discuss his work in more limited and less demanding terms: in its relationship to "imagism" and "objectivism"; in its resemblance to the work of Louis Zukofsky and William Carlos Williams; or as an early example of the American *avante garde*. In fact, these discussions have eclipsed a poetic enterprise of far more ambitious intentions; to find a body of work comparable in its seriousness and scope, we have to turn to the career of Ezra Pound.

Oppen himself has suggested this comparison with Pound, yet it has gone curiously unheeded. In an interview recorded in *Contemporary Literature*, Oppen once stated,

> It's true, of course, that Pound and Williams were both extremely important to me. But some people think I resemble Williams and it seems to me the opposite is true. Pound unfortunately defended

1. An Interview with George Oppen conducted by L.S. Dembo, *Contemporary Literature*, 10, No. 2, p. 171. Hereafter this interview will be cited as "Dembo Interview," and references will be incorporated into the text.

me against the charge of resembling him in the original preface to
Discrete Series. The fact has always haunted me.

(Dembo Interview, p. 169)

This resemblance between Ezra Pound and George Oppen, which
Oppen himself wishes us to discern, may be found, I believe, in the
similar attempts of the two poets to find a transcendent meaning
beneath the detritus of events that we call history, and in the
similar poetic strategies that the two poets employed to enact that
attempt. Although I think it is true, as Michael Bernstein argues in
his recent book, *The Tale of the Tribe*, that Pound for most of his
career sought to locate meaning within history itself,[2] there is
another aspect of Pound's poetics that valorizes the private epiphany and the mythopoeic gesture, and it is here, I think, that the
resemblance is to be discovered. For George Oppen, like the
visionary William Blake, and like other mythopoeic poets and
novelists of our own time—Pound, Eliot, Yeats, Joyce—develops
in his poetry strategies for awakening from what Joyce called the
"nightmare" of history into a deeper and more ancient reality.
If his characteristic gestures are less discernibly related to mythic
patterns than those of the other poets cited, it is perhaps because
the myths themselves to which Oppen appeals are less familiar,
or that Oppen approaches them from an oblique angle. For
George Oppen, unlike the other poets, is Jewish. It is there, in
the poet's heritage as Jew, that we will discover the poet's unique
relationship to history; and it is in the pre-Christian, Hebraic elements of the poet's imagination that we will find the source of the
mythic patterns he uses to understand that relationship. By tracing
one mythic motif (or what Mircea Eliade calls an "archetypal gesture") throughout Oppen's work, I hope to clarify my earlier suggestion that Oppen records more than simply moments of exqui-
site "perceptions" and "objective" images divorced from the rest
of his humanity; but, rather, that it records a struggle to forge a
poetic sensibility capacious enough to encompass history, and
refined enough to allow the perception of "a World in a Grain of
Sand" and "Eternity in an hour."

It is curious that we have paid so little attention to Oppen's
allusions to his Jewishness, or thought that any Jewish poet could
have lived through most of this century, fought the Nazis in World
War II (as Oppen did), and not at some point have dealt with his
unique relationship to history. It is curious because, throughout
their existence, Jews have been forced to confront their place in
history; and they are among the earliest people to have discovered,

---

2. Michael André Bernstein, *The Tale of the Tribe: Ezra Pound and the Modern Verse
Epic* (Princeton: Princeton Univ. Press, 1980).

and in a sense to have invented, history. As Mircea Eliade has pointed out, it was the Jews who first began to read a meaning in the unfolding of events. Therefore, before proceeding to a discussion of Oppen's poetry, I would first like to examine what Eliade has written about two strands in Jewish thought.

The biblical prophets, according to Eliade in *The Myth of the Eternal Return*, interpreted the historical catastrophes that the Jewish people periodically suffered as "Yah-weh's ineluctable chastisement," so that as a result "historical events acquired religious significance. . . ." He further argues that ". . . for the first time, the prophets placed a value on history, succeeded in transcending the traditional vision of the cycle (the conception that ensures all things will be repeated forever), and discovered a one-way time," a discovery, he writes, that ". . . was not fully accepted by the consciousness of the entire Jewish people, and the ancient conceptions were still long to survive."[3]

We will return to these "ancient conceptions" as they appear in Oppen's poetry later. For the moment, let us look at another aspect of the prophetic tradition's interpretation of historical significance. Eliade describes the newer conception of history as follows:

> The situation is altogether different in the case of the monotheistic revelation. This takes place in time, in historical duration: Moses receives the Law at a certain date. . . . the moment of the revelation made to Moses by God remains a limited moment, definitely situated in time. . . . it becomes precious inasmuch as it is no longer reversible, as it is historical event.
>
> (Eliade, p. 105)

Now let us see what significance Oppen chooses to emphasize in his treatment of that unique moment in history when Moses led the tribes of Hebrews out of pharaonic Egypt into the "one-way time" of recorded history. Most of the poem entitled "Exodus" appears below:

> When she was a child I read Exodus
> To my daughter   'The children of Israel . . .'
>
> Pillar of fire
> Pillar of cloud
>
> We stared at the end
> Into each other's eyes   Where
> She said hushed

---

3. Mircea Eliade, *The Myth of the Eternal Return*, trans. Willard R. Trask (New York: Pantheon, 1954), pp. 103-04. Hereafter this book will be cited as "Eliade," and references will be incorporated into the text.

                    Were the adults   We dreamed to each other
                    Miracle of the children
                    The brilliant children   Miracle

                    Of their brilliance   Miracle
                    of[4]

In a real sense, this poem emphasizes a pre-Mosaic, more ancient aspect of the historical event; it is the "miracle of," the "brilliance" of, and the childish innocence surrounding the event to which Oppen directs our attention in the poem, and this accords with what Eliade describes as the "archaic" mythical conception of time held by the Semitic tribes of the ancient Near East. As Eliade says of this more primitive conception of events which stresses the miraculous rather than the historically accurate,

> It matters little if the formulas and images through which the primitive expresses "reality" seem childish and even absurd to us. It is the profound meaning of primitive behavior that is revelatory: this behavior is governed by belief in an absolute reality opposed to the profane world of "unrealities. . . ."
>
> (Eliade, p. 92)

For Oppen, the world of events, of historical time, is the "profane world" of unrealities; time and again he opposes the "miracle" of childish innocence to this profane world of artifacts and empire. In "Philai Te Kou Philai," he contrasts the two opposing views:

                              We are
                    Lost in the childish
                    Here, and we address
                    Only each other
                    In the flat bottomed lake boat
                    Of boards. It is a lake
                    In a bend of the parkway, the breeze
                    Moves among the primitive toys
                    Of vacation . . .
                              (*CP*, p. 75)

And later, at the conclusion of the poem, he describes a "ruined ethic," implying a comparison between it and the earlier "childish" innocence of the natural scene:

                         Where can it end? Loved, Loved

                    And Hated,
                    Rococo boulevards

                    Backed by the Roman
                    Whose fluted pillars

---

4. George Oppen, *Collected Poems* (New York: New Directions, 1975), p. 22. Hereafter this book will be incorporated into the text and cited as *CP*.

> Blossoming antique acanthus
>
> Stand on other coasts
> Lifting their tremendous cornices.
>
> *(CP,* pp. 76-7)

Particularly since Oppen reminds us in poems like "The Light-houses" that his "heritage" is *"neither Roman//nor barbarian"* *(CP,* p. 251), we can be sure that the above reference to Roman empire is meant to remind us of his historical situation as Jew, or —to be more precise—as "Semite," as he reminds us in other poems (including one by that title).

It is thus as a "primitive," related to the archaic Eastern men described by Eliade, that Oppen encounters the "profane time" of history. History as duration, as linear sequence, is a veneer over reality, according to Oppen, a "silting sand of events" *(CP,* p. 119) that obliterates the real. He describes the process of history's enactment, its gradual soiling and silting of the bare ground, in these lines about the settling of America in a poem entitled "To Memory":

> And so we possess the earth.
>
> Like an army of ants,
> A multiple dry carcass
> Of past selves
>
> Moving
> Thru a land dead behind us
> Of deeds, dates, documents
>   * * *
> All that there is, is
> Yours, and in the caves of your sleep
> Lives in our permanent dawn.
>
> *(CP,* p. 66)

Here the linear movement of our progress across the continent is contrasted with a "permanent dawn"—permanent because of its continuing, cyclical recurrence. To penetrate or cut through this detritus of history—its "deeds, dates, documents"—we must, in turn, burrow down through it, either by entering the "caves" of sleep, or, as in other poems, by an actual physical "descent." It is this physical or imaginational cutting through profane time into the "real" which constitutes Oppen's most characteristic method of escaping history into a more sacred realm. Its recurrence in his writing can be defined as a poetic motif, or, to use Eliade's term, as an "archetypal gesture." In the "primitive" ontological conception, Eliade writes, "an object or an act becomes real only insofar as it imitates or repeats an archetype" (Eliade, p. 34). And further,

Eliade argues that

> . . . insofar as an act (or an object) acquires a certain reality
> through the repetition of certain paradigmatic gestures, and ac-
> quires it through that alone, there is an implicit abolition of pro-
> fane time, of duration, of "history"; and he who reproduces that
> exemplary gesture thus finds himself transported into the mythi-
> cal epoch in which its revelation took place.
>
> (Eliade, p. 35)

To locate the mythical epoch from which Oppen derived his para-
digmatic gesture, we have only to consult his poems, keeping in
mind his consciousness of himself as Semite, or Jew. Examined in
such a way, his poems begin to array themselves into larger patterns; so that looking at his latest volume, *Primitive*, we see him
repeating a gesture made in *The Materials* where he wrote, in
"From Disaster," ". . . whole families crawled/To the tenements,
and there//Survived. . ." (*CP*, p. 29). In "Disasters," the second
poem in *Primitive*, Oppen begins,

> of wars o western
> wind and storm
>
> of politics I am sick . . .

And in the conclusion of this poem Oppen alludes to the book of
Genesis and the story of Abraham and Sarah, once again finding a
refuge from history in the repetition of an archetypal gesture, a
sustained period of hiding in "caves" beneath the realm of historical events:

>   I see
>
> myself   Sarah Sarah   I see the tent
> in the desert my life
>
> narrows my life
> is another I see
> him in the desert I watch
> him he is clumsy
> and alone my young
> brother he is my lost
> sister her small
>
> voice among the people the salt
>
> and terrible hills whose armies
>
> have marched and the caves
> of the hidden
> people.[5]

---

5. George Oppen, *Primitive* (Santa Barbara: Black Sparrow Press, 1978), pp. 11-12. Hereafter this book will be cited as *P*, and all such citations will be incorporated into the text.

The passage is intended to remind us of the flight of the Jewish people of Sodom and Gomorrah into the hill-country after their military defeat by enemy kings, and of Lot (Abraham's nephew) and his similar flight from Sodom and Gomorrah after the disaster that overtook those two cities (Genesis, chapters 14 and 19). Lot, you will recall, took refuge in a cave in the hill-country with his daughters after the destruction; chapter twenty-two of Genesis further records the fact that Abraham buried his wife, Sarah, in a cave after her death.

This flight from profane time into a realm of more absolute being, which is effected by cutting through history's "rubble," is a gesture that is repeated throughout Oppen's work. In the prose passage that makes up section 5 from Oppen's poem "Route" (from *Of Being Numerous*), Oppen relates a story told to him by an Alsatian named Pierre during World War II. Learning that they were to be drafted by the German Army, Oppen recounts, "Many men, learning in their own way that they were to be called, dug a hole. The word became a part of the language: *Faire un trou.* Some men were in those holes as long as two and three years. . ." (*CP*, p. 187). In further telling his story of the Alsatians' refuge from the Nazi war-machine, Oppen, through quiet understatement, relates, "There was an escape from this dilemma, as, in a way, there always is" (*CP*, p. 188). Then he flatly describes how one man, rather than allowing the Germans to take revenge on his family for his own escape, quietly planned and executed his suicide by driving his bicycle into a tree. Pierre, Oppen relates, "knew, of course, what he was telling me"; and so, too, does Oppen know what he is telling us when in the volume which followed *Of Being Numerous* he once again repeats the "archetypal gesture" in a passage that echoes Pierre's tale:

> Fought
>
> No man but the fragments of metal
> Burying my dogtag with H
> For Hebrew in the rubble of Alsace
>
> *I must get out of here*
>
> *Father*   he thinks
>
> (*CP*, p. 211)

If there is any doubt as to what Oppen is up to in the repeated sounding of this note, we have only to study his poems for further clues that these are not hollow echoes or unconsciously repeated habits of language, but something deeper. Let us look briefly at another example of a mythic motif in Oppen's work, before further exploring the one presently under discussion. Again, Eliade's discussion of archetypal symbols is relevant to our own inquiry:

> The very ancient conception of the temple as the *imago mundi*
> . . . passed into the religious architecture of Christian Europe: the
> basilica of the first centuries of our era, like the medieval cathe-
> dral, symbolically reproduces the Celestial Jerusalem. As to the
> symbolism of the mountain, of the Ascension, and of the "Quest
> for the Center," they are clearly attested to in medieval litera-
> ture. . . ."
>
> (Eliade, p. 17)

Oppen writes of just such a "Celestial Jerusalem," aware that he is
evoking the ancient, mythic idea of the temple as sacred mountain, in his poem "Chartres": ". . . the stones/Stand where the
masons locked them," Oppen declares, "Because a hundred gener-
ations/Back of them and to another people//The world cried out
above the mountain" (*CP*, p. 56).

Although Oppen chooses to oppose history, declaring himself to be a primitive in an archetypal sense, he is too wise to believe that evasions of historical events are final, or that the archetypal gestures work as they once did. We live in a different world
from that of the Semitic tribes of pre-history, and Oppen, who has
lived through and confronted more history than most, and been
imperiled by the very heritage in which he seeks meaningful gestures, knows this. He is aware that we may now be at the end of
one of the great cosmo-historical cycles, and that the old pattern
of nestling down into the earth's crust and awaiting regeneration
may no longer apply. "We are endangered/Totally at last" (*CP*,
p. 49), Oppen declared in "Time of the Missile," and in other
poems like "The Mayan Ground," and "A Narrative," he suggests disturbing parallels to our own historical situation. Some
young men, he writes in "A Narrative," "have become aware of
the Indian," and "move across the continent/Without wealth,
moving one could say/On the bare ground . . . the land pretty
much as it was. . . ." Yet the parallel is more disturbing than
reassuring:

> And because they also were a people in danger,
> Because they feared also the thing might end,
> I think of the Indian songs . . .
>
> . . . . .
>
> Aware that the old men sang
> On those prairies,
> Return, the return of the sun.
>
> (*CP*, p. 139)

This passage cautions that the "myth of the eternal return"
may no longer hold: the end was final and irrevocable for the way
of life of the American Indians, as it was for the people of the

Mayan civilization. In section 14 of "Route" Oppen reminds us
of the "cataclysm" that followed the appearance of Cortés and
Cabeza deVaca, who "found a continent of spiritual despair"; and
in section 13 of the same poem, he treats the theme of regeneration after cataclysm explicitly. Punning on the word "plants,"
Oppen begins,

> Department of Plants and Structures—obsolete, the old name
> In this city, of the public works
>
> Tho we meant to entangle ourselves in the roots of the world
>
> An unexpected and forgotten spoor . . .
> . . . . .
>
> Tho there is no longer shelter in the earth, round helpless belly
> Or hope among the pipes and broken works . . .
> (*CP*, p. 195)

There will be no re-emergence from the rubble this time, he suggests, no new beginning.

Finally, in a poem entitled "Semite" in a volume entitled
Myth of the Blaze, Oppen sounds several of his major mythic
motifs, reminding us again of his Jewish heritage ("my distances
neither Roman/nor barbarian"), and perhaps suggesting that we
have all become like the Jews and like another tribal people, the
American Indian, a "people in danger." He begins by reminding us
of the near extinction of the Jews in World War II, and by sudden
juxtaposition, shows—through the image of the Vietnam war
coming to us on television while we eat dinner—how all of us are
endangered beings on a planet the size of a table top:

> demeaned thrown away shamed
> degraded
>
> stripped naked Think
>
> think also of the children
> the guards laughing
> . . . . .
>
>   whereupon murder
>
> comes to our dinners poem born
>
> of a planet the size
>
> of a table top . . .
> (*CP*, p. 247)

Suddenly, in this relatively late poem, we find ourselves in Marshall
McLuhan's "global village": the electronic media simultaneously

shrink the planet and unite us in archaic patterns of thought and action; we partake of common rites—the evening news, the hours of nightly entertainment, the "on the spot" coverage of "major events." Suddenly, we are back in the mythopoeic realm, each of us again a "primitive." And so George Oppen reminds us in his last volume, *Primitive*, insisting that the comparison of his own poetic "vision" with that of William Blake is not an idle one. Like Blake, he tries to persuade us in the poetry of this late volume that there is only one escape from the quotidian reality of profane time, and that it is through an awakening into a mythic realm, where things shine with the brilliance of pure being:

Tyger

> Tyger still burning in me burning
> in the night sky burning
> in us the light
>
> in the room it was all
> part of the wars
> of things brilliance
> of things
>
> in the appalling
> seas language
>
> lives and wakes us together
> out of sleep the poem
> opens its dazzling whispering hands
>
> (*P*, p. 14)

Whether or not we grant the reality of this mythopoeic realm, we must recognize its vitalizing presence in George Oppen's poetry. Like Ezra Pound, Oppen invites us not merely to look, but to change the way we see and live. To read his poetry in any other way is to dismiss the challenge his work offers, and to impoverish one of the most compelling and original bodies of poetry to have appeared in our time. In a century of evasions, it is bracing to witness such a daring endeavor. Let us then recognize and cherish it for what it is: a singular attempt to confront the terror of history, and to find beneath its waste and desolation, something at which we can still marvel—the miracle of our existence, and the precarious brilliance of our surviving humanity.

RACHEL BLAU DuPLESSIS

OBJECTIVIST POETICS AND POLITICAL VISION: A STUDY OF OPPEN AND POUND

> . . . poetry must be at least as well written as prose, etc. It must also be at least as good as dead silence.[1]

In a review of Ginsberg, McClure and Olson, published in 1962, as he was publishing the work that marked his return to a poetic career, George Oppen strongly suggests that each of these prominent figures exemplifies a tendency in current writing which he must reject. By means of this, his sole review, Oppen tacitly considers himself as a writer in relation to some significant contemporaries. "Ginsberg's mode," he says, "is often declamatory," on a line between "histrionics and openness"; indeed, "to quarrel with that is simply to quarrel with the heart of his work."[2] McClure's mode reduces poetic desire to "excitement, intoxication, meaninglessness, a destruction of the sense of oneself among things" ("Three Poets," p. 333). But what really troubles Oppen is not so much expressionism as what he takes to be filial piety; hence Olson's case is less quickly adjudicated. Oppen cites and he ponders, but he concludes that reading Olson "is simply not an encounter with a new poetry" ("Three Poets," p. 331). What, in a word, has impeded Olson's voice and vision? In a word, it is Pound. For

---

1. George Oppen, Letter to Rachel Blau [DuPlessis], 20 October 1965. Oppen here unceremoniously refers to one of Pound's aphorisms, in Letter 60, to Harriet Monroe, January 1915: "Poetry must be *as well written as prose*" (*The Letters of Ezra Pound, 1907-1941*, ed. D. D. Paige [New York: Harcourt, Brace & World, Inc., 1950], p. 48). Another likely source is Pound, "Affirmations: Analysis of this Decade," (1915), in *Gaudier-Brzeska: A Memoir* (New York: New Directions, 1970), p. 115. Hereafter cited in the text as *Gaudier-Brzeska*.
2. George Oppen, "Three Poets," *Poetry* 100, 5 (August 1962), 329-330. Hereafter cited in the text as "Three Poets."

granting once and for all that Olson is worth reading if anyone at all is worth reading, the problem remains for the reviewer and for any reader that it is impossible to confront Olson's poems without first of all acknowledging the audible presence of Pound in them. Not that Olson has not openly and handsomely acknowledged the debt to Pound in the text of the poems, but if we look to poetry as a skill by which we can grasp the form of a perception achieved, then nothing can so deaden the impact of poetic discourse as to be uncertain which of two men is speaking, to half-hear other words paralleling the words we read.

                                  ("Three Poets," p. 331)[3]

In his assessment of Olson, Oppen makes manifest a fundamental choice for his own poetry: Oppen will not be Pound.

Charles Olson probably did not realize the nature of the self-definition at stake in this review—indeed, there was no reason why he should. The Oppen review seems to have struck him as an untoward attack from someone almost without qualification to speak, that is, from a person without an oeuvre. In 1962, this was reasonably true. Hence Olson responded in a patronizing manner publicly, while privately expressing emotions which ranged from offhand tolerance to defensive annoyance that he is again taxed as Pound's epigone. Olson's visible response to "the old business of measuring me by Pound" occurs in a few tart lines from the end of Maximus VI:

>   I want to open
>   Mr Oppen
>   the full inherited file
>   of history—[4]

This suggests that the point of reference should not be Pound *per se* but the ambition which the poets shared: to write a poem including history. And in some ways, Oppen did not take up the direct and uncompromising challenge that Pound (and Williams) presented, as Olson, in contrast, did. Olson's struggle has been recently addressed by Michael Bernstein in *The Tale of the Tribe*, suggesting that Olson interpreted *Paterson* and *The Cantos* as two halves which he would be peculiarly suited to fuse in a "new epic discourse."[5] But although Oppen does not decide on the epic, for reasons which someone should examine, but rather chooses the

---

3. Oppen does seem to be using Olson mainly to measure his own danger, for he also states that "even the poems in which one is most aware of Pound assert their own musical and intellectual life" ("Three Poets," p. 332).
4. I am indebted to John Crawford for the Maximus reference. Charles Olson, *Maximus Poems IV, V, VI* (London: Cape Goliard Press, 1968), n.p. "The old business" phrase is from a letter to William Bronk, in George F. Butterick, *A Guide to The Maximus Poems of Charles Olson* (Berkeley: University of California Press, 1978), pp. 495-96.
5. Michael André Bernstein, *The Tale of the Tribe: Ezra Pound and the Modern Verse Epic* (Princeton: Princeton University Press, 1980), p. 238.

"lyric valuables," still these are for him similarly ethical and historical. Therefore the difference between Olson and Oppen may, finally, be a difference between Herodotus and Thucydides.[6] One poet engages history with a gargantuan eclecticism, combining anecdote and analysis, and saturated in myth; the other poet sees history as the study of how people choose to act, given constellated interests and forces.

For Oppen to announce, by means of that review of Olson, that he would try to avoid Pound's poetic influence involved a complicated and sticky maneuver, which is part of my topic here. First off, as we all understand, Pound is ubiquitous, a major creator of the poetics and meanings of twentieth century poetry. For Oppen to make the treacherous but enabling equation "Oppen ≠ Pound," he had to situate his vision and voice at a measured remove from this decisive, and unavoidable, influence which had, at the same time, shaped the poetic context in which Oppen could become Oppen. For Pound is the twentieth century poet who formulated most briskly, and promulgated most tirelessly, the aesthetic of visual and aural accuracy, and whose editorial grasp of the clearest word, the most succinct statement, the colloquial turn, and the lightning illumination made a broad path for his peers in his own generation, in the next—and the next. His was the way of forging a modernist rhetoric, appropriately under the banner of no rhetoric whatsoever.

More specifically, the objectivist poetics, derived in Pound's wake, was enunciated by Louis Zukofsky in an essay which profoundly affected Oppen. This poetics, which I will briefly trace, had an ethical dimension, for it began with the person, not the word, that is, began with sincerity. Pound's "credo"—"I believe in technique as the test of a man's sincerity"[7]—passes through pertinent elaborations and extensions in Zukofsky's essay "An Objective":

> In sincerity shapes appear concomitants of word combinations, precursors of (if there is continuance) completed sound or structure, melody or form. Writing occurs which is the detail, not mirage, of seeing, of thinking with the things as they exist, and of directing them along a line of melody.[8]

Sincerity is then honesty: of mind and heart, of eye and ear, not forcing the thought or making any image come out to established

---

6. Bernstein, p. 240: "Olson hoped to renew an older, and in his eyes unjustly neglected, historiographic tradition: 'I would be an historian as Herodotus was,/looking for oneself for the evidence/of what is said' ("Letter 23":100-101)."
7. Pound, *Literary Essays* (London: Faber and Faber Limited, 1954), p. 9. Hereafter cited in the text as *Literary Essays*.
8. Louis Zukofsky, "An Objective," *Prepositions* (London: Rapp & Carroll, 1967), p. 20. Hereafter cited in the text as "An Objective."

philosophic or social scripts or poetic conventions, but rather hearing the poem through to its own cadence, whose achievement will verify its honesty. Oppen has eloquently announced his participation in this endeavor:

> Modern American poetry begins with the determination to find the image, the thing encountered, the thing seen each day whose meaning has become the meaning and color of our lives. . . .It is possible to find a metaphor for anything, an analogue: but the image is encountered, not found; it is an account of the poet's perception, of the act of perception; it is a test of sincerity, a test of conviction, the rare poetic quality of truthfulness. They meant to replace by the data of experience the accepted poetry of their time, a display by the poets of right thinking and right sentiment, a dreary waste of lies. That data was and is the core of what "modernism" restored to poetry, the sense of the poet's self among things.[9]

In the objectivist statement, structure is the "objectification" or rested totality of the poem:

> its character may be simply described as the arrangement, into one apprehended unity, of minor units of sincerity. . . .
>
> ("An Objective," p. 21)

This is paralleled by Oppen's formulation in the term "discrete series," with his characteristic emphasis on the destabilized structure theoretically possible from arrangements of conflicting or cross-purposed "units of sincerity," what I have called elsewhere the structure of dilemma[10]:

> The . . . point for me, and I think for Louis, too, was the attempt to construct meaning, to construct a method of thought from the imagist technique of poetry—from the imagist intensity of vision. . . . that there is a moment, an actual time, when you believe something to be true, and you construct a meaning from these moments of conviction.[11]

Another essential term of the objectivist poetics concerns the social meaning of the ethical and structuring acts. Zukofsky is singularly intent upon making a statement about this aspect of poetry, so intent that he uses the exact same formulation three times in the essay:

> desire for what is objectively perfect, inextricably the direction of historic and contemporary particulars.
>
> ("An Objective," pp. 20, 22, and 23)

---

9. George Oppen, "The Mind's Own Place," *Montemora* 1 (Fall, 1975), 132 and 133. Originally published in *Kulchur* 10 (1963). Hereafter cited in the text as "Mind."
10. Rachel Blau DuPlessis, "George Oppen: 'What Do We Believe to Live With?' " *Ironwood* 5 (1975), 62-77.
11. L. S. Dembo, Oppen Interview, "The 'Objectivist' Poet: Four Interviews," *Contemporary Literature* 10, 2 (Spring 1969), 161. Hereafter cited in the text as "Dembo Interview."

One way of reading this difficult morsel: when a poem is "objectively perfect"—built from sincerity and the crafts of articulation toward that end—then it will of necessity embody or present some recognizable direction in life as we know it. At the very least, this would rule out surrealism, all forms of play with language alone, in the intended absence of referentiality[12]; at most this might be construed to point toward a poetics of "social awareness," articulating—or perhaps only alluding to—the possible dimensions of a Marxist poetics.[13] In any event, not trying to avoid one:

> *Impossible* to communicate anything but particulars—historic and contemporary—things, human beings as things their instrumentalities of capillaries and veins binding up and bound up with events and contingencies. The revolutionary word if it must revolve cannot escape having a reference. It is not infinite. Even the infinite is a term.[14]

("An Objective," p. 24)

The Pound on whom Zukofsky and Oppen drew was indeed the Pound of sincerity and ethical-social awareness: "technique as the test of a man's sincerity" does not separate craft from the whole social and moral being of the person. At the time of his 1929 essay on Pound, Zukofsky saw *The Cantos* as the poem of sincerity: each section or unit as the measuring of self and others by the yardstick of exact data. It is a poem which, because it embodies "a desire for what is objectively perfect," precisely shows "the direction of historic and contemporary particulars" as these are "inextricably" bonded to the articulation of statement itself. For Zukofsky, *The Cantos* are

> an ideation directed towards inclusiveness, setting down one's extant world and other existing worlds, interrelated in a general scheme of people speaking in accord with the musical measure, or spoken about in song; people, of their own weight determining or already determined.[15]

---

12. The same resistance occurs in Oppen's "Notes on Prosody?" Personal Letter, George Oppen to Rachel Blau [DuPlessis], October 1965. "And the poem is NOT built out of words, one cannot make a poem by sticking words into it, it is the poem which makes the words and contains their meaning. One cannot reach out for *roses* and *elephants* and *essences* and put them in the poem————the ground under the elephant, the air around him, one would have to know very precisely one's distance from the elephant or step deliberately too close, close enough to frighten oneself."
13. See Zukofsky on Williams in the essay "American Poetry 1920-1930," *Prepositions*, pp. 142-143.
14. Norman Finkelstein's recent article on Oppen, "Political Commitment and Poetic Subjectification: George Oppen's Test of Truth," *Contemporary Literature* 22, 1 (1981), pp. 24-41, goes far in the analysis of Oppen's political views as they emerge in the poetry and as they change throughout his poetic career.
15. Zukofsky, "Ezra Pound," *Prepositions*, p. 69.

For his quondam followers in the late twenties, Pound was the poet of sincerity because his statement of contemporary life fuses with the aesthetic and the moral, thereby making the language of poetry into a system analogous to the realistic novel.

The objectivist poetics of the late 20s and early 30s was, then, directly and irrevocably Poundian, inspired by Pound's criticism and his manifestos, and fascinated by the extension of his ambitions into *The Cantos*. A cut of literary history at that moment (say 1929-30), shows Zukofsky with deliberation and energy transposing and appropriating the Poundian position on writing, that ethical and aesthetic fusion so characteristic of Pound and so central to his achievement. It shows Oppen in a double relationship—to Pound indirectly and to Zukofsky directly, evidently inspired by both.

The poems in *Discrete Series* (dated 1932-34 in *The Collected Poems*) achieve such "contemporary particulars" as we should all be familiar with: the elevator, the telephone, the breasts facing lingerie, the steel deck, the pelvis in a city bed, the bird on the cobblestones, houses, trains, movies, all caught in the decisive "alteration of lighting."[16] The poems in that book necessarily make me think of contemporaneous work by Edward Hopper, both in the forceful sexuality and in the statement of places in which and through which awareness of the world is achieved. I mean paintings like "Two on the Aisle" (1927), "Lighthouse at Two Lights" (1929), "My Roof" (1928), "East Wind Over Weehawken" (1934), "Room in Brooklyn" (1932). And through their statements of place both Hopper and Oppen produce profound, dramatic, and almost unspeakable situations, along with the implicit web of many interacting forces: work, longing, fatigue, craft, boredom, power. From the very first poem of Oppen's oeuvre, he announces the project: to identify "what really was going on" in "the world, weather-swept, with which one shares the century." This broadly social vision is the essential Oppen. It is a vision that precisely does not make the poetry say the right thinking thing, correct "line," or pre-established statement.

Oppen has been so perfectly clear, however, about his non-relationship with the demands of a proletarian aesthetic or "socialist realism" that it might be easy to overlook the nature of the poetry he actually wrote. It is a poetry that talks about culture and society as a nexus of affiliations. I am borrowing Edward Said's honing of a Gramscian term, in order, again, to avoid the

---

16. George Oppen, *Collected Poems* (New York: New Directions, 1975), p. 9. Hereafter cited in the text as *CP*.

narrowly conceived "reflection" theory of art, while retaining the radical and fundamental definition of an artist's social vision.

Oppen writes the poetry of affiliation because he is concerned to understand and reveal.

> an often implicit network of peculiarly cultural (not natural, biological, or crudely ideological) associations between forms, statements, and other aesthetic elaborations on the one hand, and on the other, institutions, agencies, classes and fairly amorphous social forces.[17]

He writes a poetry whose effect is to pursue these analytic affiliations, while at the same time immersed in other meanings of affiliation: having to do with parenthood and personal, communal bonds. Oppen has written as follows of this project:

> One would have to tell what happens in a life, what choices present themselves, what the world is for us, what happens in time, what thought is in the course of a life and therefore what art is, and the isolation of the actual
>
> I would want to talk of rooms and of what they look out on and of basements, the rough walls bearing the marks of the forms, the old marks of wood in the concrete, such solitude as we know—
>
> and the swept floors. Someone, a workman bearing about him, feeling about him that peculiar word like a dishonored fatherhood has swept this solitary floor, this profoundly hidden floor— such solitude as we know.
>
> (*CP*, p. 168)

It is evident that Pound wanted a social and political poetry. In this he represents the world-transformative project of modernism, and this is one reason he was admired by Zukofsky and Oppen. One must criticize not this ambition but its manifestations. Pound's desire was totalitarian, heavy with what, in his view, ought to be.[18] Hence it is a poetry that propagandizes, not even so much in its content (although Mussolini wafts in and out interestingly) as secretly in its structure and in the meaning Pound

---

17. Edward Said, "Reflections on Recent American 'Left' Literary Criticism," *Boundary 2*, 8, 1 (1980), 26. Said is more interested in affiliation as "an analytico-theoretical principle of research" and the definition is slanted in that direction, rather than toward "socio-cultural process" (p. 27). But I hope the relevance of the term affiliation is clear. The only part of the definition that doesn't fit has to do with nature. Oppen writes a great deal about the ocean, first as an image of void, but second and as importantly about the ways people are in relations of craft and mastery with it. The ocean in Oppen is very often traversed by little boats and pocked with islands. A map or network of social and cultural associations is therefore traced.

18. Daniel Pearlman has analyzed the "authoritarian manner" of the essays and concludes, similarly, that there is an "unconscious parody of the style of the Fascist leader" in Pound's prose of this period. This article, a psycho-social analysis of Pound's anti-Semitism, is a very important contribution to the study of Pound. Pearlman, "Ezra Pound: America's Wandering Jew," *Paideuma* 9, 3 (1980), 461-480; citations from 464.

ascribes to his form. When Oppen rejects Pound, it is that deep political bias in Pound's use of the "epic" form that Oppen addresses. Hence in their objectivist poetics, Oppen and Pound were in fundamental agreement. In the carrying out of that poetics, they divided.

One may test Pound against what Altieri calls "the temptations of closure—both closure as fixed form and closure as writing in the service of idea, doctrine, or abstract aesthetic ideal " (Altieri, "Objectivist Tradition," p. 15). Certainly *The Cantos* is an endless poem in formal terms, presenting "complex" by "instant" in a fusion of spatial network with temporal articulations of the self and its changes. Yet as certain values or discoveries are treated as settled, Pound's poetry can settle into his own repeating codes, with only perfunctory (dare I even say, only rhetorical) engagement with the tactic of beginning from poverty over again. From

Charles Altieri has defined the symbolist and the objectivist world views of modern poetry in ways pertinent to this discussion of Oppen and Pound. The romantic-symbolist approach values the mind's shaping and interpretive capacities as it reflects upon the meaning of perceptions; this mode increases "the distance between the empirical and a realm of imaginative values."[19] The objectivist begins with the detail, the seen or perceived unit, and proceeds by "thinking with the things as they exist" and as the person in context registers them. In this process, the poet abstains from "predatory intention," without teaching, converting, or hectoring the reader.[20] Presentations—not the rhetorics of self-expression or confession—become the poet's most exacting and comprehensive task. There is, then, in the purest objectivist poetics, an implied interrogation of the self and of any stated position or system because of this "sincerity." Sincerity can pull the poetic project back to unpredictable starting points: such a poet's test of vocation may then be that s/he is always beginning in "poverty" once again, that poetic closure is unstressed, and that the encapsulation of idea into system is avoided, for all would distort the poet's task. An example is the characteristic bewildered pleasure of Oppen "left with the deer, staring out of the thing, at the thing, not knowing what will come next."[21]

19. Charles Altieri, "The Objectivist Tradition," *Chicago Review* 30, 3 (Winter 1979), 9. Hereafter cited in the text as Altieri, "Objectivist Tradition."
20. Louis Zukofsky, "Sincerity and Objectification" (1931), cited by Altieri, p. 6; Louis Zukofsky, "An Objective," p. 26.
21. For the word "poverty," see Oppen, *CP*, p. 213. For the deer, see Dembo interview, p. 163. J. Hillis Miller's formulation is deservedly classic, if based on that saturating sexual plunge most characteristic of Williams: ". . . the mind must efface itself before reality, or plunge into the density of an exterior world, dispersing itself in a milieu which exceeds it and which it has not made" (*Poets of Reality* [Cambridge, Mass.: Harvard University Press, 1966], p. 8).

the inter-war period on, I would argue, while the collaged form of the poem did not change, the meaning which Pound gave to his formal acts did indeed alter. In the mid-twenties, that is, *The Cantos* modulated from an early concern for re-illuminating moments of full cultural and emotional achievement (moments of renaissance), to the concern which controls the bulk of the poem: making a "totalitarian synthesis" by the didactic insistence upon certain verities.[22]

Before and possibly even during World War I, Pound thought that the modern renaissance, for which he had long been preparing himself, was arriving. The War, to his shock and terror, made him see how easily that renaissance could be broken by political and social forces. This realization was symbolized for him in the death of Gaudier-Brzeska. In some sense Pound—as perhaps also the Eliot who responded in a similar way to the death of Jean Verdenal, "Mort aux Dardenelles"—seems to have been afflicted with the guilt of the survivor. The war, in any event, deeply affected the writing of the modern period, on every level—personal, social, aesthetic. In consequence, Pound turned to the problem of finding a favorable political context for art—investigating with which of the two parties (Communist or Fascist) the Poundian "Party of Intelligence" would affiliate.[23] In the 1934 Postscript to the 1916 Gaudier memoir, a rare reassessment of his own position which indicates a change of emphasis, Pound feels that the revolution in art, in which he and Gaudier participated, was a prefiguration of a "volitionist" social revolution. The artists had been, gratifyingly, at the revolutionary vanguard. Reassessing the earlier manifesto in this light, he writes that Vorticist formal ideas really had an ideological function. Vorticism

> meant a complete revaluation of form as a means of expressing nearly everything else, or shall we say of form as a means of expressing the fundamentals of everything, or shall we say of

---

22. Ezra Pound, *Guide to Kulchur* (London: Peter Owen, 1938), p. 95. Hereafter cited in the text as *Guide*.

23. In the *Exile* period, Pound proposed that there were three political parties: Marxist, Fascist, and his own, the "Party of Intelligence," which was conducting an investigation of both. By the mid-thirties, the Party of Intelligence had chosen Fascism for a variety of reasons which are not my subject here. One reason: Pound felt that "Mussolini is the first head of state in our time to perceive and to proclaim *quality* as a dimension in national production."("Murder by Capital" (1933), *Impact: Essays on Ignorance and the Decline of American Civilization*, ed. Noel Stock [Chicago: Henry Regnery Company, 1960], p. 87. Hereafter cited in the text as *Impact*.) That is, Pound felt Mussolini would be in charge of a renaissance parallel in intensity and meaning to the one in the 15th century. Pound personally identified with Mussolini as late as *Drafts & Fragments*; there is an element of narcissistic hero-worship in his keeping of a scrapbook on the hero (reported by Noel Stock in the Pound biography)—narcissistic because Pound felt that Mussolini achieved in the political sphere what Pound had achieved in the aesthetic. Thus Pound essentially saw himself as Mussolini's corresponding half.

form as expressing the specific weights and values [of?] total consciousness.

(*Gaudier-Brzeska*, p. 144)[24]

The Cantos, than, take on this function: they offer "a complete revaluation of life in general. . . ." (*Gaudier-Brzeska*, p. 144).

The double meaning of Pound's term *paideuma* can also indicate the play between the historical and the static in Pound's poetics from the late twenties on. The view that an organic culture comprises the values, attitudes and assumptions held in any historical period, along with their interrelations and their products, Pound (with Frobenius' term) described as "paideuma," "the tangle or complex of the inrooted ideas of any period" (*Guide*, p. 57).[25] In Pound's view, a new paideuma—cultural or social change—can be achieved through historically rooted realizations. This was probably the definition with which Zukofsky and Oppen would have agreed. However, Pound also used "paideuma" to mean a universal, transhistorical set of values in action, which are kept alive by an elite group. Not organic in the sense of being "inrooted," they are instead perpetually reaffirmed, the "recurring decimals" of wisdom and good government (*Guide*, p. 249). The arithmetical analogy conceals the religious structure of thought. For Pound eventually explains the existence of these ideas in mystical terms, and their believers become initiates in a mystery which unifies the elites of many times and places. As he says, "A conspiracy of intelligence outlasted the hash of the political map." (*Guide*, p. 263) After Pound reaches this point in his poetics, *The Cantos* are increasingly based on pre-existing convictions of will and desire, rather than on the investigation of a field of densely inrooted particulars. This is the moment that Oppen will reject Pound.[26] Because of his moral and political convictions, Pound the objectivist became Pound the symbolist, intent—in Altieri's words—on "raising particulars to the level of universals whereby they come to provide models for experience."[27] Hence the purpose Pound ascribes to poetry in general and the actual texture and approach of his poetry are in major contradiction.

For the Oppens, trying to read *The Cantos* might well have been like experiencing Pound's magisterial sweep out to the water

---

24. *Gaudier-Brzeska*, 144. I have supplied a conjectural word for the missing one.

25. Another historical definition occurs in "For a New Paideuma," *The Criterion* XVII, 67 (Jan. 1938), 205: "the active element in the era, the complex of ideas which is in a given time germinal. . . ."

26. Hence when Dembo asked Oppen about a resemblance between the idea of a discrete series and the ideogrammic method, he received a response criticizing Pound's organization of the poem by ego; Dembo interview, p. 170.

27. Charles Altieri, "From Symbolist Thought to Immanence: The Ground of Postmodern American Poetics," *Boundary* 2, I, 3 (Spring 1973), 611.

when they visited him at Rapallo: "From there came the Greek ships."[28] Too much of a gesture, for he was pointing in the wrong direction. Almost fifty years later, they remember: "We weren't wowed by *The Cantos*. We saw that it was magnificent poetry; it was as if someone had played the piano. Didn't mean we had to buy a grind organ."[29] Yet even though he distances himself from *The Cantos*, still, references to Pound do appear, especially in Oppen's recent work. Oppen seems to have been completely moved by Pound's apologia, in which a fragmented reading of the major poem is favored, and in which Pound reveals that although he always wanted an ending of major proportions, yet he was forced by circumstances to renounce this ambition:

> But the beauty is not the madness
> Tho' my errors and wrecks lie about me.
> And I am not a demigod,
> I cannot make it cohere.
> If love be not in the house there is nothing.[30]

Oppen refers to these very lines in "The Speech at Soli," asking Pound "What do you want/to tell." He posits Pound's answer as the intolerable alternative "as against the Populism in my poem"[31]:

> mad kings
>
> gone raving
>
> war in incoherent
> sunlight it will not
>
> cohere it will NOT that
> other
>
> desertion
> of the total we discover
>
> Friday's footprint is it as the sun moves
>   *(CP*, p. 234)[32]

---

28. Mary Oppen, *Meaning a Life* (Santa Barbara: Black Sparrow Press, 1978), p. 132. Hereafter cited in the text as *Meaning*.
29. "Talking with George and Mary about Pound," author's notes, made 16 May 1980, San Francisco. Hereafter cited in the text as "Talking." How then did Oppen "get" his Pound? To some degree it was through Zukofsky. For, as I have implied in the discussion of poetics, the Oppens and Zukofsky were the strongest and deepest friends at the time when Zukofsky was writing the important study of Pound which appeared in *The Criterion* in 1929. Further, Oppen "gets" Pound in "passages and lines. Just about the time I'm beginning to consider Pound an idiot, I come to something like the little wasp in the *Pisan Cantos*, and I know I'm reading a very great poet." Dembo interview, p. 170.
30. Ezra Pound, Canto 116, *Drafts & Fragments of Cantos CX–CXVII* (New York: New Directions, 1968), pp. 25-26. Hereafter cited in the text as *Drafts*.
31. Kevin Power, "An Interview with George & Mary Oppen," *Montemora* 4 (1978), 200. Hereafter cited in the text as "Power interview."
32. The Friday/Crusoe reference recalls the poem "Of Being Numerous," sections 6, 7 and 9. In the early part of "The Speech at Soli," which I've not quoted, the various lines

What, in Oppen's view, is wrong with Pound's alternative? One answer may occur in the apparently innocuous word "want": "What do you want/to tell." For that word carries a double force. It might signal the desire to conform to some pre-existing system, wanting to tell a certain message, wanting to affirm a certain idea. This would be "desertion of the total" because it does not account for the affiliations of the ensemble addressed, but privileges one aspect for willful reasons. Oppen's position should not be confused with barefoot empiricism, I think, but should rather be viewed as a statement of the unending dialectic between inductive and deductive reasoning, observation and analytic models, both tested against each other and against a sense of wholeness or totality. Pound got stuck in deduction and therefore in the insistence that things come out as he wanted, as his model predicted; this led to "madness" and "raving." The judgment could not be clearer. In contrast, the other meaning of the word "want" is—again—a statement of sincerity, establishing again and again what the person at a given moment can want, as situations, moments, perceptions change:

> A social ethic cannot be constructed unless we know, finally, what we want [33]

And what we want changes, situationally, in time. It is only possible to live morally if one recognizes that different situations and historical moments demand different responses. This adaptability, I think, should not be reduced to opportunism.

Oppen returned to the word "want" in letters in the late 60's. He argued that the force of the New, as opposed to the Old, Left was that the people of the New Left were not speaking for others—as, say, a petty bourgeois would claim to be speaking for the working class—but were instead saying what they themselves wanted:

> A fake ethic, a forced ethic, we cannot construct an ethic unless we know what we want and how much we want it. [34]

One of the largest differences between Oppen and Pound is that Pound was perplexed by, and resistant to, historical fluidity and its demands on praxis. He wanted things settled once and for all. Oppen did not resist that fluidity, but was always fascinated by the ways the dimensions of "want" changed and could be

from "a letter"—"young girls fell into [open] wells," "in the green [spring] storm," and "bringing to birth" are all from my poem "Elegies" (*Wells*, New York: Montemora, 1980). The last phrase appeared in an early version of "Elegies" but has been cut from the published version.

33. Personal letter, George Oppen to Rachel Blau [DuPlessis], 24 Jan. 1969.
34. Personal letter, George Oppen to Rachel Blau [DuPlessis], 14 March 1969.

reassessed. That is probably why Oppen has quoted, so approvingly, Hugh Kenner's remark about his taking 25 years to write the next poem (Dembo interview, p. 174). For Oppen, Kenner may have seemed to understand Oppen's changing wants; however, Kenner's remark may equally come from the aesthetician's attempt to avoid discussing the political commitment in those intervening years.

The compact between George and Mary Oppen, fairly fresh at the time they first met Pound in Rapallo in 1930, was a primary bond of defining importance. The couple took risks for it; they fought its disruption. This will help measure the force of what occurred then, as they remember it now. "There were two of us, and in Pound there is no feminine," they told me in 1980. Pound had strong male bonding relations with Zukofsky and Bunting. There was no reason in Pound's mind why Oppen should not fit this pattern of discipleship, especially as Pound also thought that TO Press was prepared to publish his collected works. But it bothered the young couple that Pound excluded Mary from conversation, and also, as Oppen said, that "he invited me to call, not Mary." In having extricated themselves from Oppen's family, by whom they had been financially and emotionally "seduced," the Oppens had affirmed their "resistance" and self-sufficiency.[35] They were not to give any other paternal figure power over them. Hence Oppen resisted the preferred attractions of personal connection with Pound. By immersion in political activity and by paying its political cost, Oppen then sought a forum for his instruction outside literary tradition. Neither a poet nor a critic need assume that a sense of cultural authority can alone come from the consideration of texts, from discipleship in education, or from the apostolic succession of poet to poet. Immersion in collective struggles (the milk strike in New York State, Depression organizing in New York City, the Second World War) and saturation in the felt experiences of every social class were what the Oppens selected as their cultural instructors in the 30s and 40s.

When Pound and Oppen met for the second time, in 1969 at New Directions, the two wept together, over each other. Oppen's poem "Of Hours," first published in *Seascape: Needle's Eye* (1972), explores that oppositional contact and mutual grief in the context of Pound's work, especially *The Pisan Cantos* (*CP*, pp. 210-212).[36] For in the 30s not only had George and Mary

---

35. These words come up in conversation as they come up in Mary Oppen, *Meaning a Life*.
36. In the version of this article published in *Paideuma* 10, 1, I attempted to show the way the whole poem could be interpreted as a commentary on the Oppen-Pound relationship.

Oppen resisted the personal attractions of the "father poet," but they had found the politics damaging, both as statements and for what they said about Pound. By 1930, Pound was well into the romance of fascism. Mary Oppen has commented how revealing it was to hear Pound talk fondly about Mussolini as "the Boss." Probably the core of rage ("o rage/of the exile") which Oppen offers in this poem has to do with two issues: himself as Jew and Pound as anti-Semite; himself as marxist-democrat, and Pound as fascist. Indeed, symbolically speaking, putting Oppen next to Pound creates, in little, the most defining confrontation of twentieth century history: the right reactionary philo-fascist and the left revolutionary communist. However, the core of grief in the poem is articulated by the fact that "rage/of the exile" could apply equally to Pound as expatriate and Oppen as Jew; the grief comes with empathy for the person:

Holes   pitfalls open
In the cop's accoutrement

Crevasse

The destitute metal

Jail metal

Impoverished   Intimate
As a Father did you know that

Pound's several confinements—political and psychological, from the post-war detention center to the Washington hospital— are engaged in these lines. Oppen's challenge to Pound is based, interestingly, on paternity, and recalls, therefore, Oppen's yearning towards "the children" in his poems, children as the palpable future. He could be asking whether Pound ever saw the way the role of "cop," of keeper of order, would tend. Are not the "pitfalls," the "holes" in the argument visible? Didn't you know, he asks Pound obliquely, what fascism was (all that "destitute metal," all the trappings, the terror)? And if you knew, why did you believe? Is this what you *want*?

Indeed, Pound was not unaware of the tactics of the Fascists in Italy. The Matteoti murder (1924, the year Pound settled in Rapallo) caused a crisis in Italy; Mussolini responded by a rightward move. Within the next few years, the fascists established totalitarian control. In later comments on this period, Pound saw internal terror as an aberration which he was willing to justify because of his hope that the renaissance for which *he* had long been ready had, in fact, arrived. His letter to Basil Bunting from

1938 evinces a forceful blindness to the implications of the
curious analogy he chose to explain this.

> You will never get the hang of fascism if you persist in the
> habit of regarding every act as a precedent.
> Surgeon amputates leg/NOT as a precedent/he don't mean to
> go on amputating the patient's leg every week or year.
> Operations to save life/ONLY in an emergency/What are called
> CONTINGENT. Things to be done ONCE and not erected into a
> system.[37]

Of course, the point is that for any one patient there is only
one operation. The leg once amputated is not available again; the
precedent occurs perforce in cutting off one of the two to begin
with. The power relation in this citation is worth noticing.
Occurring between the professional and the patient, this exemplum
presents a hierarchy of decisive knowledge in which the metaphorically ill one has no control and no choice. This kind of
system is consistent with other of Pound's structures—is not, in
short, *aberrant*.

In the poem "Of Hours," Oppen thinks about the Second
World War in the context of himself as a Jew:

> Fought
>
> No man
> but the fragments of metal
> Tho there were men there were men   Fought
> No man but the fragments of metal
> Burying my dogtag with H
> For Hebrew in the rubble of Alsace.

When the metal which is being fought becomes, in the repetition
of that line, one's own identity, the metal tag which characterizes
oneself as anathema, torturable, vulnerable in an imposed way,
then the war and fascism live in the sword against oneself, and in
the degree to which one fears one's own identity because it is
one's otherness.[38] In the *no man*, Oppen is recapitulating the

---

37. Pound's letter to Bunting, *Impact*, 263. "Matteotti, an exceptionally brave Socialist
Deputy, exposed the electoral practices by which the Fascists had gained some 65 per-
cent of the vote. He was murdered by Fascist toughs. The response of the still relatively
free press, public and parliament was such as to shock Mussolini into the realization that
he could not expect to rule without total controls." Consequently, "the one-party state
moved to total control over press, judiciary, educational, trade union, cultural, propaganda, and youth activities." John Weiss, *The Fascist Tradition: Radical Right-Wing
Extremism in Modern Europe* (New York: Harper & Row, Publishers, 1967), pp. xxi-
xxii. Especially pertinent is Pound's defensive confession that he did know about, without learning from, the terror tactics; the reference here is to a famous tactic—forced
diarrhea: "Nobody hit me with a club and I didn't see any oil bottles" (*Jefferson and/or
Mussolini* [New York: Liveright, 1935], p. 51.)
38. In his essay on Edmond Jabès, Maurice Blanchot cites Robert Misrahi, *La condition
réflexive de l'homme juif* (ed. Juilliard): " 'To be a Jew' is something that cannot be

otherness of the Jew, the anonymity of war, and the Odyssean moment in *The Cantos*; ΟΨ ΤΙΣ is *no man*, Pound's hero Odysseus. So Oppen remembers the war, remembers thinking

> that the lives of all Jews were endangered by fascism; our lives were in danger, and not to fight in the war was to ask of others what we would not do for ourselves.
>
> (*Meaning*, p. 173)

It is hard to be kind to Pound on the subject of Jews, although in the recently published "Addendum for Canto C" he states that usury is "beyond race and against race" (*Drafts*, p. 28). There are, over all, too many nasty quotations, despite the honorable, but rather oft-repeated assurances that he lacked *personal* anti-Semitism. In some curious way, this is not as exculpatory as it has sounded, for it isolates the good Jews (my friends, the elite) from all the others (the enemy), and gives the anti-Semite control of the choice, defining who is who, which is which. The political anti-Semitism of fascism—a universal pogrom—was not Pound's solution; he wanted, however, a limited antisepsis, aimed at the Jews at the top. But beyond Pound's solutions, final or semi-final, those poor, much maligned Jews in Pound's cantos are symptomatic of a mode of thought far removed from Oppen's and which makes another distinction between them. A conspiracy theory is, after all, so monocausal as to almost miss being termed analytic.

Pound's conspiracy theory, as Daniel Pearlman has pointed out in his important article, was pointedly anti-Semitic, but one would have to add that it was not exclusively so. The Jews were the focus of the long-standing pseudo-analysis Pound had been making since World War I of the "obstructors" of various sorts. That is, not to mince words, a conspiracy theory lies at the center of Pound's intellectual life for most of his active years. This kind of analysis, with its urgencies and frustrations, contributes to the crusading tone of Pound's prose, for he is constantly giving his readers the lowdown on those pertinacious, but so visible, forces which block the otherwise magically achievable new society. Pound hardly had any kind of structural or systemic analysis— these being the polar opposite of conspiracy theory—so the simplicity of getting rid of the highly personalized obstructors was, in his view, patent. It is as if they could be "popped" out of place.

Conspiracy theory and anti-Semitism enter Pound's *Cantos* of course in their content. But more centrally, conspiracy theory enters the invisible threads of the poetry, in those mental habits

---

defined for the cultured, assimilated Jew, except paradoxically and circuitously: by the *mere fact* of always being susceptible to gratuitous murder 'because of being Jewish' . . . ", *Montemora* 6 (1979), 80.

and perceptions that help the poet create the structural systems of statement which constitute the poem. So the degree to which a conspiracy theory, with its familiar scapegoats, is injected into Pound's poem, in both content and deep structure, is the degree to which he could be one of the objects of Oppen's brief manifesto:

> We, the poets, change the accents, change the speech. We change the speech because we are not explaining, agitating, convincing: we do not write what we already knew before we wrote the poem.[39]

Pound does indeed write what he knew before he wrote the poem. For Oppen, this represents a failure to create poetry from the objectivist poetics which Pound had, in effect, invented.

Syntax in poetry, like narrative choices in fiction (e.g. coincidences, the nature of beginnings, what is resolved or excluded at conclusions), is the area where ideology or world view is most keenly revealed. What then is it like to read *The Cantos*, to read Oppen's *Collected Poems*? What world views does the poetry convey?

On site, inside the poem page by page, *The Cantos* are the location of tremendous poetic conflicts pulling the work in opposite directions. The major stress comes between the ideogram and the summary category, that is, between structuring by the presentation of particulars in a field (comparable to objectivist practice) and by the representation of already formulated statement. A field structure is heuristic and process-oriented, its paratactic arrangements allowing an intimate relation between reader and writer, sustained by the poet's tact and by a deep commitment to equalizing access to information and vision. Capitalizing on Fenollosa's analysis of syntax, Pound developed that poetic structure by dissociating the energies of words (interpreted as variants of verbs) from the presumably limiting and deadening patterns of sentences in which words were enclosed. Yet, as I've suggested, as Pound's political ideas became more fixed, the poet violated or drastically modified this imagist or objectivist poetic procedure by summarizing or asserting ideas. Thus he limited his words in their meaning, while still attempting to free them by his structure.

The Cantos often makes shorthand allusions to and oblique summaries of arguments already elliptical in Pound's prose. In practice, therefore, many words appear to the untutored reader as if in a code. Pound compels at least temporary discipleship for this reason: only by learning Poundian references as if learning a

---

39. Oppen, "A Letter," *Agenda* (1973), 59.

foreign language can a reader fully comprehend key words and thematic references in the poem. For instance, the word *metath-emenon*, whenever it appears, indicates a passage in Aristotle which discusses the altering of currency values. In order to read this contextless word, one must search for the anecdote, connota-tion or reference in other works by Pound. So the unit of compo-sition of the poem approaches being a unit of a special language: a poundeme. A good number of words do not yield meaning until a special referent is discovered for them.

Pound's cantos certainly present a horizontal vista of multi-ple potential relations created by the juxtaposition and thematic resonance of lines. In this he is like the *Paterson* poet. But while both poets create an endless poem about change and of change, Williams was committed to a process of decreation and invention, while Pound desired that his poem should show change—once and for all. Terms such as "totalitarian synthesis" (*Guide*, p. 95) and "hierarchy of evaluation" (*Impact*, p. 177) testify to the rich verticality and didactic intention of Pound's coordinates.

Pound took these risks for his poem because he wanted it to have a social function, to make the old world new. If one may properly speak of a historical time of transition, perhaps *The Cantos* are one of the first poems to try to function as a "text of transition" in a period of historical crisis. Pound achieved a prob-lematic work because of his tremendous and insistent direction: to allow for the use of the work—"that I tried to make a paradiso// terrestre " (*Drafts*, p. 32). Not, that is, the paradise of a funished object, but a living society adumbrated, a new and total culture which could exist in reality, conjured by the magic of the poem. So Pound risked the poem for the world.

Indeed, by the late thirties, Pound seems to have lost interest in the general reader, and to have wanted to use his poem as a tool to build up and fortify the new elite, which he sometimes termed *le beau monde*. This became Pound's main political reform, done through the screening process of the poetic text itself. He seems to have viewed his fragmented lines, clear images, and key facts as a special shorthand message to the elite and if you could read his poem, you were qualified for membership. And the mode of the work is, then, not fiction or story, but a series of true state-ments, functioning as directives to the men on the job.[40] The

---

40. As in the following passage from the essay "We Have Had No Battles But We Have All Joined In And Made Roads," *Polite Essays* (London: Faber and Faber, 1937), p. 55. "It may be even that the serene flow of a sentence is more exciting to the reader than are words set down in anger. But when one is not narrating? When one specifies the new life or the new temple? When one talks to the capo maestro, that is to the building foreman as distinct from making architectural pictures that one knows will remain for ever (or

poetics of the ideogram gets assimilated to the politics of a real, earthly paradise. The "detached phrase"—really the syntactic unit of *The Cantos*—is redefined as the means of communication "half way between writing and action" (*Impact*, p. 40) since it gives the elite "condensed knowledge" (*Literary Essays*, p. 408):

> *Le beau monde* governs because it has the most rapid means of communication. It does not need to read blocks of three columns of printed matter. It communicates by the detached phrase, variable in length, but timely.
>
> (*Impact*, p. 50)

Pound thus grew to justify his uses of juxtaposition and fragmentation—tactics after all used by many modernists—by their political usefulness to select and train cadres, and he staked all on the validation of the poem through the future historical realizations and changes which he desired to induce those cadres to achieve. The poet is not simply the unacknowledged legislator, but the unacknowledged executive director, of the world. And the poem then becomes literally dependent on the future for its ending and its coherence, which will be achieved only when its prophecy of change and its manifesto for change emerge victorious, so that the poem ends as the celebration of those political and social changes which it would have the peculiar satisfaction of having induced.

Therefore the tragedy of Pound, who staked too little on his poem *as* poem and too much on a narrow understanding of the historical realities with which he was confronted. Pound's *Cantos* have the shape and meaning they do because Pound's political desires overrode, eroded, and negated his poetic practice—the poetic practice which was the major source for the Objectivist position. And this gradually intensifying encapsulation of the poem was the result of a profound choice made in the inter-war years in response to the disaster of World War I. Thereupon follow a series of tragic ironies. The poet who wanted the end of a symbolist poetics, the end of a hermetic, unrealistic poetry, the end of the poet's ivory-tower seclusion becomes more hermetic, more arcane, and inaccessible than he had ever desired. The poet who railed against allegorical equivalencies created a poetry of scholastic signals, to which one must be specially trained to respond. The poet who wished to convert readers and energize them into action ends by sapping the readers' strength or at least preoccupying them permanently in the very consideration of the poem. And the poet who wanted to educate a politically active elite has educated a far more inturning elite of Poundians.

---

for ages) unrealized, one may have other criteria? Risking the END of the reader's interest when the house or palace is up?" (Il Capo was a well-known name for Mussolini.)

But Pound's legacy is neither his hierarchy of values nor his own hectoring insistences which could be written as mottos on half a page. Rather it is the flat, vast, uncoordinated canvas of poetry into which one steps as into world itself. Pound's legacy, then, is not his content, but his struggle within form, recorded on the level of syntax. He is such fecund soil for poetry because he struggled so hard with the seriousness of his objectivist poetics and of his political vision. And *The Cantos* are a ragged and bloody record of that struggle—between imposed categories and immanent lyric experiences, between kinesis and stasis, between the totalitarian and the democratic worlds, between the imposition of knowledge and the discovery of knowledge. Pound, indeed, thought that his achievement was in "totalitarian categories"; his readers generally think otherwise. The fact that no formula or structure can resolve Pound's major conflicts of purpose does create the formal endlessness of his poem, which is of itself crucial to contemporary poetics. Yet Pound, unlike Williams, would have liked to solve that endlessness; Williams, in contrast, embraced it.[41] As for *The Cantos*, its epigraph may well be that it has "the defects inherent in a record of struggle" (*Guide*, p. 135).[42] Or, as Basil Bunting said, "There are the Alps."[43] Pound the grappler with the enormity of a vocation and an ambition—this is Oppen's Pound: the Pound of struggle itself.

The formation of meaning in Oppen occurs in linearity or forward movement, as the formation of meaning in Pound occurs by networks clotted around categories. In Oppen, the reader experiences a forward pulse of language, especially marked in *Seascape* and *Primitive*:

> if you want to say no say
> no if you want to say yes say yes in loyalty
>
> to all fathers or joy
> of escape
>
> from all my fathers I want to say

---

41. What is interesting about the "abandonment" of the *Cantos* (Hugh Kenner's word on the final pages of *The Pound Era* [Berkeley: University of California Press, 1971]) is that Pound did not permanently accept the moral and emotional stance of the *Pisan Cantos*, yet could not negotiate the rest of the poem in the way he had planned. For I think the paradiso was to be a paradiso *cum* Mussolini; hence, after World War II, he was "stuck." That word, of course, comes from Donald Hall's interview with Pound, *Paris Review*, no. 28 (1962).

42. These summary pages on Pound were written in 1975. Now Wendy Stallard Flory's book (*Ezra Pound and The Cantos: A Record of Struggle* [New Haven: Yale University Press, 1980]) has this title. My comments may be construed to "second" her use of that phrase. Any overlap in our conclusions is unintentional.

43. Basil Bunting, "On the Fly-Leaf of Pound's Cantos," *Collected Poems* (Oxford: Oxford University Press, 1978), p. 110.

>   yes and say
>   yes the turning
>   lights
>
>   of oceans in which to say what one knows and to
>   limit oneself to this
>
>   (*CP*, p. 250)[44]

This pulse is ur-syntactic, seeking connectedness, yet a-syntactic because suppressing certain conventions for connection:

> That most complex thing of syntax, of those connections which can't be dealt with outside the poem but that should take on substantial meaning within it.
>
>   (Power interview, p. 198)

Oppen's poetry is built with strongly marked line breaks and a rejection of terminal punctuation in sentences: this takes place on a canvas with an uncompromising use of white space to solemnize the encounter between the chosen and the void.

>   Song?
>
>   astonishing
>
>   song?   the world
>   sometime be
>
>   world the wind
>   be wind o western
>   wind to speak
>
>   of this
>   (*CP*, p. 249)

The vocation of poetry is never taken for granted: it is, in fact, reinvented at every turn. It is never a tool to get something else accomplished; it accomplishes only itself. Yet it is not an aesthetician's poetry, because through language it is announcing the world as ensemble. The syntax engenders that poetry of affiliation. By consistently placing the first words of a subsequent thought on the same line with the end of the last thought, a simultaneous hovering-over and forward-pulsing is created on the scale of the smallest unit. Further, a ratio or metonymic resonance is created between the words on any given line.[45] And finally, there is

---

44. This poem, dedicated "To LZ in time of the breaking of nations," certainly contains more material on which analyses of the Pound/Zukofsky/Oppen relationship could be built.

45. "The meaning of many lines will be changed—one's understanding of the lines will be altered—if one changes the line-ending. It's not just the line-ending as punctuation but as separating the connections of the progression of thought in such a way that understanding of the line would be changed if one altered the line division. And I don't mean just a substitute for the comma; I mean with which phrase the word is most intimately connected—that kind of thing" (Dembo interview, p. 167).

almost no descriptive amplification of any unit of meaning. These tactics create three feelings in the reader: mental weightlessness, physical density or pressure, and a sense of the void.

The mental weightlessness of this syntactic movement occurs because no thought closes before it gets pushed past the possibility for such closure or terminus. One has a sense of freedom, of risk and also of the connectedness of things. These feelings become associated in their turn, and it is the connectedness and affiliations of the world as ensemble that Oppen is addressing, and which subsequently, and simultaneously, cause this sense of freedom and risk—a sense of possibility and of awe.

> inshore,   the rough grasses
> rooted on the dry hills or to stand still
>
> like the bell buoy   telling
>
> tragedy so wide
> spread so
>
> shabby a north sea salt
> tragedy 'seeking a statement
>
> of an experience of our own' the bones of my hands
>
> bony   bony   lose me the wind cries   find
> yourself   I?
>
> this?   the road
> and the travelling   always
>
> undiscovered
> country forever
>
> savage   . . . .
>
> (*CP*, pp. 239-240)[46]

When I think about the physical density of the experience of reading Oppen, I do not mean the richness of a cultural and mytho-historical circuit, the Poundian periplum, but rather a sense of navigation itself. Say when we sailed in the boat, going from Sunset Cove to Eagle Island, George handed me the tiller. Not sure what I expected, but the sea pulled hard in every which direction. It was heavy and it pulled. The poem is then the person on the sea, steering, the sea pulling: the poem changes force and weight at every word but moves on its way, forward. Indeed, many of

---

46. Taken together, these syntactic features make Oppen as difficult to excerpt as any poet I know (except possibly prime Wordsworth), and this in itself makes the reader confront the temporal ensemble which he creates.

Oppen's poems have the sea as that force or element against which and in which all is tested. Syntactically and intellectually, the poems create a tension-filled vector: "trying to find the thought that will take us somewhere" (Mary Oppen in Power interview, p. 203).

A sense of the void is, of course, hard to describe. I am talking of the illuminated blankness before an image, an accident, an event. This is a defining moment in which the self is elected (out of its own resistances) as the explorer of that silence in which it is also dissolved. And from which it may emerge, stammering the relation of poetry to aphasia. This is the point at which Oppen's "take" on Pound cited as epigraph here—that poetry should be at least as well written as silence—becomes a serious matter of approaching a mystery of being without having to populate it with opinion and strained hope. Pound was, finally, not a poet of negative capability, for he did not want to wait!

> Clarity
>
> In the sense of *transparence*,
> I don't mean that much can be explained.
>
> Clarity in the sense of silence.
>
> (CP, p. 162)

An exacting and tender guide to the void occurs in a recent review by Gustaf Sobin; I will modify his terms to fit Oppen. Linearity or a sense of forward movement is achieved with the knowledge of contradictory pulls of meaning or possibility, and by the excision of traditionally binding elements, whether in syntax, in explanation, or in ideas which might be good for the reader to absorb. This procedure creates

> between or even "behind" the words an emptiness, a "void." The use of this void as *dimension* completely modified the expression of man's relationship with the world. . . .[47]

For one, it allows for the expression of spiritual heights and depths without assigning to these a structure from religion or myth as such. For another, it creates, within the texture of affiliation, spaces that prevent the social and ethical world depicted from seeming simply busy, chattering. For a third, it allows a space against which contradictions play, and which accords them the fullest possible force precisely because they are weighted against the void itself.

---

47. Gustaf Sobin, "Review of *L'Ecriture Poétique Chinoise* by François Cheng," *Montemora* 5 (1979), 248.

Part of what Oppen achieves is a constant set of contradictions created within syntax, and these are, at the same time, the ethical experiences he proposes: love and rage, alienation and populism, the singular and the multitude, the "level of art" and the "me-too of art," the children and the cataclysm.[48] These contradictions simply continue, unresolved.[49] It is a world view quite different from Pound's. In his, one side is consciously chosen; both sides are not maintained except as dualistic and highly contrasted elements: "we know that there is one enemy" (*Guide*, p. 31). In Oppen, the movement from word to word, the question where a sentence ends or whether it ends, the hovering created by removing a question mark from a syntactically created question, the multiple readings possible with intonation shifts—these are some of the syntactic ways that contradiction is organized and sustained. So the contrast Pound/Oppen begins with an apocalyptic poet who thought he discovered the truth in (reactionary) revolution, who wanted to effect the sudden ending of one world and the beginning of another, and whose poem, in consequence, has the inner dynamic of a manifesto. He is opposed to a historical poet who inhabits time by writing as if navigating a vector of conflicting forces, whose morality it is to work for statements fit to be tested as truth, and whose poems, in consequence, have the inner dynamic of gnomic fragments.[50]

And so Oppen's poem to Pound, "Of Hours"—of the pulse of time moving forward—gathers force as it states the doubleness of revulsion and love at the moment when the two faced each other, almost forty years after their first meeting:

I must get out of here

Father   he thinks   *father*

Disgrace of dying

---

48. "The level of art," *CP*, p. 168. The "me-too of art," George Oppen, letter to Rachel Blau [DuPlessis], Sept. or Oct. 1965: "Poetry seems to me a thing to do when it is absolutely beyond, out of sight beyond the me-too of art."

49. In his desire to pursue the non-ironic presence of full contradiction, Oppen recalls the Enzensberger of "Summer Poem": "Literary language has a tendency to tie down anything that can be said. This text opposes the tendency by breaking up sentences. That is why the poem is dominated by a kind of syntax which classical grammar calls *apo koinou*: four sentence parts are related in such a way that the sentence can be read in several different ways. The repetitions in the poem serve to subject the experiences dealt with to doubt, to contradiction, to questioning." Hans Magnus Enzensberger, *Selected Poems* (Harmondsworth: Penguin Books Ltd., 1967), p. 90.

50. "It is part of the function of poetry to serve as a test of truth. It is possible to say anything in abstract prose, but a great many things one believes or would like to believe or thinks he believes will not substantiate themselves in the concrete materials of the poem" (Oppen, "Mind," p. 133). Every time Oppen talks about truth, he raises the spectre of the absolute idea; one must, I think, read the word as true-at-the-time or truth as "moments of conviction," as he said in the Dembo interview, p. 161.

And here Oppen dramatizes his final question to Pound before the painful last word:

> Old friend   old poet
> If you did not look
>
> What is it you 'loved'
> Twisting your voice   your walk

This quoted word can refer to two essential moments in Pound's *Cantos.* It may evoke almost the last words on the last page of *Drafts & Fragments.*

> M'amour, m'amour
>   what do I love and
>   where are you?
> That I lost my center
>   fighting the world.
> The dreams clash
>   and are shattered—
>
> and that I tried to make a paradiso
>   terrestre.
>   (*Drafts*, p. 32)

Given these realizations, one may project several responses from Oppen. One is certainly tears of empathy and grief. Another might be tears of rage. Why? Unkindly, it's a little late in the day to be asking that question.

And the fact that the word "loved" may refer to the climax of *The Pisan Cantos* startles with the critical edge of Oppen's question and his dramatic assertion: that Pound did not really look, with the acute perception—with that perceptual sincerity beyond system—which was his gift to poetry. Therefore how could he know what he loved?[51] The turn away from Pound's poetic diction (*lov'st* to *loved*; *thou* to *you*) seems apropos.

> What thou lovest well remains,
>   the rest is dross
> What thou lov'st well shall not be reft from thee
> What thou lov'st well is thy true heritage[52]

What did Pound love? There are so many answers. Beauty; order; the fecundity of the earth. But also a political order that would sculpt people like art. And as well, a social hierarchy which privileges the artifax (leader or artist). The past, but the attempt to

---

51. In his criticism of Pound, Oppen has emphasized the visual impact of things in the world; Zukofsky, at a similar juncture, takes up the aural. "When [Pound] asked me [in 1939] if it were possible to educate certain politicians, I retorted, Whatever you don't know, Ezra, you ought to know *voices.*" "Work/Sundown," *Prepositions*, p. 157.
52. Ezra Pound, *The Cantos* (New York: New Directions, 1970), pp. 520-521. Hereafter cited in the text as *Cantos.*

restore such values in the present. Understanding—but how garnered? With the exasperated tone of the autodidact, Pound used his whole life and much of his poem to tell us: "with one day's reading a man may have the key in his hands" (*Cantos,* p. 427).

For Oppen, the idea of any "key" to understanding is equally exasperating, a violation of the poetics and the world view which the two poets began by sharing:

> Wet roads
>
> Hot sun on the hills
>
> He walks the twig-strewn streets
> Of the rain
>
> Walks homeward
>
> Unteachable

ERIC MOTTRAM

THE POLITICAL RESPONSIBILITIES
OF THE POET: GEORGE OPPEN

In a 1968 interview George Oppen uses characteristic evaluative terms for his position, so that poetry and politics are not separated. He speaks of the necessity for "a position of honesty" and a method of thought for "forming a poem properly, for achieving form."[1] The result is to retain "the imagist intensity of vision" and be "a test of truth," "a test of sincerity" (Dembo Interview, p. 161). The prosody emerges from a prime Oppen fact: "you believe something to be true, and you construct a meaning from these moments of conviction" (Dembo Interview, p. 161). *Discrete Series* is titled to refer to "a series of empirically true terms" (Dembo Interview, p. 161). Oppen explains this concept by a quotation from Hegel: "Disagreement marks where the subject matter ends. It is what the subject-matter is not" (quoted in Dembo Interview, p. 162). This means that the poem apprehends substance which is not comment or argument. But in some of his later poems Oppen will engage in argument. For example, *Of Being Numerous* "asks the question whether or not we can deal with humanity as something which actually does exist" (Dembo Interview, p. 162). Oppen comes back to the value of the act of poetry, not its possibility: "a test of whether one's thought is valid . . . whether or not one will consider the concept of humanity to be valid, something that is, or else have to regard it as being simply a word" (Dembo Interview, p. 162). How many poets have ever gone to such roots with such directness? The instance follows—"Psalm" in *This In Which*: "The small nouns/ Crying faith/In this in which the wild deer/Startle, and stare

---

1. L. S. Dembo, "The Objectivist Poet: Four Interviews," *Contemporary Literature*, 10:2 (Spring, 1969), 160. Hereafter cited in the text as "Dembo Interview."

out."[2] Doubts included: "we have a kind of feeling that the absolutely unitary is somehow absolute, that, at any rate, it really exists" (Dembo Interview, p. 163). So the world is demystified. "The life of the mind" is awareness of this physicality: "nearly a sense of awe, simply to feel the thing is there" (Dembo Interview, p. 164). Or, in *Of Being Numerous*: "Tell the life of the mind, the mind creates the finite" (*CP*, p. 193).

This is Oppen's basis for "all the struggles for happiness, all the search for a morality of altruism, all the dependence on the poor to confer value" (Dembo Interview, p. 164). So that the political enters poetry and truth just here, in "an ethic of altruism," embodied, for instance, in the young Americans who went into Mississippi during the 1960s civil rights movement, who "were heroic and were doing what needed to be done" (Dembo Interview, p. 165). But the ethic is neither permanent, nor does it answer "the problems . . . the outcome of the process of humanity" (Dembo Interview, p. 165). The static Socratic view that in injuring society you injure your own interests is useless if you believe "there is something we want humanity . . . to become" (Dembo Interview, p. 165). Commitment begins here; beyond the mere feeling that you cannot stand children being napalmed any more, you cease to be an ethical observer and begin to discriminate. Commenting on the image of the car in the seventh poem of *Discrete Series*, Oppen says: "there is a feeling of something false in overprotection and overluxury—my idea of categories of realness" (Dembo Interview, p. 168).

Thirty-eight years later, in "From a Phrase of Simone Weil's and Some Words of Hegel's," Oppen's commitment remains steady:

> Ob via   the obvious
> Like a fire of straws
> Aflame in the world or else poor people hide
> Yourselves together
>
>   (*CP*, p. 205)

In *Of Being Numerous* he cites a favorite passage from Kierkegaard which summarizes his commitment to a work democracy, to an active life of the mind, and to action in and against society:

> '. . . he who will not work shall not eat,
> and only he who was troubled shall find rest,
> and only he who descends into the nether world shall
>   rescue his beloved,

---

2. George Oppen, *Collected Poems* (New York: New Directions, 1975), p. 78. Hereafter cited in the text as "*CP*".

> and only he who unsheathes his knife shall be given
>   Isaac again. He who will not work shall not eat . . .
> but he who will work shall give birth to his own father.'
>   (*CP*, p. 158)

Back in 1934, *Discrete Series* opens with "The knowledge not of sorrow, you were/saying, but of boredom/Is . . . Of the world, weather-swept, with which/one shares the century" (*CP*, p. 3)— "phrases," Oppen says in the 1968 interview, "from Heidegger's Acceptance Speech [of the Chair of Philosophy at Freiburg] made in 1929, the year I was writing the poem" (Dembo Interview, p. 169). Knowledge of boredom becomes a philosophic tool to ascertain what the facts are. In *Of Being Numerous* this is transmuted into

> The sea anemone dreamed of something, filtering the sea
>   water thru its body,
>
> Nothing more real than boredom—dreamlessness, the
>   experience of time, never felt by the new arrival,
>   never at the doors, the thresholds, it is the native
>
>
> Native in native time . . .
>
> The purity of the materials, not theology, but to present
>   the circumstances
>   (*CP*, p. 186)

Hegel, Heidegger, Weil and, as epigraph to *The Materials* in 1962, Maritain: "We awake in the same moment to ourselves and to things" (from *Creative Intuition in Art and Poetry*, the Mellon lectures first printed in 1953). The ego and dogma are both subdued in the necessity of analysis and action. When Oppen reads, the steadying calm and lowered tone of deliberateness, of deliberation, refuses ego in the performance of social truth through poetry. Ego is pared down to skill, the condition of the political without Pound's "ego system" or what Olson called "the EGO AS BEAK":

> Ez's epic solves problems by his ego: his single emotion breaks all
> down to his equals or inferiors. . . .the methodology of *The
> Cantos* [is] a space-field where, by inversion, though the material
> is all time material, he has driven through it so sharply with the
> beak of his ego, that, he has turned time into what we must now
> have, space & its live air.[3]

Oppen adds a further and far more political objection—to Pound's heroic vitalism, his belief in chthonic leadership rights, the origins

---

3. Charles Olson, "Mayan Letters," in *Selected Writings*, ed. Robert Creeley (New York: New Directions, 1966), pp. 81-2.

of infatuation with male dominant rule: "Pound's ego system, Pound's organization of the world around a character, a kind of masculine energy, is extremely foreign to me" (Dembo Interview, p. 170). His "objections to parts of *A* " are not detailed in the interview.[4] For the rest, Blake, Wyatt, and "several Middle English poems" mean more than most contemporaries (Dembo Interview, p. 171). Oppen is not explicit—nor is he, here, on Olson and Duncan, for example. But the inferences are clear enough, and what the problem might be emerges in his origins for the story in part 5 of "Route": "It's the kind of story any existentialist—Sartre specifically—might tell except that it did happen to me. . . .Pierre [Adam] knew the point he was making. He knew I was very positive about politics, about social and political morality—very positive about judgments concerning the war" (Dembo Interview, p. 172). The existentialist—Sartre specifically—places the self in a detailed awareness of historical society, without excuses of class and expedience, and certainly not of political dogma. This is, for example, the existential factor in René Char, poet and maquis leader, whose later and political poems complement Oppen's. In Oppen's words: "the learning that one is, after all, just oneself and in the end is rooted in the singular, whatever one's absolutely necessary connections with human history are" (Dembo Interview, p. 172). When he adds "Not the symbol but the scene," and "what happened and the place it happened in" (Dembo Interview, p. 172), we can juxtapose Zukofsky writing in the middle of the periodic collapse of American capitalism: "the only form that will include the most pertinent subject of our day—/The poor," and "the facts are not a symbol . . . No human being wishes to become/An insect for the sake of a symbol."[5]

The life of the mind for Oppen is seeing—the articulated vision—things and facts. His response to "large sections of humanity" may therefore be "despair" (Dembo Interview, p. 173). He refuses any populist stance and understands the seriousness of the fact that poetry may be "actually destructive for people. . . .It does lead to the growing isolation of the poet; there's no question in my mind about it" (Dembo Interview, p. 173). As for his own direct political action in the thirties, fifteen million families starving in the Depression needed action, action beyond writing: "In a way I gave up poetry because of the pressures of what for the moment I'll call conscience" (Dembo Interview, p. 174)—itself a result of working in factories, having a child, feeling that there

---

4. Cf. Eric Mottram, "1924-1951: Politics and Form in Zukofsky," *Maps*, No. 5.
5. Louis Zukofsky, "Mantis, An Interpretation," *All: The Collected Shorter Poems, 1923-1964* (New York: Norton, 1971), pp. 77-78.

would be time ahead to write poems. Poems are not politically "efficacious." Further details appear in "The Mind's Own Place" in 1963: "The emotion which creates art is the emotion which seeks to know and disclose"[6]—exactly that "opening up of the horizon of meaning which habitual expectations and forms close off" which causes Oppen's poetics to resist "New Critical and structural attempts to impose upon them the teleological, ironic, atemporal, distanced structures of the reifying West."[7] (In an interview of 1975, Oppen, in connection with "Civil war photo . . ." in *Discrete Series*, speaks of "meaning, conviction, emotion—the immediate emotional response"[8] as a part of necessary clarity). Although "the artist is not dependent on his subject in the sense that he can be judged by its intrinsic interest" ("Mind," p. 2), what he discloses, his knowledge, is to the point, as a reading of any major artist confirms. There is a politics of the restricted and narrow, of clinging to the familiar in the name of "tradition" or dogma, of propaganda or manipulation. To the authoritarian, political or religious, freedom to know and disclose has to be restricted. To the dominance of Philistia and Bohemia which Oppen castigates in this essay, the inventive imagination is a danger; it threatens dogma. If "it is the nightmare of the poet or the artist to find himself wandering between the grim grey lines of the Philistines and the ramshackle emplacements of Bohemia" ("Mind," p. 2)—which are "never endangered by the contest" ("Mind," p. 2)—it is because they are aspects of the same authoritarian urge. "New vision" and the "act of vision" in the new style which Oppen discovers in Dante, modern French art, the Ash Can school, the poets of *Others* magazine (Lindsay, Sandburg, Kreymborg, Williams), Pound and Eliot—all in their particularities moved away from that fatal contest, got "their heads above—or below—the terrible thin scratching of the art world" ("Mind," p. 3). Their aim: "to replace by the data of experience the accepted poetry of their time, a display by the poets of right thinking and right sentiment, a dreary waste of lies" ("Mind," pp. 3-4).

If your aim is "to construct a form out of no desire for the trick of gracefulness, but in order to make it possible to grasp, to hold the insight which is the content of the poem" ("Mind," p. 4), the authoritarian will try to prevent you, in social-political action as in the arts: no distinction can be made. The Beats, as Oppen says, assailed "the so-called Academic poets" ("Mind," p. 4) who

6. George Oppen, "The Mind's Own Place," *Kulchur* 3:10 (1963), p. 2. Hereafter cited in the text as "Mind."
7. Paul Bové, *Destructive Poetics*, (New York: Columbia University Press, 1980), p. xv.
8. Kevin Power, "An Interview with George and Mary Oppen," *Montemora* 4 (1978), p. 188. Hereafter cited as "Power Interview."

dominated the 1940s and early 1950s—and in fact still do, poets of Auden's derivations from Eliot, and Frost's from Edward Thomas and Hardy. If in 1963 "the people on the Freedom Rides are both civilized and courageous [and] the people in the Peace Marches are the sane people of the country" ("Mind," p. 7), their "terrifying necessity" is beyond the contests of the authoritarians. Oppen gave up poetry in the Depression; now in 1963 he agrees with Brecht's lines in "An die Nachgeborenen": "What times these are/when to speak of trees is almost a crime/Since it is a silence against so many enclosing injuries." Oppen writes: "there are situations which cannot honorably be met by art" ("Mind," p. 7), although "there is no crisis in which political poets and orators may not speak of trees" ("Mind," p. 7), even if they do speak propaganda. We may recall Lenin on aesthetics being the ethics of the future when Oppen says:

> . . . the definition of the good life is necessarily an aesthetic defi-
> nition, and the mere fact of democracy has not formulated it,
> nor, if it is achieved, will the mere fact of an extension of democ-
> racy, though I do not mean of course that restriction would be
> better. Suffering can be recognized; to argue its definition is an
> evasion, a contemptible thing. But the good life, the thing wanted
> for itself, the aesthetic, will be defined outside of anybody's
> politics, or defined wrongly.
>
> ("Mind," p. 8)

Oppen's "good life" is near Arendt's definition of authority as against the authoritarian in her essay "What is Authority?"[9] He speaks from the authority of non-engagement in the varieties of political verse in the 1930s, of being hounded by his country for his political action, of exile. His existentialism is a position many Europeans of his generation would recognize as necessary. The result is not "proletarian verse" or the aesthetic compromises of *New Masses*, or socialist realism; nor is it in any way similar to the sardonic lyrics of Fearing and Cummings, and the bourgeois whinings of a Robert Lowell. Oppen's work became silence and political action: "The situation of the Old Left was the theory of Socialist Realism, etc. . . .Its seemed pointless to argue [with political friends]. We stayed carefully away from people who wrote for the *New Masses*."[10] The poets he "looked up to" had a very small public, and it certainly did not include politicized popu-lists (Ironwood Interview, p. 23). As Orwell wrote in 1940, "the

9. Hannah Arendt, *Between Past and Future* (New York: The Viking Press, 1969), pp. 91-141.
10. Charles Amirkhanian and David Gitin, "A Conversation with George Oppen," *Iron-wood*, 5 (1975), p. 21. Hereafter cited in the text as "Ironwood Interview."

'democratic vistas' have ended in barbed wire."[11] It was impossible for Oppen to write such abject propaganda for the Communist Party as, for example, Langston Hughes's "Ballad of Lenin" or Spender's lines in *Trial for a Judge*, which Orwell quotes:

> We are nothing
> We have fallen
> Into the dark and shall be destroyed.
> Think, though, that in this darkness
> We hold the secret hub of an idea
> Whose living sunlit wheel revolves in future years outside . . .
>
> (Orwell, p. 233)

Orwell noted that between 1935 and 1939 "the Communist Party had an almost irresistible fascination for any writer under forty," in spite of the fact that what began as "a movement for the violent overthrow of capitalism" degenerated within a few years into "an instrument of Russian foreign policy," making party members and fellow-travellers "mentally subservient" to Russia, a state just as unscrupulous as any other "great power" (Orwell, pp. 234-5). Orwell concluded that what attracted British writers, at least, to "a form of socialism that makes mental honesty impossible" must have been "middle-class unemployment"—by which he meant that "by about 1930 there was no activity, except perhaps scientific research, the arts, and left-wing politics, that a thinking person could believe in" (Orwell, p. 236).

But for a writer determined to maintain "a position of honesty" as Oppen knew, the issue was complicated: "Any Marxist can demonstrate with the greatest of ease that 'bourgeois' liberty of thought is an illusion. But when he has finished his demonstration there remains the psychological *fact* that without this 'bourgeois' liberty the creative powers wither away" (Orwell, p. 241). Orwell found Henry Miller's "passive, non-cooperative attitude" preferable to unthinking support for dogma or for anything that did not recognize actively "the age of totalitarian dictatorships" (Orwell, p. 249). Miller worked it out in Paris, Orwell in Spain, Oppen in New York: "We joined the movement to help organize the unemployed." No poems could tell that definiteness: "We wanted to gather crowds of people on the simple principle that the law would have to be changed . . . when they involved someone's starvation. And we were interested in rioting . . . under political discipline. Disorder . . . —to make it impossible to allow people to starve" (Dembo Interview, p. 175). "[The] Depression . . . was not something in the newspapers. There were actually

---

11. George Orwell, "Inside the Whale," in *A Collection of Essays* (New York: Harcourt Brace, 1946), p. 219. Hereafter cited in the text as "Orwell."

hungry people in the streets under one's window. And people who were not 'the poor,' I realize there're all sorts of implications in my saying this, but one does become inured to the poor, and one was absolutely shocked by seeing men one could recognize as carpenters, as masons, as small business men, asking us at the age of twenty, twenty-one, around there, for a dime. . . .You either did something or you didn't do something" (Ironwood Interview, p. 23).

Oppen briefly sketches in what followed: the difficulty in "escaping" Communism, "difficulty with our own thinking," the impossibility of working in the American situation, McCarthyism, exile in Mexico between 1950 and 1958. With a child, being jailed would have been impossible: "That is in its own way political, too." (Dembo Interview, p. 176). Oppen's humanity as poet and political activist is integrated: "It's part of the whole pragmatism of social and political attitudes, the test of goodness, which extends awhile when one is thinking of a child" (Dembo Interview, p. 176).

In 1958 in Mexico he wrote a poem again: "Blood from the Stone" (*The Materials*) which cites the 1930s—the unemployed, war, the comradeship of those "Deserted like ourselves and therefore brothers":

Yet

So we lived
And chose to live

These were our times.

(*CP*, p. 33)

Oppen's poetry is neither that of the existentialist intellectual nor that of a soldier or activist off-duty, but a rare form of intellectually committed, socially responsible work which considers the issue of a human future within a precise and ecological sense of men and women among the facts and objectives of the world. As Maritain observes at the beginning of *Creative Intuition in Art and Poetry*, poetry is "that intercommunication between the inner being of things and the inner being of the human Self"[12] which relates the poet to the *vates*, the poet as diviner of that inner energy which Plato called *mousiki*. The intensity of concentration in Oppen's poetry, and in his reading of it, arises from this sense of double responsibility—to the disinherited and to the definition of the human. This is not simply Duncan's well-known definition—"the ability to respond"—but the ability to respond with political

12. Jacques Maritain, *Creative Intuition in Art and Poetry* (New York: Meridian Books, 1953), p. 3.

commitment against poverty, unemployment and exploitation, an action clearly focussed in socialism, rather than dispersed in egoism, protest, or careless tacit support of capitalist democracy and its international interventionist policies. In Maritain's opening chapters Oppen must have recognized a position he had already reached and which his later poetry explores, challenges and reassembles. *Of Being Numerous* and what follows may be read as a radical challenge to the ego-centered poetry of the American mainstream and its liberal self-expressive preoccupations which avoid true responsibility. Given the self-conscious protest poetics of the Beat stance—exhausted and confused in a mess of religiosity and unfounded politics—it is salutary to read Oppen, in the *Ironwood* interview, speak of his sense of San Francisco, primarily in connection with "Some San Francisco Poems" in *Seascape: Needle's Eye*. New York City and San Francisco have become increasingly meaningless and useless; earlier historical meaning had been circumvented; London, who once ran for Communist mayor of San Francisco, "addressed himself to the pulps"; cleverness dominates; sophistication and finance rule. But the western city has a certain isolation at the Pacific edge of the United States which Mark Twain and Bret Harte thought comical but which does help the city to retain some unguarded openness. The disastrous Altamont festival (1969),[13] which Oppen attended, is recognized both in the *Ironwood* and Power Interviews and in the first poem of the "Seascape" sequence as a political event: "We left before the murder took place. I wrote the poem before I knew about it. . . .We knew something was wrong. It's just the incident, I'm not exactly philosophizing. There was no more innocence. Just those millions of dollars spread out in front of us. . . .The poem finishes with 'Miracle/of.' I didn't quite know what the miracle would be, but it had to be within the young children" (Power Interview, pp. 202-3):

> *the songs they go to hear on*
> *this occasion are no one's own*
>
> *Needle's eye   needle's eye   but in the ravine*
> *again and again on the massive spike the song*
> *clangs*
>
> *as the tremendous volume of the music takes*
> *over obscured by their long hair they seem*
> *to be mourning*

> *(CP*, p. 214)

---

13. Cf. Eric Mottram, "Dionysus in America," *Other Times*, No. 1 (Nov., 1975-Jan., 1976), p. 3.

Oppen comments: " . . . everyone turned very sharply into himself or herself. Kind of a masturbatory atmosphere. Banging upon the spike was pretty literal" (Ironwood Interview, p. 22). Altamont continued the poverty of American life into the 1960s, that capitalist alienation which had previously climaxed in the 1930s. It takes a socialist poet to realize that. But the issue is as complex as "Populist"[14] explores, placing the poet's identification with "the people," with working people, the figure of that search for "the concept of humanity" which has remained his basis, within the democrat's need for the right poem. That need is not simply to reflect a populist position but to write a possible "song of myself"—Whitman's title is built into the poem, with a question mark—which would include an intuitive, skilled penetration the worker might recognize as a legitimate necessity. The existentialist and socialist poet cannot speak his magic just to himself, remain a lonely analyst of sickness or lonely appreciator of natural or cultural splendour:

> into the cities in that word blind
>
> word must speak
> and speak the magic
>
> infants' speech driving
> northward the populist
> north slowly in the sunrise the lapping
>
> of shallow
> waters tongues
>
> of the inlets glisten
>
> (*Primitive*, p. 21)

The poet is only too aware of life which actually maintains the society in a basic way:

> over the flatlands poems piers foolhardy
>
> structures and the lives the ingenious
> lives the winds
>
> squall from the grazing
> ranches' wandering
>
> fences young workmen's

---

14. George Oppen, *Primitive* (Santa Barbara: Black Sparrow, 1978), p. 20. Hereafter cited in the text as *Primitive*.

loneliness on the structures has touched
and touched the heavy tools   tools
in our hands in the clamorous

country birth-
light savage

light of the landscape magic

page the magic
infants speak

(Primitive, pp. 21-2)

So the poem finally returns to those "empirically true terms" Oppen requires, but this time the roots of clear speech under necessity are traced to the child. The page, the writing structure is, for the seventy-year-old poet, more strenuous an act than ever. The explorative pacing of the cadences is the prosody of respect for work and the poetic process, a condition prior to "the good life."

Behind this fine poem lies that multiple social experience which engages us in Mary Oppen's *Meaning A Life*, a pattern of extraordinary confidence and strength in hardship and continuous ascertaining of moral action. The political points are clear: George and Mary expelled and suspended from Corvallis agricultural college for a dormitory meeting; experiencing oppressive law and the nature of capitalist labour while hitch-hiking in the late 1920s; experiencing the restriction of information on and apparatus for birth control and abortion; deciding to live economically on George's small inheritance "to free us from meaningless work, so that we would not have to follow a profession as William Carlos Williams did or try to seek political power as Pound later did, or do tedious work, as Reznikoff did at the law book company. We agreed that we would work when necessary to augment this income."[15] In this process they changed class, away from the comfortable bourgeois and towards the Left. In 1929 they were in France:

> We were in pursuit of a style of life for ourselves, for we did not yet see ourselves in the perspective of our own culture or of our own country's history; we were searching for something more than a life of "making a killing," as my mother said. The United States we had just left was rich, with an affluence of new cars and talk of the stock market. We wanted a way of life that allowed us to paint, write, think and converse in friendship with those who were on our same path.

(Meaning, p. 121)

15. Mary Oppen, *Meaning A Life* (Santa Barbara: Black Sparrow, 1978), p. 90. Hereafter cited in the text as "*Meaning*."

The vision of an alternative life suggested by living in France played into their political vision–traditions which the Depression and poverty of the 1930s could not entirely disrupt. Pound's *ABC of Economics* they found absurd, a circumvention of Marx by a man who lived on "income derived through capitalism." "His grandfather's system of scrip issued to workers for trade at his grandfather's store" was only a version of workers bound to the company store (*Meaning*, p. 136).

With Europe threatening Jews, the Oppens returned to New York in 1933, in mid Depression: "we felt we were in a nightmare, our fathers impoverished" (*Meaning*, p. 144). Fascist organizations were active. They contacted the Socialist Labor Party but it was doing "nothing at the time to alleviate the problems of the workers with whom they planned one day to ride to power" (*Meaning*, p. 146). In California, strike-breakers broke up Berkeley meetings and threatened workers' families. When, in 1935, the 7th. World Congress of the Communist Parties called for a united front to defeat fascism and war, the Oppens "decided to work with the Communist Party, not as artist or writer because we did not find honesty and sincerity in the so-called arts of the left" (*Meaning*, p. 151)–the exceptions were Brecht and some Soviet films. "We said to each other, 'Let's work with the unemployed and have our other interest in the arts for a later time' " (*Meaning*, p. 151). Friends and family would have to decide what their response would be. The physically dangerous life of activists followed. The Oppens were arrested, tried over a two-year period for attacking the police; then, though without "special skills," they decided to go to Spain. By now they began to understand their special position as Jewish anti-fascist Communist workers who "intended to find their way back to a life in poetry and the arts" (*Meaning*, p. 158).

In Utica they encountered the American tradition of working-class radicalism just at the time when the Roosevelt administration's work to alleviate the Depression rejuvenated liberal tendencies to believe that capitalism could be adjusted to democracy. In Utica their Communism was far less opposed than in New York. George next worked a seventy-hour week in Detroit, a "crowded wartime city" (*Meaning*, p. 169), but he decided to be drafted in 1942, fought in the Vosges, was severely wounded, and did not return to America until 1945. The Oppens then found work in California factories and in building houses. In 1950 "the FBI began its visits" (*Meaning*, p. 193). George and Mary were now part of an anti-war movement, and that included, for a time, support for Henry Wallace. But under the 1960s pressures, they left for Mexico—followed by both FBI and CIA agents. In 1958 they achieved passports.

Exile and political life combined to occupy "the life of the mind" with what Mary Oppen calls "expedients" not conducive to art: "We have always felt that our writing required distance from the politics of experience. Even the ideology of day-to-day politics is not a far-reaching truth. . . .We needed to be freely in our own country, to have time to assimilate the violent years before turning them into thought and poetry" (*Meaning*, p. 200). When George Oppen did return to poetry, the achievement had none of the noisy rhetoric of the Black and Beat protesters, and nothing of their refusal of socialism. For example, where LeRoi Jones (now Imamu Amiri Baraka) excoriated Michael Schwerner and other white Civil Rights organizers who penetrated the South to help people to their rights and the vote, Oppen is more accurate. In "The Book of Job and a Draft of a Poem to Praise the Paths of the Living," which is dedicated "in memory of Mickey Schwerner" (*CP*, pp. 236-41), in *Of Being Numerous*, and in other poems, Oppen is more accurate and grasps with a more generous understanding the facts of the young's need to challenge national oppression—in a word, their responsibility. The pivot of morality here is, again, poverty, the unforgivable action of decay in any society, the central hypocrisy of a democracy which proclaims its egalitarianism as a permission to intervene in the rest of the world:

> Our
> lady of poverty the lever the fulcrum
>
> (*CP*, p. 236)

Finding a form for political feeling, his hope, especially given his committed past, is beautifully impressive. The young are his inheritors; naming is again possible:

> what is the form
> to say it there is something
> to name Goodman   Schwerner   Chaney
> who were beaten not we
> who were beaten   children
> not our
> children   ancestral
> children rose in the dark
> to their work there grows
> there builds there is written
> a vividness   there is   rawness
> like a new sun the flames
> tremendous the sun
> itself ourselves ourselves
> go with us *disorder*

> *so great the tumult wave*
>
> *upon wave* this traverse
>
> this desert   extravagant
> *island of light*
>   (*CP*, pp. 236-7)

Here in the magnificent lines of "The Book of Job and a Draft of a Poem . . . " Oppen's memory of unemployment and oppression in the 1930s moves accurately into the present:

>   carpenter
> mechanic   o we
> impoverished we hired
> hands that turn the wheel   young
> theologians of the scantlings   wracked
> monotheists of the   weather-side   sometimes I imagine
> they speak
>   (*CP*, p. 238)

The presence of poverty continued, and the guilt shown before "the unthinkable hunger." If we are to say "tragedy" or make a poem, it must be " 'seeking a statement/of an experience of our own' the bones of my hands": in the words of the *Kulchur* essay, "determination to find the image, the thing encountered" ("Mind,", p. 2). "It is possible to find a metaphor for anything, an analogue: but the image is encountered, not found; it is an account of the poet's perception, of the act of perception; it is a test of sincerity, a test of conviction, the rare poetic quality of truthfulness" ("Mind," p. 3):

> to know   to know   in my life to know
>   (*CP*, p. 242)

This poem, "Myth of the Blaze," is an extraordinary self-examination, without egoism because it is dedicated to the knowledge by which I becomes Another—the essential act of the social:

>   lost to be lost   Wyatt's
> lyric and Rezi's
> running thru my mind
> in the destroyed (and guilty) Theatre
> of the War   I'd cried
> and remembered
> boyhood   degradation   other
> degradations and this crime I will not recover
> from that landscape it will be in my mind
> it will fill my mind and this is horrible
> death bed   pavement   the secret taste
> of being lost
>   (*CP*, p. 242)

Oppen's naming of experience places him with Adam naming the animals and with Blake's questioning definition of "Tyger" in the "blaze of changes," the ability to cut through to the existential: "bread each side of the knife." Once the naming of experience led to the clearsighted abandonment of poetry; now we have the equally clear assessment of a point at which to take it up—to reach, as it were, beyond the renunciation—which Laura Riding came to out of a sense of

> a discrepancy, deep-reaching, between what I call the creed and the craft of poetry—which I might otherwise describe as its religious and its ritualistic aspects. . . .what compatibility can there be between the creed offering hope of a way of speaking beyond the ordinary, touching perfection, a complex perfection associable with nothing less complex than truth, and the craft tying the hope to verbal rituals that court sensuosity as if it were the judge of truth? . . .If poets strain hard enough they must reach the crisis-point at which division between creed and craft reveals itself to be absolute.[16]

But in fact Riding's poetic ambition simply outstripped the limits of art: "looking to an eventual solution in poetry of the universal problem of how to make words fulfil the human being and the human being fulfil words" (Riding, p. 15). Such a classicist aim is impossible in a period with "so great a variety of individual poetic styles, and so much poverty of thematic content" (Riding, p. 13).

Stevens's response was to pare his technique to an iambic formula—itself a kind of classicism—which just encompassed his need to play variations on existential themes in a world he took to be essentially balanced: a platonic vision which made him an exceptional poet, for whom "poverty" hardly meant, as it did for Oppen, the national disgrace of unemployment, and "soldier" did not infer the futile ideological warfare of his time. Oppen knows precisely where the poetic limits are because he is a political man from direct Depression and World War II experience. At the end of "Route," having cited "madmen [who] have burned thousands of men and women alive," and other "despairs," he writes:

> These things at the limits of reason, nothing at the limits
> of dream, the dream merely ends, by this we know it is the
> real
>
> That we confront
>
>   (*CP*, p. 196)

---

16. Cf. Laura Riding, preface to *Selected Poems: In Five Sets* (New York: W. W. Norton, 1973), pp. 11-12. Hereafter cited in the text as "Riding."

And in a letter to Rachel Blau DuPlessis in 1965, Oppen writes: "There is a point at which one reaches what one meant to reach, the thing that the poetry was for. One *gets* there, and can throw the rest away. At that moment nothing that went before matters."[17] Oppen knows that you do not have to speak publicly, but if you do it is a responsibility not so much to existing self and existing order but to possible self and future order, since the history of his time has been as intolerable to the majority as to himself: a fact which Pound nearly awakes to in *Pisan Cantos* and actually does awake to in *Drafts and Fragments*—with remorse. The wary spacing, the run-on and hesitant pacing of syntax, and the sense of arguing positions, with himself as much as others, in Oppen's poetic forms is an explorer's poetics, remote from the cheapening fixed metrics of dogma so familiar during the past four decades. Systematic order forced him into exile, and the poets he admired (Reznikoff, Rakosi, Zukofsky, Bunting) by and large could not speak to the people. "Gift: the Gifted"[18] ends with a possible miracle of change in the "myopic" horizons of the popular:

> among the people
> they have never spoken to therefore run away
>
> into everything the gift
>
> the treasure is
>
> flight my
> heritage

"Miracle" in this poem and in "Exodus" (*Seascape: Needle's Eye*) implies a future in which our children have learned the democratic *potentialities*. Children are the constant gift to the world, a possible hope; and behind them, the constancy of love, whose example throughout the poems, is—if one may say it so bluntly, but without the least sentimentality—George and Mary Oppen, a ground base to all the inventions. Oppen has a right to advise sternly in *Of Being Numerous*—advice given to all of us, but especially to the tampering scientists:

> Love in the genes, if it fails
>
> We will produce no sane man again
>
> I have seen too many young people become adults, young
>   friends become old people, all that is not ours,

17. Rachel Blau DuPlessis, "George Oppen: 'What Do We Believe to Live With?' " *Ironwood*, 5 (1975), p. 62.
18. George Oppen, "Gift: the Gifted," *Ironwood*, 5 (1975), pp. 38-9.

> The sources
> And the crude bone
>
> —we say
>
> *Took place*
>
> Like the mass of the hills.
>
> > (*CP*, p. 184)

That italicized passive phrase pinpoints that conservatism—that sense of the social world as a natural phenomenon—which social-ism challenges. Nothing socially human *takes place*. Society, con-trary to Burkeian tradition, is not Nature. The factors of choice out of social conscience define the human against the animal. If Oppen, in this same poem, re-emphasizes clarity as his aim, "clar-ity" must be placed within the social responsibility; clarity "is/Of what is not autonomous within us." If there are to be "doors" and "thresholds," we must resist naturalist conservatism, or false ecology, as well as "theology" or dogma (the limits of tolerating the Communist Party in the 1930s): "The purity of the materials, not theology, but to present/the circumstances." Being a soldier in World War II is still a subject for doubts as to justification— "what was I doing there? . . . we are brothers? . . . A man will give his life for his friend provided he wants to"—just as he will want to kill a German, or not. Glib "epiphany"—the sense of resolution which the weak poet continually yearns for (it is the core of the weak intellectualist Auden tradition, the "mainstream" of British and American poetry) is resisted. What is true is not necessarily good; the true political action begins here, against Nature and the *faits accomplis* called History. To Oppen's question here—"Whom shall I speak to"—his poems give an answer: he will speak to the young, who will listen to his poems because they open up the rigidities of American failure in "miracle." Reading the end of section 13 of "Route" in London in 1973, Oppen used a line omitted from the published version and which does help us to understand that sense of political solidarity his work implies, and without which "miracle" would be merely a utopian dream (the line is italicized):

> 'Substance itself which is the subject of all our planning'
>
> *and our most profound companionship*
>
> And by this we are carried into the incalculable

The next section begins:

> There was no other guarantee
>
> (*CP*, pp. 195-6)

"Of Being Numerous" (a reworking of "A Language of New York") (*CP*, pp. 94-101) is Oppen's primary instance of articulating the issues between "despairs" and productive knowledge: "There are things/We live among 'and to see them/Is to know ourselves'." (*CP*, p. 147) The initial sections define "humanity" between infinite occurrence, actual wickedness and theological or rooted wickedness (inherent human evil). Existence given as "unmanageable," an arid absolute, or "matter" cannot be a generative fact: the city is not merely a "locality," but corporations and populace interacting. Mere "satirical wit"—the anarchic refuge of evasive bourgeois particularly in the 1960s—cannot "serve." The constant pressure of media-information makes us passive to event and to power: "Crusoe/We say was/ 'Rescued'." "Obsessed, bewildered/By the shipwreck/Of the singular/We have chosen the meaning/Of being numerous" (*CP*, pp. 150-1)—one more populist version of saving face. It is the poet's function now to know his singularity within "man's way of thought" (*CP*, p. 152), the language, and his own particular experience. That triad is the only possible way to hold to the singular. "A crowd is nothing" (*CP*, p. 153) but "numerous." But "numerous" can be translated into people participating in an arts performance in "the new arts," an example of social possibility. The crux of this section is related by rhythm and cadence, it seems, to Stevens, and to Eliot through his disquisition on what humanity may bear, or not, archaic forms of philosophic individualism. "City" is not exemplified and then despised, but recognized as house, neighborhood and docks—"And it is not 'art' " (*CP*, p. 154). The tribal may be order and respected patience, but it is also repetiton. The city can make life "unreal" as argument, baseball, and differences of opinion—the false sense of the generative which sterilizes in "stale" atmosphere, another form of repetition: "one may honorably keep/His distance/If he can" (*CP*, p. 156). But the poet's war experience is a true community experience which prevents distancing into the singular or the numerous: "How talk/Distantly of 'The People'/Who are that force/Within the walls/Of cities/Wherein their cars/Echo like history/Down walled avenues/In which one cannot speak" (*CP*, p. 157). But the poet has to speak, and speak in city language: "It is not easy to speak/A ferocious mumbling, in public/Of rootless speech" (*CP*, p. 159).

The poetic is dialectical, the order of the language is explorative. "Of Being Numerous" exemplifies the late twentieth-century necessity for positive knowledge placed at the disposition of a third position between the authoritarian and the individualistic. "People burn" (*CP*, p. 160); the atrocity inside the media-event, the official helicopter, the president's order, "insanity in high places" (*CP*, p. 160); "the news/Is war/As always" (*CP*, p. 161) but the poem combats war. Failure, guilt, knowledge of the unforgivable, the absence of traditional salvations (Oppen refuses fashionable Buddhism, the drug cult, the so-called politics of "rock," and any authoritarian junk masquerading as panacea): but to order these as a gloomy fatalism would merely cut across humanity with false pessimism which fogs "clarity" and breaks "silence" with cliché—the media-processing of "the people" and their dissatisfying pleasures. Williams's Elsie of 1923 is given a later application to the failure of the American covenant of hope— "The pure products of America" now live out their sacrificed lives. And then, in section 26, Oppen brings his thematic materials into overt discussion: how to remake relationships between the individual and the social, between limitation and a future. It resolves into a question of what generation is—the generative, a new generation, what to place against waste, war, and sacrifice: "We want to say/ 'Common sense'/And we cannot" (*CP*, pp. 165-6). Clarity, at the conclusion of this poem, can only be imaged from pebbles seen clearly through water. To transfer that to "the level of art," to see "the one thing" through corrupt processes of the social and political many, is "difficult" (*CP*, p. 168).

How does the poet, therefore, and this one in particular now, the father, pass on knowledge to his daughter, to continue generation? And what knowledge will not prejudice the unknown and therefore prevent the possible "ennobling" clarity, the act of knowing itself? Alternatives are briefly stated—that Crusoe may not be "rescued" or solved; that we may remain, like the man, helpless in a paranoid vision of conspiracy or the pressures of the non-human, of natural process. The work ends with Whitman writing, during the Civil War, of the Capitol's figure of the Genius of Liberty glowing at sundown "like a big star: it looks quite/curious" (*CP*, p. 179). But in Oppen's text "curious" is given a final large isolating space. The star has become arcanely symbolic since the war between the States destroyed the covenant. And the space itself is an extension of the procedures of the whole work whose careful argument is itself the groundwork of the political, a production of objects which will not slip inside the transience of media-democracy or be smashed against the totalitarianism of dogma.

EDWARD HIRSCH

"OUT THERE IS THE WORLD":
THE VISUAL IMPERATIVE IN THE POETRY OF
GEORGE OPPEN AND CHARLES TOMLINSON

The eye *sees*!
—George Oppen, "Time of the Missile"[1]

Perfect is the word I can never hear
Without a sensation as of seeing—
—Charles Tomlinson, "Rhymes"[2]

I

When Charles Tomlinson opened *The Materials* (1962) to find Maritain's statement that "We awake in the same moment to ourselves and to things" poised against "They fed their hearts on fantasies/And their hearts have become savage," he responded immediately to a sensibility very much like his own. Indeed any number of assertions from *The Materials*—from "Ultimately the air/Is bare sunlight where must be found/The lyric valuables" (Oppen, *CP*, p. 29) to "What I've seen/Is all I've found: myself" (Oppen, *CP*, p. 40)—could stand as fitting epigraphs to Tomlinson's own *Selected Poems* (1978).[3] By 1962 Tomlinson had

---

1. George Oppen, *Collected Poems* (New York: New Directions, 1975), p. 49. Hereafter all references to Oppen's poetry will be to this edition, and all such citations will be incorporated into the text.
2. Charles Tomlinson, *The Shaft* (New York: Oxford University Press, 1978), p. 21. All references in this paper to Tomlinson's poetry will be to the *Selected Poems: 1951-1974* (New York: Oxford University Press, 1978) for his poems through 1974, and to *The Shaft* for his poems from 1974 through 1978. Hereafter all such citations will be abbreviated as *SP* and *Shaft* respectively, and all such citations will be incorporated in the text.
3. For Tomlinson's account of his relationship to the Objectivists see his piece "Objectivists: Zukofsky and Oppen, a memoir," *Paideuma* 7, #3 (Winter 1978), pp. 429-446. Of particular interest are pp. 431-432 for an account of Oppen's poem "To C. T." (*CP*, p. 142). This may be read in conjunction with Tomlinson's poem for the Oppen's, "Elegy

already published three books—*Relations and Contraries* (1951), *The Necklace* (1955), and *Seeing Is Believing* (1960), the last two of which are very much about the necessity and the implications of the difficult, creative act of seeing. The very title *Seeing Is Believing* suggests that the poet's job is to render, with attentive care and fastidiousness, the world as it appears because appearances *are* reality ("what appears, is"), though this is a statement that must not be interpreted innocently: Tomlinson's poems are filled with Stevensian propositions like "Six points of vantage provide us with six sunsets" (Tomlinson, *SP*, p. 3) and "No single reading renders up complete/Their shifting text" (Tomlinson, *Shaft*, p. 29). Sight is the privileged faculty for both Oppen and Tomlinson; they are poets concerned with the visually given, with what Tomlinson tends to refer to as "facts" and Oppen as "the world." That the poet can transcend his own subjectivity to see things as they really are, however, is an idea that both poets call into question in their later work: always the isolated mind remains the constituent witness of reality, the eye faces the impenetrability of the Other. To borrow a phrase from Donald Justice's elegy for Stevens, "the *the* has become an *a*." What this translates into, in Oppen's severe formula, is that "the world, if it is matter,/Is impenetrable" (Oppen, *CP*, p. 148).

Both Oppen and Tomlinson write an austere phenomenological poetry not so much of things as of the process of the mind encountering those things. They both strive to erase the lyrical ego from their poems and deny the Romantic idea of transcendence: sincerity demands truthfulness to one's own local reality, one's own perceptions. "Who shall say/How the Romantic stood in nature?" (Oppen, *CP*, p. 62) Oppen's poem "California" asks. Or as Tomlinson puts it in an early Ars Poetica: "The fact being, that when the truth is not good enough/We exaggerate. Proportions/Matter. It is difficult to get them right" (Tomlinson, *SP*, p. 7). As poets of exteriority they are scrupulously concerned with registering the felicities of the thing seen, the world's patterns, surfaces, textures. The sometimes chill atmosphere of their poems manifests their care for exactitude and "objectivity." For Oppen this often means observing razed buildings and square slabs of concrete as well as New England boats and the California coast line; for

for Henry Street," in *SP*, p. 132. In this essay I am interested not so much in the influence of one poet on the other as in their fundamental shared premises, the way in which their ideas of poetic immanence correspond and interrelate. The correlation of their ideas is not surprising since in crucial ways both poets derive their aesthetics from Pound and Williams. One way to account for the different textures of their work—apart from national differences—is the fact that Tomlinson's modernist inheritance was filtered through the sensuous influence of Stevens, whereas Oppen's poetics were partially shaped by the intellectual stringencies of Zukofsky.

Tomlinson's painterly eye it means a continual return to the "minute particulars" of the natural world seeking "a language of water, light and air" (Tomlinson, *SP*, p. 135). Both poets continually affirm the *presence* of external reality, yet remain committed to surveying the difficult relationship between that reality and the singular perceiving self. Here is Oppen registering precisely the rhythm of the mediating mind going about the business of moving beyond itself:

> consciousness
>
>   in itself
>
> of itself carrying
>
>   'the principle
>   of the actual' being
>
> actual
>
> itself . . .
>
>   (Oppen, *CP*, p. 253)

The principle of the actual being actual demands that the poet seek transparency, perfect visual clarity, but honesty demands attentiveness to the process of consciousness registering and thus defining that actuality. In one of his few prose pieces Oppen has written:

> Modern American poetry begins with the determination to find the image, the thing encountered, the thing seen each day whose meaning has become the meaning and colour of our lives—it is possible to find a metaphor for anything, an analogue: but the image is encountered, not found; it is an account of the poet's perception, as the act of perception; it is a test of sincerity, a test of conviction, the rare quality of truthfulness.[4]

Both in its emphasis on the relationship between the observer and the observed and in its predisposition to local reality (both natural and man-made), Oppen's concept of modern American poetry stands close to Tomlinson's own postmodern aesthetic stance. It is this account of the mind in the act of encountering an image that must suffice which characterizes the ethics and the metaphysics of both Oppen's and Tomlinson's poetry.

---

4. "The Mind's Own Place," *Kulchur* 3, #10, as cited in Tomlinson's essay, "An Introductory Note on the Poetry of George Oppen," *Ironwood* 5 (1975), p. 12.

II

> There are things
> We live among 'and to see them
> Is to know ourselves'.
> —Oppen, *CP*, p. 147

By the time he published *Discrete Series* (1934) Oppen's poetics of encounter was already well established: the sincerity of attending to "vital particulars," the objectification of hammering those particulars into completed verbal artifacts. The key to that poetics was already manifest in the second section of "1930'S," the poem of Oppen's which Louis Zukofsky published in the Objectivist issue of *Poetry* (February 1931). Oppen implicitly acknowledged how much the poem reveals by deleting its title and moving it to a privileged position as the opening fragment of the book. It is thus as the first empirical statement of the *Collected Poems* (1975) that the reader finds it, a single convoluted sentence of sixty-eight words linking "knowledge" to "the century": "The knowledge not of sorrow, you were saying, but of boredom/Is . . . Of the world, weather-swept, with which one shares the century." Thirty-eight years after they first appeared Oppen glossed these lines by invoking his kinship with Heidegger:

> The word "boredom" is a little surprising there. It means, in effect, that the knowledge of the mood of boredom is the knowledge of what *is*, "Of the world, weather-swept." But these phrases I use here to paraphrase the poem are phrases from Heidegger's acceptance speech made in 1929, the year I was writing the poem. And the words "boredom" and "knowledge" are, in their German equivalents, the words he used. So I feel I have a natural sympathy with Heidegger—that he should use as a philosophic concept a mood of boredom.[5]

The Heideggerian idea picked up by Oppen is that the mood of boredom also is part of the recognition of what is. This helps to define what the Objectivists meant by sincerity: no ideas but in one's own experiential definition of things. Oppen's poems phenomenologically explore the world of things by exploring his own experience of those things. The poet writes, in Heidegger's

---

5. See L. S. Dembo's interview with George Oppen, *Contemporary Literature* X, #2 (1969), p. 169. My discussion of Oppen's phenomenology is also indebted to Dembo's fine essay, "The Existential World of George Oppen," *The Iowa Review* 3, #1 (Winter 1972), pp. 64-91. It was just the sort of Heidegerrian metaphysics implicit in Oppen's poem that may have caused one Long Island editor to mail back the Objectivist issue of *Poetry* "first class" to ask for his money back. Another reader could mistake a seemingly mathematical precision for "technical inability." To which Louis Zukofsky characteristically replied, "The writer believes Oppen's contributions qualify as to objectification by nature of their rhythmic and logical structures," *Poetry* XXXVIII, #1 (April 1931), pp. 51-58.

formulation, to "discover the thingly character of the thing," and he does this by bringing those things out of their silence, by naming them and thus nominating them to their own "being."[6] The phrase of Heidegger's which Oppen uses as the epigraph to *This In Which* (1965)—". . . the arduous path of appearance"—suggests that this nominating can only be done by a rigorous *seeing*, by struggling to find the essential being in appearance. In *An Introduction to Metaphysics*, from which this epigraph is taken, Heidegger expounds Parmenides' idea of the hidden unity of being and appearance: "the third path is that of appearance, but in a particular way, for on this path appearance is experienced *as* belonging to being."[7] This concept of appearance as a showing forth of being is set against the preliminary delineation that sets the real and the authentic (internal reality) against the unreal and inauthentic (the "merely" external). So, too, it is anti-Platonic in its rejection of the Idea and its advocacy of appearance as the essence of what is. For Oppen consciousness is always consciousness of something and the poet's job is to watch whatever happens as it happens:

> The mind is capable not only of thinking but has an emotional root that forces it to look, to think, to see. The most tremendous and compelling emotion we possess is the one that forces us to look, to know, if we can, to see.[8]

Or, in the words of "World, World—", " ' Thought leaps on us' because we are here. That is the fact of the matter" and "The self is no mystery, the mystery is/That there is something for us to stand on." (Oppen, *CP*, p. 143)

The enormous human loneliness at the heart of Oppen's poetry—wholly devoid of Romantic despair or elevation—is the result of his recognition that the something where we stand cannot ever be known. His poems have increasingly related a knowledge of the isolation of the self, of what in "Of Being Numerous" he

---

6. See Heidegger's essay "The Origin of the Work of Art," in *Poetry, Language, Thought*, translated by Albert Hofstadter (New York: Harper and Row, 1971), esp. pp. 20 and 73. In his poem "Melody" Tomlinson translates Rilke's "Song is being" into "Song is the measure, rather/Of being's spread and height . . ." In their particular brand of phenomenology both Oppen and Tomlinson emphasize the encounter between mind and matter. In Tomlinson's rendering the mind as a hunter of forms binds itself to rescue matter from decay and thus present substance ("Oppositions").
7. *An Introduction to Metaphysics*, translated by Ralph Manheim (New Haven: Yale University Press, 1959), pp. 112-113.
8. "Interview with George Oppen," *Contemporary Literature*, p. 173. The ethical imperative in this is also clear. In the same interview (p. 174) Oppen says: "I think that what we really want is not to establish a definition of the good and then work toward it, but rather to see what happens happen, to go wherever we are going." Oppen's idea that the mind sees through the eye is paralleled in the third paragraph of Tomlinson's prose poem "Skullshapes," which contains the lines "It is the mind sees. But what it sees consists not solely of that by which it is confronted grasped in the light of that which it remembers. It sees possibility." Oppen and Tomlinson are united in their idea that perception involves the whole man—his past, present, and future.

calls "the shipwreck/Of the singular" (Oppen, *CP*, p. 151). The perceiving self is incapable of contact except in single incidents. Oppen's nominalist idea is that matter is, by its very nature, impenetrable: it cannot be reduced to "meaning" or recovered through language. "Words cannot be wholly transparent. And that is the 'heartlessness' of words" (Oppen, *CP*, p. 186). The logical steps towards individual isolation are set forth with mathematical precision in "Parousia":

> Impossible to doubt the world: it can be seen
> And because it is irrevocable
>
> It cannot be understood, and I believe that fact is lethal
>
> And man may find his catastrophe,
> His Millennium of obsession.
>
> (Oppen, *CP*, p. 83)

In the failure of understanding all the poet can affirm is, in Oppen's philosophical formulation, "We want to be here" (Oppen, *CP*, p. 143).

Oppen's poems participate in what he calls "the life of the mind" in order to point his readers beyond their own consciousness. The quest in his work is for clarity in relationship, for the "this in which," the determination of the human in relation to the Other. The ethical imperative in his work is always to reach for the actual. For this reason Oppen treats language with circumspection and distrust, questioning the ability of words to escape their current debasement and once more render up what is "out there," to again "name" the world. In this he shows himself to be an American urban poet, trying to trust to a poetry of simple statement but always cognizant of how the language has lost its truthfulness before the daily onslaught of newspapers, advertising, and institutional "brochures." In "A Language of New York" he has set forth his (deconstructive and reconstructive) task:

> Possible
> To use
> Words provided one treat them
> As enemies.
> Not enemies—Ghosts
> Which have run mad
> In the subways
> And of course the institutions
> And the banks. If one captures them
> One by one proceeding

            Carefully they will restore
            I hope to meaning
            And to sense.

                                                        (Oppen, *CP*, p. 97)

Oppen's self-reflexive and spare poetry of consciousness strives to
restore meaning and sense to language by calmly and faithfully
using it to refer outwards to a world of things, "perfectly simple,
perfectly/impenetrable" (Oppen, *CP*, p. 189). There is both danger
and enormous power in his persistent confrontation with external
particulars. As he says in "Route": "I might at the top of my
ability stand at a window/and say, look out; out there is the
world" (Oppen, *CP*, p. 186).

III

            Judge, as you will, not what I say
            But what is, being said.
                                    —Tomlinson, *SP*, p. 30

    The phenomenological imperative behind all of Charles Tom-
linson's work is to measure and say being, to render the actual. At
all points Oppen's notion that the journey outwards is also the
journey inwards informs that imperative. The first subject of Tomlinson's poems is the physical and metaphysical act and art of
seeing. His aesthetic goal is to define relations and contraries, to
articulate space by attempting to understand the object in its
relationship to other objects, the self in relationship to the world.
The moral posture of his work is always to save the appearances,
to encounter being as it exists physically in external particulars.
In a recent memoir Tomlinson reformulates his essential idea that
"one does not need to go beyond any sense experience to some
mythic union, that the 'I' can be responsible only by relationship
and not by dissolving itself away in ecstasy." Tomlinson's anti-
Romanticism, like Oppen's, helps him to define a poetics of
immanence against a poetics of transcendence.[9]

---

9. See Tomlinson's essay "Some American Poets: A Personal Record," *Contemporary
Literature* 19, #3 (June 1977), p. 284. In his rejection of the transcendental Idea and his
commitment to immanence Tomlinson shares an ethical base with other postmodern
poets. See Charles Altieri, "From Symbolist Thought to Immanence: The Ground of
Postmodern American Poetics," *Boundary 2*, 1, #3 (Spring 1973), pp. 605-641. Also for
an insightful discussion of what he calls the dialectical relationship between two fundamental modes of awareness in Tomlinson's work, see Merle Brown, "Intuition and Perception in the Poetry of Charles Tomlinson," *The Journal of Aesthetics and Art Criticism* XXXVII, #3 (Spring 1979), pp. 277-293. For a chronological discussion of Tomlinson's visual concerns as they unfold through his *Selected Poems*, see my essay "The
Meditative Eye of Charles Tomlinson," *The Hollins Critic* XV, #2 (April 1978), pp. 1-12.

The visual ethic is so strong in Tomlinson's work that almost
all of the exemplary artistic presences in his poems are painters
who have sought to record the difficult physicality of nature in
all of its essential otherness: Constable, Eakins, Cézanne. The task
of the artist is set forth precisely in "Cézanne at Aix" (Tomlinson, *SP*, p. 22):

> And the mountain: each day
> Immobile like fruit.   Unlike, also
> —Because irreducible, because
> Neither a component of the delicious
> And therefore questionable,
> Nor distracted (as the sitter)
> By his own pose and, therefore,
> Doubly to be questioned: it is not
> Posed. It is. Untaught
> Unalterable, a stone bridgehead
> To that which is tangible
> Because unfelt before. There
> In its weathered weight
> Its silence silences, a presence
> Which does not present itself.

Cézanne is Tomlinson's exemplary artist precisely because he
labors at observation, patiently responsible to the unselfconscious,
irreducible (and thus impenetrable) presence of the mountain.
Tomlinson's particular brand of aestheticism demands a measured
encounter with appearances: the slow, pondered rhythms of his
poetry define a scrupulous attentiveness to his experience of the
thing seen. His poetry argues that the first task of perception is
to erase the Romantic self, obliterate mythology, undermine
Imagination: "A dryad is a sort of chintz curtain/Between myself
and a tree./The tree stands: or does not stand:/As I draw, or
remove the curtain" (Tomlinson, *SP*, p. 8).[10] This is Tomlinson's
version of Objectivist sincerity: to destroy received "myths" by
truthfulness to one's own perception of particulars. Much of his
poetry arises directly from something seen ("I want to register
that in all its clarity and in all its implications") and strives in both
its ethics and its enactment to celebrate contact with primal
things. The act of looking immediately engages the observer in a
relationship. In fact, it is Tomlinson's idea that the self can only

---

10. In "An Interview With Charles Tomlinson," Jed Rutsula and Mike Erwin, *Contemporary Literature* XVI, #4 (Autumn 1975), pp. 407-408, Tomlinson glosses these lines
by referring to the section "I consider a tree" in Martin Buber's *I And Thou*. What Tomlinson particularly responds to is Buber's notion that "the tree is no impression, no play
of my imagination, no value depending on my mood." Tomlinson's suspicion of myth
suggests his trust in sensation. Whereas Tomlinson attempts to erase "mere mood"
because of the particularities it conceals, Oppen suggests that mood too is part of the
language of the senses, the recognition of what is.

know itself through encounters and relations with what it is not. The language of the senses encountering the Other allows us to construct ourselves:

> In my own case I should add that the particular, rather than existing in its own isolate intensity, means first of all the demands of a relationship—you are forced to look, feel, find words for something not yourself—and it means, like all relationships, a certain forgetfulness of self, so that in contemplating something, you are drawn out of yourself towards that and towards other people—other people, because, though the words you use are *your* words, they are also *their* words; you are learning about the world by using the common inheritance of language. And once you are moving on into your poem, rather than "isolate intensity," you are aware of belonging among objects and among human beings and it is a great stay for the mind, this awareness.[11]

For Tomlinson the act of engaging the particulars of external reality also engages the poet in community with other men. In the same interview he tells us that "The celebration here is not only a celebration of objects, but of the forms of language we choose to articulate the sense of objects bodied over against us." The painter relies on paint, as the poet relies on his language, to wake us to what is real.

It is noteworthy that Tomlinson's celebration of particulars is seldom informed by the same overwhelming solitude that defines Oppen's idea that the mind can never transcend its own nominalist encounters. Nor does the gaping void between words and things ("the void eternally generative" as Oppen cites it in "Route") seem to trouble Tomlinson with the same force as it does Oppen. Indeed it is their different attitudes towards the language which they use that marks the essential difference in their sensibilities and their poetics. That difference is both temperamental and metaphysical. Tomlinson posits for the poet a shared Wordsworthian language where "word and world rhyme (Tomlinson, *Shaft*, p. 21). For Oppen that shared language is more problematic and consequently called into question ("Whom shall I speak to" one fragment ends). His poetry continually affirms that it is necessary to speak but reminds itself that speech is difficult both because of the "heartlessness" of words (their lack of transparency) and because of the uneasy, anti-ontological status of the American language. The seventeenth section of "Of Being Numerous" is explicit.

---

11. "An Interview With Charles Tomlinson," *Contemporary Literature*, p. 406. Tomlinson's idea of the necessary relationship between the self and what surrounds it corresponds to Heidegger's idea that man *is* his relationship of encounter and correspondence.

Anti-ontology —

He wants to say
His life is real,
No one can say why

It is not easy to speak

A ferocious mumbling, in public
Of rootless speech

                                   (Oppen, *CP*, p. 159)

Oppen's distrust of language is reflected in the spareness of his
poetic—each phrase blocked and weighed, questioned, often isolated on the page. Tomlinson's aestheticism is of a different order:
instead of isolate phrases, a suspicion of words as "enemies" or
"ghosts," he relies on what he calls "the chastity of the formal
means." Often this means that his poems rely on a calm, flexible
four stress line that is simultaneously fluid and ceremonious.[12]
It is precisely this qualified fluidity which Oppen's poetry refuses,
continually questioning its own ontological status. These different
attitudes towards shared language may partially be attributable to
Tomlinson's sense of an audience that Oppen's poetry has generally lacked (hence Oppen's warm response in "To C.T." to "the
pleasure of being heard,/the pleasure/of companionship" (Oppen,
CP, p. 142) when Tomlinson stands in as Oppen's audience). Or
it may be that Oppen's American poetics, confronted with "a city
of the corporations" and "the brutal . . . without issue" (Oppen,
CP, pp. 94-5) requires a language that must reflexively question and
deconstruct itself in order to reaffirm value in a way that is not
crucial for Tomlinson. In Tomlinson's work the mind, too, can be
brought "half way to its defeat" (Tomlinson, *Shaft*, p. 29) by the
shades and shadows of a landscape that defies linguistic rendering,
and yet his poetry is infused with a hard won sense of reciprocity
utterly foreign to Oppen. This is evident in his many "images of
perfection."

> Perfect, then, the eye's command in its riding,
> Perfect the coping hand, the hillslopes
>   Drawing it into such sight the sight would miss,
> Guiding the glance the way perfection is.
>   (Tomlinson, *Shaft*, p. 21)

The fundamental premise that both Oppen and Tomlinson
share is that the human can only know itself through relationship
to the non-human and through the faithful attempt to make language escape its self-contained nature by referring to the world

---

12. Ibid, p. 413.

referentially. There can be no reduction of that world, but there can be a naming, a bringing forth of being out of appearance. Tomlinson's is explicit: "We bring/To a kind of birth all we can name/And, named, it echoes in us our being." (Tomlinson, *SP*, p. 90) This idea of the poet as the namer of things rhymes with Oppen's idea that to encounter those things is to discover ourselves. It also implies Heidegger's formulation that language is the house of our being. For it is language that embodies things and allows us, as best we can, to know them. And that knowing, that bringing forth by naming, that taking hold of the physical moment is dependent on the primary act of perception. For both Oppen and Tomlinson perceiving is an activity that engages the whole man giving birth to meaning. And that giving birth, that calling forth of the world, is a defense of poetry.[13]

IV

> The act of being, the act of being
> More than oneself.
> —Oppen, *CP*, p. 143

Both George Oppen and Charles Tomlinson have written a poetry of visual imperatives that simultaneously enacts and meditates on its own procedures. For both poets the essential principle is the human mind struggling to see through the eye purely, to discover what is as it emanates out of what appears. The world may not ever be known, but as Oppen says, "I do believe that consciousness exists and that it is consciousness of something, and that is a fairly complete but not very detailed theology, as a matter of fact."[14] The poet's job is to name the world as

---

13. In his interview (p. 416) Tomlinson tells how he has returned again and again to a key passage in Merleau-Ponty's *The Primacy of Perception*. Tomlinson calls this passage "one of our great defenses of poetry." The idea of the primacy of perception as a task for poetry is also reflected in Oppen's statements that "I have not and never did have any motive of poetry/But to achieve clarity" (Oppen, *CP*, p. 185) and "We are concerned with the given" (Oppen, *CP*, p. 198).

14. "Interview with George Oppen," *Contemporary Literature*, p. 163. Oppen's statement of his "theology" suggests the importance of belief in his affirmation that we are capable of talking about the nature of reality (and not just our comments about it). Indeed he has already anticipated a possible Derridean critique of his "metaphysics of presence" by emphasizing that his metaphysics *is* a theology. As he says: "I realize the possibility of attacking many of the things I'm saying and I say them as a sort of act of faith. The little words that I like so much, like 'tree,' 'hill,' and so on, are I suppose just as much a taxonomy as the more elaborate words; they're categories, classes, concepts, things we invent for ourselves. Nevertheless, there are certain ones without which we really are unable to exist, including the concept of humanity" (p. 162). Oppen has also explained the exact nature of that faith (p. 163): "that the nouns do refer to something; that it's there, that it's true, the whole implication of these nouns; that appearances represent reality, whether or not they misrepresent it; that this in which the thing takes place, this thing is here, and that these things do take place."

accurately as possible by entrusting to the actual, to the essential "whatness" of things. Each poet tells us in his own way that this task demands faith as well as perception. That faith is manifested in Tomlinson's translation of Stevens' "Let be be finale of seem" into "Let be be its being" ("Antecedents"). It is also there in the closing lines of Oppen's little religious poem, "Psalm":

> The small nouns
> Crying faith
> In this in which the wild deer
> Startle, and stare out.
>
> (Oppen, *CP*, p. 78)

ERIC HOMBERGER

GEORGE OPPEN
AND
THE CULTURE OF THE AMERICAN LEFT

During his great years as editor of *The Masses* and *The Liberator*,
Max Eastman combined the roles of radical political advocate and
romantic poet. In the first number of *The Liberator* in March
1918, Eastman committed the magazine to the cause of social and
political equality for blacks, to the liberation of women, to the
nationalization of public utilities, mines and railroads, and to the
ownership and control of industry by the workers. Eastman was
perhaps the most outspoken defender of Lenin in America. He
viewed poetry, however, as mainly being concerned with those
moods and perceptions which were not usually nourished by social
concerns. In the same issue in which he outlined the program of
the magazine, he published a sonnet on Isadora Duncan:

> You bring the fire and terror of the wars
> Of infidels in thunder-running hordes,
> With spears like sun-rays, shields, and wheeling swords
> Flame shape, death shape and shaped like scimitars,
> With crimson eagles and blue pennantry,
> And teeth and armor flashing, and white eyes
> Of battle horses, and the silver cries
> Of trumpets unto storm and victory!
>
> Who is this naked-footed lovely girl
> Of summer meadows dancing on the grass?
> So young and tenderly her footsteps pass,
> So dreamy-limbed and lightly wild and warm—
> The bugles murmer and the banners furl,
> And they are lost and vanished like a storm![1]

---

1. Max Eastman, "Isadora Duncan," *The Liberator*, 1 (March 1918), p. 21.

The cult of Duncan was widespread among young artists and writers, who saw in her dancing the promise of a new, liberated life devoted to honest self-expression, high art, and progressive social ideals. William Carlos Williams saw her dance in 1908, and wrote:

> Isadora when I saw you dance the interrupting years fell back,
> It seemed with far intenser leave than lack
> Of your deft step hath e'er conferred no flaw. . . .[2]

Writing to his brother, Williams said that her performance "doubly strengthened my desire and my determination to accomplish my part in our wonderful future."[3] In 1913 Floyd Dell wrote that Duncan "made us despise the frigid artifice of the ballet, and taught us that in the natural movements of the body are contained the highest possibilities of choreographic beauty."[4] Rather less susceptible to Duncan's cult of classicism, Eastman emphasized the contrast between the energy and martial flamboyance of her dance and the "dreamy-limbed" barefooted dancing girl. Eastman was working well within familiar lines: behind his observation of the tension between the dancer and the dance lay the late romantic and symbolist cult of the dancer, about which Frank Kermode has written so brilliantly.[5] His poem was a slight, graceful footnote to great poems by others, and even lacked the sense of personal discovery which Williams's youthful lines convey. Eastman collected "Isadora Duncan" in *Colors of Life* (1918), to which he contributed a "Preface About American Poetry" written in a defensive tone, and it is not hard to see why. It was widely noted, even by disciples and friends of Eastman's, that there was a glaring contradiction between his tame, aesthetic poetry and his radical politics. Even so enthusiastic a protégé as Michael Gold regarded Eastman's poetry as old fashioned and inappropriate for a serious communist:

> This man, who could think on politics with the clean beauty of a running athlete, had the flabbiest, most reactionary notions of poetry. It was something that had no connection with the struggle of human beings, with their epic moments, with their dramatic aspirations and day by day labors. Poetry was a mere langourous sensual melancholy, in Eastman's eyes; why he believed so I

---

2. Quoted by Reed Whittemore, *William Carlos Williams: Poet from Jersey* (Boston: Houghton Mifflin, 1975), p. 52, from an unpublished letter to his brother Edgar of 21 October 1908.
3. Quoted from the same letter to Edgar Williams by Bram Dijkstra, *Cubism, Stieglitz and the Early Poetry of William Carlos Williams: The Hieroglyphics of a New Speech* (Princeton: Princeton U.P., 1969), p. 127.
4. Floyd Dell, *Women as World Builders* (Chicago: Forbes, 1913), p. 43.
5. See Frank Kermode, *Romantic Image* (London: Routledge & Kegan Paul, 1957).

could understand, and I was one of those who esteemed his intellect this side of idolatry. . . . [But his poems] seem as anachronistic as the poetry of Oscar Wilde, or Arthur Symons.[6]

In his preface to *Colors of Life* Eastman explained that his poems reflected his own "too easy taste of freedom" rather than the world's struggle:

> That struggle has always occupied my thoughts, and often my energies, and yet I have never identified myself with it or found my undivided being there. I have found that rather in individual experience and in those moments of energetic idleness when the life of universal nature seemed to come to its bloom of realization in my consciousness. Life is older than liberty. It is greater than revolution. It burns in both camps.[7]

Eastman's humane and fair-minded point was fairly surprising from such a devoted follower of Lenin (as he was in 1918: by 1925 he was an avid partisan for Trotsky). In the increasingly polarized atmosphere of the American left in the 1920s it was frankly unsupportable.

The face which radical politics turned towards art, and that which artists showed to politics, radical or otherwise, may be suggested by two meetings.

"Stieglitz, this is Bill Haywood." Years later, when Stieglitz wrote his memoirs, he recalled his meeting with the tall, burly leader of the Wobblies. Haywood looked around the 291 Gallery and asked Stieglitz why he was wasting his time in such a "dinky little place." "True workers," he said, "don't believe the artist will ever win the fight for what we're after" and asked why a big man like Stieglitz did not "leave this place and join the real fight." Stieglitz's reply was carefully measured:

> Mr. Haywood, I don't believe you understand. You don't believe that my way is the way. You believe that your way is the only way. . . . You believe you have followers, hundreds of thousands, maybe millions. I make no distinction between classes and races and creeds. There is no hatred in me unless it be a hatred of pretense and hypocrisy and maybe a hatred of stupidity. Even my own. When the day arrives and what you are doing proves to be true and what I am attempting to do proves to be equally true we'll be standing shoulder to shoulder wherever we meet.[8]

Until then, however . . . Haywood shook his head. "Too bad," he

---

6. Michael Gold, "May Days and Revolutionary Art," *Modern Quarterly*, 3 (January-April 1926), p. 161. By the mid-1920s Gold was within the orbit of the Communist Party, if not yet a member, while Eastman had broken conclusively with the Stalinists. Their relations at an earlier period are suggested in Gold's "Max Eastman: A Portrait," *New York Call Magazine*, 9 February 1918, pp. 6, 16. Gold was at that time still using his given name, Irwin Granich.
7. Eastman, "A Preface," *Colors of Life* (New York: Alfred A. Knopf, 1918), n.p.
8. Alfred Stieglitz, "Ten Stories," *Twice-a-Year*, Nos. 5-6 (1940-1), pp. 136-7.

said, walking out of the gallery.

Margaret Anderson described an even more disastrous meeting in her autobiography. She had long looked forward to introducing her friend and assistant on the *Little Review*, Jane Heap, to the renowned anarchists Emma Goldman and Alexander Berkman. She hoped that Goldman and Berkman would find Heap, a stylish and clever lesbian, to be "an incentive toward their clearer thinking." When they finally met, Heap teased Goldman and playfully appealed to Berkman for sympathy. This subsequently produced a complaint from Emma Goldman to Anderson about Heap's aggressiveness. When they met a day later, Anderson recalled that they argued bitterly about art:

> They had tried to maintain that "The Ballad of Reading Gaol" was better art than "Salome." When I used the black swan in Amy Lowell's "Malmaison" to illustrate a certain way of pointing emotion there was a general uprising. E. G. was a little beside herself.
> The working-man hasn't enough leisure to be interested in black swans she thundered. What's that got to do with revolution? . . . If only a few people understand the art you talk about that's proof that it's not for humanity, said Berkman.[9]

Anderson and Heap, the most energetic and assiduous groupies of *avant-garde* art in America, were hardly to be persuaded by the earnest utilitarian artistic ideas of the anarchists. An unexpected consequence of this meeting, as it filtered into the pages of the *Little Review*, was a famous exchange between Upton Sinclair and Margaret Anderson. It succinctly captured the spirit of the uneasy relations between radicals and the *avant-garde* in the 1920s. Sinclair wrote, cancelling his subscription: "I no longer understand anything in it, so it no longer interests me." Anderson's reply was brusque and unequivocal: "Please cease sending me your socialist paper. I understand everything in it, therefore it no longer interests me."[10]

There were a small number of people in the 1920s who were attracted by the Russian experiment, and among these some who were seriously trying to transplant Soviet artistic practice and literary theory into America.[11] Michael Gold was among the

9. Margaret Anderson, *My Thirty Year's War: An Autobiography* (London: Alfred A. Knopf, 1930), pp. 119, 125-7.
10. *Ibid.*, p. 128.
11. Among the most fascinating and elusive of such figures was David Burliuk (1882-1976). Born in Kiev, between 1912 and 1914 he became the chief organizer and propagandist for Russian futurism. Invited by Kandinsky to participate in the Blaue Reiter exhibition in Munich, Burliuk was a friend of Mayakovsky and Khlebnikov. He settled in New York in 1922, and when Mayakovsky visited America in 1925, it was in Burliuk's apartment that the young proletarian poets of the "Hammer and Sickle" group, including Gold and Joseph Freeman, met the Russian poet. Burliuk organized an American branch of LEF.

first to recognize the importance of the Proletcult, and to advocate the creation of an American proletarian literature. He came
back from Russia in 1924 with the example of the Workers' Art
Theater in Moscow very much on his mind, and wrote to Upton
Sinclair that he hoped to start a similar theater in New York in
which revolutionary plays might be produced.[12] Em Jo Basshe,
John Howard Lawson and John Dos Passos were drawn into the
enterprise, eventually called the New Playwright's Theater.[13] For
a brief moment when the N.P.T. was busy with productions of the
plays of Dos Passos and Upton Sinclair, and when *The New Masses*
was launched, one saw the possibilities of radical literary and
theatrical practice and revolutionary politics working in tandem.

Unlike *The Liberator* in its final phase, when it was under the
domination of the Communist Party, *The New Masses* was initially
edited by figures such as Egmont Arens and John Sloan who had
been prominent contributors to the old *Masses* before the war. Of
the 56 identified contributors, only two were party members, and
only a dozen were known to be sympathetic to communism. The
venture was energized by an openness and optimism. Gold wrote
to Sinclair, when the magazine was in the planning stages, that
there were

> one or two good leads here toward getting a big bunch of money
> to start a new free non-partisan revolutionary Masses in New
> York. The old artists and writers are crazy to be talking out
> again. . . .[14]

One can get a good sense of the spirit of *The New Masses* from the
various contributors, from W. C. Williams to Allen Tate; and an
even better indication of the mood of the magazine from poems
such as "Vitagraph" by Carl Rakosi, which appeared in the fourth
number in August 1926:

> Out in God's country where men are men,
> the terror of Red Gap used to ride on his
> bulletsodden roan.
> He was called God damn Higgins
> and was said to have faith only in his gun,
> his horse, and Denver Nan.
> It turned out she was in cahoots with Gentleman Joe
> who could shuffle a deck faster than you can count,
> and one day the two of them cleaned the poor sucker
>   out of his last red cent.
> But it was the last time Gentleman Joe
> hung his thumb into the armpit of his vest

---

12. Michael Gold to Upton Sinclair, 7 January 1924. Lilly Library, Indiana University.
13. See Daniel Aaron, *Writers on the Left* (1961; New York: Avon-Discus ed., 1969),
p. 459 n. 10.
14. Gold to Sinclair, n.d. [1925]. Lilly Library, Indiana University.

and snickered behind his nibbled tooth pick,
for a masked stranger showed up in the barroom
that night, with his hand on his hip pocket.
Years later the Reverend Marcus Whitney
pitched his tent in town,
And Denver Nan had her only chance to go straight,
And made good,
And married Good Deed Higgins,
And three cheers for the star spangled banner.
And how about God damn Higgins?
O he used to be hard all right.
He could draw a gun faster than any man in Arizona.

Rakosi's language, as befits the future author of the "Americana" sequence, celebrates its own clichés. Each is savored, but wholly without highbrow contempt.

Within the notoriously humorless Party, and on the left generally, there was considerable skepticism about the value of such bourgeois literary productions as "Vitagraph." Fellow-travellers such as Michael Gold and Joseph Freeman were confronted with philistines within the Party who dismissed (or had never heard of) Toller, Piscator, Becher, Grosz and Mayakovsky. Literature for such people was basically a waste of time, a pointless indulgence.[15] As younger radicals and intellectuals drew closer to the Party on political grounds, in the aftermath of the execution of Sacco and Vanzetti and the Passaic textile strike, they were faced with the need to defend revolutionary politics among their literary acquaintances, and to defend art among their Party comrades.

From 1928 *The New Masses* moved steadily to the left. Arens and Sloan resigned. There were appeals for worker-correspondents, and much talk about proletarian literature. The editors of the magazine founded the John Reed Club in New York, and sought in a variety of ways to foster a proletarian and revolutionary culture in opposition to bourgeois values.[16] The open hand extended to bourgeois radicals by *The New Masses* in 1926 was rapidly closing. Periodicals and cultural organizations within the influence of the Party were being Stalinized. At the Kharkov Congress of the International Union of Revolutionary Writers in 1930, the

---

15. Joseph Freeman, *An American Testament: A Narrative of Rebels and Romantics* (London: Victor Gollancz, 1938), p. 355.
16. See Eric Homberger, "Proletarian Literature and the John Reed Clubs 1929-1935," *Journal of American Studies*, 13 (August 1979), 221-44; Lawrence Schwartz, *Marxism and Culture: The CPUSA and Aesthetics in the 1930s* (Port Washington, N.Y.: Kennikat Press, 1980); Daniel Aaron, *Writers on the Left*; and Richard Pells, *Radical Visions and American Dreams: Culture and Social Thought in the Depression Years* (New York: Harper & Row, 1973) is good on the larger outlines of the radicalization of the intellectuals. Despite its Cold War bias, Irving Howe and Lewis Coser, *The American Communist Party: A Critical History (1919-1957)* (Boston: Beacon Press, 1957) provides a useful account of the shift to the left in this period.

American delegation was among the most unyielding and doctrinaire—to the point where the chairman at one of the sessions rebuked the young Americans for their excessive leftism.

The changes in political line, and rapid shifts of mood among the members of the John Reed Club, were dismaying to people like Gold and Freeman, who had been instrumental in the change of policy in 1928. By 1931 Gold wrote to Upton Sinclair with annoyance and contempt about the youthful sectarians who were increasingly dominating the John Reed Club and who threatened to take over *The New Masses*:

> You get a bourgeois college boy who's never seen a strike or worked in his life—he gets to be a Communist (not party member however) & in 3 months he is patronizing Lenin & improving on Marx & hunting heresies. It gets boring sometimes—but we mean to keep as commonsense a line as we can against some of this stuff.[17]

Throughout this period Joseph Freeman was waging a lonely battle against "vulgar" Marxist literary criticism (such as the attempt to explain the evolution of literary patterns "by the simple method of describing the economic conditions under which a book is written"[18]), and in 1932 he unsuccessfully tried to return *The New Masses* to a more serious intellectual level.[19]

Against this climate, the publication in 1929 and 1930 of the Rebel Poets' anthologies, edited by Ralph Cheyney and Jack Conroy, was a rather curious anachronism. The editors were unable to interest any American publisher in an anthology of radical poetry, and the volumes eventually appeared in London. They represent the final phase of the older populist way of thinking about poetry as versified social criticism. The theme, and title, of both anthologies was "unrest": poems were included which portrayed and satirized bourgeois manners, upper-class pretension, hedonistic college life, pretentious poets, and a wide variety of social ills. This was socially-committed poetry in the traditional sense, with poems on the wrongful imprisonment of a black in South Carolina, and a poem describing a funeral in an urban ghetto. There was nothing Marxist about such poems, most of which were simply humane literary protests against inhumanity. But in the changing literary climate of the American left, in which younger writers were trying to write in a more overtly political manner, and were seriously trying to become Marxist poets, the old mix of traditional verse forms and social-protest sentiment

---

17. Gold to Sinclair, n.d. [1931]. Lilly Library, Indiana University.
18. Joseph Freeman, "Literary Patterns," *New Masses*, 5 (June 1929), p. 14.
19. Joseph Freeman, "Ivory Towers—White and Red," *New Masses*, 12 (11 September 1934), pp. 20-24.

was no longer viable.[20] Under the pressure of the collapse of the economy in 1929, there was a growing feeling that writers had to take sides; to earn their place within the movement, a harder, more programmatic opposition to capitalism was expected, as was a more direct concern with putting literature at the service of the class struggle.

The most interesting example of the new mood was *We Gather Strength* (New York: Liberal Press, 1933), an anthology of poems by Herman Spector, Joseph Kalar, Edwin Rolfe and S. Funaroff. The political themes are visible and insistent in Rolfe's "Kentucky—1932," Spector's "Anarchist Nightsong," and Funaroff's "An American Worker." The Russian *mythos*, as Orwell was later to describe it, was a new element (Funaroff's "Dnieprostroi"), and with Rolfe's "Homage to Karl Marx" a new hero steps to stage center. No less interesting than the changed political tendency is the (belated) influence upon the *We Gather Strength* poets of T. S. Eliot and modern poetry in general. Funaroff's "What the Thunder Said: A Fire Sermon" is a conscious pastiche of Eliotian techniques and imagery. None of the poems in this anthology rhyme, and there are no sonnets; free verse is the order of the day; the imagery is often quite "modern":

> within these urban angularities
> and geometric patterns of despair,
> the flowing lines of music trace
> emotion in sinuous, vague curves through garbage-air
>
> and a squat guy in a straw hat passing
> flips a stub of cigarette to the street . . .
> (Spector, "Saturday Eve, East-Side")

Many of the traditional and clichéd images of social-protest poetry live on, with emphasis on "rotting structures," the "sure advance" of the proletariat, and the "crimson banner/flying in the wind." But *We Gather Strength* is alive to the achievement of modern American poetry, and though there is hardly a poem in the anthology which is not flawed in some important respect, at least the flaws are interesting ones. Michael Gold was convinced the book represented something new within the culture of the American left: in the past, he wrote in the introduction to *We Gather Strength*, "in our revolutionary movement only doggerel has been esteemed."

---

20. In addition to the publication of the *Unrest* anthologies in 1929 and 1930, N. Guterman and P. Morhange translated a selection of *New Masses* verse as *Poèmes D'Ouvriers Américains* (Paris: Les Revues, 1930). No similar collection of leftwing writing on this scale appeared in the United States between Upton Sinclair's *The Cry for Justice* (1915) and *Proletarian Literature in the United States* (1935). The contrast between these in content and intention is highly suggestive.

Arguably the flowing crimson banners and the urgent cry of "Defend the Soviet Union!" were ritualistic gestures, concessions made obligatory by the political moment. Within what is often a mechanical use of leftwing imagery, there is occasionally a frantic and despairing urgency:

> Out of darkness, out of the pits now—
> Foreigners only to the light of day—
> claiming the mountains in the sudden glow
> of battle, welded in a mass array,
> shouting!
>
>> This is our land, we planted its first seed!
>> These are our mines, our hands dig the coal!
>> These roads are ours, the wires across the land
>> are ours! THIS IS OUR EARTH!
>>   (Rolfe, "Kentucky—1932")

More fastidious literary consciences might indeed be moved by the strike in Harlan County, Kentucky, and want to join Rolfe's cry. But there was a more persuasive master, William Carlos Williams, who taught in "Spring and All" that "One by one objects are defined." The massive acts of appropriation in the Rolfe poem were more immediately satisfying (as was the famous conclusion of Odets's *Waiting for Lefty*, with its dramatic calls for a strike) than the modest suggestion of Williams that "so much depends" upon the seeing of a red wheelbarrow. But it would take a megaphone-art akin to Mayakovsky's to make it work. As poetry, Rolfe is scarcely using the medium. Williams had much to teach the younger poets, and the history of poetry in the interwar years might be written in terms of his example and influence. What was perhaps most important in the early 1930s was the way he combined powerful social criticism with a spare, disciplined technique.

This is not the place to rehearse the history of the Objectivist movement, or its aesthetic principles. Many of the leading Objectivists were either sympathizers or actively engaged in leftwing politics. That well-known poet, "Louis Zukonski" [sic], was reported in the *Daily Worker* of 2 July 1937 to have been elected by the Middle Atlantic Division of the League of American Writers to an Official Committee to organize support for steel strikers. Reznikoff published a poem dedicated to the martyred socialists of Vienna in *Separate Way* (1936). Yet their literary efforts were rebuffed by the Communist literary establishment, and contemptuously dismissed by roughnecks like Herman Spector. Spector's review of two volumes by Charles Reznikoff in the Summer 1934 issue of *Dynamo* was essentially a political argument against Objectivism:

> Charles Reznikoff expresses in his poetry the limited world-
> view of a "detached" bystander: that is, of a person whose flashes
> of perception for the immediate esthetics of the contemporary
> scene are not co-ordinated in any way with a dialectical compre-
> hension of the life-process. . . . The fatal defect of the Objectivist
> theory is that it identifies life with capitalism, and so assumes
> that the world is merely a waste land. The logical consequence is
> a fruitless negativism. . . . Impartiality is a myth which defeatists
> take with them into oblivion.[21]

"Objectivism" was one of the many failings which Henri Barbusse's
journal, *Monde*, was accused of at the Kharkov Congress in 1930:

> . . . *Monde* . . . should have regarded all the phenomena of the
> surrounding bourgeois life from the class point of view, this being
> the only attitude to take towards the objective world at the
> present historical stage; from the standpoint, that is, of the pro-
> letariat armed scientifically with dialectical materialism. Its ob-
> jectivism should have been the "objectivism of the class struggle"
> (Lenin).[22]

The term "objectivist" was, on the left, a damaging confession of
neutrality. There is no reason to assume that Zukofsky was aware
of this when the term was first used in the February 1931 number
of *Poetry*. Within the terms of the Party, however, Spector's comments were fairly predictable. When Williams reviewed *An "Objectivists" Anthology*, he addressed the problem which Spector
pointed out in Reznikoff: the absence of a connecting link between the "flashes of perception" and the meaning of such perceptions within the "life-process." Williams saw Objectivism as "the
presentation, simply, of certain new objects without obvious connection with the classics and which he [the Objectivist poet]
entitles 'poems'."[23] Williams goes on to suggest that paradoxically the perception of the newness of the new affirms the "continued existence of the old." With a nice example of Eliot-like
legerdemain, the Objectivists can thus have their cake and eat it.
At the end of the review Williams suggests another definition of
the term "Objectivist":

> . . . they are successfully displayed to hold an objective view of
> poetry which, in a certain way, clarifies it, showing it to be not a
> seductive arrangement of scenes, sounds and colors so much as a
> construction each part of which has a direct bearing on its mean-
> ing as a whole, an objectification of significant particulars.

---

21. Reprinted in *Bastard in the Ragged Suit: Writings of, with drawings by, Herman Spector*, ed. Bud Johns and Judith S. Clancy (San Francisco: Synergistic Press, 1977), pp. 104-5.
22. "Resolution on *Monde*," *Literature of the World Revolution*, Special Number 1931 (Reports, Resolutions, Debates of the Second International Conference of Revolution-ary Writers), p. 105.
23. *The Symposium*, 4 (January 1933), p. 114.

The formalist way of viewing the term was certainly more con-
genial to the principals in later years, and probably comes close to
the central point of the anthology itself, and to the ideas which
held the Objectivists together in the 1930s. The "political" meaning of Objectivism kept the poets and the Communist Party at
arms' length.

The criticism Spector makes of the "detached bystander"
aspect of Reznikoff's poetry is not without sense, though for
Reznikoff detachment was a complex aesthetic and psychological statement of the man himself. Reznikoff's *Testimony*, in the
prose version which appeared in *An "Objectivists" Anthology* and
which Spector reviewed, was not a politically committed work in
the obvious sense. It revealed a conception of art as the expression of a subtle and intense humanism—an art, in other words, for
which the megaphone and waving crimson banner were less than
useless. For a wide variety of reasons it is true that Reznikoff
shied away from the provision of meanings in his poems. Spector,
and other leftwing critics of the 1930s, were asking whether, in
a world threatened by Fascism and in which millions were unemployed, it was enough merely to see (however clearly) the

> Round
> Shiny fixed
> Alternatives
> (Oppen, *Discrete Series*, p. 3)

as one would see a red wheelbarrow or "the senseless/unarrange-
ment of wild things,"[24] but not feel called upon to take a stand
on the larger public concerns. It is hard not to feel that the left
were asking important questions about Objectivism; but scarcely
waiting for an answer.

Discrete Series was published by the Objectivist Press in 1934.
The proletarian literary movement was in high gear, with novels
that year by Robert Cantwell, Edward Dahlberg, James T. Farrell,
Waldo Frank, Albert Halper and Josephine Herbst. It was the year
of Kenneth Burke's "My approach to Communism" and Philip
Rahv's declaration that he hoped to become "an intellectual assistant of the proletariat."[25] John Strachey's *Literature and Dialectical Materialism*, and Stanley Burnshaw's "Notes on Revolutionary Poetry" were published, and the *Partisan Review* was founded.
The "Call" went out for the League of American Writers.

Oppen's slender book did not make much of an impression

---

24. W.C. Williams, "This Florida: 1924," *An "Objectivists" Anthology*, ed. Louis Zukofsky (Le Beausset, Var: To, 1932), p. 103.
25. "For Whom Do You Write? Replies from Forty American Writers," *The New Quarterly*, 1 (Summer 1934), p. 12.

on bourgeois critics. William Rose Benet thought that Oppen's writing was like "listening to a man with an impediment in his speech."[26] Williams, who had kept up intermittent relations with the left in the early 1930s,[27] took the occasion of a review of *Discrete Series* to make an important statement about art and revolution:

> An imaginable new social order would require a skeleton of severe discipline for its realization and maintenance. Thus by a sharp restriction to essentials, the seriousness of a new order is brought to realization. Poetry might turn this condition to its own ends. Only by being an object sharply defined and without redundancy will its form project whatever meaning is required of it. It could well be, at the same time, first and last a poem facing as it must the dialectic necessities of its day. Oppen has carried this social necessity, so far as poetry may be concerned, to an extreme.[28]

To look at Edwin Rolfe's "Kentucky—1932" through Williams's eyes is to see how little it achieves sharp definition, and form without redundancy. Its effects are achieved at the cost of a blurring of perception, for only thus would we miss the way it is caught up in a web of clichés and unrealized social emotion. *Discrete Series* represents precisely the "sharp restriction to essentials" which Williams indicates. If anything, those essentials, those images through which Oppen works are too spare. He describes people in a theater removing their coats and sitting down as a "semaphoring chorus." In another poem a social portrait (reminiscent of rather wordier things in Pound's *Lustra*) turns upon a single word, "Pertain," and its elusive connotation:

> Your breasts
> > Pertain to lingerie.
> > > (*CP*, p. 13)

Discrete Series is a book which omits the explanations which we have usually come to expect from poetry. A point which Williams made in his review of *An "Objectivists" Anthology* provides us with an essential term: "These pieces, these lines, these words, neither are they fragments but their power is cumulative [,] rather

---

26. W. R. Benet, "The Phoenix Nest," *The Saturday Review of Literature*, 10 (24 March 1934), p. 580.
27. See Dickran Tashjian, *William Carlos Williams and the American Scene 1920-1940* (Berkeley: University of California Press, 1979); Mike Weaver, *William Carlos Williams: The American Background* (Cambridge: Cambridge U.P., 1971); and Robert von Hallberg, "The Politics of Description: W. C. Williams in the Thirties," *ELH*, 45 (Spring 1978), 131-151. For the generally sympathetic attitude towards Williams on the left, see Michael Gold in the *Daily Worker*, 12 October 1933, Milton Howard's review of Williams's *Collected Poems* in the *Daily Worker*, 10 February 1934, and Edwin Seaver's review of *White Mule, Daily Worker*, 28 July 1937.
28. W. C. Williams, "The New Poetical Economy," *Poetry*, 44 (July 1934), pp. 223-4.

in tension than in story." By *story* Williams identified what Spector felt was missing from Objectivism: the connections and explanation which would have clarified and asserted the meanings of the things seen. Oppen has never felt the need to thicken the outline of the sharply-defined object. Perhaps he has seldom felt a hunger for the completeness and artifice of the story in his poems.

There is a sense in which the early Oppen was a poet of estrangement—not, as Williams suggested, because the Objectivist poet presented objects "without obvious connection" and called them "poems," but because he was writing in a society in which the connections, explanations and stories had been corrupted, distorted, mystified, turned into ideology. *Discrete Series* embodies a revolutionary art in which the links between objects and meanings can no longer be asserted (as Spector thought) as a matter of "dialectical comprehension." In the face of a comprehensive and radical epistemological uncertainty (though there is a danger in exaggerating the extent to which Oppen is a philosophical poet), he sought an art which was free from the smothering cloud of anecdote and story which envelopes our culture.

He found no place in the leftwing literary movement of the 1930s, which was an ironic blessing. He had nothing to repent when repentence was in season. Mary Oppen describes the fate of *Discrete Series* in two sentences: "The Gotham Book Mart bought some of the books; very few were sold, and the rest were stored. Politics were dominant and danger was imminent."[29]

29. Mary Oppen, *Meaning A Life: An Autobiography* (Santa Barbara: Black Sparrow, 1978), p. 146.

THE METHOD

George Oppen. Photograph circa 1955, courtesy of Mary Oppen.

L. S. DEMBO

OPPEN ON HIS POEMS: A DISCUSSION

According to Mary Oppen, Louis Zukofsky once asked her husband, "Do you like your own poetry better than mine?" George replied, "Yes." "George," Mary continues, "insisting on clarity and understanding, speaking of his difficulty in knowing if the readers would understand; Louis, with a shrug replying, 'It doesn't matter, they don't care if they understand you or not.' . . . Not knowing how to say it without insulting Louis, but implying that Louis used incomprehensibility and obscurity as a tactic, George said, 'You're tougher than I am, Louis,' referring to Louis' disregard of the reader."[1]

To anyone who has looked into Oppen's first collection, *Discrete Series* (1930), to say nothing of later work like *Seascape: Needle's Eye* (1972) or *Primitive* (1979), this distinction surely must seem to be between pot and kettle. Many of Oppen's poems are no less obscure than any to be found in Zukofsky. Yet, Oppen did say in "Route," "I have not and never did have any motive of poetry/But to achieve clarity,"[2] thereby confirming that, whatever Zukofsky's attitude, the issue was scarcely one that Oppen considered peripheral. Indeed, his cry for "the most beautiful thing in the world,/A limited, limiting clarity" (*CP*, p. 185) is integral with his "poetics of veracity" and arises from the core of his emotional life.

Simply: "He wants to say/His life is real,/No one can say why//It is not easy to speak" (*CP*, p. 159). Or, to elaborate:

---

1. Mary Oppen, *Meaning A Life: An Autobiography* (Santa Barbara: Black Sparrow, 1978), p. 209.
2. George Oppen, *Collected Poems* (New York: New Directions, 1975), p. 185. All quotations from Oppen's poetry will be from this edition, which will be cited hereafter as *CP*. All such citations will be incorporated into the text. The poems by Oppen reprinted in the text of this interview are copyrighted   1934 by the Objectivist Press and 1975 by George Oppen, and are reprinted here by permission of the author and New Directions.

"One would have to tell what happens in a life, what choices present themselves, what the world is for us, what happens in time, what thought is in the course of a life and therefore what art is, and the isolation of the actual" (*CP*, p. 168). And always the same problem: "One must not come to feel that he has a thousand threads in his hands,/He must somehow see the one thing" (*CP*, p. 168); just as always the same hope: "The light/Of the closed pages, tightly closed, packed against each other/Exposes the new day,//The narrow, frightening light/Before a sunrise" (*CP*, p. 169).

Ideally, the "public utterance" that is the poem is the "reportage" of an actuality or truth experienced, felt, or perceived by the poet. More often, however, such utterance is nothing but the "ferocious mumbling, in public/Of rootless speech" (*CP*, p. 159). This is so because in Oppen's existential world only the individual man can determine what is meaningful and of value in his own life and he is beset by confusion and doubt. "I stumble over these stories," Oppen writes, "—/Progeny, the possibility of progeny, continuity,//Or love that tempted him//He is punished by place, by scene, by all that holds/all he has found" (*CP*, p. 193). Place and scene are the "materials" of reality or truth; they punish the poet because they stubbornly remain matter rather than allowing themselves to be rendered into form: "this pavement, the silent symbols//Of it, the word it, never more powerful than in this/ moment. Well, hardly an epiphany, but there the thing/is all the same" (*CP*, p. 193). Earlier, Oppen had said, "Not the symbol but the scene this pavement leads/To roadsides—the finite//Losing its purposes/Is estranged" (*CP*, p. 192).

It is precisely the finite in its limited, limiting clarity that Oppen seeks, but "infiniteness is the most evident thing in the world," (*CP*, p. 174) and the poet cannot find his bearings: "We want to defend/Limitation/And do not know how. . . . And cannot defend/The metaphysic/On which rest//The boundaries/of our distances" (*CP*, p. 165). Oppen's desire to discover whether or not the "numerosity" of human beings constitutes a unity called "humanity," whether the Seascape is more than the needle's eye of waves (or whether the sea is "capable of contact save in incidents"), whether the "thousand threads in his hands" can be woven into one whole fabric are all expressions of his lifelong attempt to attain the certain knowledge in which finitude is joined to purpose and the obscurities of the material world as well as those of symbols that have no connection with lived reality are dispelled.

Obscurity is as inevitable a part of Oppen's poetry as of his life—indeed, paradoxically, it is part of the "meaning" in both.

The illumination that brings definition and certitude eludes the poet, and the poem is "messed." (This is Oppen's own word, as we will see in the interview that follows.) Thus understood, the poem demonstrates its own theme. And here we return to the original point, Mary Oppen's assertion about her husband's concern for clarity, with a fuller appreciation of its accuracy. At least we can appreciate that Oppen does not revel in being obscure, nor is he indifferent to his audience. The text that follows is in its very existence proof enough of that. Having already submitted himself to two hours of general questions in a seminar interview, Oppen agreed to an additional session in which he would be asked to elucidate specific poems.

That was more than twelve years ago—May, 1968, to be exact. The seminar interview became part of the "Objectivist" Poet series published in *Contemporary Literature*[3]; the hour-long discussion of the poems was filed away for future reference. At that time the situation called for the general material; today, in light of Oppen's reputation and given the present context, it seems to me that the opposite is true. I do not believe that the remarks are either dated or, addressed as they are mainly to *Discrete Series*, overspecialized. Quite the contrary, they are the *limited, limiting clarities* that help light the way to the later poems as well as to illuminate *the mind's own place* of a poet who has known and *reported* on *the outer limits of ego, reason, dream,* and *devotion to life.*

† † † † †

D. I wonder if you'd mind talking first about some of the more difficult poems in *Discrete Series*. I know that in these poems you often see things in terms of motion and gestures and shapes but there usually seems to be more that is going on. For instance, you write,

> Who comes is occupied
> Toward the chest (in the crowd moving
>   opposite
> Grasp of me)
>   In firm overalls
> The middle-aged man sliding
> Levers in the steam-shovel cab,——
> Lift (running cable) and swung, back
> Remotely respond to the gesture before last
> Of his arms fingers continually——
> Turned with the cab.

3. *Contemporary Literature*, 10, 2 (Spring 1969), 159-177. Reprinted in *The Contemporary Writer: Interviews with Sixteen Poets and Novelists*, ed. L. S. Dembo and Cyrena N. Pondrom (Madison, Wisc.: Univ. of Wisc. Press, 1972), pp. 172-190.

And the poem ends:

> But if I (how goes
>   it?)——
>   The asphalt edge
> Loose on the plateau,
> Horse's classic height cartless
> See electric flash of streetcar,
> The fall is falling from electric burst.

                                    (*CP*, p. 7)

The streetcar image, in which the electricity falls from the top of the trolley, is vivid, but I couldn't quite understand what you meant here by "The asphalt edge/Loose on the plateau" or the "Horse's classic height cartless." I wonder if you can recall what motivated these lines.

O. I'd just say it's a matter of recalling. I have a sort of a double vision of these poems. I don't feel as if I wrote them, and yet I can so easily guess that I had because the themes are familiar. The real question is simply, whether the poem is successful or not, and I can't quite make up my mind. That's specifically something I've said since, I think, of the vision of the raw land under that asphalt. There's the asphalt but under it is really what was, or even is, just a prairie, just the raw land. There's a double consciousness there where you see the road is a road and then begin to see just the raw land. And the "Horse's classic height" is messed, I would say; "cartless," I just meant, and imagine on the prairie a horse, not a horse pulling a cart. Remember there were carts at the time, though not many. But just a plain horse. It's messed, so I can tell you only what I think I meant. The word "classic," I tried to create the meaning by some vague association in my own mind, I suppose, with the height of a horse.

D. Well, of course the word "classic" does have a special meaning in your poetry. I remember in the poem "Philai te kou philai" (*CP*, p. 75) you mention the classic columns of Rome.

O. That's right. On the other hand, in that poem I described Mary's and my love for Maine as the other antiquity, the non-classic antiquity. I think that line's also messed. I too, like the electric burst. There's some pretty bad syntax, though; and I don't know if the image works. In a way, there's the confusion of the city and so on. I think the cadences of the man working the levers of the cab is fairly well done. And then as against this the motion of traffic, which maybe creates too much incoherence, I don't know. It's simply a crowd of men coming straight towards you, a stranger, trying to get the experience of a city.

D. Of course, this poem is written very "discretely" because you have a series of images just juxtaposed, whereas you know the normal tendency would be for the reader to follow the poet throughout the entire poem as though it were a progression. But it's not a progression. It's a discrete series of images.

O. In a way it's more conventional than some of the other poems, I think, which is what I was objecting to a little bit. It's a sort of "montage," because there's just the city and I'm jumping around like the fashionable camera of that time.

D. What would the prairie have to do with the city, then?

O. It's there. It's just there, under the pavement. It is that ground.

D. I'm not sure I follow you.

O. I just meant, my eye sees the plain land. It's just land after all, even though they've paved this thing and created all this complication on it.

D. I see. The land is just *there*, an actuality, like the deer in "Psalm"—"That they are there." I also want to ask you about "Party on Shipboard" (*CP*, p. 8). You said that the whole *Of Being Numerous* was contained in that poem.

O. Yes, that was my first attempt. I don't know whether it's clear as symbolism, I think there are some lines that say it. The people, one sees these individual people at a party jumping around and the image justified. I really was remembering a send-off party on a ship. If not, I was using that. You see the separate waves but somehow there is *the sea,* just as you see people and somehow there is, or could be found, *humanity*.

D. Specifically in this poem you use the line, "Like the sea incapable of contact/Save in incidents." You use the same line again in a poem in *The Materials*, in quotation marks.

O. Oh, yeah. I've several times quoted from myself.

D. Yes, I know that. But I was interested in what the import of this image was to you, "incapable of contact/Save in incidents," as a description of the sea.

O. The waves are the individual person. Humanity can't be encountered as an incident or something that has just happened. But all one has is "this happened," "that happened"; and out of this we try to make a picture of what a man is, who these other people are, and even, what humanity is. Actually, it is from the hills that people speak of "the sea." When you're in the sea, there's this wave and that wave and that breaker and the other breaker.

D. This seems to be an example of *discrete* perception again.

O. I may be encountering . . . (no, I was going to say the "limitations") not the limitations, but the difficulties of imagist sincerity. Because one does have to know a wave is just a wave; one doesn't experience "the sea." Except . . . you know, of course you know, I'm using "image" in Pound's sense, not Amy Lowell's.

D. Well, this really goes back to the whole idea of the perception of particularities. "The sea" is a generalization but "the wave" as it occurs when you're on the sea is not a generalization; it is a particularity.

O. Yes, right. And the sea as a whole . . . I don't accept it, I don't accept it unless it is also a perception, an image in Pound's sense, though in the narrower sense, it's not an image. But unless one actually experiences the fact of the weight and solidity and unity of the sea, if one actually experiences it, then it's an image as I'm using the word.

D. I see. This is a mode of seeing that we talked about before.

O. The "Party on Shipboard,"—I just remembered it better—records the failure of that perception of the sea, though the concept is still in my mind. But it ends with just the waves homogeneously . . . they just leap about. At least within that image I didn't . . . I left it as a contradiction, that I *know* there is such a thing as "the sea," the whole. But the poem doesn't manage to see it, and it records the poet's—my own—inability to see it. So that it leads directly to what I've told you about my giving up poetry. At least, again directly, to substantiating the accurate intuition of Kenner's statement.[4] It was the last poem I wrote in that book.

D. I see. How about this poem:

> She lies, hip high,
> On a flat bed
> While the after-
> Sun passes.
>
> Plant, I breathe———
> O Clearly,
> Eyes legs arms hands fingers,
> Simple legs in silk.
>
> (*CP*, p. 9)

---

4. Oppen was explaining his decision to abandon poetry in the thirties, in favor of social action, when Hugh Kenner observed, "In brief, it took twenty-five years to write the next poem." See the Oppen interview in the *Contemporary Literature*, p. 174, or *The Contemporary Writer*, p. 187.

Again, this seems to be particularistic perception: "Eyes legs arms hands," the immediate image, immediate contact. I'm probably quite wrong but this appeared to be a humanized vision of one plant by another.

O. Oh, that does come into it. I was going to answer you, I was all prepared to say, well, if such things enter, then it's just a factor of my personality, my peculiarities, that what I was doing was writing an erotic poem, that I hope it's a dirty poem. But the plant, it's true . . . I was just describing my presence there, my sense of my own presence. That's all I was saying. It's not me, but this girl lying there, which I'm talking about. My own presence is like a plant, just breathing, just being, just seeing this. Well, no, I was talking about eroticism, just internal sensations, like a plant. I don't exist otherwise. It's the closure of eroticism within oneself. It's two things, the tremendously sharp vision of erotic desire, together with a kind of closing of one's self, within oneself emotionally.

D. I hope I'm not wearing you out, but these poems have been really interesting to me.

> Town, a town,
> But location
> Over which the sun as it comes to it;
> Which cools, houses and lamp-posts,
> during the night, with the roads———
> Inhabited partly by those
> Who have been born here,
> Houses built—. From a train one sees
> him in the morning, his morning;
> Him in the afternoon, straightening———
> People everywhere, time and the work
> pauseless:
> One moves between reading and re-reading,
> The shape is a moment.
> From a crowd a white powdered face,
> Eyes and mouth making three———
> Awaited—locally—a date.
>
> (*CP*, p. 11)

O. I do know what I meant. I don't know why I know. You can see all those themes there, and they get rattled around. But the thing of place, which even in that early book I've repeated, the mystery of place, the feeling about place, the stasis of place. . . . And a man seeing just in his place one's separation from him. . . . I think I was seeing him from a train window or something.

D. Yes. "From a train one sees/him in the morning, his morning." So it's as though you're observing a figure. . . .

O. His place, therefore his morning, a place he's familiar with. This whole feeling of place as enclosed car, and in a lot of the later poems, and then the immediacy of someone, that face there. One sees this man in his place, which excludes you, as a traveler through it. By the way, I noticed when you were reading, and I agree, it's totally equivocal; I know that I meant to say, "between reading and re-reading one moves." One moves, one always moves, one's always this guy on the train.

D. Then in the poem there actually are two separate subjects. One is the man in the town, the other is the isolated man observing him from the train, from his world.

O. From place.

D. From his place.

O. And then there's a sudden vividness there, her eyes coming toward me or whatever you read. And then it ends—how does it end?

D. "Awaited—locally—a date."

O. I guess that's just a place. She's locally awaited, and there's a date, and so this is her place, but place in a very different way. Place by the boys she knows. It doesn't work, I know. It seems I happen to remember what I was feeling.

D. Perhaps it doesn't work in that sense, but it is still a very characteristic poem for the collection because the way things are perceived is again particularistically. It's like arms, legs, etc., hand; here, it's eyes and mouth. She appears not as a coherent whole but by her parts, so to speak, to the perceiver.

O. Right. As you were reading that poem I kept hoping it was going to work out. I sort of liked it. But then I kept feeling that it rattled around quite a bit.

D. Well, it was just my poor reading.

O. No, . . . I have no great investment in these poems so long after.[5]

D. Well, you have to give them their due.

O. I give them their due. It was the way I wrote them. The problem, I said to the seminar, the chief problem was simply that of honesty. What I couldn't write I scratched out. I wrote what I could be sure of, what I *could* write. I'm not speaking of just what they call now language skills, but what I could think, could say, could do.

---

5. In May, 1968, almost forty years had elapsed since the appearance of *Discrete Series*.

D. But now you feel you can sit in judgment on them and wonder if you actually could have done it after all. So you're saying, for example, that this poem you feel didn't work.

O. My judgment is still a little subjective. It's like looking at a picture of oneself.

D. Can you say something about "Eclogue" (*CP*, p. 17)? I wrestled with this poem for. . . .

O. I don't remember that one.

D. The men in the uproar of the living room, pinpointing an assault . . .

O. Yes, I remember. The title because—it's almost ironic—my version of a bucolic poem, a rural scene, looking out the window.

D. It seemed to me that here again two worlds are being portrayed, the human world and the rock outside, the natural, contingent world, so to speak.

O. Yes. The humans talking of deals and triumphs as a kind of artillery bombardment against that indestructible natural world.

D. The "Image of the Engine" seemed to me to be a very charming poem, the first section in any case. "Likely as not a ruined head gasket/Spitting at every power stroke, if not a crank shaft" (*CP*, p. 18). And you talk about the operation of this creaky engine, and then you conclude, quite spectacularly, "There hovers in that moment, wraith-like and like a plume of steam, an aftermath,/A still and quiet angel of knowledge and of comprehension."

O. The question is the image of man as a machine. That has been said before, but I think the poem works anyway. It's just the image of man as a machine, with a ghost, the ghost in the machine, that's the phrase. It's the image of man as a machine, and it asks the question, Does one believe, then, just because one *can* believe? Does one believe just because one is almost *forced* to believe—in the case of the motor too, is my point. I am a fairly passionate mechanic, but I think anyone will experience that. When the motor finally starts, it's different, it's itself, and it's very different from a lump of steel. Some old-timers used to refuse to feel that about a motor. I remember a fisherman who described—when I was a kid—he had finally gone out on a power fishing boat. "Well, she—yeah, it had a motor, I guess, it had a big lump of steel in it somewhere, a big lump of iron in it somewhere." He was consciously refusing to see a motor. Well, I was using that fact to alter a little bit that phrase about the image of man as a machine. I was saying maybe the image of a machine can hardly be held even in quite that way.

D. Well, that's very interesting. I had been reading the poem completely differently. What baffled me was that I had been reading the engine as an image of the mind, the way the mind works, and the mind really doesn't work well. It works, but it's a blundering machine, the "flywheel blundering/Against compression," for example. That's why it seemed to me that when there was knowledge and comprehension at the end, which all of your poetry denies, I was a little surprised.

O. Well, shall we imagine, then, just because we can imagine it? It's a rather wistful line. Remember Yeats chained to a dying animal? I'm describing the same thing in different terms. A body, and it may be breaking down; it's just a machine. One is tied to this machine. I mean it's implied all the time in the metaphor there. The motor may have something wrong with it, and if it stops, it becomes rather an exact metaphor of a man dying and of the thing blundering, the cough in the manifold. Almost too good, maybe.

D. Then where does the knowledge and compression come in? That's what I'm interested in.

O. Then it finally stops. The man finally dies, the motor finally stops. Shall one imagine then, shall one? In the case of the motor, obviously, one shall not. I mean one knows it isn't true. In the case of the man, just the question, shall one imagine just because one can imagine? There's no reason to believe it, except that one can, or except that there's this impulse to believe. That's really what I meant to say. Even in the case of a motor there's this impulse to feel that. It's difficult to believe in death. I'm just saying that. I didn't try to settle the question. I wouldn't dream of trying to settle the question. If asked the direct question, does one live after death? I would say, I don't know.

D. That's what I didn't understand. It's the knowledge and comprehension of death, not the meaning of life?

O. No, is there a soul which exists, is there a mind which exists, as knowledge, as comprehension? I'm describing the Christian view which suddenly achieves knowledge, comprehension.

D. A soul, a spirit?

O. A spirit that sees eternity, that sees infinity, that knows. The direct question I wouldn't try to answer, except as against occult stories. I would say the evidence is preponderantly that, on the event of death, changes do take place. I doubt very much if people find jewels for their relatives and so on, which seems an inadequate change. But the other question I just wasn't trying to answer.

D. The poem is so simple yet so elusive, I didn't really quite know what to make of it.

O. I suppose I was tempted by a conceit there. . . . And I'm not sure that, if someone asked me, I would say I wasn't clear of conceits or allegories. But the roots of a tree as compared to a child, the metaphor, the conceit just worked out in my mind so compellingly in this motor, I'm really doing a little injustice to myself there. The motor really *is* the same experience as this experience. I used it for that, not for the cleverness of the conceit.

D. I see. What about the poem called "The Undertaking in New Jersey"?

> Beyond the Hudson's
> Unimportant water lapping
> In the dark against the city's shores
> Are the small towns, remnants
> Of forge and coal yard. The bird's voice in their streets
> May not mean much: a bird the age of a child chirping
> At curbs and curb gratings,
> At barber shops and townsmen
> Born of girls—
> Of girls! Girls gave birth . . . But the interiors
> Are the women's: curtained,
> Lit, the fabric
> To which the men return. Surely they imagine
> Some task beyond the window glass
> And the fabrics as if an eventual brother
> In the fields were nourished by all this in country
> Torn by the trucks where towns
> And the flat boards of homes
> Visibly move at sunrise and the trees
> Carry quickly into daylight the excited birds.
>
> (*CP*, p. 42)

O. I like the poem. It just moves. . . . Maybe it's clear, it doesn't exactly lend itself. . . . I think you see all these themes, the village, the community, the thing we're doing, all these things we're building in the houses. I'm taking one thing now. And what is the feeling of what we're ultimately doing? We imagine something, someone, like a brother out there, who will be the meaning of all this, beyond the faint dissatisfaction with the

curtains, and we don't really mean these curtains as our purpose. It is as if . . . I don't think the poem lends itself to paraphrase too easily. And then all the many contradictions in this
which I've sort of touched on in other spots; these were just
girls who had the babies, and that this is a woman's house;
they were just kids who got pregnant, produced a baby. And
out of that came this whole elaboration of the curtains and the
men down to this—I forget how it went. The men come home
and enter this woman's world, and must, to live, to live in anything, to live in a purpose at all. And yet it's really very alien
to them. The men come home from their jobs with other
things they could describe with maybe a touch of dissatisfaction, but which lead nowhere. And do we imagine? And the
sparrows, again, they're just the raw . . . they can be treated
just as plain objects. The sparrows just sit on the street because it's there.

D. I see. "The Undertaking in New Jersey" then is the undertaking of community.

O The undertaking that is maybe barely adumbrated there in our
feeling that outside the window is the inheritor of something
of . . . however I put it. Yes, that's the undertaking: to make a
community, to make a community which will lead to . . . to
what? I mean, I don't say to what, just a question mark.

D. To a "still and quiet angel of knowledge and of comprehension."

O. Oh, yes, right. Out there in the fields. I realize I keep saying
the same few things. With three thousand years of literature
behind us, I don't feel ashamed if I manage to say only one
thing.

D. I don't think you're saying the same few things. I really think
there is a great deal of innovation in the poetry and in a whole
way of looking at experience.

O. Oh, I think it's my own. The same few things that I say, not
the same few things that other people have said. But some of
your students do oversearch for philosophizing.

D. That's really my fault.

O. They're afraid by then, and were afraid to say a poem was
simple.

D. Right. Well, one of them came to me after class and said, "He
didn't mean anything by it. He said he just felt it."

O. Yes, well, that doesn't mean anything either.

D. Well, as you can see, my weakness is for the conception in a poem.

O. I don't think it's a weakness; I think they have to be shaken. So, it's just an emotion. Well, what's an emotion? You know it's strange; in a way you teach them very rigorously, and yet what you're after is the sense of wonder. You tell them, "Yes, well then, the simple fact that somebody didn't like to be killed, or . . ."

D. It does come down to that.

O. That's what it is.

D. "Technologies," I had a terrible time with this poem. It's rather long so I better not read the whole thing, but if you could talk about the small hard blossoms of "feminine profusion//The 'inch-sized/Heart,' the little core of oneself,/So inartistic//The inelegant heart/Which cannot grasp/The world /And makes art//Is small" and then there's the hawk image, and a "small hawk/Lighting disheveled on a window sill" (*CP*, p. 71).

O. This doesn't explain the poem, but I don't mind a certain amount of literary gossip, either. After a bitter argument with me, Denise Levertov wrote a poem in which a hawk howls on the window sill, "Nothing matters, *timor mortis conturbat me*," and so on. I think Denise was pretty mad at me. I was pretty mad at her when I wrote this poem, too, and said, so I'm a hawk, and so forth. But as for the feminine technologies . . . the feminine technologies I take to be a kind of medical pragmatism. . . . There are times one is infinitely grateful for the feminine contribution, and times one just has to fight about it, and this poem was more or less fighting. But the poem moves along fairly freely; I wasn't really conducting a crusade.

D. Well, then "feminine technologies" is something bad in this particular poem.

O. A kind of pragmatism, an unrecognized pragmatism. "What's true is what's good for us." And "why will you be a hawk yelling *timor mortis conturbat me*? What's the use of yelling that? What's the use of saying that?" That's what nice women say to us, women as nice as Denise Levertov is, but sometimes one objects.

D. Well, then there's a poem we've been talking about in passing ever since you arrived, and I wonder if we could look at it a little more closely. A poem I've found fascinating and baffling at the same time: that's "Philai te kou philai." You mentioned something about taking this poem from a. . . .

O. . . . from a movie. I really know extremely little Greek, exactly enough to be able to use a lexicon. I was faintly embarrassed about a Greek tag, except that it was that phrase in the movie that I responded to. It was Electra speaking about her mother, after she had killed her. I'm not qualified to interpret the Greek tragedies, and I don't mean to. It meant to me—to me she was speaking also about mother earth, the mother universe, loved and not loved, she cried out, . . . loved and hated.

D. I don't see the significance of the portrait of the "Intellectual Man" by Eakins, who "might be a school teacher." . . . and then you said "How have we altered." And then the subject changes again, "As Charles said/Rowing on the lake/In the woods, 'if this were the country,/The nation, if these were the routes through it—'" (*CP*, p. 75).

O. It's all about mother nature, mother earth, the universe. It starts—where did you say it started—even as you said it, I was putting it together.

D. "There is a portrait by Eakins/Of the Intellectual."

O. Yes, well this is the realist artist, you see. It's all about this thing, the world which is so loved and so hated and the poem wanders deliberately because it sort of must. There we are on the lake with my friend Charles Humboldt, and this is the natural world and all, except really under modern conditions and, in fact, it's a little lake, just stuck in, almost as a decoration. We haven't yet reached this, which we love and which we hate. And if I remember, the poem, by the end of it, really begins to rise. Or right through, I think, is rising, to try to reach this thing in mother earth, the real thing there, not the little lake in the park. This little lake is just one of the "toys/Of vacation"; in fact, the whole "circle of the visible" has become mere toys; it doesn't count any more, the circle of the visible, the primitive. What was there to the primitive is nothing to us now. You speak by telephone and it's just a game to pretend that only the tree within sight is present.

D. Would this be like that poem in *Discrete Series* where you see the asphalt loose on the plateau?

O. Yes. And Maude Blessingbourne looking out the window at the real world, the plain world, in all of them (*CP*, p. 3). The poem finally reaches even the ancient temples on other coasts and the history of the earth and, I think, it does begin to evoke the earth. I'm aware it moves in a winding line, but I felt it had to, or certainly I meant it to.

D. I had been under the impression, that you were contrasting civilization with nature here.

O. Yes, well it keeps moving that way too, and resolves it in civilization *and* the earth, the cornices which stand on other coasts. They become, they also are a toy, but by then I depend on the lyric, "their tremendous cornices," historically tremendous, emotionally tremendous.

D. This is part of the earth, part of nature.

O. It's become a big thing to the world, though it's artificial, as artificial as the lake. Let me take a look at the poem and I'll undoubtably be a little more coherent. Oh yes, well, I think it's all here. It begins with the realist artist and these little— just what our eyes see, and as Charles said, how different it would be if just this little place were the real world and it's not. And I go back to Eakins and his day; yes, how firm he felt, the pedagogic intellectual, and he lived in a little place like this little vacation point, and these are the primitive toys now of vacation the circle of the visible itself is a toy of vacation. But the real world—the one the animal looked across and saw my eyes in terror—was that "vacation's interlude?" The animal ran! "What entered the mind" too when we saw the iron locomotives and the . . . we're beginning to get into terror here. The animals' bare eyes in the woods, that's no joke. " 'The relation of the sun and the earth//Is not nothing!' " The great, tremendous astronomic relations, they're not nothing in our lives. " 'The sea in the morning'/And the hills brightening"—they're not only not nothing, because they're so tremendous, but they're not nothing within a little place where we sit. The relation between the sun and the earth is the morning and the hills growing, children waking, and it shifts a little. "Children waking in the beds of the defeated"—I'm thinking of the city, yes, a "million//Windows and the grimed sills/Of a ruined ethic." It's not the greatness of our ethic which is making this burst. That ethic is "Bursting with ourselves." And as for the myths, they've been murderous; where will it end? We love and we hate reality. And just breaks into history. . . .

D. Philai te kou philai—it really sums up the whole vision of experience and man's relation to reality that you've been talking about. Even what seems to be a toy in reality is actually something tremendous.

O. Right. And in using my voice a little dramatically I'll confess
    that most of the meaning is in the cadences where it rises,
    which, of course, you know—I'm just saying that I know, too.
    Yes, in the cadences and in the shape of the lines, in the pulse
    of the thought which is given by the lines. The line ending is
    not just punctuation but separates the connections of the pro-
    gression of thought in such a way that again and again one's
    understanding of the poems would be changed if one altered
    the line division. And I don't mean just as a substitute for a
    comma; I mean with which phrase the word is most intimately
    connected—that kind of thing.

D. Well, I have several dozen more questions I'd like to ask you,
    but you've been more than generous already. I'm deeply grate-
    ful to you, and I know this feeling will be shared by students
    who listen to these tapes in times to come.

O. Well, I can understand what people who object to taking a
    poem apart are saying. On the other hand, I don't think a
    poem is all that fragile. The poem remains and the poem is a
    poem. I certainly wouldn't want it to be all that fragile. And
    I have, just on a human basis, a kind of liking for openness
    and a willingness to talk and question; and if one says some-
    thing that is wrong, so one says something that is wrong. I try
    not to write anything that's wrong but conversation is another
    matter. I'm objecting a little bit to preciousness and exag-
    gerated delicacy. I don't feel one is going to destroy a poem all
    that easily even if one does speak foolishly about it. And I
    don't think this has been a bad . . . I've enjoyed the conver-
    sation, too. I'm not saying otherwise, not apologizing. Just
    commenting on this idea of one's freedom with a poem, like
    one's freedom with anything. It doesn't need to tiptoe about.
    The poem does remain if it has any right to remain.

D. Well, of course I'm very much committed to the position of
    understanding poetry on a conceptual level. This is not the
    way poetry was meant to be responded to, but in some ways it
    is, it seems to me, especially when the poetry is subtle.

O. Or to bridge certain gaps between temperament to reach com-
    mon ground, in spite of differences in temperament. After
    all, it's one of the very crucial and difficult questions of that
    poetry, whether within these differences in one's personal
    vision, etc., one can reach common ground. One always finds
    that one can—that's the very wonderful thing.

D. That's a very refreshing attitude. It's a truism that poets har-
    bor a profound hostility to the very idea of criticism.

O. I would be tempted to call that attitude a self-protective device or a sphere.

D. Well, I think that your idea of communication is really the crucial one here. If we can communicate through a third medium . . .

O. It's interesting that we do reach . . . there is—to reverse myself—there are ways in which one is superstitious about poetry. It's true one sees afterwards that one has carefully and deliberately said what he didn't know he was saying. It's true that in one case at least I dreamt a line. I thought I had read it. I spent two weeks trying to find it and realized finally that I had dreamt it. I am as superstitious as anyone. It's true that one can hear a false statement in a poem. One can work and work and work and if one can't make the line decent, one knows there's something wrong with what he was trying to say. I mean I believe in the efficacy of poetry as poetry; nobody believes in it more than I do. All the questions they ask: "What if red doesn't mean to him what it means to me?" and so on. Well, all these questions get answered. It turns out it's true that one can find common ground, provided only that the mind possesses that virtue, which is just to say provided people give a damn, really. If they're bored, there's nothing you can do about that.

MARJORIE PERLOFF

"THE SHAPE OF THE LINES":
OPPEN AND THE METRIC OF DIFFERENCE

> —I see the difference between the writing
> of Mr. Oppen and Dr. Williams, I do not
> expect any great horde of readers to notice
> it. They will perhaps concentrate, or no,
> they will concentrate, they will coagulate
> their rather gelatinous attention on the
> likeness.
>
> —Ezra Pound, Preface to
> *Discrete Series* (1934)[1]

Pound was quite right. From the beginning, the "likeness" between Williams and Oppen has been accepted as axiomatic; Williams himself, for that matter, introduced *Discrete Series* to the audience of *Poetry* magazine in a review that devoted more space to "our" Objectivist aims than to Oppen's poems, praising the latter rather off-handedly for their use of "plain words" and their "metric . . . taken from speech."[2]

Oppen himself has regularly protested to the contrary. In a 1968 interview, he tells L. S. Dembo,

> . . . some people think I resemble Williams and it seems to me that the opposite is true. Pound unfortunately defended me against the possible charge of resembling him in the original preface to *Discrete Series*. The fact has always haunted me. At any rate, my attitudes are opposite those of Williams. Certainly one would have needed a great deal more courage without his example, to begin to find a way to write. He was invaluable and many of his poems are beautiful, though I've always had reservations about *Paterson*.[3]

1. (New York: Objectivist Press, 1934), p. v; rpt. *Paideuma*, 10 (Spring 1981): *Special Issue: George Oppen*, ed. Burton Hatlen, p. 13.
2. "The New Poetical Economy," *Poetry*, 44 (July 1934), 224.
3. L. S. Dembo, "George Oppen" (interview conducted on 25 April 1968), *Contemporary Literature*, 10 (Spring 1969), 159-77. Subsequently cited as *CL*.

When Dembo remonstrates, "I was under the impression that one
of the basic themes of *Paterson*, 'No ideas but in things,' would
appeal to you," Oppen replies,

> I have always wondered whether that expression didn't apply to
> the construction of meaning in a poem—not necessarily that there
> are out there no ideas but in things, but rather that there would
> be in the poem no ideas but those which could be expressed
> through the description of things. I took it that he meant the
> latter. . . .

(CL, p. 170)

Oppen's desire to separate himself from what he takes to be
Williams' Imagist aesthetic is not just a case of the Anxiety of
Influence, the need to dissociate oneself from the threatening
Precursor. For although his poems may look on the page like
Williams' lyrics—minimalist, jagged, free verse units, surrounded
by much white space—Oppen's language, his syntax, and especially
his prosody are really quite different. For one thing, the stress on
"plain words" and a "metric taken from speech," attributed to
Oppen by Williams, the faith that, as Williams puts it, "The pro-
nunciation as spoken must make [the poet's] line,"[4] is one that
Oppen emphatically rejects. "I don't subscribe," he tells Dembo,
"to any of the theories that poetry should simply reproduce
common speech and so on" (*CL*, p. 167). On the contrary, "I
learned from Louis [Zukofsky], as against the romanticism or
even the quaintness of the imagist position, the necessity for
forming a poem properly, for achieving form" (*CL*, p. 160).
Which is to say that the making of a poem inevitably involves artifice. In a "Statement on Prosody" made in a recent interview,
Oppen says,

> I try one word and another word, reverse the sequence, alter the
> line-endings, a hundred, two hundred rewritings, revisions—This
> is called prosody: how to write a poem. Or rather how to write
> *that* poem.[5]

And again, "every *and* and *but* must be revelatory—a music. We
must think what is being asserted in the 'little' words." For
"primarily and above all, and note by note, the prosody carries

---

4. For a good summary of Williams' view of the relation of poetry to actual speech, see
Mike Weaver, *William Carlos Williams: The American Background* (Cambridge: Cam-
bridge University Press, 1971), pp. 78-84. As early as 1913, Williams sent an essay called
"Speech Rhythms" to Harriet Monroe for publication in *Poetry*, but, according to
Weaver, she found it incomprehensible. See also "The Poem as a Field of Action," *The
Selected Essays of William Carlos Williams* (New York: Random House, 1954), p. 290.
5. Reinhold Schieffer, "Interview with George Oppen conducted on 1 May 1975."
Unpub. MS, Archive of New Poetry, University of California at San Diego, n.p. Quoted
by permission of Michael Davidson, Director of the Archive for New Poetry. Subse-
quently cited as "Schieffer interview."

the relation of things and the sequence." Prosody is "the instant of meaning, the achievement of meaning and *presence*, the sequence of disclosure which comes from everywhere" (Schieffer interview, n.p.). And, in articulating that *sequence of disclosure*, nothing is more important than the decision where to break the line:

> . . . I do believe in a form in which there is a sense of the whole line, not just its ending. Then there's the sense of the relation between lines, the relation in their length; there is a sense of the relation of the speed, of the alterations and momentum of the poem, the feeling when it's done that this has been rounded. I think that probably a lot of the worst of modern poetry . . . uses the line-ending simply as the ending of a line, a kind of syncopation or punctuation. It's a kind of formlessness that lacks any sense of line measure.
>
> The meaning of a poem is in the cadences and the shape of the lines and the pulse of the thought which is given by those lines. The meaning of many lines will be changed . . . if one changes the line ending.
>
> (*CL*, p. 167)

Or, to put it another way, "The line-break is just as much a part of the language as the period, comma, or parenthesis, and it shows that there are things that can only be said as poetry."[6] In this context, "syntax" refers to "those connections which can't be dealt with outside the poem but that should take on substantial meaning within it" (*Montemora*, p. 198).

To compare Oppen's line divisions and syntactic patterns to those of Williams is to learn a great deal about the fuzziness of the Objectivist label. Here is Williams' "Nantucket," which first appeared in *Poems 1921-31*, published by George Oppen's Objectivist Press in 1934.

> Flowers through the window
> lavender and yellow
>
> changed by white curtains—
> Smell of cleanliness—
>
> Sunshine of late afternoon—
> On the glass tray
>
> a glass pitcher, the tumbler
> turned down, by which

---

6. Kevin Power, "An Interview with George and Mary Oppen, *Montemora*, 4 (1978), 195. Subsequently cited as *Montemora*.

a key is lying—And the
immaculate white bed[7]

Both rhythmically and visually, "Nantucket" is characterized by stability of pattern. Despite a somewhat variable syllable count (6-6; 5-5; 7-4; 7-4; 7-6), each of the five couplets contains a three-stress followed by a two-stress line, the exception being line 10 which has three primary and one secondary stress—"immáculàte whĭte bĕd"—and which therefore provides at least a degree of closure. The first couplet, for that matter, is made up of two identical prosodic units:

$$\diagup x \quad \diagup x \quad \diagup x$$
$$\diagup x \quad \diagup x \quad \diagup x$$

with the final words linked by rhyming feminine endings.

In the first half of the poem, the line breaks coincide with phrasal units, culminating in "Smell of cleanliness" and "Sunshine of late afternoon." But in the second half, the movement accelerates: cuts now come between noun and verb or between article and noun, as words in final position reach out for completion: "On the glass tray→," "by which→," "the tumbler →," "And the →." In Williams, says Hillis Miller, "the word reaches out with all its strength towards the other words which are for the moment absent. Conjunctions, prepositions, adjectives, when they come at the end of a line, assume an expressive energy as arrows of force reaching towards the other words."[8]

In reading "Nantucket," we are propelled forward by precisely such "arrows of force," as the camera eye of the poem pans from outside ("flowers through the window") to inside by means of the "white curtains" that connect the two, coming to rest on what we might call the still-life of the "glass tray," with its "glass pitcher, the tumbler/turned down, by which/a key is lying." This last clause contains the first indicative verb in the poem: indeed, the key is the poetic point of focus, and it leads, hesitantly but tantalizingly, to "the/immaculate white bed." Thus, although the poem can be read as no more than a charming verbal painting of an interior, of one of those simple and hence delightful rooms in which one spends a Nantucket holiday, it also has Williams'

7. *The Collected Earlier Poems of William Carlos Williams* (New York: New Directions, 1951), p. 348. Subsequently cited as *CEP*. For publication dates and information, see Emily Mitchell Wallace, *A Bibliography of William Carlos Williams* (Middletown, Conn.: Wesleyan University Press, 1968).
8. *Poets of Reality: Six Twentieth-Century Writers* (1965; rpt. New York: Atheneum, 1969), pp. 299-300. Subsequently cited as "Miller."

characteristic erotic overtones. In a neighboring poem, we are presented with "Gay Wallpaper" that bears "cerulean shapes/laid regularly round" and a "basket floating/standing in the horns of blue" (*CEP*, p. 345). "Nantucket" begins with the word "flowers" and ends with the word "bed." Perhaps the white bed won't, after all, remain "immaculate," especially with that key so near by. The erotic tension of the ending is, in any case, heightened by the line break after "And the" and the increasingly choppy rhythm:

x /   x / x //   x x

x / x   // / /

One would think that a poem like "Nantucket" would answer perfectly to Oppen's own demand for a "prosody that carries the relation of things and sequence." "The little words I love so much"[9]—surely we find them in "Nantucket" or in a related poem of the thirties like "Between Walls":

> the back wings
> of the
>
> hospital where
> nothing
>
> will grow lie
> cinders
>
> in which shine
> the broken
>
> pieces of a green
> bottle
>
>   (*CEP*, p. 343)

Yet the scrupulous bareness of these poems is oddly different from Oppen's own kind of minimalism. Here is a poem from *Discrete Series*, published the same year as "Nantucket":

> She lies, hip high,
> On a flat bed
> While the after-
> Sun passes.
>
> Plant, I breathe——
>   O Clearly,
> Eyes legs arms hands fingers,
> Simple legs in silk.[10]

9. See *Montemora*, pp. 198 and 203. The point is also made in the Dembo interview (*CL*, 1968) and the Schieffer interview (1975).
10. George Oppen, *Collected Poems* (New York: New Directions, 1975), p. 9. Subsequently cited as *CP*. Because the *CP* obscures the original divisions between poems, I

Perhaps the first thing that strikes us as we read this unnamed poem is that Oppen's bedroom scene is much more disjointed than Williams'. For although Williams' lines are often fragmentary bits of incomplete grammar ("turned down, by which"; "of the"; "will grow lie"; "the broken"), the syntax itself, overriding line units, is perfectly straightforward. "Nantucket" is framed as a simple catalogue of noun phrases, into which a single clause is inserted in the ninth line: "by which/a key is lying." We can read the poem as a list:

> Flowers through the window . . .
> Smell of cleanliness . . .
> Sunshine of late afternoon . . .
> On the glass tray a glass pitcher . . .
> And the immaculate white bed

Again, "Between Walls" is, despite the fragmentation of its line units, a complete sentence. We need only supply the word "of" at the beginning of the poem in order to read it as follows: "Between walls of the back wings of the hospital where nothing will grow, lie cinders in which shine the broken pieces of a green bottle." To destroy Williams' lineation in this way is, of course, to make a travesty of his poem;[11] I merely want to point out that "Between Walls" has a definite forward movement, a straight propulsion. Hillis Miller writes:

> When nothing remains but the bits of glass and the poet fixes these with his full attention, the presentness of things present becomes a revelation of that fugitive radiance which all things hide. The poem means, [Williams] says, "That in a waste of cinders loveliness, in the form of color, stands up alive" [*Selected Letters*]. In the same way words, cut off from past and future,

---

cite the original text (New York: Objectivist Press, 1934), subsequently noted as *DS*, as well. "She lies, hip high" is found on *DS*, p. 21.

11. The definitive statement on the function of lineation in Williams is made by Hugh Kenner in his discussion of "The Red Wheelbarrow" in *A Homemade World* (New York: Alfred A. Knopf, 1975), p. 60:

> . . . art lifts the saying out of the zone of things said. For try an experiment. Try to imagine an occasion for this sentence to be said:
>
> > So much depends upon a red wheelbarrow glazed with rainwater beside the white chickens.
>
> Try it over in any voice you like: it is impossible. It could only be the gush of an arty female on a tour of Farmer Brown's barnyard. . . . Not only is what the sentence says banal, if you heard someone say it you'd wince. But hammered on the typewriter into a *thing made*, and this without displaying a single word typographically, the sixteen words exist in a different zone altogether.

Precisely, but this is not what Oppen's lineation does. In his case, the words are lifted, not out of "the zone of things said," but, so to speak, out of the poet's imagination, for his phrases and clauses are often non-grammatical.

and from all preformed literary tradition, are freed to reveal their innate linguistic energy as nodes of power in a verbal field.

(Miller, p. 346)

But what is the "revelation" that "all things hide" in Oppen's gnomic poem? Here lineation is not, as in Williams, a release of the "innate linguistic energy" of words, a removal of those words from their usual contexts so as to create new relationships between them. Rather, in *Discrete Series*, line division is, so to speak, the meaning of each poem. For try to transpose the eight lines of "She lies, hip high" as prose and see what happens:

> She lies, hip high, on a flat bed while the after-sun passes. Plant, I breathe—. O Clearly, eyes legs arms hands fingers, simple legs in silk.

It makes no sense: "Plant, I breathe—" and "O Clearly" follow neither from what comes before nor relate, in any reasonable way, to "Eyes legs arms. . . ." Indeed, when we try to define what is happening in Oppen's poem, we find no reliable guide-posts. "She lies, hip high/On a flat bed"—a woman in labor, perhaps, with "after-Sun" being some kind of play on "after-birth." But the poet's response to this woman (his wife, Mary Oppen) is so sexual ("Plant, I breathe—"), he is so interested in enumerating the parts of her body (hip, eyes, legs, arms, hands, fingers), that it seems more plausible to read the poem as describing a love scene: "She lies, hip high/On a flat bed"—a man is about to enter a woman. It is perhaps a late, lazy afternoon, the "after-/Sun" that "passes" referring to twilight. "O Clearly" the speaker is full of want, and yet the last line presents a puzzle. "Simple legs in silk"—the wearing of stockings—makes one wonder if the poet is, after all, describing an afternoon's love making or whether he is simply observing the object of his desire from a distance, taking pleasure in her movements. Perhaps he has just been with her; perhaps he is going to be. There is no way to be sure, and the exclamation "O Clearly," withheld as it is from the left margin and floating in space, functions as a false lead.

Now let us see what role sound structure plays. "She lies, hip high" is, strictly speaking, written in free verse, the syllable count being 4, 4, 4, 3 in the first stanza; 3, 3, 6, 5 in the second, and no two lines having precisely the same pattern of stresses. At the same time, the first stanza looks like a square and its qualitative sound features create a densely interwoven system of recurrences:

> She lies, hip high,

Four monosyllables with two punctuation breaks, the fourth word chiming with the second (assonance of long i's) as well as with the third (alliteration of h's). A phonemic transcription[12] of the line gives us:

šiy layz ‖ hip hay ‖

What is startling is the way the poem now modulates these initial sounds. The following phonemes are foregrounded:

/iy/ glide:	breathe—clearly
/ay/ glide:	lies—high—while—I
high front vowel (/i/):	hip—fingers—simple— in—silk
lateral (/l/):	lies—flat—Plant—clearly —legs—simple—legs— silk
voiceless spirant (/z/):	sun—passes—simple—silk
voiced spirant in final position (/z/):	lies—passes—eyes—legs— arms—hands—fingers —legs

Sometimes more than one kind of sound repetition is involved: thus "eyes" rhymes with "lies"; there is consonance in "lies" / "legs," chiasmus in "lies" / "while," and so on.

When the recurrence of sound is so pervasive, one looks for places where the sounds don't chime. The final word of the poem, the word that gives an odd perspective to the whole "love scene," is "silk," which contains the only instance in the poem of the phoneme /k/. Again, Oppen's first word, "She," contains the only instance of /š/ and the "O Clearly" of line 6, the only instance of /ow/. When we look at these isolated instances against the larger structure of recurrence, we discover a kind of subtext that conveys

---

12. The notation used is based on George L. Trager and Henry Lee Smith, Jr., *An Out-line of English Structure* (Washington: American Council of Learned Societies, 1957). Trager and Smith use the following stress marks: primary / ⁄ /, secondary / ⋏ /, tertiary / ⋱ /, and weak / ∪ /. In this essay I don't mark tertiary stresses and I use / x / rather than / ∪ / for weak stress because it can be typed. The notation / ‖ / designates plus juncture or pause—in conventional metrics, the caesura. I also use conventional metrical terms like "amphibrac" where relevant. The Trager and Smith terminology for the phonemic transcription of vowel and consonant sounds is widely accepted: see, for example, H. A. Gleason, *An Introduction to Descriptive Linguistics* (New York: Holt, Rinehart and Winston, 1961).

the urgency of the poet's desire: "She—O—silk." The "little words" that Oppen loves so much—a vocabulary that looks like Basic English but that in fact deviates sharply from the inflections of common speech that Williams advocated—are welded into a tensile verbal structure, a carefully planned suspension system. We can see now what the poet means when he says, "I try one word and another word, reverse the sequence, alter the line-endings. . . This is called prosody: how to write a poem. Or rather how to write *that* poem." "She lies, hip high" is purposely set up as a structure of possible contradictions: its presentation of desire is arresting precisely because we don't know whether it has been or will be satisfied. Or even if it wants to be.

From the beginning, then, Oppen has displayed a penchant for what we might call a poetic of "discrete series." As he explains the term to L. S. Dembo,

> A pure mathematical series would be one in which each term is derived from the preceding term by a rule. A discrete series is a series of terms each of which is empirically derived, each one of which is empirically true. And this is the reason for the fragmentary character of those poems. I was attempting to construct a meaning by empirical statements, by imagist statements.
>
> (CL, p. 161)

Here the term "imagist" is misleading, for the point about a poem like "She lies, hip high" is precisely that the poem does not proceed, as do Williams' "Nantucket" or "Between Walls," from image to related image. Rather, Oppen lays out, side by side, a "discrete series" of empirical statements, of fragments that seem unrelated and that tend to be conceptual rather than sensuous:

> From this distance thinking toward you,
> Time is recession
>
> Movement of no import
> Not encountering you . . .
>
> (DS, p. 26; CP, p. 10)

The very titles of Oppen's volumes—*The Materials, This in Which, Of Being Numerous, Primitive*—express a concern for cognition: the poem, Oppen implies, is the only way to reconcile one's disparate and contradictory perceptions of the external world, for here the recurrence of sound can mitigate against the undecidability of experience. Consider another love poem in *Discrete Series*:

> Near your eyes— —
> Love at the pelvis
> Reaches the generic, gratuitous
>   (Your eyes like snail-tracks)

> Parallel emotions,
> We slide in separate hard grooves
> Bowstrings to bent loins,
>   Self moving
> Moon, mid-air.

                       (*DS*, p. 28; *CP*, p. 11)

Here the fragmentary prepositional and noun phrases that make up most of the nine lines are suspended both phonically and visually, and yet forms of recurrence, unobtrusive as they seem, play a central role. Stress count, for example, brings items together that syllable count would distinguish. Thus "Near your eyes" (3 syllables) and "Love at the pelvis" (5 syllables) have corresponding stress patterns:

$$\diagup \ \text{x} \ \diagup$$
$$\diagup \ \text{x} \ \ \text{x} \diagup \ \text{x}$$

and even the long third line (10 syllables) has only three primary stresses:

$$\diagup \ \text{x} \ \Vert \ \ \text{x} \ \ \text{x} \diagup \text{x} \ \Vert \ \ \text{x} \diagup \text{x} \ \ \text{x}$$

"the generic" repeating the rhythm of "at the pelvis." Again, the first line of the second stanza, "Parallel emotions," echoes the first line of the poem, repeating the amphimac (/ x /) and adding its mirror image in the form of an amphibrac (x / x). In the last three lines, the recurrence of what we might call "envelope" groups (/ x / /) and (/ /) balanced by the falling rhythm of the enclosed line (/ / x) provides a sense of arrest and coalescence, a coalescence emphasized by the marked alliteration of b's and m's, the consonance of "strings"/"loins," and the assonance of "bent"/ "Self," the two words forming a column. The final words, "moving" and "moon" nearly rhyme, "mid-air" breaking up this chiming ever so slightly.

Just as the relationship among the elements along the speech chain is thus repeated—but not quite—in the course of the poem, so the semantic elements involve both recurrence and suspension. "Near your eyes," to begin with, would seem to go with "Love," but "Love at the pelvis" is hardly a very pretty image, despite the near-rhyme of "Love" and "pelvis." What seems to be a suspended noun phrase, "Love at the pelvis," now turns out to lead to a complete sentence unit, but a sentence whose meaning is indeterminate. Love "Reaches the generic," the root, that which makes the woman what she really is. But why is the "generic" "gratuitous"? The two words, joined as they are by the alliteration of g's and r's—an alliteration that makes the line turn back upon itself to "Reaches"—are a puzzling pair. Is the generic gratuitous because freely given? Obtained without charge? For no apparent cause? Or given without receiving any return value? We cannot tell. We know only that the poet somehow hangs back, perceiving his beloved's eyes quite unromantically as "snail-tracks"—which is to say that her eyes follow his movements very slowly. But "snail-tracks" also looks ahead to the "separate hard grooves" of line 7, the "parallel" and hence never meeting "emotions" of the two lovers.

Is theirs then a failed love act? One might say yes and no. "Bowstrings to bent loins" suggests close and loving conjunction: the playing upon each other's instrument. In this context, "Self moving" may refer to the moment of orgasm, but the word "Self" also suggests separation, possibly isolation. The final line, "Moon, mid-air" does not dispel the mystery. The reference may be to the ejaculation of seed. But also, perhaps more humbly, to a mere shift in position of one or the other lover. Does the woman, like her counterpart in "She lies, hip high," thrust her legs into "mid-air"? Is she the moon? Or is the moon literally shining?

"The meaning of a poem," says Oppen, "is in the cadences and the shape of the lines." Certainly in "Near your eyes" each line break acquires meaning, emphasizing a "discrete series" of emotions and perceptions that could not be stated in any other way. Making love, the poem implies, is at once an act of conjunction and separation. Love "Reaches the generic"—"Bowstrings to bent loins"—yet somehow the lovers' emotions remain parallel, a "sliding" in "separate hard grooves" like the "snail-tracks" of the woman's eyes. Just so, on the sound level, there is a rhythmic recurrence, a coming together that is consistently offset by the "separate hard grooves" of the unequal line lengths, the variation of syllable count, the move away from the left margin as the poet discovers the "Self moving." "Prosody," as Oppen says, "is the achievement of . . . *presence*, the sequence of disclosure that comes from everywhere."

Such "achievement of presence" often depends upon parody, the sly undermining of a traditional topos:

> Her ankles are watches
> (Her arm-pits are causeways for water)
>
> When she steps
> She walks on a sphere
>
> Walks on the carpet, dressing.
> Brushing her hair

> Her movement accustomed, abstracted,
> Declares this morning a woman's
> "My hair, scalp——"
>
>   (*DS*, p. 11; *CP*, p. 5)

Here Oppen begins with a series of extravagant conceits: his wife, evidently emerging from the shower or bath in what is her morning ritual, is quite literally a kind of wet dream; the flow of her body (arm pits become "causeways for water" and ankles tick as she moves) meets the flow of his desire so that her mere footsteps across the room have the grace of a goddess "walk [ing] on a sphere." It is the sort of metaphoric indulgence Williams scorned, believing, as he did, that "the coining of similes is a pastime of very low order,"[13] that instead the poet's attention should attach itself to the forms of nature themselves—a young sycamore, a lily, a cat climbing over the top of a jamcloset—so as to extract their particularity, their unique erotic force. Indeed, reading the first half of Oppen's poem, one thinks of Yeats's tributes to Maud Gonne:

> For she had fiery blood
> When I was young
> And trod so sweetly proud
> As 'twere upon a cloud . . .[14]

But unlike Yeats, Oppen can't hold such a thought for more than a moment; he knows that women don't really walk on spheres, that in fact his wife "Walks on the carpet, dressing./Brushing her hair." And now something happens. Once dressed, his wife has lost the capacity for metaphoric transformation; the fanciful conceits of the opening couplet give way to hard facts:

> Her movement accustomed, abstracted,
> Declares this morning a woman's
> "My hair, scalp——"

Here the word "scalp" functions rather as does "silk" in "She lies, hip high." The first three couplets have stressed the recurrence of sounds (*watches—water—walks*; *ankles—watches—arm-pits—steps—walks*; *dressing—brushing*; *sphere—hair*); what is ironically "accustomed" turns out to be the dissonance of the tercet: the nine syllables of line 7 yield only three stresses, arranged, so to speak, in clumps:

$$x \; \diagup \; x \quad \| \quad x \; \diagup \; x \quad \| \quad x \; \diagup \; x$$

13. "Prologue," *Kora in Hell: Improvisations* (1920), in *Imaginations* (New York: New Directions, 1970), p. 18.
14. *The Collected Poems of W. B. Yeats* (New York: Macmillan, 1950), p. 88.

and the truncated last line comes down heavily on the hard voiceless stop /p/ of "scalp." It is not the first /p/ in the poem, but the others ("arm-pits," "steps") are not in final position, and "scalp" also contains a second voiceless stop /k/ following a spirant. The effect is harsh and it is meant to be. What was once flowing (armpits as causeways for water) gives way to a substance that is hard and possibly scaly: we prefer the scalp to be concealed by hair. Nor do we know what the woman, who speaks for the first time in the last abbreviated line of the poem, is about to say about her "scalp." We only know that the liquid flow of desire is, at least for the moment, suspended.

Oppen's best poems regularly display this curious tension between the image of desire and the hard fact, between metrical and phonemic recurrence and a curious disruptiveness. Here is a later poem called "A Theological Definition":

> A small room, the varnished floor
> Making an L around the bed,
>
> What is or is true as
> Happiness
>
> Windows opening on the sea,
> The green painted railings of the balcony
> Against the rock, the bushes and the sea running[15]

Thematically, this poem recalls Williams' "Nantucket"; indeed, Williams might have written the first couplet with its precise and loving description of the L-shaped varnished floor surrounding the bed. Again, the reference to the "green painted railings of the balcony" in the tercet bring to mind such Williams poems as "The Poor," with its reference to the "cast iron balcony/ with panels showing oak branches/in full leaf" (*CEP*, p. 415).

But the middle couplet, which shifts abruptly from image to concept, reflects Oppen's own personal conviction that the "bare image," as Stevens called it, is not enough. The syntax of the passage is impossible to unravel because the "or" is equivocal: Oppen may be saying that "What is" (the phenomenology of perception) is the only truth since it can give us happiness. Or again, the other way around: "What is" (the delightful little room with its varnished floor and ocean view) is just an appearance but since it brings us happiness we accept it as "true." However we take these words, they clearly place the title of the poem in an ironic perspective: the only theological definition Oppen can give us is that there is none. The mono-syllabic line "What is or is true as," with its

---

15. It appeared in *Of Being Numerous* (1968). See *CP*, p. 197.

function words and auxiliaries, suggests that knowledge comes
only by fits and starts, and that, in any case, words like "true" and
"happiness" are not sufficiently delimited. This suggestion is
borne out by the last line of the poem, which is a pseudo-alexan-
drine, its twelve syllables containing no more than five primary
stresses, and the dying fall of its feminine ending ("running"),
gently mocking the preceding rhyme, "sea"/"balcony."

Oppen is not always able to sustain a syntax in which the
"connections which can't be dealt with outside the poem . . . take
on substantial meaning within it." "The Forms of Love," which
appeared in *This In Which* (1965), is one of his better known
poems, but I don't think it can match the formal achievement of
the love lyrics in *Discrete Series*:

> Parked in the fields
> All night
> So many years ago,
> We saw
> A lake beside us
> When the moon rose.
> I remember
>
> Leaving that ancient car
> Together. I remember
> Standing in the white grass
> Beside it. We groped
> Our way together
> Downhill in the bright
> Incredible light
>
> Beginning to wonder
> Whether it could be lake
> Or fog
> We saw, our heads
> Ringing under the stars we walked
> To where it would have wet our feet
> Had it been water

(CP, p. 86)

Questioned by L. S. Dembo as to the meaning of this poem,
Oppen replies:

> The car is detached from emotion, from use, from necessity—
> from everything except the most unconscionable of the emotions.
> And that lake which appears in the night of love seemed to me
> to be quite real even though it was actually fog.

(CL, p. 168)

And when Dembo suggests: "But only two lovers—because of their
heightened state of mind or heightened sensitivity—would have

thought that the fog was a lake," that "the vision was actually a form of love," Oppen agrees.

It is a lovely poem but after a decade of Deep Image and Confessional poetry, we are perhaps inured to such lyrics of "heightened sensitivity," lyrics in which "vision" becomes "a form of love" somewhat too easily. Of the first stanza of "The Forms of Love," one might say what Oppen said in criticism of much contemporary poetry: "the line ending [is used] simply as the ending of a line, a kind of syncopation or punctuation" (*CL*, p. 167). "Parked in the fields/All night/So many years ago"—these lines merely continue, phrases like "So many years ago" and the repetitive "I remember" acting as little more than padding. "We groped/Our way together/Downhill"—any number of poets might have written those lines. Only in the last stanza does Oppen's characteristic rhythm of suspension return. "We saw," for example, refers back to the fog, but the lineation also makes us read it as "We saw our heads . . ." By the time we reach the penultimate line:

> to where it would have wet our feet

with its eight hesitant monosyllables, at once disjointed and yet united by the repeated chiming of w's and t's, we know we are back in Oppen country.

In a five-part poem called "Image of the Engine," that appears in *The Materials* of 1962, we find these lines:

> *Also he has set the world*
> *In their hearts.* From lumps, chunks.
>
> (*CP*, p. 21)

I can think of no better description of Oppen's characteristic prosody, his way of proceeding through a given poetic structure. If Williams' is a metric of action, the creation of a field of force in which the presence of the moment is made manifest, Oppen's "discrete series" of lines remains disjunctive, discriminatory, abrupt—a movement of fits and starts, "From lumps, chunks." Ellipsis, riddle, radical condensation, abstraction, equivocal syntax, and the fragmentation of semantic units—all these pull against the coalescence of sound, often extremely delicate, and the hammering of words into the firm structure of the line. Oppen wants us to pause on every word, to try to understand how and why just these words could possibly coexist in the same text, so far removed are his "connections" from those of ordinary discourse. The text itself is thus called into question even as the poet *"sets the world/In our hearts."*

MICHAEL ANDRÉ BERNSTEIN

RETICENCE AND RHETORICS:
THE POETRY OF GEORGE OPPEN

Mais Racine? . . . Lequel des deux prefereriez vous? ou qu'il eut
été un bon homme . . . bon mari, bon pere, bon oncle, bon
voisin, honnete commerçant, mais rien de plus; ou qu'il eut été
fourbe, traitre, ambitieux, envieux, mechant; mais auteur d'*Andromaque*, de *Britannicus*, d'*Iphigenie*, de *Phedre*, d'*Athalie*.[1]

So entirely has Diderot's preference become part of our pre-judg-
ment about how to engage a work of art properly that it may almost stand as a kind of antonomasia for all the diverse arguments
designed to secure the aesthetic as a category independent of other
modes of cognition and other kinds of response. But in so unre-
flecting an acceptance of this division, salutary, perhaps even indispensable, though it undoubtedly is, we risk forgetting the whole
complex network of historical forces within which the argument
was initially articulated and the pressures that remain to contest
it today. Still, to reopen the question, even in a discussion of
George Oppen, is to risk both misunderstanding and a certain embarrassment. After all, no one can have much confidence in a criticism presumptuous enough to include, as one of its central exhib-
its, the reader's (inevitably distorted and partial) sense of an artist's
"exemplary conduct" or "personal integrity." Even the more
fashionable decision to limit the commentary to impulses and
attitudes expressed purely within the work itself, categorically
excluding any moralizing about the biography of its creator, does
not provide a more secure foundation. Not only would this

---

1. Denis Diderot, *Le Neveu De Rameau*, ed. Jean Fabre (Genève: Librairie Droz, 1963),
pp. 11-12. ("But what about Racine? Which of the two would you prefer? That he
would have been a good man, a good husband, good father, good uncle, good neighbour,
trustworthy businessman, but nothing more; or that he would have been a swindler, a
traitor, a careerist, envious and evil, but the author of *Andromaque, Britannicus, Iphi-
génie, Phèdre*, and *Athalie*?) The peculiarities of spelling and accentuation in the French
are those of Diderot himself as established in Fabre's brilliant edition of *Le Neveu*.

criticism still find itself subject to the same risks of arbitrariness, cultural blindness, etc., but (1) strictly speaking, it would have to be mute in the face of any art that does not articulate a recognizable ethics, and (2) it would have no means, short of a blanket condemnation or facile recuperation, to confront texts which deliberately assault our habitual assumptions about human motivation and desires (e.g., writers as diverse as Flaubert, Céline, Beckett, et. al., to say nothing of De Sade or William Burroughs).

And yet the impulse remains. Rightly so, as well, for our use of words like "sincerity" and "honesty" is not always a mere recitation of cant phrases best set aside when we talk seriously about art. Rather, these words define one kind of response, a reaction to something vital in an artist's work which it is simply fatuous to ignore.

Because the poetry of George Oppen raises all these issues with a quiet, unhectoring insistence unrivaled by any of his living peers except Basil Bunting, I can think of no honest way to avoid them here. And if I spoke earlier about a certain embarrassment, it is because I think the very language of modern criticism, for all its theoretical subtlety, has shown itself remarkably impoverished at registering the authority of a work compelling precisely because of its commitment to what one can only call the "common decencies" of a shared discourse and world. It is these very words, "sincerity," "honesty," and "clarity" that recur throughout Oppen's famous 1968 interview, always enunciated in consort with the strictest notion of the poem as an articulated, crafted ("objective," if you will) structure:

> What I felt I was doing was beginning from imagism as a position of honesty. The first question at that time in poetry was simply the question of honesty, of sincerity. But I learned from Louis [Zukofsky], as against the romanticism or even the quaintness of the imagist position, the necessity for forming a poem properly, for achieving form. That's what "objectivist" really means.[2]

Or, in the words of one of his poems from the collection *Of Being Numerous* (1968):

> Clarity, clarity, surely clarity is the most beautiful
>   thing in the world,
> A limited, limiting clarity
>
> I have not and never did have any motive of poetry
> But to achieve clarity[3]

---

2. George Oppen Interview in *Contemporary Literature*, 10:2 (Spring, 1969), 159-177. The passage quoted is on p. 160.
3. George Oppen, *The Collected Poems of George Oppen* (New York: New Directions, 1975), p. 185. All references are to this edition and are acknowledged directly after the quotation in the text as *CP*.

In a sense, the issue in both of these quotations is one of decorum in its full, classical sense: an obligation to find the particular words, tones, rhythms and shapes most suitable to the subject matter at hand. The best criticism of Oppen somehow must also show, in its own articulation, the imprint of such a decorum. Hence the exact justice of Hugh Kenner's comment about Oppen's many years of political exile and poetic silence: "Hugh Kenner interrupted my explanation to him of these years by saying, 'In brief, it took twenty-five years to write the next poem.' Which is the way to say it."[4]

Decorum may seem like an unusual term to apply to the work of a poet famous initially for having emerged as the printer of such iconoclastic volumes as Pound's *ABC of Reading* and *An "Objectivists" Anthology*, and as the author of the slim but technically adventurous collection, *Discrete Series* (1934). But neither this beginning, at the vanguard of experimental verse in the early 1930s, nor the subsequent decision to set aside his art for immediate political and social imperatives, qualifies the impression that Oppen has always written—and acted—out of a scrupulous respect for the tact his diverse tasks enjoined. Thus, although he was ready to make immense personal renunciations for his politics, he refused to write the kind of polemical, socialist poetry that filled American literary journals throughout the Depression. As he explained years later,

> I didn't believe in political poetry or poetry as being politically efficacious. I don't even believe in the honesty of a man saying, "Well, I'm a poet and I will make my contribution to the cause by writing poems about it." . . . If you decide to do something politically, you do something that has political efficacy. And if you decide to write poetry, then you write poetry, not something that you hope, or can deceive yourself into believing, can save people who are suffering.[5]

In many ways this is an admirably lucid realization, but it is also more problematical than Oppen's admirers have been ready to acknowledge, and its ambiguity is centrally linked to the sustaining tensions at the core of the poetry itself. I doubt that Oppen means here exactly what W.H. Auden did in writing, "For poetry makes nothing happen" ("In Memory of W.B. Yeats"). Clearly our century alone has provided numerous examples of verse which are both politically committed and aesthetically satisfying (Pound, Brecht, Neruda, Mayakovsky, to name only some obvious examples). Instead, it seems to me that Oppen is, at least in part, speaking out of a recognition that his own individual skill

---

4. Oppen Interview, *op. cit.*, p. 174.
5. Oppen Interview, *op. cit.*, p. 174.

as an artist depends upon establishing a poetic voice that renounces the conclusive, the unwavering certainties any immediately exhortative verse must be able to summon. In fact, much of Oppen's writing is balanced within a seemingly contradictory epistemology whose distinct impulses provide the poem with its characteristic energy and tone. On the one hand, Oppen is committed to a view of consciousness as inherently inter-subjective, as bound up, from the outset, with the existence of the world and its other inhabitants. The very first poem in *Discrete Series* already announces a decision to see, as sharply as possible, the multiplicity "Of the world, weather-swept, with which/one shares the century" (*CP*, p. 3), and all of the subsequent volumes remain faithful to that first urging. The lures of preciosity or pure self-reflexivity which have, for the past fifty years, compromised a great deal of the best American poetry held no fascination for a writer convinced —and able to state with such calm assurance—that

> The self is no mystery, the mystery is
> That there is something for us to stand on.
>
> We want to be here.
>
> The act of being, the act of being
> More than oneself.
> (*CP*, p. 143)

Because Oppen is certain that "it is the/real//That we confront" ("Route," *CP*, p. 196), rather than some solipsistic "dream," an abiding attentiveness to the physical details of the world, its natural and man-made variety, marks his verse at both the lexical and the thematic level. So well-known is Oppen's reputation as a complex, "experimental" poet that the verse's sheer sensual delight in light and water, in sexuality and landscape, is often overlooked. But his writing is a store-house of gatherings from different domains of experience, ranging in one typical piece from

> And every crevice of the city leaking
> Rubble: concrete, conduit, pipe, a crumbling
> Rubble of our roots

to a vision of

> Earth, water, the tremendous
> Surface, the heart thundering
> Absolute desire.
> (*CP*, p. 21)

On the other hand, balanced against this confidence there tugs an equally strong sense of the limitations in any one man's mind or language, limitations that severely restrict how much of that larger world he can honestly (again, the unavoidable word) grasp. Thus, the superficial paradox of the Marxist poet who has never written a party strophe, and thus, also, the more important paradox of the poet committed to the world beyond his own artistic compatriots announcing with wry dignity

> One imagines himself
> addressing his peers
> I suppose. Surely
> that might be the definition
> of 'seriousness'? I would like,
> as you see,
> to convince
> myself
> that my pleasure in your response
> is not
> plain vanity
> but the pleasure of being heard,
> the pleasure
> of companionship, which seems
> more honorable.
>
> (*CP*, p. 142)

Indeed, many of Oppen's most touching poems enact their openness towards others not by moving such large counters as "class conflict" or "historical inevitability," but rather by commemorating the field of personal loves and friendships that have given shape to his emotional life. The splendid pieces to Mary Oppen— splendid in their gentleness and humanity—seem to me to stand, along with Williams' poems to Flossie and Zukofsky's to Celia, as among the best love poetry American verse has given us in this century:

> To find now depth, not time, since we cannot, but depth
>
> To come out safe,   to end well
>
> We have begun to say good bye
> To each other
> And cannot say it
>
> (*CP*, p. 220)

At the same time, however, I think that it is Oppen's resistance to the rhetoric of assertion, a rhetoric one aspect of his epistemology could easily have encouraged, that enabled him to fashion a new and quite different rhetoric, one which succeeded in making notions like "honesty," "sincerity," and "clarity" not only components of the work's intended effect, but also constituent thematic and stylistic elements of its very structure as an utterance. The "difficulty" of some of Oppen's verse (usually a question of punctuation and transitions rather than of complex imagery) is one

attempt—not always his most convincing—to create this new rhetoric in which language both seeks to engage "Not the symbol but
the scene this pavement leads/To . . ." ("Route," *CP*, p. 192) and
yet stay aware of its status as only the articulation of one man
writing from the particularities of his time and perception.[6]

In 1965, Frank O'Hara perceptively defined one of the principal dangers attendant upon any poetics which seeks to make out
of its very fidelity to a modest, unassertive tone, a new claim to
authority.

> But of course . . . you have another element which is making *con-
> trol* practically the subject matter of the poem. That is your *con-
> trol* of the language, your *control* of the experiences and your
> *control* of your thought. . . . the amazing thing is that where
> they've pared down the diction so that the experience presum-
> ably will come through as strongly as possible, it's the experience
> of their paring it down that comes through more strongly and
> not the experience that is the subject.[7]

Although both Robert Creeley and Denise Levertov, the two poets
to whom O'Hara was referring in the interview, clearly have
managed to rise above such limitations in their best work, there is
all too much evidence that many of their less talented imitators
have not. (The charge also seems to hold more for younger writers
intent upon aping Creeley than for those who have taken Levertov's quite different poetics as a primary model.) Similarly, however, poems by some of George Oppen's disciples reveal a tendency towards the same kind of misdirection of attention that
O'Hara criticized. But in their case, I think one can more readily
indicate just how carelessly they have read their master. For ultimately, the honesty about which I have been writing is not at
all the result of the poet's "paring down" of his diction, nor of his
substituting a virtuoso's "control" for the integrity of his subject.
Oppen's strength has little to do with the creation of any simplistic "anti-poetical" strategy. Rather, it emerges out of a precarious intersection of urges and in the rigorous fidelity to an
epistemology in which one is always both alone and numerous,
confined within one's language and open to the world with which
those words retain an indissoluble bond. Balanced between the
many and the one, the intimate and the panoramic, a rhetoric
and its reticences are simultaneously crafted giving Oppen's

---

6. For a more detailed discussion of the attack upon rhetoric as inherently "anti-poetical," and a defense of the rhetorical element in Pound, Williams, and Olson, see the
author's, *The Tale Of The Tribe: Ezra Pound And The Modern Verse Epic*, Princeton:
Princeton U. Press, 1980, esp. Chapter Ten, "The Old Measure Of Care."
7. Frank O'Hara Interview with Edward Lucie-Smith, in Donald Allen (ed.), *Standing
Still And Walking In New York*, Bolinas: Grey Fox Press, 1975, pp. 3-26. The passage
quoted is from p. 23.

Collected Poems their particular and hard-won "sincerity." And perhaps only someone who has disciplined himself so strenuously within this double duty can, at the end, maintain the tentative, secular decorum of his poetic line and still sustain a tone of celebration:

> We stared at the end
> Into each other's eyes   Where
> She said hushed
>
> Were the adults   We dreamed to each other
> Miracle of the children
> The brilliant children   Miracle
>
> Of their brilliance   Miracle
> of
>
>   *(CP*, p. 229)

HUGH SEIDMAN

"BOY'S ROOM":
A NOTE ON CLARITY AND DETACHMENT

George Oppen's poetry has always been "political," or one might say "moral," in its evocation of the actual against the self-satisfying ego. In "The Building of the Skyscraper," such a task is named:

> There are words that mean nothing
> But there is something to mean.
> Not a declaration which is truth
> But a thing
> Which is. It is the business of the poet
> 'To suffer the things of the world
> And to speak them and himself out.'[1]

Oppen is distinguished from other contemporaries in his commitment to an intensely personal moral vision and yet, paradoxically, by his detachment from the sentimentality of morality through "objective" clarity. He is immediately uncompromising, direct, and totally serious (transcending self-mockery and rhetorical wit), yet he escapes the tendentious.

Consider the small poem, "Boy's Room," from *This In Which:*

> A friend saw the rooms
> Of Keats and Shelley
> At the lake, and saw 'they were just
> Boy's rooms' and was moved
>
> By that. And indeed a poet's room
> Is a boy's room
> And I suppose that women know it.

---

1. George Oppen, *Collected Poems* (New York: New Directions, 1975), p. 131. Hereafter all references to Oppen's poetry will be to this edition, and such citations will be incorporated into the text.

> Perhaps the unbeautiful banker
> Is exciting to a woman, a man
> Not a boy gasping
> For breath over a girl's body.
>
> (*CP*, p. 104)

The rooms of a boy and a poet are alike relative to the implication of the last stanza: if money (and power) defines masculinity, then poets lacking sufficient means do not live as men but in rooms no better than a boy's. Note that Oppen avoids equating boys and poets in favor of relating the objectively verifiable character of their quarters. And, "unbeautiful" occurs both as a precise adjective (whatever beauty is, the banker lacks it) and as an indirect irony on Romantic conceits (poets are beautiful), the "ugliness" of Capitalism, and so on.

Furthermore, even though the use of the boys and the banker has the potential for soap-opera inflation, the tactic of reportage (an element named elsewhere in the poem "Route") saves the speaker from becoming the self-pitying victim of his own judgements; that is, a "friend" is quoted or the speaker appears to merely confirm what we all fear to be true: money makes the sexual world turn. The possible anger or other reaction in the lines " . . . And indeed a poet's room/Is a boy's room" is quickly undercut by the ironic "suppose" and "perhaps." Obviously, only someone who had "suffered" such boyhood (at least imaginatively) could have written "Boy's Room," yet Oppen has taught himself the lesson of self-effacement; and what is done here is done elsewhere. In the remarkable poem "Route"—mentioned above—he speaks directly of those qualities that resist our intrusion:

> We are brothers, we are brothers?—these things are
> composed of a moral substance only if they are untrue. If
> these things are true they are perfectly simple, perfectly
> impenetrable, those primary elements which can only be
> named.
>   —Section 6
>   (*CP*, p. 189)

And in a similar gesture he explicates "clarity":

> Clarity
>
> In the sense of *transparence*,
> I don't mean that much can be explained.
>
> Clarity in the sense of silence.
>   —Section 22, "Of Being Numerous"
>   (*CP*, p. 162)

> Clarity, clarity, surely clarity is the most beautiful
>   thing in the world,
> A limited, limiting clarity
>
> I have not and never did have any motive of poetry
> But to achieve clarity
>   —Section 1, "Route"
>   (*CP*, p. 185)

Still, the poet worries:

> . . . One man could not understand me because I was saying
> simple things; it seemed to him that nothing was being
> said. I was saying: there is a mountain, there is a lake
>   —Section 6, "Route"
>   (*CP*, p. 190)

So the careless might ask—being used to the fireworks of more obvious writers—is such limitation really poetry? Whatever the answer that anyone wishes to make, it is clear that Oppen's discourse thwarts preconceptions, while establishing excellences such as a flawless ear, often memorable line breaks, and an extraordinary intellective complexity via syntax. But finally, as we have noted, it is his reverence for human conduct that is the deep measure of his genius.

Looking at "Boy's Room" again, for example, simple diction is disturbed in line 5 by the enjambed "by that" which rhythmically emphasizes the sympathy of a witness for the state of the rooms, although why he is so touched is not stated. And when "indeed a poet's room/is a boy's room"confirms the condition in the speaker's mind, we are also forced to confront such possibility.

Yet so what? Certainly, we know that money talks, but what is it to us how poets live or die, or with whom bankers sleep? But suddenly, "a boy [is] gasping/for breath over a girl's body" (one assumes that the final two lines are meant as printed—i.e. no comma follows "boy"), and the image seems to come, not from the context of the poem, but from the speaker's own experience— as if his previous judgements reflected, in some way, himself as a "boy" rather than as a man who does the world's sexual and economic work. And who, whether male or female, cannot identify with such a conflict. So that, if the poem is successful, Oppen will have won our empathy for the poets and for the speaker; and, in eleven brief lines through his "isolation of the actual" (Section 27, "Of Being Numerous"), he will have registered a Freudian complex ("boy" versus "banker"), the sexism of patriarchal culture (women are aroused by power rather than by beauty), and the life of the artist.

It is just this kind of empathy, on the part of the poet, that Oppen invokes in "Of Being Numerous":

> I would want to talk of rooms and of what they look out on
> and of basements, the rough walls bearing the marks of the
> forms, the old marks of wood in the concrete, such solitude
> as we know—
>
> and the swept floors. Someone, a workman bearing about
> him, feeling about him that peculiar word like a dishonored
> fatherhood has swept this solitary floor, this profoundly hid-
> den floor—such solitude as we know.
> —Section 27, "Of Being Numerous"
> (*CP*, p. 168)

And the final stanza of Section 27, with its eye on that isolated "workman" (for whom one might read "poet" without embarrassment), enunciates the ultimate striving in all of Oppen's work:

> One must not come to feel that he has a thousand threads
>   in his hands,
> He must somehow see the one thing;
> This is the level of art
> There are other levels
> But there is no other level of art
> (*CP*, p. 168)

ABBY SHAPIRO

BUILDING A PHENOMENOLOGICAL WORLD:
CUBIST TECHNIQUE IN THE POETRY OF GEORGE OPPEN

> 6
>
> Silver as
> The needle's eye
>
> Of the horizon in the noise
> Of their entrance row on row the waves
> Move landward   conviction's
>
> Net of branches
> In the horde of events the sacred swarm avalanche
> Masked in the sunset
>
> Needle after needle more numerous than planets
>
> Or the liquid waves
> In the tide rips
>
> We believe   We believe[1]

What do we do with lines of poetry such as these? How do we proceed to grasp and know, if only momentarily, the becalmed yet elusive world created in George Oppen's poems? Separated from each other, the poem's "objects" seem perfectly ordinary (the horizon, the waves, branches, a sunset, a belief), but the relationships created by their conjunction form a puzzle of entanglements. Attempting to sort out syntax (we find a scarcity of verbs), to discover what each of the many prepositional phrases modifies, we may think that we "have something" only to find ourselves thrown into new "territory" by another preposition or noun or space between words or lines. What, for example, is "silver as the

---

1. George Oppen, from "Some San Francisco Poems," *The Collected Poems of George Oppen* (New York: New Directions, 1975), p. 223. (Hereafter cited as *CP.*)

needle's eye"? The waves? The waves would appear to be "conviction's net of branches," but what is "masked in the sunset"? The "sacred swarm avalanche"? The "horde of events"? "Needle after needle"? The waves? Are some or all of these equivalent? What is the seemingly fervent belief?

The difficulty in these poems would seem to be this: Oppen's is a precisely constructed world, each word in its place, yet often, as in this "San Francisco" poem, a world of ambiguous relationships and a seeming absence of logic. Less "legible" than other poetries, Oppen's seems less "teachable." "An academic poetry? Hardly," Hugh Kenner writes—for Oppen's poems, which come to rest unexpectedly but with great assurance, resist easy diagramming; "wit," "paradox," "irony," even "myth"—these terms the poetry will not tolerate. Rather, for Oppen, "A structure of words, that's the aim, and the meaning is whatever applicability they attract."[2]

Poems with conditional meanings, then; poems which "can be about" or "may be about" something. The world of poems such as these, L. S. Dembo writes, is an existential world, even a phenomenological world, and he suggests that the difficulty in understanding Oppen's poetry, indeed the paradox found within Oppen's work is the following:

> For Oppen, appearance is what is *seen*, and what is seen intensely, as far as the poet is concerned, *is*. This is what Oppen means when he asserts his faith in the reality of the perceived world, while remaining wholly aware that his vision may have significance only to himself.[3]

I wish to examine one of the ways in which Oppen creates this "real" and hence undecipherable world: his use of techniques which strongly resemble those used by the cubist painters, thus, his participation in "collage construction," suggested by Charles Altieri as the basic "mode of relatedness" for Objectivist poetry.[4] I will also examine the way in which these techniques, which have been suggested but not yet fully explored, inform and effect Oppen's phenomenological poetics. Although it would seem that the Cubists did not directly influence Oppen, the similarity between their art and his poetry is in some ways great; the cubist analogy offers us, I think, a way of approaching a poetry which may at times seem too personal to be significant, as well as a way into Oppen's "constructing" and the phenomenological world

---

2. See Hugh Kenner, *A Homemade World* (New York: Alfred A. Knopf, 1975), pp. 173-74, 186.
3. L. S. Dembo, "The Existential World of George Oppen," *Iowa Review*, 3 (Winter 1972), 66.
4. See Charles Altieri, "The Objectivist Tradition," *Chicago Review*, 30 (Winter 1979), 13.

which results. Oppen's early poems (*Discrete Series*, 1934) and latest poems (*Seascape: Needle's Eye*, 1972; *Myth of the Blaze*, 1972-1975) seem to me to be the most "cubist," the poems in *The Materials* (1962), *This in Which* (1965), and *Of Being Numerous* (1968) less so. This paper does not deal with the changes in Oppen's poetry; I wish to suggest that the methods of "construction" discussed here inform Oppen's poetry in varying degrees throughout his work.

In *Art and Illusion*, E. H. Gombrich writes:

> Cubism has sometimes been explained as an extreme attempt in compensation for the shortcomings of one-eyed vision. The picture embodies clues of which we could become aware only through movement or touch. . . . the visible world of our experience is a construct made up of memories of movement, touch, and sight. . . . Where (cubism) succeeds is in countering the transforming effects of an illusionist reading. . . . by the introduction of contrary clues which resist all attempts to apply the test of consistency. Try as we may to see the guitar or jug suggested to us as a three-dimensional object and thereby to transform it, we will always come across a contradiction somewhere which compels us to start afresh. . . . our interpretation can never come to rest and our "imitative faculty" will be kept busy as long as we join in the game.[5]

We perceive the world (and art) via a system Gombrich calls "schema and correction"—that is, by trial and error, or a kind of "twenty questions." When faced with something unfamiliar we immediately begin attempts to categorize according to familiar concepts, for "without some starting point," some initial schema, we could never get hold of the "flux of experience." We also perceive and make sense out of the chaos of the world's sensations in terms of relationships between colors and shapes, rather than in terms of individual elements. Our eyes are never unbiased or "innocent," nor are our minds passive, because we are constantly testing and projecting, transforming on the basis and power of suggestion.[6] This testing is a game which can be enjoyable, "especially when the effort required . . . amounts to a pleasurable flexing of our mental muscles rather than a painful straining."[7]

To avoid the mimetic and illusionist, to effect a response to a work of art other than "transformation" or familiarization, then, the Cubists reduced familiar objects, including persons, to geometric shapes, fragments, and swatches of color, juxtaposing and fitting the pieces back together in ways which totally altered

---

5. E. H. Gombrich, *Art and Illusion* (New York: Pantheon Books, Inc., 1960), pp. 281-85.
6. See Gombrich, pp. 82-88, 298.
7. See Roger Cardinal, "Enigma," *20th Century Studies*, Dec. 1974, p. 42.

conventional relationships. In Georges Braque's *Femme à la Guitare* (1913), for example, a kind of symbiotic relationship exists between the woman and the guitar. Given certain identifiable features or signs with which to begin—the woman's eyes, her lips, the hole and strings of the guitar—one attempts to sort out which facets, textures, lines, and colors belong to which objects. The forms resist reconstitution, however. Not only do many remain illegible, but others assert multiple identity, informing the woman, the guitar, and the background in which together they face us. Thus the curves and hole of the guitar recur, it seems, as the woman's torso, and the curves of hair, neckline, eyelid, and shoulder recall each other, as well as the guitar. Parallelograms echo in guitar, sheets of music, the woman's face and nose, and what appears to be her hat. Similarly, what seems to be a hand with fingers curved around the neck of the guitar reminds us of other forms perceived within the painting, forms which suggest the foot of a chair or music-stand or the curl of a treble clef. Textures (wood, cloth, paper) and colors (ochres, blues, browns) assert themselves, then give way to each other: representational perspective abandoned, the layers of facets cannot be differentiated.

Thus the forms, illuminated, but from no determinate source, seem movable, capable of many combinations; we are struck by the ingeniousness of the objects, by how little we knew of their versatility, by how hidden they were, and by how many possible occurrences this set of objects, dismantled and explored, might inform. And yet, the seemingly mobile fragments also seem perfectly lodged, perfectly ordered as the particular composition demands. In *Femme à la Guitare*, we are not sure exactly what is occurring but we sense, nonetheless, that something definitely is. A partially revealed newspaper title in the lower half of the painting reads LE REVE. Are the woman's eyes closed? Or is one eye open? Perhaps the completed title reads LE REVEIL. Does the woman sit in a chair and dreamily play the guitar? One cannot say for sure. Although the clues are there, the exact place or occurrence cannot be pinned down. The reality achieved in cubist paintings is, Picasso wrote, "not a reality you can take in your hand. It's more like a perfume—in front of you, behind you, to the sides. The scent is everywhere, but you don't quite know where it comes from."[8]

Like the Cubists, Oppen also wishes to get at the "sense behind" the appearance of the thing—not "behind" in the modernist sense where poems and the objects within the poems serve symbolically as "Keys to relationships behind and beyond the

---

8. See Max Kozloff. *Cubism/Futurism* (New York: Harper & Row, 1973), p. 116.

particulars,'' but to get at the meaning in or of the thing itself, to get to the "immediate relationships with particulars in process."[9] In describing his poems in *Discrete Series*, Oppen discussed the meaning of that mathematical term:

> A pure mathematical series would be one in which each term is derived from the preceding term by rule. A discrete series is a series of terms each of which is empirically derived, each of which is empirically true. And this is the reason for the fragmentary nature of those poems. I was attempting to construct a meaning by empirical statements, by imagist statements.[10]

Discrete Series is the most fragmentary of Oppen's books, but many of his later poems seem to "construct meaning" in this manner as well. Oppen takes these "true statements" and puts them together mosaically, splicing together cinematic "takes" of closely and carefully observed phenomena: inanimate objects, animals, humans, conversation. These phenomena he shows only partially, however, fracturing them into pieces which serve, again, as clues to the mysterious whole:

> She lies, hip high,
> On a flat bed
> While the after-
> Sun passes.
>
> Plant, I breathe——
>   O Clearly,
> Eyes legs arms hands fingers,
> Simple legs in silk.
>   (from *Discrete Series*; *CP*, p. 9)
>
> of the Tiger   blaze
> of the tiger   who moves in the forest leaving
>
> no scent
>
> but the pine needles' his eyes blink
>
> quick
> in   the shack
> in the knife-cut
> and the opaque
>
> white
>
> bread each side of the knife
>   ("Myth of the Blaze"; *CP*, p. 244)

---

9. See Charles Altieri, "From Symbolist Thought to Immanence: The Ground of Postmodern American Poetics," *Boundary 2*, 1 (Spring 1973), 609.
10. See L. S. Dembo, "Interview with George Oppen," *Contemporary Literature*, 10 (1969), 161.

Here words, treated with utmost care as the links to objects and the first step to the "sincerity" so important to the Objectivists, seem almost to be used as *objets trouvés*, like the bits of burlap or paper used by the Cubists in some of their collages.[11] Also syntax is fractured in odd ways, and punctuation functions very carefully, selectively joining and separating:

> A car
>   (Which.
> Ease; the hand on the sword-hilt
>   (from *Discrete Series*; *CP*, p. 4)

> Save the pulse cumulates a past
> And your pulse separate doubly.
>   (from *Discrete Series*; *CP*, p. 10)

> Truth also is the pursuit of it:
> Like happiness, and it will not stand.
>   ("Leviathan"; *CP*, p. 68)

"One-point linear perspective" is gone in many of the poems, resulting in a feeling that "anywhere is everywhere,"[12] and the poems exist in what Oppen calls "open time" (*CP*, p. 171), or what Zukofsky calls "keeping time with existence,"[13] where past, present and future exist simultaneously and the "mind vaults from one place to another":[14]

> The knowledge not of sorrow, you were
>   saying, but of boredom
> Is—aside from reading speaking
>   smoking—
> Of what, Maude Blessingbourne it was,
>   wished to know when, having risen,
> "approached the window as if to see
>   what really was going on";
> And saw rain falling, in the distance
>   more slowly,
> The road clear from her past the window-
>   glass—
> Of the world, weather-swept, with which
>   one shares the century.
>   (from *Discrete Series*; *CP*, p. 3)

The poem shifts in its focus from "you" to "Maude" to "one," from "Maude" to "the window" to "the rain" to "the world." The verb tense also shifts, from "you were saying" to "Maude

---

11. See J. Hillis Miller, *Poets of Reality* (London: Oxford University Press, 1965), p. 293.
12. See Miller, p. 9.
13. Louis Zukofsky, "A Statement for Poetry," in Donald Allen and Warren Tallman, eds., *The Poetics of the New American Poetry* (New York: Grove Press, 1973), p. 143.
14. Kozloff, p. 52.

Blessingbourne it was" to "with which one shares."

A new "logic," an immediate logic, emerges in many of the poems, resulting from the juxtaposition and coexistence of dissimilar objects:

> The fly in the bottle
>
> Insane, the insane fly
>
> Which, over the city
> Is the bright light of shipwreck
> > > (from *Of Being Numerous*; *CP*, p. 160)
>
> There can be a brick
> In a brick wall
> The eye picks
>
> So quiet of a Sunday
> Here is the brick, it was waiting
> Here when you were born
>
> Mary-Anne.
> > (from *Of Being Numerous*; *CP*, p. 162)

> Leaving the house each dawn I see the hawk
> Flagrant over the driveway. In his claws
> That dot, that comma
> Is the broken animal; the dangling small beast knows
> The burden that he is: he has touched
> The hawk's drab feathers. But the carpenter's is a culture
> Of fitting, of firm dimensions,
> Of post and lintel. Quietly the roof lies
> That the carpenter has finished. The sea birds circle
> The beaches and cry in their own way,
> The innumerable sea birds, their beaks and their wings
> Over the beaches and the sea's glitter.
> > ("Workman"; *CP*, p. 41)

Each "thing" in "Workman" has its own meaning: "the dangling small beast *knows* the burden that he is" (emphasis mine) (and then comes the colon which joins the beast to its reason for knowing): "he has touched/The hawk's drab feathers." *But* the carpenter's is a less violent, more quiet culture "Of post and lintel." Meanwhile the sea birds "cry in their own way" in another "culture": "Over the beaches and the sea's glitter." The parts of the poem fit together simply because all of its parts are true, or at least as Dembo, discussing the difference between truth and sincerity, points out, *"true as encountered"*; each occurrence is really happening or has happened, at least to the "sincere" poet attempting to be empirical. The "reporter" poet can at best, however, Dembo writes, report only "his own perceptions and feelings."[15] The logic in the poem is, of course, the poet's logic; each thing's "meaning" (what it does) emerges as a part of a whole —the whole of the poet's biological world or the whole of the poem.

Oppen also juxtaposes sections of longer poems against each other, using the separate "fields" as clues to each other, so that each part can gather more "meanings," can be seen from more angles. In the section of *Discrete Series* beginning on page three of *CP*, the "camera" moves slowly and sensuously, taking in shapes, textures, colors:

1

White. From the
Under arm of T

The red globe.

Up
Down. Round
Shiny fixed
Alternatives

From the quiet

Stone floor . . .

Something is being described very carefully and very definitely (the periods used ensure that). But what? The words "Under arm" suggest a human being as well as the space under the letter T, while "shiny fixed alternatives" suggests something inanimate.

In the series' next section, which seems to occur at lunch time, a new mood ensues—some logic seems to be occurring:

2

Thus
Hides the

Parts—the prudery
Of Frigidaire, of
Soda-jerking——

Thus

Above the

Plane of lunch, of wives

---

15. See Dembo, "Existential World," p. 65.

```
                Removes itself
                (As soda-jerking from
                the private act

                Of
                Cracking eggs);

                big-Business
```

"Discrete" and thus distinct, this section nonetheless introduces objects that seem to function in part suggestively: possible relationships, including relationships with the previous section of the series, begin to appear, although nothing is certain. The "White," the "Shiny fixed/Alternatives/From the quiet/Stone floor . . ." may now suggest a "Frigidaire." Big-business seems linked to soda-jerking, cracking eggs to wives. Prudery recalls underarms, underarms seem related to refrigerators, refrigerators to wives. The "red globe" seems somehow connected to "shiny fixed alternatives," to frigidaires, to soda-jerking. Perhaps the handle on a soda-jerking machine? The quiet in the previous section of the series seems related to "the private act of cracking eggs," to wives; "big-Business" seems noisy. Dissimilar objects begin to share the same shapes and qualities and boundaries.

A cinematic cut occurs between "big-Business" and the next section of *Discrete Series*, which occurs in the evening; "they" (the speaker and a woman? his wife?) are in a car:

```
                The evening, water in a glass
                Thru which our car runs on a higher road.

                Over what has the air frozen?

                Nothing can equal in polish and obscured
                        origin that dark instrument

                A car
                        (Which.
                Ease; the hand on the sword-hilt
```

In the first two lines Oppen juxtaposes "The evening" (a time of day), "water in a glass" (an inanimate object), and "Thru which our car runs on a higher road" (an action). A startling image, the comparison seems too fragile to be pushed. The lines

```
                The evening was like water in a glass
```

Or

```
                Our car runs thru the evening which is like water in a glass
```

won't work. Nor will:

```
                The gear shift was like a sword-hilt
```

for the simile does not seem to exist in "open time," whereas Oppen's mosaic association does.

Oppen also seems to redefine metaphor in the next part of the series, which takes place in the morning:

> Her ankles are watches
> (Her arm-pits are causeways for water)
>
> When she steps
> She walks on a sphere
>
> Walks on the carpet, dressing.
> Brushing her hair
>
> Her movement accustomed, abstracted,
> Declares this morning a woman's
> "My hair, scalp——"

The woman in the poem is described as another object intricately involved with all the other objects in the world, not just reminiscent of or like them: "Her movement" (what she does in this world, her interaction with the world—the cracking of eggs, the brushing of hair) "declares this morning a woman's." And, the images in the lines

> Her ankles are watches
> (Her arm-pits are causeways for water)

seem to be not so much comparisons as "overlays" from other places or times.

This section of *Discrete Series* forms relationships with the previous sections: "causeways for water" recalls the "water in a glass," the "sphere" recalls the "red globe," the woman the "wives," the morning the evening. Capable of "dissolving into each other," of "coming forward" to be remembered so that an "illegible" object, scenario, or moment seems familiar or known, the pieces of *Discrete Series* function, then, both separately and collectively. Images of a woman, of water, of a machine, of a car found throughout *Discrete Series* or in Oppen's other books seem both unique and reminiscent:

> A world around her like a shadow
> She moves a chair
> Something is being made ——
> Prepared
> Clear in front of her as open air
>
> The space a woman makes and fills
>   ("O Western Wind"; *CP*, p. 53)

> Closed car——closed in glass——
> At the curb
> > (from *Discrete Series*; *CP*, p. 6)

> It is you who truly
> Excel the vegetable,
> The fitting of grasses——more bare than
> > > that.
> Pointedly bent, your elbow on a car-edge
> > (from *Discrete Series*; *CP*, p. 12)

> Leaving that ancient car
> Together. I remember
> Standing in the white grass
> Beside it.
> > ("The Forms of Love"; *CP*, p. 86)

A static, completely "solved" picture never emerges, however, from our contemplation of the poems' fragments. Perhaps the sections of *Discrete Series* describe a marriage, or a period of time, or a journey by car, but the moods and occurrences of that marriage or period or journey revealed to us (most carefully) in part are also "re-veiled" at the same time.[16]

But Oppen's poetry does more than simply force us to play a game, to say "I think I'm getting something here" or "you win; I give up." Because of his use of fragmentation and juxtaposition, we are allowed to observe the world in a new way. There is no "mystery monger" here[17]; this is a poet who trusts in words and their power to name, the power to join us with the thing named. Oppen says,

> They're categories, concepts, classes, things we invent for our-selves. Nevertheless, there are certain ones without which we are really unable to exist. . . . All the little nouns are the ones that I like the most, the deer, the sun, and so on. You say these per-fectly little words and you're asserting that the sun is ninety-three million miles away, and that there is shade because of shadows, and more, who knows? . . . I do think they exist and it doesn't particularly embarrass me; it's certainly an act of faith.

For central to Oppen's desire to take something apart to really see it is the belief that there is something there worth seeing. In answer to the question, "Well what exactly do you mean by 'the life of the mind'?", Oppen answered,

> I mean the awareness . . . I suppose it's nearly a sense of awe, simply to feel that the thing is there and that it's quite something to see. It's an awareness of the world, a lyric reaction to the world. "Of Being Numerous" ends with the word "curious" . . .

---

16. See Cardinal, p. 45.
17. See Cardinal, p. 47.

because men are curious, and at the end of a very long poem, I couldn't find anything more positive to say than that.[18]

"That they are there!" writes Oppen in "Psalm" (*CP*, p. 78) and in "World, World——":

> Soul-searchings, these prescriptions,
>
> Are a medical faddism, an attempt to escape,
> To lose oneself in the self.
>
> The self is no mystery, the mystery is
> That there is something for us to stand on.
>
> We want to be here.
>
> The act of being, the act of being
> More than oneself.
> > (*CP*, p. 143)

To look outside at the world ("What will she make of a world/Do you suppose, Max, of which she is made." *CP*, p. 30) is to see the stuff of which we are made and with which we share the "act of being." It is important to begin with the small nouns Oppen loves so much, "the small nouns crying faith" (*CP*, p. 78), because these contain "the mystery." To look closely at the familiar—at a car, a woman, a deer—is to see the mystery in it:

> The new wood as old as carpentry.
> . . . .
> Carpenter, how wild the planet is.
> > ("Carpenter's Boat"; *CP*, p. 110)
>
> the alien small teeth
> . . . .
> the strange woods
> > ("Psalm"; *CP*, p. 78)
>
> In the bright simpleness and strangeness of the sands.
> > ("California"; *CP*, p. 62)

Ernest Fenollosa complained, "We do not say 'a tree greens itself',"[19] but Oppen, through his use of language, does ascribe to objects their innate power:

> Cell by cell the baby made herself, the cells
> made cells.
> > ("Sara in Her Father's Arms"; *CP*, p. 30)
>
> Quietly the roof lies
> That the carpenter has finished.
> > ("Workman,"; *CP*, p. 41)

---

18. See Dembo, "Interview," pp. 162-64).
19. Ernest Fenollosa, "From *The Chinese Written Character as a Medium for Poetry*," in Allen and Tallman, p. 20.

> Her movement accustomed, abstracted,
> Declares this morning a woman's
> > (from *Discrete Series*; *CP*, p. 5)

> It brightens up into the branches.
> > (*CP*, p. 13)

The recognition of and faith in the power of words is a first step in what J. Hillis Miller calls "walking barefoot into reality" or "abandoning the independence of the ego . . . abandoning the will to power over things."[20] It is what Richard Pevear means, I think, when he says that Oppen is involved in a "worlding"—the opening of a place which we share with things—a "common world," "the place of humanity."[21] And it is what Oppen means when he says, "It's certainly an act of faith." For "walking barefoot into reality" involves giving up so much.

It is the getting outside of oneself that is important here—the discovery of the value inherent in participation with the world as opposed to creation of the world; the discovery that "the world can get on quite nicely without our expressive efforts,"[22] the discovery "that they are there!" Oppen's poems allow us to look closely at those things with which we are most familiar and not recognize them, and thus, to "give them up." In this way comes the realization, as Picasso states, that "the form is there to live its own life."[23] The "form" asserts its independence, and a getting away from the human, a "decreation"[24] or what Miller calls "the effacement of the ego" occurs.[25] For the forms which "come into being" in the poems (and which, cell-like, make the poems which contain them into objects with perimeters, objects to be reckoned with) demand our full attention; we must relinquish our "soul searchings" to concentrate fully on them in their new, mysterious ways.

It is in the recognition of a world shared with things that participate in "Being" that Oppen's poetry becomes, as Dembo and Altieri have pointed out, Heideggerian, "religious," phenomenological.[26] "I do believe that consciousness exists," Oppen states, "and that it is consciousness of something, and that is a very complete but not very detailed theology."[27] Objects that have entered

20. Miller, p. 7.
21. See Richard Pevear, "Poetry and Worldlessness," *Hudson Review*, 29 (Summer 1976), 317-18.
22. See Kenner, p. 65.
23. Pablo Picasso, "Statement, 1923," in Herschel B. Chipp, ed., *Theories of Modern Art* (Berkeley: University of California Press, 1968), p. 265.
24. Altieri, "From Symbolist Thought," p. 612.
25. Miller, p. 8.
26. See Altieri, "Objectivist Tradition," p. 13; "From Symbolist Thought," pp. 620-25.
27. See Dembo, "Interview," p. 163.

the "light of Being" invoke the sense of "awe" in the world, the sense of wonderment at the "this in which," become "numinous."[28] But only human beings who enter into a Heideggerian "state of "unconcealedness" can participate in "Being," can feel the mystery around them.[29]

Oppen's poems assert quietly and sincerely that what is being described is "true," exactly as it has occurred; we believe them. The ambiguities which occur through Oppen's use of cubist techniques—collage-like juxtapositions, "open time" in which memories come forward to mingle freely with the rest of the poem, strange moments and inter-relationships that we "know but can't quite place . . ."—guard against a description becoming too familiar and, thus, meaningless, merely absorbed by our will to power and made "human." For we must concentrate on his poems and in doing so we recognize the power within the words—the power to denote things other than ourselves which really do exist. Because we cannot "unlock" the poems and understand their "hidden meanings," they also become objects (an exercise in paint, not illusion, was what the Cubists wanted), asserting their independence from us. In his book, E. H. Gombrich discusses the way, after being in an art gallery, we may, at least for a while, see the world as art[30]: "A Picasso clarinetist, a Braque landscape," we might think. Oppen's poems allow us to see the world as, in some ways, "cubist"; the poetry invites us to give over with pleasure to that world's intriguing, perhaps mystifying relationships.

28. Altieri, "From Symbolist Thought," p. 614.
29. See Martin Heidegger, "The Way Back into the Ground of Metaphysics," in Walter Kaufmann, ed., *Existentialism from Dostoevsky to Sartre* (New York: World Publishing Co., 1956), pp. 207-8.
30. See Gombrich, p. 316.

HARVEY KAIL

A TEST OF IMAGES:
GEORGE OPPEN'S "VULCAN"

I would like to put a poem of George Oppen's to the test, an examination using his own criterion that "a test of images can be a test of whether one's thought is valid, whether one can establish in a series of images, of experiences . . . whether or not one will consider the concept of humanity to be valid, something that is, or else have to regard it as being simply a word."[1] If I understand this correctly, the test of truth (or at least of "sincerity") in a poem is its ability to establish for the poet and for the reader a tangible awareness of shared experiences among men and women that defines each of us as members of a human community. This community, Oppen insists, must actually assert itself in our consciousnesses, thereby demonstrating that we are not single, isolated things like rocks, but are instead a class of beings with a history and with a future, so that when we talk about "common humanity" or "humankind" we are not simply engaging in a process of semantic wishful thinking, but are showing that we truly cannot exist without this concept of each other.

Somehow, the poem must be "proved," perhaps in a sense that a mathematical theorem is proved, if it is to contain "valid thought." In a mathematical proof, we discover that our theorem is true if we end up with a statement that contains all of the previous statements within it, and at the same time is something else again, a new true statement. To do this one applies a set of rules (of logic, in mathematics) to a series of statements (themselves based on axioms, which are unprovable assumptions, or on previously "proven" statements) in order to arrive at a final statement that must also be considered true. The manner in which one manipulates these statements depends on the mathematical system being used. In short, there must be internal consistency.

---

1. Quoted from an interview with L. S. Dembo, Oppen Interview, "The Objectivist Poet: Four Interviews," *Contemporary Literature*, 2 (Spring 1969), p. 161.

In a "poetic proof," we substitute for mathematical statements (say $\frac{dx}{dt} = a_1 x_1 + a_2 x_2$) what Oppen calls imagist statements. These statements are, in turn, based on "moments of conviction," the axioms of Oppen's verse.[2] The rules by which he will manipulate these statements are, of course, the rules of syntax (up to a point) and what for lack of a better phrase I am going to call the logic of emotion. In effect, what I would like to do in this paper is to examine the calculus of George Oppen's poetry.

To look at simply one poem, and a fairly short one at that, as I propose to do, is certainly a narrow basis for examination of a poet's method of thought. But Oppen's work is in many important ways one long poem, and placing a bit of it under a microscope should be somewhat like studying a sample of DNA; everything in the organism is therein contained. "Vulcan," the poem I have chosen to examine, carries, I think, a particularly high concentration of Oppen's way of thinking, yet it is brief enough to discuss in the necessary detail. Besides, the poem still puzzles me. For those readers who are not familiar with or who have not read it recently, here it is:

Vulcan

The householder issuing to the street
Is adrift a moment in that ice stiff
Exterior. 'Peninsula
Low lying in the bay
And wooded —' Native now
Are the welder and the welder's arc
In the subway's iron circuits:
We have not escaped each other,
Not in the forest, not here. The crippled girl hobbles
Painfully in the new depths
Of the subway, and painfully
We shift our eyes. The bare rails
and black walls contain
Labor before her birth, her twisted
Precarious birth and the men
Laborious, burly — She sits
Quiet, her eyes still. Slowly,
Deliberately she sees
an anchor's blunt fluke sink
Thru coins and coin machines,
The ancient iron and the voltage
In the iron beneath us in the child's deep
Harbors into harbor sand.[3]

---

2. Dembo, Oppen Interview, *Contemporary Literature*, p. 161.
3. *Collected Poems* (New York: New Directions, 1975), p. 46.

Reading this poem is somewhat like walking slowly along a huge mural separated into distinct panels. (I am reminded of the WPA art projects that decorated the walls of the post offices of my youth.) As we move through the poem, the images, at first apparently unconnected, begin to fit into a pattern. The poem takes us via these images through a series of "events" separated both in time and in space, and it is not until we have been through the entire poem (more than once) that the relationships among the parts become clearer, and the poem takes on a shape of its own. Like the "mineral world" that Oppen talks about so much in his work, the poem too is finally impenetrable, but not completely so. The act of examination and "proof" is, I believe, vital to reading Oppen, and a genuine part of the process of validating a concept of humanity.

The first part of this examination, then, will be simply to see what is here, to walk through the poem.

It begins by evoking man's mythic history, calling up the ancient story of Vulcan (Haephestus, in the Greek legend), the crippled craftsman thrown off Mt. Olympus by his mother, Hera, who was displeased by her own child's ugliness. Indeed, Vulcan is the only God born on Olympus unbeautiful. Yet, in spite of his deformity, or perhaps because of it, he becomes the smith to the immortals, fashioning out of fire and metal their weapons and their furnishings in his subterranean workshop. In one version of his story, he makes for his lame legs golden braces; in another he smelts golden handmaidens to help him at his forge. In either case, he is a craftsman who makes things of beauty in order to "support" himself.

Juxtaposed against the smoky, forge-bound image of Vulcan, we meet the first figure of the poem proper, a very common soul, an everyman, an anyman, coming onto a street, any street, not quite sure where he is going: "The householder issuing to the street/Is adrift a moment in that ice stiff/Exterior." Who is this person? "Householder" is the name of a class of people, not an individual, and Oppen gives us no individualizing visual cues—the line is, in fact, stubbornly non-visual. All that we might sense about the figure at this point is a faint air of domesticity: he/she is a householder. The participle describing the action seems more promising of elucidation. The householder doesn't simply emerge into the street, but "issues," a word that describes not only a physical action but has connotations of birth as well. And from where does the householder issue? A house? An apartment building? A subway entrance? Wherever, the moment he emerges into the street he is "adrift," a curious nautical term that keeps

the householder poised for a second on the top of a wave of inde-
cision: shall he go up the street or down the street, east or west,
left or right? In that moment of deciding, or not deciding, the
householder enters the "ice stiff/Exterior."

Exterior is an important word in Oppen's lexicon (they are
all important, of course), one of those small nouns that carry such
a potent meaning-making power. On the one hand, the exterior is
a kind of place; it is the outside of something—a building, an automobile—the opposite place from "interior." As we see often in
Oppen's work, two words really define each other; there is an
exterior of things and an interior of things. Also, the movement
from the implied interior into the "ice stiff/Exterior" suggests a
coming to the surface, a brief moment of being, in a sense, outside the interior of the self, an unselfconscious awareness of the
world—that place where, for instance, weather happens, in this
case perhaps very frigid weather, ice stiff. The householder issues
into this exterior because there is an exterior there for him to
emerge into. His is a particular awareness of being alive in the
world in that moment during which one chooses in which direction one is going to set sail, this way or that. It is, if nothing else,
a cold awakening.

The slight nautical flavor of the opening statement serves (in
retrospect) as one possible link to the next image: " 'Peninsula/
Low lying in the bay/And wooded—' " The single quotation
marks indicate that the speaker or writer of the lines is someone
other than the speaker of the poem, while the dash at the end of
the statement might indicate that the entire quotation is not given,
that this section has been lifted from a longer descriptive passage.
Who is the speaker of this line and to what does he refer? Certainly, this is not the householder speaking; the street and the view
of the peninsula seem disconnected both in time and in space.
Their neighboring positions on the same line—"Exterior. 'Penin-
sula/"—does, however, hold them in some relationship to each
other, one panel of the mural butted up against the next. Throughout the poem, in fact, Oppen never begins a new sentence on a
new line; the thoughts are connected by their mutual presence if
in no other immediately discernible fashion. The view we get of
the land seems, itself, to be waterborn, as if we are viewing a
peninsula, or what appears to be a peninsula, from the vantage
point of a boat out in the bay. The matter-of-factness of the line
calls to mind a ship's log written in a curious, antique style. At
this point in the poem, we can surmise little else, and move on.

It is not until we read the third sentence that the second
becomes more definitely located: "Native now/Are the welder and

the welder's arc/In the subway's iron circuits:/We have not
escaped each other,/Not in the forest, not here." The first half of
this sentence establishes a relationship between "now" and, presumably, "then." "Then" may have been when the peninsula was
wooded, inhabited by a different set of natives using a different
kind of tool native to them, not the technologically sophisticated
welder arcing electricity into the subway's iron circuits, joining
them together into one continuous loop. "Native," like "exterior,"
is a particularly high energy word in Oppen's poems, calling up the
image of the aboriginal (the Indian in America prior to European
exploration?) and also the sense of people who are wholly a part
of the time in which they live, "native in native time" as Oppen
puts it in another poem.[4] Finally, a figure from another time is
also suggested in these lines—Vulcan, the metal worker, melting
and reforming iron in his grotto workshop.

All of this leads to the colon and the summary remark "We
have not escaped each other,/Not in the forest, not here." "Here"
is, perhaps, the present, the "now," the subway, the modern subterranean; the forest is "then," the wooded pristine peninsula, or
possibly even the mythological time and place of Vulcan. But who
is this "we"? Why does the poet speak to us now in the third
person? Does he dare presume to speak for *us*, for humanity? The
tone of the statement is flat and matter-of-fact; there is nothing
speculative about it. It is as if the voice of the poem is saying, "All
this is history. This is empirical fact. We have failed in our
attempts as human beings to escape from each other, to lose each
other in the forests, say, of a younger America. We seem to insist,
instead, on living among each other, together even in the spacious-
ness of the forests and certainly 'here' in the subway's iron
circuits."

It is in the subway that we meet the major figure of the
poem—a daughter of Vulcan, surely—a "crippled girl" who "hob-
bles/Painfully in the new depths/Of the subway." Like Vulcan, the
girl is lame, misformed. And like Vulcan's mother, we react with
aversion: "and painfully/We shift our eyes." All of the events of
the poem up to this point—the householder set adrift, the sighting
of the peninsula, the welder's arc, our own shared inability to
escape each other—seem to lead to this image of a crippled girl.
We see her against the backdrop of the subway which, even though
it is "new," is older, far older than she is. The subway's "bare
rails/And black walls contain/Labor before her birth, her twisted/
Precarious birth and the men/Laborious, burly—" The work that
has gone into the making of the subway, an electric-like energy, is

---

4. "Route," *Collected Poems*, p. 186.

seen as only the latest in a series of workmanlike efforts in the
metal-crafting tradition of Vulcan. And the energy seems still to
be there, "contained" in the black walls. The circuit that the
welder melts together runs·not only to the next station down the
line, but through history as well, connecting us with our common
past. It is all still there.

If only we could "see" it. The girls's function in the poem
seems to be to help us to see. From the point that she enters the
poem, what happens happens in the "deep harbors" of her mind:

> She sits
> Quiet, her eyes still. Slowly,
> Deliberately she sees
> An anchor's blunt fluke sink
> Thru coins and coin machines,
> The ancient iron and the voltage
> In the iron beheath us in the child's deep
> Harbors into harbor sands.

The crippled girl sees—not with the eyes but with the mind—
the fluke of an ancient anchor (perhaps the anchor of the boat
from which hundreds of years ago an explorer might have written
of the vista before him, "Peninsula low lying in the bay and
wooded"); and she sees this anchor, itself the product of metal
working, sink through a layer of coins and coin machines, the
subway itself, the modern, into the sand at the bottom of the
harbor: all of it, even the voltage in the iron rails, settling together
into history.

II

So, we have been through the poem. No doubt we have
missed much, but we have seen as well. Now, how do the things
we have seen in the poem fit together? What are the rules, what is
the calculus, that holds them together and proves them to be true
imagist statements? What is the emotional logic among and
between

   a.   a man frozen in a characteristic human moment, stepping
        into a street,
   b.   a peninsula seen perhaps for the first time by alien eyes,
   c.   a welder kneeling over the arc of his work, and
   d.   the continual allusions to Vulcan?

These images or statements are one half of the equation. They lead
up to the colon, the equals sign, if you will, at the end of the
seventh line of the poem. On the other side of the equation, a
statement: We have not escaped each other, then or now, not in

the forest and not here in the subway. How can Oppen "prove" that the equation—this human equation, as it were—is true, that it balances?

Only through the emotion of vision, Oppen seems to be saying. One can prove this theorem that humanity does, in fact, exist, only through an act of "seeing" in the same sense that we "see" a tree or any other object, by filling our eyes and our minds with it. History is a thing that is in reality just as palpable (to use one of Whitman's words) as any other object or thing, an elbow, a rock, a Bach cantata. We can "see" this concept of humanity everywhere, even in the subway, where history is buried alive in the walls.

This act of vision is the function (both "mathematical" and poetical) of the girl in the poem; she is a see-er. Where Vulcan forges metals, the crippled girl in the poem is a kind of craftsman of the mind. She molds purposefully a mental image of events buried in the human consciousness in the same way that the labor of the workmen who built the subway (who gave "birth" to it) is "contained" in its walls. She sees with a kind of intent singleness of purpose this vision of an ancient anchor, product of Vulcan's craft, sinking through archeological layers, even through the archaeology of the present moment, sinking into the rich muck of history.[5]

Our relationship with the girl is ambiguous. She is part of "us," down in the subway, but we refuse to look at her, even though it causes us pain to look away! She is crippled (by her vision?) and we don't want to see that, so we look away, or perhaps we are afraid to stare. And so the see-er, the craftsman of the mind, is both part of this concept of humanity and outside it. A terrible position, a painful one, paradoxical but perhaps unavoidable. If one is to prove that humanity, its history and its future, is not simply a word but an actual thing, perhaps it is necessary to be at least in some way separate from and outside that concept. This seems to be the fate of the poet in George Oppen, "suffering the things of the world and speaking them out of himself."

---

5. This complex image reminds me of a story about an ancient ship from out of New York's Dutch ancestry that had, miraculously, been discovered by workmen digging out one of the subway tunnels in the lower end of Manhattan. It seems that over the years the New York harbor facilities had slowly been extended into the bay by successive land-fills, and this boat, sunk in what must have once been the harbor, had slowly "moved" inland until it was discovered hundreds of years later by workmen hacking out the I.R.T. It was decided (at who knows what level of the bureaucracy) too expensive or inexpedient to remove the old ship from its grave, so it was simply walled back in. And to this day, so the story goes, subway trains careen within inches of this ancient, landlocked ship. I don't know if the story is true, but it serves to illustrate a context out of which Oppen frequently constructs his thought, a sense of place in which history keeps intruding into the present and the present population, in its turn, tries to wall the past back in.

Well.   Has Oppen flunked or passed? Is his method of
thought valid? He attempts to prove that human history is real,
that there is a valid concept of humanity by seeing it as something
that actually occurs. For Oppen, ideas are real, concepts take
place. Yet, the concept of humanity is one that Oppen has
struggled with all of his life. In "Pro Nobis," a poem written after
"Vulcan," Oppen says,

> Tho I had hoped to arrive
> At an actuality
> In the mere number of us
> And record now
> That I did not.
>
> Therefore pray for us
> In the hour of our death indeed.[6]

In mathematical proofs as well as in poetical proofs, when
there is doubt one comes back to the axioms. There is, Oppen
says, "a moment, an actual time, when you believe something to
be true, and you construct meaning from these moments of conviction."[7] These moments of conviction—are they replaced or
superceded by other moments that invalidate their predecessors?
Do things change through time, or is it merely our perception of
them that changes? All that one can do, according to Oppen, is to
report on what it is one actually believes to be true at the moment
he believes it, native thought in native time. When he no longer
believes it, it won't be true for him anymore. He'll believe something else.

The theorem that Oppen wishes to prove—i.e., that the concept of humanity is valid—may be similar to one of those propositions in mathematics that Gödel tells us are *undecidable*. George
Oppen went on from "Pro Nobis" to write his long metaphysical
poem on the same subject as "Vulcan," "Of Being Numerous,"
a poem which ends on the word "curious." Oppen is ever curious
to test his images, his language, against the "fatal rock of the
world." That is his great victory, for in doing so, even when he
fails, George Oppen passes.

---

6. *Collected Poems*, p. 141.
7. Dembo, Oppen Interview, *Contemporary Literature*, p. 161.

THE CANON
I.
DISCRETE SERIES

George Oppen. Photograph circa 1941, courtesy of Mary Oppen.

WILLIAM CARLOS WILLIAMS

THE NEW POETICAL ECONOMY[1]

Mr. Oppen has given us thirty-seven pages of short poems, well printed and well bound, around which several statements relative to modern verse forms may well be made.

The appearance of a book of poems, if it be a book of good poems, is an important event because of relationships the work it contains will have with thought and accomplishment in other contemporary reaches of the intelligence. This leads to a definition of the term "good." If the poems in the book constitute necessary corrections of or emendations to human conduct in their day, both as to thought and manner, then they are good. But if these changes originated in the poems, causing thereby a direct liberation of the intelligence, then the book becomes of importance to the highest degree.

But this importance cannot be in what the poem says, since in that case the fact that it is a poem would be a redundancy. The importance lies in what the poem *is*. Its existence as a poem is of first importance, a technical matter, as with all facts, compelling the recognition of a mechanical structure. A poem which does not arouse respect for the technical requirements of its own mechanics may have anything you please painted all over it or on it in the way of meaning but it will for all that be as empty as a man made of wax or straw.

It is the acceptable fact of a poem as a mechanism that is the proof of its meaning and this is as technical a matter as in the case of any other machine. Without the poem being a workable mechanism in its own right, a mechanism which arises from, while at the same time it constitutes the meaning of, the poem as a whole, it will remain ineffective. And what it says regarding the

1. Reprinted by courtesy of the Williams estate from *Poetry*, 44 (July 1934), pp. 220-225.

use or worth of that particular piece of "propaganda" which it is detailing will never be convincing.

The preface seems to me irrelevant. Why mention something which the book is believed definitely not to resemble? "Discrete" in the sense used by Mr. Oppen, is, in all probability, meant merely to designate a series separate from other series. I feel that he is justified in so using the term. It has something of the implications about it of work in a laboratory when one is following what he believes to be a profitable lead along some one line of possible investigation.

This indicates what is probably the correct way to view the book as well as the best way to obtain pleasure from it. Very few people, not to say critics, see poetry in their day as a moment in the long-drawn periodic progress of an ever-changing activity toward occasional peaks of surpassing excellence. Yet these are the correct historic facts of the case. These high periods rest on the continuity of what has gone before. As a corollary, most critics fail to connect up the apparently dissociated work of the various men writing contemporaneously in a general scheme of understanding. Most commentators are, to be sure, incapable of doing so since they have no valid technical knowledge of the difficulties involved, what has to be destroyed since it is dead, and what saved and treasured. The dead, granted, was once alive but now it is dead and it stinks.

The term, technical excellence, has an unpoetic sound to most ears. But if an intelligence be deeply concerned with the bringing up of the body of poetry to a contemporary level equal with the excellences of other times, technique means everything. Surely an apprentice watching his master sees nothing prosaic about the details of technique. Nor would he find a narrow world because of the smallness of the aperture through which he views it, but through that pinhole, rather, a world enormous as his mind permits him to witness.

A friend sticks his head in at the door and says, "Why all the junk standing around?"

The one at work, startled perhaps, looks up puzzled and tries to comprehend the dullness of his friend.

Were there an accredited critic of any understanding about, he might be able to correlate the details of the situation, bringing a reasonable order into these affairs. But the only accredited critics are those who, seeking order, have proceeded to cut away all the material they do not understand in order to obtain it. Since man has two legs, then so also must the elephant. Cut off the ones that are redundant! Following this, logically, they describe a hollow tail and a tassel sticking out just above the mouth. This is my considered opinion of the position of the formerly alert critic, T. S. Eliot.

Then there are the people who do reviews for the newspapers. They haven't the vaguest notion why one word follows another, but deal directly with meanings themselves.

An imaginable new social order would require a skeleton of severe discipline for its realization and maintenance. Thus by a sharp restriction to essentials, the seriousness of a new order is brought to realization. Poetry might turn this condition to its own ends. Only by being an object sharply defined and without redundancy will its form project whatever meaning is required of it. It could well be, at the same time, first and last a poem facing as it must the dialectic necessities of its day. Oppen has carried this social necessity, so far as poetry may be concerned in it, over to an extreme.

Such an undertaking will be as well a criticism of the classics, a movement that seeks to be made up only of essentials and to discover what they are. The classics are for modern purposes just so much old coach.

And once again, for the glad, the young and the enthusiastic, let it be said that such statement as the above has nothing to do with the abiding excellence of the classics but only with their availability as a means toward present ends. In the light of that objective, they are nostalgic obstacles.

Oppen has moved to present a clear outline for an understanding of what a new construction would require. His poems seek an irreducible minimum in the means for the achievement of their objective, no loose bolts or beams sticking out unattached at one end or put there to hold up a rococo cupid or a concrete saint, nor either to be a frame for a portrait of mother or a deceased wife.

The words are plain words; the metric is taken from speech; the colors, images, moods are not suburban, not peasant-restricted to serve as a pertinent example. *A Discrete Series*. This is the work of a "stinking" intellectual, if you please. That is, you should use the man as you would use any other mechanic—to serve a purpose for which training, his head, his general abilities fit him, to build with—that others may build after him.

Such service would be timely today since people are beginning to forget that poems are constructions. One no longer hears poems spoken of as good or bad; that is, whether or not they do or do not stand up and hold together. One is likely, rather, to hear of them now as "proletarian" or "fascist" or whatever it may

be. The social school of criticism is getting to be almost as sub-
versive to the intelligence as the religious school nearly succeeded
in being in the recent past.

> The mast
> Inaudibly soars; bole-like, tapering
> Sail flattens from it beneath the wind.
> The limp water holds the boat's round sides.   Sun
> Slants dry light on the deck.   Beneath us glide
> Rocks, sand, and unrimmed holes.

Whether or not a poem of this sort, technically excellent, will
be read over and over again, year after year, perhaps century after
century, as, let us say, some of Dante's sonnets have been read
over and over again by succeeding generations—seems to me to be
beside the point. Or that such a test is the sole criterion of excellence in a poem—who shall say? I wish merely to affirm in my own
right that unless a poem rests on the bedrock of a craftsmanlike
economy of means, its value must remain of a secondary order,
and that for this reason good work, such as that shown among
Mr. Oppen's poems, should be praised.

TOM SHARP

GEORGE OPPEN, DISCRETE SERIES, 1929-1934

> *Among the heaps of brick and plaster lies*
> *a girder, still itself among the rubbish.*
>
> —Charles Reznikoff, *Jerusalem the Golden*

I. Principles.

On 6 March 1930, Louis Zukofsky wrote to Ezra Pound, announcing that he might have for Pound thirty-two pages of poems by George Oppen, whose occasional imprecisions and stylistic peculiarities Zukofsky excused because of the unique way he managed a certain type of "void."[1] These pages were a manuscript of Oppen's first book, *Discrete Series*, which was published by the Objectivist Press in 1934, with a preface which had been volunteered by Pound.

The last poem in Oppen's most recent book, *Primitive*, describes writing *Discrete Series*:

> . . . and writing
>
> thru the night (a young man,
> Brooklyn, 1929) I named the book
>
> series empirical
> series all force
> in events the myriad
>
> lights have entered
> us it is a music more powerful
>
> than music[2]

---

1. Unpublished letter in the Beinecke Rare Book and Manuscript Library, Yale University. Paul Zukofsky, the executor of the Zukofsky estate, has refused permission to quote this letter.
2. (Santa Barbara: Black Sparrow Press, 1978), pp. 30-31.

As Oppen here describes the process, the poems of *Discrete Series* were the results of the myriad lights in events entering his consciousness. The effect is musical because the process recognizes and taps the music inherent in the heart of things and of language itself.

Pound, describing his poem "In a Station of the Metro," wrote:

> In a poem of this sort one is trying to record the precise instant when a thing outward and objective transforms itself, or darts into a thing inward and subjective.[3]

A poem of this sort is an act of what I will here call "inspiration," an inward movement of an objective thing such as myriad lights or faces in a crowd. "Objectivist" and Imagiste poems both rely on inspiration. In contrast, Symboliste poems are acts of what I call "projection," the outward movement of a subjective thing. Symbolisme remakes the world in the image of the poet's prior psychic state, but Imagisme and "Objectivism" are based upon the recognition that our psychic states are remade by the world with each fresh perception.[4]

Imagisme and "Objectivism" differ, however, regarding the allowable nature of the "thing," the Image. The first Imagiste proposition permitted the "thing" to be "subjective or objective."[5] In "Affirmations . . . IV. As for Imagisme" (1915), Pound wrote:

> The Image can be of two sorts. It can arise within the mind. It is then 'subjective'. External causes play upon the mind, perhaps; if so, they are drawn into the mind, fused, transmitted, and emerge in an Image unlike themselves. Secondly, the Image can be objective. Emotion seizing up some external scene or action carries it intact to the mind; and that vortex purges it of all save the essential or dominant or dramatic qualities, and it emerges like the external original.[6]

The "Objectivists" generally, and Oppen especially, believed more than the Imagistes in the virtues of original external causes; that is,

3. *Gaudier-Brzeska: A Memoir* (NY: New Directions, 1974), p. 89.
4. I use quotation marks around "Objectivist" in respect for Zukofsky's distinction "between its particular meaning in the Program of Feb. *Poetry*, and the philosophical etiquette associated with objectivist" ("'Recencies' in Poetry," *An "Objectivists" Anthology*, p. 9). The word is not used in its common sense.
   I capitalize "Image" to distinguish Pound's concept from the common sense of the word. The "Image," the intellectual and emotional complex, is not simply an "image," a visual impression.
5. F. S. Flint, "Imagisme," *Poetry: A Magazine of Verse*, 1, 6 (March 1913), 199; Ezra Pound, *Pavannes and Divisions* (NY: Alfred A. Knopf, 1918), p. 95; Ezra Pound, *Literary Essays*, ed. T. S. Eliot (NY: New Directions, 1968), p. 3.
6. Ezra Pound, *Selected Prose 1909-1965*, ed. William Cookson (NY: New Directions, 1973), pp. 374-375.

their Image was usually objective, and their world full of form.

A further distinction between Imagisme and Symbolisme also tells something about "Objectivism." Even the Imagiste's subjective Image is not an act of projection. It is not misrepresented as the world. Subjective experience is not justified by claiming priority over objective things. Instead, the Imagistes emphasized the dynamic and emotive properties of the poem's structure.

The first principle of the composition of a poem such as "In a Station of the Metro" is the belief that each element of one's art can have a precise intellectual and emotional effect on the reader. The complex of such effects, as Pound defined the term, is the Image.[7] An Image in this technical sense is not, as many poets and readers, beginning with Amy Lowell, have mistakenly thought, a visual impression of something objective. It exists in the poem as the poet's representation of an ur-Image: his impression of the object if the Image is objective, or his impression itself if the Image is subjective.

The second principle of the composition of such a poem is that, to have the effect of the thing the poet wishes to express, the elements used in the poem must be derived from or exactly correspond to the ur-Image of that thing. Pound's concept of an "absolute" embodies both these principles. In "Credo," he wrote: "I believe in an 'absolute rhythm', a rhythm, that is, in poetry which corresponds exactly to the emotion or shade of emotion to be expressed."[8] And in his introduction to *Cavalcanti Poems* he extended this idea: "I believe in an ultimate and absolute rhythm as I believe in an absolute symbol or metaphor."[9] This term is a metaphorical application of a concept in music theory, absolute pitch. It is an ability to sense the exact form required to reproduce the object.[10]

These principles survived the twenties in the work and mentorship of Pound and Williams, descending directly, and also indirectly through Zukofsky, to Oppen. Oppen was aware of the "Objectivists" common reaction against the dilutors of Imagisme. In his interview with L. S. Dembo, when asked about the attitude which he claimed characterized the writers in *An "Objectivists" Anthology*, he made two points which the Amygists had never understood:

> A. Let me see what we thought and whether I can generalize about it. I'll just put it in personal terms. What I felt I was doing

---

7. *Literary Essays*, p. 4.
8. *Literary Essays*, p. 9.
9. Ezra Pound, *Translations* (NY: New Directions, 1963), p. 23.
10. See Ezra Pound, *Antheil and the Treatise on Harmony, With Supplementary Notes* (Chicago: Pascal Covici, Publishers, 1927), pp. 13, 21.

was beginning from imagism as a position of honesty. The first
question at that time in poetry was simply the question of
honesty, of sincerity. But I learned from Louis, as against the
romanticism or even the quaintness of the imagist position, the
necessity for forming a poem properly, for achieving form. That's
what "objectivist" really means. There's been a tremendous misunderstanding about that. People assume it means the psychologically objective in attitude. It actually means the objectification of the poem, the making an object of the poem.

Q. Williams, in fact, speaks of the poem as object.

A. Right. And this existed in the context of the sloppy American
imagism descending out of Amy Lowell and a thousand others.
The other point for me, and I think for Louis, too, was the
attempt to construct a meaning, to construct a method of thought
from the imagist technique of poetry—from the imagist intensity of vision. If no one were going to challenge me, I would say,
"a test of truth." If I had to back it up I'd say anyway, "a test of
sincerity"—that there is a moment, an actual time, when you
believe something to be true, and you construct a meaning from
these moments of conviction.[11]

Oppen's point about "the necessity for forming a poem properly,
for achieving form" was based on the three Imagist propositions:

1. Direct treatment of the "thing," whether subjective or objective.

2. To use absolutely no word that did not contribute to the
   presentation.

3. As regarding rhythm: to compose in sequence of the musical
   phrase, not in sequence of a metronome.[12]

The "Objectivists" avoided metrical superfluity as well as ornamental verbosity, although not by foregoing structural necessity.
Only by an idea of form does one know what to avoid. Pound
wrote,

By 'direct treatment', one means simply that having got the
Image one refrains from hanging it with festoons.[13]

All the elements of poetry, not only diction (*le mot juste*) and
rhythm (the musical phrase), are seen as capable of corresponding
absolutely to the thing the author wishes to express, which was for
Oppen an objective thing. If these correspondences are established,

11. George Oppen, Interview with L. S. Dembo, *Contemporary Literature*, 10, 2 (Spring
1969), 161; reprinted in *The Contemporary Writer: Interviews With Sixteen Novelists
and Poets*, eds. L. S. Dembo and Cyrena N. Pondrom (Madison: The University of Wisconsin Press, 1972), pp. 173-174.
12. *Poetry*, 1, 6 (March 1913), 199.
13. *Selected Prose*, p. 375.

one has "sincerity." Moreover, if one establishes correspondences to all essential qualities of the object, one achieves form, one creates "the poem as object," one has "objectification."

Williams spoke of the poem as object in his autobiography. There "Objectivism" was "an antidote, in a sense, to the bare image haphazardly presented in loose verse."[14] He also spoke of the poem in terms of a machine. His best-known application of this metaphor is to his own work, in the introduction to *The Wedge* in 1944,[15] but he had previously applied it to the work of George Oppen, in his review of *Discrete Series* in 1934.[16] Here Williams suggested that Oppen's book is "of importance to the highest degree" because "necessary corrections of or emandations to human conduct" originate "in the poems, causing thereby a direct liberation of the intelligence." He continued:

> But this importance cannot be in what the poem says, since in that case the fact that it is a poem would be a redundancy. The importance lies in what the poem *is*. Its existence as a poem is of first importance, a technical matter, as with all facts, compelling the recognition of a mechanical structure. A poem which does not arouse respect for the technical requirements of its own mechanics may have anything you please painted all over it or on it in the way of meaning but it will for all that be as empty as a man made of wax or straw.
>
> It is the acceptable fact of a poem as a mechanism that is the proof of its meaning and this is as technical a matter as in the case of any other machine. Without the poem being a workable mechanism in its own right, a mechanism which arises from, while at the same time it constitutes the meaning of, the poem as a whole, it will remain ineffective. And what it says regarding the use or worth of that particular piece of "propaganda" which it is detailing will never be convincing.[17]

In his interview with Dembo, Oppen expressed in another way his sense of the meaning of form:

> Yes. Well, I do believe in a form in which there is a sense of the whole line, not just its ending. Then there's the sense of the relation between lines, the relation in their length; there is a sense of the relation of the speed, of the alterations and momentum of the poem, the feeling when it's done that this has been rounded. I think that probably a lot of the worst of modern poetry, and it would be true of some quite good poetry, such as Creeley's, uses the line-ending simply as the ending of the line, a kind of

---

14. *The Autobiography of William Carlos Williams* (NY: New Directions, 1967), pp. 264-265.
15. *Selected Essays of William Carlos Williams* (NY: New Directions, 1969), pp. 255-257. See also "An Essay on Virginia," *This Quarter*, Paris, 1, 1 (Spring 1925), 173-175; *Imaginations*, ed. Webster Schott (NY: New Directions, 1971), pp. 319-322.
16. "The New Poetical Economy," *Poetry*, 44, 4 (July 1934), 220-225.
17. *Poetry*, 44, 4 (July 1934), 221.

syncopation or punctuation. It's a kind of formlessness that lacks
any sense of line measure.

The meaning of a poem is in the cadences and the shape of the
lines and the pulse of the thought which is given by those lines.
The meaning of many lines will be changed—one's understanding
of the lines will be altered—if one changes the line-ending. It's not
just the line-ending as punctuation but as separating the connections of the progressions of thought in such a way that understanding of the line would be changed if one altered the line
division.[18]

According to metrical prosody, one simply looks at the poem to
see if it has form: one counts syllables and charts accents and
rhymes. But one can not simply look at an "Objectivist" poem to
see if it has form. "Objectivist" form is the realization of a gestalt:
the "thing" by which all the elements of the poem—semantic,
syntactic, phonemic, and phonetic—cohere.

Oppen's second point—"beginning from imagism as a position of honesty," and constructing "a method of thought from the
imagist technique of poetry"—was based on the "Doctrine of the
Image"[19] as a serious epistemological discipline, avoiding the
Amygist idea of the image as the passively transmitted visual impression. One can see the germ of Oppen's "moments of conviction" in Pound's original definition of the "Image":

An "Image" is that which presents an intellectual and emotional complex in an instant of time. I use the term "complex"
rather in the technical sense employed by the newer psychologists, such as Hart, though we might not agree absolutely in
our application.

It is the presentation of such a "complex" instantaneously
which gives that sense of sudden liberation; that sense of freedom
from time limits and space limits; that sense of sudden growth,
which we experience in the presence of the greatest works of
art.[20]

A moment of conviction is the experience of the objective Image,
an experience strictly faithful to empirical fact. The presentation
of the Image, its realization in form, gives a sense of revelation—
"causing thereby," wrote Williams, "a direct liberation of the intelligence." This formal realization is the object of the discipline of
Discrete Series.

In his interview, Oppen continued,

My book, of course, was called *Discrete Series*. That's a phrase
in mathematics. A pure mathematical series would be one in
which each term is derived from the preceding term by a rule. A
discrete series is a series of terms each of which is empirically

18. *The Contemporary Writer*, p. 180.
19. F. S. Flint, "Imagisme," *Poetry*, 1, 6 (March 1913), 199.
20. *Poetry*, 1, 6 (March 1913), 200-201.

derived, each of which is empirically true. And this is the reason for the fragmentary character of those poems. I was attempting to construct a meaning by empirical statements, by imagist statements.[21]

"Imagist," for Oppen, meant "empirical." An "imagist statement" is absolute, a statement which precisely corresponds with the empirical observation. This discipline avoids through its reliance on the substantive the falseness to which abstract language becomes subject. Oppen said,

> A statement can be made in which the subject plays a very little part, except for argumentation; one hangs a predicate on it that is one's comment about it. This is an approximate quotation from Hegel, who added (I like the quote very much): "Disagreement marks where the subject-matter ends. It is what the subject-matter is not." The important thing is that if we are talking about the nature of reality, then we are not really talking about our *comment about it*; we are talking about the apprehension of some *thing*, whether it *is* or not, whether one can make a thing of it or not.[22]

Oppen's test of reality is whether he can make of it a "thing," whether he can make of it a poem which achieves form.

The objects for Oppen's empirical series derived from his experience of New York City in 1929. Mary Oppen, in her autobiography, wrote:

> We didn't yet know the subway system, and we got off at stations at random just to see what was above ground. Once we stuck our heads out into a cemetery, another time we were on clay fields with standing pools of water, and once we were among gigantic identical apartment buildings in the Bronx, block after block.[23]

When I suggested to the Oppens that this was a prototype for *Discrete Series*, George said "That's Rezzy," and Mary added, "That's Charles Reznikoff. He comes up and he sees the streetlight or he comes up and sees the moon."[24] Oppen learned the value of empirical observation partly from Reznikoff. The work of both realizes moments of revelation of (in Oppen's words) "the things which one cannot not see."[25]

---

21. *The Contemporary Writer*, p. 174.
22. *The Contemporary Writer*, p. 175.
23. *Meaning A Life* (Santa Barbara: Black Sparrow Press, 1978), p. 89.
24. Personal interview, 28 November 1978, San Francisco. See *Poems 1918-1936, Volume I of the Complete Poems of Charles Reznikoff*, ed. Seamus Cooney (Santa Barbara: Black Sparrow Press, 1976), p. 111, No. 20.
25. *The Contemporary Writer*, p. 185. Oppen is remembering section 36 in "Of Being Numerous," *Collected Poems* (NY: New Directions, 1975), p. 176.

II. The Problem.

Each poem of *Discrete Series* makes an objective Image of a
direct observation by the young George Oppen of New York City
—except for the first poem, which, instead, prepares us for these
observations by addressing the problem of seeing what is really
in the world:

> The knowledge not of sorrow, you were
>   saying, but of boredom
> Is—aside from reading speaking
>   smoking—
> Of what, Maude Blessingbourne it was,
>   wished to know when, having risen,
> "approached the window as if to see
>   what really was going on";
> And saw rain falling, in the distance
>   more slowly,
> The road clear from her past the window-
>   glass——
> Of the world, weather-swept, with which
>   one shares the century.[26]

Maude Blessingbourne is a character in Henry James's "The Story
In It."[27] She is a sweet young widow who is staying at Mrs.
Dyott's country home. After a visit by Mrs. Dyott's secret lover,
Colonel Voyt, in which Maude and the Colonel argue about
whether women in the French romances in which Maude vicari-
ously lives need be immoral, Mrs. Dyott learns that although
Maude is passionately in love, she prefers that the man not know
it. Maude's indulgent withdrawal into the pleasures of her subjective romance protects her from the danger which her pessimistic fears would involve her in, if she were to "live." She fears a
real relationship would be a threat to her "honesty," that is, her
virtue; however, her "honesty" is less at stake than her fantasy. By
not honestly admitting it, she protects it from the test of reality.
At any rate, her pleasure in being the mistress of her own passion
compensates for her unhappiness and boredom. Her withdrawal,
her abstinence from expressing her passion, is symbolized by her
gesture of approaching the window to look at the storm, knowing
beforehand what she would see. The weather, if not a projection
of her psychic state, is at least consonant with her inner, though
not her outer, nature. It is not something that has entered her
and changed her in the way the impressions of New York City

---

26. From *Discrete Series*, reprinted in *Collected Poems*, p. 3. All citations from *Discrete
Series* will be from the *Collected Poems*, and will be incorporated in the text.
27. Barrett H. Clark and Maxim Lieber, eds., *Great Short Stories of the World* (NY:
Garden City Publishing Co., 1938), pp. 970-984.

changed the young George Oppen in 1929.

This poem serves as Oppen's preface to *Discrete Series*. As such, it is different, in several ways, from the thirty poems which follow it. To begin with, we are given, in addition to the speaker and his listener, addressed as "you," a persona, Maude Blessingbourne, with whom the mood of boredom is identified. Moreover, she is mentioned by the author to illustrate a philosophical concept previously expressed by his listener: "you were/saying," he says. This distances that mood and that concept from the speaker. Secondly, the poem directly states this concept—that is, that the knowledge of the mood of boredom is the knowledge of the world. To state the concept is to break the discipline which is maintained in the thirty subsequent poems, which present, without comment, the Image encountered in the concrete experience. Each of the other poems in the series is precisely *not* the objective correlative of a subjective thought or state of feeling, but the objective itself, presented to show its significance. Thirdly and as a consequence, in this poem, which quotes and even parodies the prose of Henry James, the rhythms are more extended and less broken, the syntax more convoluted and less elliptical, than in the poems which follow.

The irony of the quotation adds to the distance created by James's language, by Maude's mood, and by the ascription of the philosophical concept in the poem—i.e., the "knowledge of boredom"—to an unidentified interlocutor, the "you" of line one. The poem's total emotional effect is one of curiosity, an effect appropriate to the manner in which the "you" to whom the poem is addressed makes distinctions: "Not of sorrow, you were/saying, but of boredom." The alliteration and the repetition of the musical phrase: / x / x, reinforces a deliberateness not associable with Maude's fond vagueness.

Oppen spoke of this poem in his interview with Dembo. He said that "The word 'boredom' is a little surprising there"; also that it is "rather strange."[28] I suggest that it seemed strange to Oppen because it represented the fulfillment of Maude's desire to know, not Oppen's. The degree to which her social class removes her from the rabble is also the degree to which she is removed from her own basic needs. It can be assumed safely that Oppen understood this problem, for it is the reason he left his financially successful and socially prominent family in San Francisco to hitchhike with Mary across the country and to find in

---

28. *The Contemporary Writer*, p. 182.

New York poets who insisted on "contact." As Mary Oppen wrote
in her autobiography,

> We were searching for a way to avoid the trap that our class back-
> grounds held for us if we relented in our attempts to escape from
> them. We understood from our experiences while hitchhiking
> that in the United States we were not required to remain in the
> class into which we were born. We wanted to see a great deal of
> the world, and the education of which we talked for ourselves
> was to leave our class and learn our life by throwing ourselves
> into it.

And speaking of George's father's reaction to their commitment,
she wrote:

> I know now that we must have seemed to him vulnerable and too
> young to be out in a world of which he knew nothing. I think
> now that he was afraid for us. But we had found people out in
> the larger world to be open and friendly to us wherever we had
> been; his life did not hold for us this wealth of people of all
> classes that we wanted to know. I think we felt the world was
> ours, and that it was not his to give to us.[29]

Maude Blessingbourne had been contented to love from a distance,
but Oppen felt more a part of "the world, weather-swept, with
which/one shares the century," the world he threw himself into.

    Speaking of the spirit which he feels offsets "a kind of pessi-
mism" in his later poems, Oppen has said that he enjoyed life
"very, very much," and he has defined his feeling about life

> by the word "curious" or, as at the end of "A Narrative," "joy,"
> joy in the fact that one confronts a thing so large, that one is
> part of it. The sense of awe, I suppose, is all I manage to talk
> about. I had written that "virtue of the mind is that emotion
> which causes to see," and I think that perhaps that is the best
> statement of it.
>
> * * * * *
>
>   Yes, it is an emotion. The mind is capable not only of think-
> ing but has an emotional root that forces it to look, to think, to
> see.[30]

Maude's gesture, made "as if to see/what really was going on," is
ironic and pathetic. Her boredom is perhaps the "void" which, as
Zukofsky wrote to Pound, Oppen handled in a unique way.
The poem, though expressing knowledge of the world, is not
boring. The poet has chosen not withdrawal but involvement, not
subjectivity but objectivity, not pessimism but curiosity; and the

---

29. *Meaning A Life*, p. 76.
30. *The Contemporary Writer*, pp. 185-186. The word "curious" occurs at the end of
"A Language of New York," and "Of Being Numerous," *Collected Poems*, pp. 101,
179. "A Narrative" ends with "Of clarity, and of respect," *Collected Poems*, p. 140. The
passage "The virtue of the mind//Is that emotion//Which causes/To see" occurs in
"Guest Room," *Collected Poems*, p. 87.

consequence of this is not boredom but joy.

III. The Unreal.

In his brief preface to *Discrete Series*, Pound complained:

> . . . the cry for originality is often set up by men who have never stopped to consider how much. I mean how great a variant from a known modality is needed by the new writer if his expression is to be coterminous with his content.[31]

Oppen succeeded in that reformation in 1929 by providing an "adequate variation from a known mode of writing"—from, that is, the mode of Dr. Williams.[32]

The similarity is clear. In his *Novelette*, Williams wrote that his poems are neither symbolic nor evocative of images; they are "pure design" having only the effect of themselves.[33] The second poem in *Discrete Series* is such a pure design:

1

White. From the
Under arm of T

The red globe.

Up
Down. Round
Shiny fixed
Alternatives

From the quiet

Stone floor . . .
(*CP*, p. 3)

Even though, for the present-day reader, this poem has an appreciable purity as design, it can remain obscure because it neither names nor creates a visual image of its object. This obscurity has increased with time, because the object from which the poem arose, once common, is now esoteric. On the newer elevator portals in Manhattan in the late twenties was a decorative device shaped like a "T" and under its "arms" were two shiny round globes, one white and one red, which lit to signal the direction of the passage of the elevator, up or down. With this knowledge, the poem gains for the present reader total clarity.

Although unfamiliarity with essential factual details increases

---

31. *Discrete Series*, pp. v-vi.
32. *Discrete Series*, p. vi.
33. *Imaginations*, pp. 299, 288, 287.

with time, there is another kind of seeming obscurity more daunt-
ing to readers in the thirties,. who were not as accustomed as are
present-day readers to poetry which enacts the process of perception. Pound tried to counter this obscurity in his preface:

> Bad criticism emerges chiefly from reviewers so busy telling
> what they haven't found in a poem (or whatever) that they have
> omitted to notice what is.
> The charge of obscurity has been raised at regular or irregular
> intervals since the stone age, though there is no living man who is
> not surprised in first learning that KEATS was considered "ob-
> scure." It takes a very elaborate reconstruction of England in
> Keats' time to erect even a shaky hypothesis regarding the prob-
> able fixations and ossifications of the then hired bureaucracy of
> Albermarle St., London West.[34]

This obscurity arises from the reader's "fixations and ossifica-
tions," his outdated, inappropriate expectations about the poem.
Few readers in the thirties, even though they would have recognized the device on the elevator, were prepared to appreciate a
poem without "poetic" ornaments or rhetorical devices, without
symbol, metaphor, or simile, without impressions of simple emotional suggestiveness, without traditional themes or subject-matter,
and without abstract fundamentals like Truth or Beauty. They did
not know how to "read" a poem which strives to be a verbal
equivalent of a perception brought into being by the changing
lights of elevator signals in a skyscraper.

In *An "Objectivists" Anthology*, Zukofsky put this poem in
the section devoted to the "epic,"[35] which was his term for
poetry which recognizes the poetic value of the facts around us,
contemporary or historical particulars, be they things or events.
Zukofsky wrote to Carl Rakosi that Oppen would be represented
in the anthology by

> a short poem presenting the modern skyscraper—the sense of
> being inside it.[36]

For Zukofsky, the poem does not simply record the elevator
portal. The poem is synecdochic; the part represents the whole.
If concrete experience is a test of more conceptual observations,
then we are justified in seeing the poem as a part of more inclusive

---

34. *Discrete Series*, p. v. Pound's criterion for bad criticism was derived from Williams'
position in "George Antheil and the Cantilene Critics: A Note of the First Performance
of Antheil's Music in N Y C: April 10, 1927," *transition*, 13, American Number (Summer 1928), 237-240; in *Imaginations*, pp. 351-355. See Pound, "Dr Williams' Position,"
Selected Essays (NY: New Directions, 1968), p. 393.
35. *An "Objectivists" Anthology*, ed. Louis Zukofsky (NY and Le Beausset, Var, France:
TO Publishers, 1932; rpt. Folcroft Library Editions, 1975), p. 43.
36. Humanities Research Center, University of Texas at Austin; 7 October 1931.

wholes. Indeed, the poem's title in the anthology is "1930s,"[37] and it states a frame of mind which during the years of the Great Depression was fascinated with devices by which one could swiftly rise—or just as swiftly fall.

The next poem, the third, linked with the second by the numbers which precede them, is an observation about how "big-Business," with a capital "B," removes itself from public view:

2

> Thus
> Hides the
>
> Parts—the prudery
> Of Frigidaire, of
> Soda-jerking——
>
> Thus
>
> Above the
>
> Plane of lunch, of wives
> Removes itself
> (As soda-jerking from
> the private act
>
> Of
> Cracking eggs);
>
> big-Business

(*CP*, p. 4)

The objects of this poem are more recognizable than the object of the previous poem. The previous poem seemed mildly ironic because it used Pound's "direct treatment" (avoiding ornament, stripping the verse to its functionally essential parts) to present a device which was partly ornamental. Here Oppen presents an observation of the same kind with, however, a more critical intent. Oppen reflects on the location of a public soda-fountain on the first floor of a large office building. The businessmen above are removed from the "Plane of lunch, of wives," just as the working parts of Frigidaire's refrigerators are hidden within aerodynamically designed curves of white enamel, and as a common act like cracking eggs is made by the soda-jerk to appear to be an act of magic. Big-Business in its tower is removed from the plane of private experience just as the products of big-Business induce a withdrawal which protects us from that kind of experience.

---

37. This title was also used for the third and first poems of *Discrete Series* in the "Objectivists" issue of *Poetry*, 37, 5 (February 1931), 256-257.

What is "really going on" is that we are removed from the actual
by the mystiques of architecture, design, and showmanship whose
intent is to hypnotize us into paying for what we could either do
without or, like cracking eggs, do for ourselves. This poem, as
others in the series, directly presents an aspect of reality antithetical to the honesty and sincerity of direct and objective experience. The "Objectivist" presentation contributes critically to
the ongoing investigation of the book into the question of what is
real.

For Oppen, the real exists on three interdependent levels: the
formal, the epistemological, and the social. Accordingly, the poem
must rest on three interdependent disciplines: meaning must be
resolved into matters of form; thought must be expressed in terms
of lower levels of abstraction; and the object must be in accord
with a kind of populism which Oppen feels he shares with the
poets in his tradition. Oppen summarized his populist principles
as follows:

> The early moderns among painters of the United States found
> themselves promptly identified as the Ash Can school, and it
> happens that Lindsay, Sandburg, Kreymborg, Williams—the poets
> of the little magazine *Others* which came off a hand press in a
> garage somewhere in New Jersey about 1918—were almost a
> populist movement. Though it is hard to register now, the sub-
> jects of Sandburg's poems, the stock-yards and the railroad
> sidings, gave them their impact. Of the major poets it is only
> William Carlos Williams, with his insistence on "the American
> idiom," on the image derived from day to day experience, on
> form as "nothing more than an extension of content," who shows
> a derivation from populism. But it is the fidelity, the clarity,
> including the visual clarity and their freedom from the art subject
> which is the distinction also of Pound and Eliot and the force
> behind their creation of a new form and a new prosody; the
> "speech rhythms" of Pound, the "prose quality" of Eliot.[38]

Populism is a belief in the rights, wisdom, or virtues of the common people. For Oppen, this belief connects his own work with
the work of Pound and Eliot, of the *Others* group, of the Chicago
literary renaissance, and, later, of "the San Francisco School, the
poets called Beat."[39] The term "populism" labels Williams' social,
epistemological, and formal virtues: "his insistence on 'the American idiom,' on the image derived from day to day experience, on
form as 'nothing more than an extension of content.'" Similarly,
he approves Pound's and Eliot's "fidelity" and "clarity," "their

---

38. "The Mind's Own Place," *Montemora,* 1 (Fall 1975), 133. The quotation "nothing
more than an extension of content" derives from Robert Creeley, in Charles Olson,
"Projective Verse," which Williams quoted in his *Autobiography,* p. 330.
39. *Montemora,* 1 (Fall 1975), 134.

freedom from the art subject," and "their creation of a new form and a new prosody," again, reflecting the same three mutually dependent aspects of poetic meaning: the social, the epistemological, and the formal.

This is not to say that Oppen's poetic is identical to that of any other poet in his tradition. For one thing, Oppen did not share Williams' self-conscious need, as a first-generation American, to embrace and reflect the American character. Williams' belief that the language of the poem should be the language of speech is a restriction by which Oppen does not abide. Oppen believes that the language of the poem should be the language of thought, that is, of experience. Although the sounds and rhythms of the poem are part of the structure that gives the meaning, Oppen's test is never whether one would actually *say* the poem. When asked whether he agreed with Williams about the great importance of overthrowing the iambic pentameter, he replied,

> I don't subscribe to any of the theories that poetry should simply reproduce common speech, and so on. My reason for using a colloquial vocabulary is really a different one. It may be touched by populism as Williams' is, but in general I don't agree with his ideas on the subject.[40]

In short, Oppen's poetic is, just as Pound wrote in the preface to *Discrete Series*, "the adequate variation from a known mode of writing," and is certainly not identical to Williams' or any other writer's. Pound wrote,

> I salute a serious craftsman, a sensibility which is not every man's sensibility and which has not been got out of any other man's books.[41]

Oppen's sensibility, the root of his own "Objectivism," was established prior to contact with Zukofsky, and before he had extensive contact with the work of Pound and Williams. In an interview with Charles Amirkhanian and David Gitin, Oppen recalled,

> We had come to New York from San Francisco with the sense of the necessity of what one encountered, what one saw, the reality of the world. I was supposing then it was a Western confrontation. One imagines New York City dwellers involved most of the time with artificial concepts, the game, the definitions. So did I remember the root of my own Objectivism.[42]

Oppen brought this populist root, "the sense of the necessity of what one encountered," to his observation of New York City

---

40. *The Contemporary Writer*, p. 180.
41. *Discrete Series*, p. vi.
42. Charles Amirkhanian and David Gitin, "A Conversation with George Oppen," *Ironwood* 5, 3, 1 (1975), 24.

dwellers. He presents, in *Discrete Series*, the reality of their involvement with abstraction, their detachment from direct experience.

Asked by Dembo what he meant by "populism," Oppen discussed the epistemological virtue of populism as embodied in *Discrete Series*:

> Williams likes to name those objects: wheelbarrow, white chickens, etc. I, too, have a sense—I hesitate to say it because I have no way of defending it—of the greater reality of certain kinds of objects than others. It's a sentiment. I have a very early poem about a car closed in glass. I felt that somehow it was unreal and I said so—the light inside that car.
>
> * * * * *
>
> In fact a lot of the poems talk about that sort of thing.

> Closed car—closed in glass—
> At the curb,
> Unapplied and empty:
> A thing among others
> Over which clouds pass and the
>   alteration of lighting,
> An overstatement
> Hardly an exterior.
> Moving in traffic
> This thing is less strange—
> Tho the face, still within it,
> Between glasses—place, over which
>   time passes—a false light.

> There is a feeling of something false in overprotection and overluxury—my idea of categories of realness.[43]

As do the first three poems, this poem (the ninth) is an ironic presentation of the unreal. It presents a direct experience of an aspect of reality which removes one from direct experience. Like Maude behind her window-glass, the occupant of the car is protected from the true light, the light of "immediate emotional response," "the meaning in the thing itself."[44] Oppen elaborated:

> The car in the poem I just quoted is detached from emotion, from use, from necessity—from everything except the most unconscionable of the emotions.[45]

IV. The Real.

Oppen does not dwell exclusively on the unreality of urban experience; he also dwells on its realness. He presents not only

---

43. *The Contemporary Writer*, pp. 180-181.
44. Kevin Powers, "An Interview with George and Mary Oppen," *Montemora*, 4 (1978), 187.
45. *The Contemporary Writer*, p. 181.

things which detach one from direct experience, but also things which attract us to it. Here, for example, is the sixteenth poem, one of the book's love poems:

> She lies, hip high,
> On a flat bed
> While the after-
> Sun passes.
>
> Plant, I breathe——
>   O Clearly,
> Eyes legs arms hands fingers,
> Simple legs in silk.
>
>   (*CP*, p. 9)

The meaning is in the scene itself, which is presented as clearly and sincerely as it is apprehended by the speaker. The single non-literal word is "Plant," metaphorical shorthand for something like "Quiet as a plant," or, from an early manuscript of the book, "As in a closed room a plant/In darkness growing. Nightcloud."[46] But the plant's qualities need not be explicitly stated; they are implicit in the word itself. We have here only the essentials. "Afternoon" has been reduced to "after-." The terms in "Eyes legs arms hands fingers" are not separated by commas, for they are organically parts of one body.

In his review of *Discrete Series*, Williams wrote:

> An imaginable new social order would require a skeleton of severe discipline for its realization and maintenance. Thus by a sharp restriction to essentials, the seriousness of a new order is brought to realization. Poetry might turn this condition to its own ends. Only by being an object sharply defined and without redundancy will its form project whatever meaning is required of it. It could well be, at the same time, first and last a poem facing as it must the dialectic necessities of its day. Oppen has carried this social necessity, as far as poetry may be concerned in it, over to an extreme.[47]

The form of the poem expresses the epistemological and social realizations which were the conditions of its creation.

The awareness of form that registers "the sense of the whole line, not just its ending," and "the sense of the relation between lines," also registers the sense of the page and the relation between pages. That this series is discrete does not mean that its terms are unrelated; it means that they are as related as are their counterparts in the real world. The twenty-ninth poem illustrates this sense of form:

---

46. The Charles Reznikoff Archive at the Archive for New Poetry, University of California—San Diego.
47. *Poetry*, 44, 4 (July 1934), 223-224.

DRAWING

Not by growth
    But the
Paper, turned, contains
This entire volume
                (*CP*, p. 14)

In *Collected Poems*, *Discrete Series* loses the sense of being a volume of discrete but related parts. It is like a poem whose lines are written out as prose with only longer spaces between the lines. The deleterious effects of the cramped design are more serious than the occasional confusion about where one poem ends and another begins and about whether the end of the page and the end of the poem coincide. In the book's original form, each poem, however small, was printed on a page, and had a single poem facing it on the opposite page. Each leaf turned revealed two new pages. The book unfolded not organically, "by growth," but mechanically, by "drawing," as of cards from a deck, an induction and an accumulation.

When Oppen was asked whether in this poem he were "making a statement about the fragmentary nature of the poem and, by extension, of perception and truth," he replied,

> In a lot of the poems that's said isn't it? I don't know that I was thinking of it there. I was just speaking about "pointing," the poems have that quality of simply pointing at the thing as a way of constructing a poem. It's an imagist base that I'm making use of there. But I'm also talking about form, and maybe even primarily, since that's a major preoccupation of this whole volume.[48]

To justify assertions pertaining to things external to the poem, we must identify their formal equivalents. The fourth poem in the book reads as follows:

The evening, water in a glass
Thru which our car runs on a higher road.

Over what has the air frozen?

Nothing can equal in polish and obscured
        origin that dark instrument
A car
        (Which.
Ease; the hand on the sword-hilt
                (*CP*, p. 4)

The first sentence is elliptical and incomplete. Its verb has apparently suffered the fate of the rhetoric which would customarily

---

48. *Montemora*, 4 (1978), 186.

link "The evening" to "water in a glass," for example, "still, liquid, and contained as." The verb and the rhetoric are inessential. (Just as are the additional letters spelling "through.") Instead, "The evening," the substantive, is emphasized, and "our car" running "on a higher road" is subordinate. The "evening" is the occasion for two observations: one about the frozen air, an unresolved question, and the other about the car, a determined declaration: "Nothing can equal in polish and obscured/origin that dark instrument/A car." The car's polish (hiding its working parts) and its obscurity of origin make its mechanics seem magic, echoing the theme of the previous poems. That the car is a "dark" instrument suggests that this magic isn't white magic. The following two lines contain instances of the stylistic peculiarities of which Zukofsky complained. The parenthesis, capital, period, and lineation of "(Which."—not witch—confer an independent existence upon the relative pronoun, which suggests that the car's independent existence is also the fix and fiction of convention. The juxtaposition of substantives suggests both qualities and verbs, latent, not suppressed. The last line confers upon the car the ease, the simplicity and latent power, of "the hand on the sword-hilt," cutting through the evening.

The efficient formal reliance on the substantive is Oppen's answer to "the first question at the time in poetry"—"the question of honesty, of sincerity," a dialectic necessity of his day. He achieves this by efficiently presenting the concrete experience, refraining from comment. Even a phrase that has the appearance of being comment, such as "a false light," is meant to be a shorthand expression of the feeling of the concrete thing. It is the difference between saying "it was unreal" and "I felt at the time that it was unreal."

V. Meaning.

Oppen's populist sentiment "of the greater reality of certain kinds of objects than others" finds concrete expression throughout the book. We have seen two methods that he uses, the ironic presentation of the unreal, and the direct presentation of the real. He also uses a third method of presentation, juxtaposition, which invites comparison of different categories of realness. An example is the nineteenth poem:

>Bolt
>In the frame
>Of the building——
>A ship
>Grounds

Her immense keel
Chips
A stone   ˖
Under fifteen feet
Of harbor
Water——
The fiber of this tree
Is live wood
Running into the
Branches and leaves
In the air.

(*CP*, p. 10)

The dashes here divide the poem into three terms whose shared element is wood. The terms, as I see it, are arranged in order of ascending value: the inert, the dynamic, and the organic. The tree's vitality excels the ship's force, which excels the building's harnessed stresses.

The following poems about women, the twenty-third, twenty-fourth, and twenty-fifth, are another such triad:

Fragonard,
Your spiral women
By a fountain

'1732'

Your picture lasts thru us

         its air
Thick with succession of civilizations;
And the women.

             * * *

No interval of manner
Your body in the sun.
You? A solid, this that the dress
                insisted,
Your face unaccented, your mouth a mouth?
             Practical knees:
It is you who truly
Excel the vegetable,
The fitting of grasses—more bare than
                that.
Pointedly bent, your elbow on a car-edge
Incognito as summer
Among mechanics.

             * * *

'O city ladies'
Your coats wrapped,
Your hips a possession

Your shoes arched
Your walk is sharp

> Your breasts
> > Pertain to lingerie
>
> The fields are road-sides,
> Rooms outlast you.
> > > (*CP*, pp. 12-13)

These poems present three moments of conviction, the clarity of Oppen's immediate emotional response to a painting by Fragonard, to a photograph of a woman, probably Mary Oppen, leaning on a car, and to a line of verse attributable to the women of New York City streets. These three moments, if the criteria is duration, are in order of descending value. But, if the criteria is realness, the middle woman, excelling the vitality of the vegetable, is most real. Oppen agreed that the intention of the Fragonard poem was the clarity of his immediate emotional response, "the light coming off what is seen":

> Yes, the picture, the actual picture. But I was also interested there in the women themselves as almost a mediation of the culture. I see it as coming down through the women.[49]

If so, then the culture comes down through the type of woman in the second poem above, and through the type of art in the first, not through the women or the art of the third, which even rooms outlast.

These and all the poems of *Discrete Series* are the concrete results of Oppen's empirical investigation into the nature of what is real, of his ability "to construct a method of thought from the imagist technique of poetry—from the imagist intensity of vision," and of his honest presentation, by each of the three methods I've discussed, of the meaning of what truly excels the vegetable, the meaning of the things in which our culture is mediated, the meaning of the apprehensions resolvable into form, and the meaning in "the sense of the necessity of what one encountered, what one saw, the reality of the world."

There are twenty more poems in *Discrete Series* (in addition to the poems already here discussed). They present in the fifth the intimate abstraction of a woman dressing, in the sixth a deck hand on a modern ship taking a break compared to the scene at the sailor's rest home, in the seventh the lights put up for a race, in the eighth a small boat sailing, in the tenth a steamshovel and operator compared to a horse and rider moving through the crowd watching the excavation, in the eleventh a "Party on Ship-board" in relation to the sea, in the twelfth a family laundry in the country, in the thirteenth a couple hypnotized by a stage-show,

---

49. *Montemora*, 4 (1978), 187.

in the fourteenth the juxtaposition of the ocean and somebody's lawn, in the fifteenth a tug moving upriver, in the seventeenth a "Civil war photo," in the eighteenth a new bird on the cobbles, in the twentieth the distance which separates two lovers, in the twenty-first a town seen from a train, in the twenty-second the sexual act, in the twenty-sixth a sign of the depression—a man selling postcards, in the twenty-seventh a tug with two barges and a shoreward movement, in the thirtieth death and geraniums, and in the last, self-reflexively, the formality of these poems:

> Written structure,
> Shape of art,
> More formal
> Than a field would be
> (existing in it)——
> Her pleasure's
> Looser;
> 'O—'
>
>   'Tomorrow?'—
>
> Successive
> Happenings
> (the telephone)
>   (*CP*, p. 14)

One recognizes in the last three lines a description of (and a model for) a discrete series. The series is like successive calls on a telephone, events which might have no relation to each other except that their medium is the same and that their audience holds the same receiver.

VI. Epilogue.

George Oppen stopped writing after *Discrete Series* was published by the Objectivist Press in March 1934. In 1958, when he took it up again, the world had only begun to understand, by confirming the importance of his immediate predecessors, the significance of his work. *Discrete Series* still stands as a testimony to the value of the objective Image and the power of language to register not the fiction but the fact. Oppen cleaved the clean—the essential, the concrete—from the unclean. In the eighties, we still must understand Oppen before we can adapt with integrity old words to our new world in a new way, as Oppen, in his time, had to understand Pound and Williams. Our concern must be to build upon "Objectivism" as the "Objectivists" built upon Imagisme.

HAROLD SCHIMMEL

(ON) DISCRETE SERIES

I. Pointes of the memoriall . . .

> What may I concluden of this long serye
> —Chaucer

Like a boy given his father's tool box after his father's death—
"Sonny!" and out of that he builds his poems; or a child with an
attractively boxed set, "Village," replete with Post Office, City
Hall, Fire Department and shining red engines—George Oppen has
remained the arch-demographer of his poetic polis. Urban planner,
civic geographer and small town topographer responsible that

> Street lamps shine on the parked cars
> Steadily in the clear night[1]

Location has been bolted, lest it fly off into an amorphous realm
of "metaphysical."

He is that soldier in the movie on a map-reading course surveying the lay of the land, raised hand shielding his eyes from glare,
before glancing down at the unwieldy paper; and the soft-hel-
meted, goggled pilot leaning over the side of his biplane, pinpointing live targets with hawkeye against the aerial photograph
on his lap—buildings, highway, road, river, fields, trucks, barges,
hills, cars, curbs, tenements, sidewalks, tract houses, streets, parks,
harbor, stairs, hallway, plumbing:

> There had been trees and people,
> Sidewalks and roads
>
> (CP, p. 60)

Is this urban planner aspect something he shared with Williams

---

1. George Oppen, *Collected Poems* (New York: New Directions, 1975), p. 166. All subsequent references to Oppen's poetry will be to this edition, which will hereafter be cited
as *CP*. All such citations will be incorporated into the text.

and Olson? Only superficially, for the specific angle of vision in
Oppen is entirely his own. In one sense there is no objective world
for him—except that form shaped by the moment—since vision is
multiple. There is the same element of geography in "The World
too short for trend is land" (*CP*, p. 14) as in "Pointedly bent, your
elbow on a car-edge" (*CP*, p. 12). Twenty-five years later he will
quote himself—"No interval of manner"—testing himself for
verity; qualifying, and admiring "A limited, limiting clarity" (*CP*,
p. 185).

* * * * *

Discrete Series, in a light sea-green cloth binding bleached
apple-green at the edges, lies open on my table. One cannot but
regret the penny-wise economy of its reprinting in the New Directions *Collected Poems*. The serial aspect of the meticulously elegant *Series* is all but lost. The considered, faced pages no longer
exist, but most seriously, in this for-the-most-part untitled mode,
it is impossible to tell where a poem ends and where a new poem
begins (cf. "O city ladies" [*CP*, p. 12] which runs on to the top
of page 13, or "2" of the series [*CP*, p. 5] which runs over to page
6). Constructed as independent grouped structures, the poems
cry out for free-circulating air—*lebensraum*. To have missed the
importance of Oppen's first book (or to have, unknowingly,
slighted it) is to have misunderstood Oppen's career as a poet.
Slender as *Discrete Series* was, it embodied the materials and
mechanics of all Oppen's later work. References back to it are
conscious and real, just as Mary Oppen's dedication of 1978,
"To George, whose life and mine are intertwined"[2] is the exact
and essential counterpart to George Oppen's dedication of 1975,
"For Mary/whose words in this book are entangled/inextricably
among my own." But this meshing of "life" and "words," doubly,
is contingent with both their books and at every level.

The obviousness of the Williams affinity seems less apparent
to us today than Pound assumed it would, in his introduction to
Discrete Series. Seeing "the difference" seems no great feat,
especially as Zukofsky hinted at the natural, colloquial, voiced
side of Williams in pointing out that "Against obvious transitions,
Pound, Williams, Rakosi, Bunting, Miss Moore, oppose condensation."[3] Williams was seemingly the opposite of a classicist—casual
disposition fixed—whereas the young Oppen erects temples (little
paestums) on the page. *Discrete Series*, at least, is all condensation,

---

2. Mary Oppen, *Meaning A Life* (Santa Barbara: Black Sparrow, 1978), p. 7. Hereafter
this book will be cited as *MAL*, and all such citations will be incorporated into the text.
3. Louis Zukofsky, " 'Recencies' in Poetry," in *An "Objectivists" Anthology* (New
York: TO Publishers, 1933), p. 22. Hereafter this book will be cited as *AOA*, and all
such citations will be incorporated into the text.

all composition—or if composition can be said to be a habit of the eye, then *Discrete Series* is all construction. The true colloquial flavor of the "I" is what is carefully absent. In this sense he is much closer to Gertrude Stein when she says, "I made it stay on the page quite composed." There is also a strain of composed formality in *Discrete Series* which touches back to Henry James via Marianne Moore. Such a line as

> Like the sea incapable of contact
> Save in incidents
>
> (*CP*, p. 8)

could be the opening of a poem by Marianne Moore. The diction, "incapable of contact/Save," is formidable—formal, odd, proper, elaborate. But there is also a shared bent for precise statement:

> The sea is a constant weight
> In its bed
>
> (*CP*, p. 8)

It is possible, with hindsight, to take Oppen at his word when he says (c. 1969), "really Blake is more important to me than Williams, and several philosophers may be more important to me than Pound" (quoted in *MAL*, p. 94). The Blake of *Thel*, for instance—"I ponder, and I cannot ponder; yet I live and love"—is miles from Williams and close to what Tomlinson so brilliantly described (in Oppen's speech) as "exact with a pondered exactness like his poetry." As for his "several philosophers"—why yes, in the disposition of the argument, in the tactics behind the placement of such pivotal words and phrases as "Thus," "Tho," "Save," "Which," "truly," "against," "Than," "here," "however," "But if," "Thru which." Definition, delineation and qualification are habits of apprehension in *Discrete Series*. There is also his tendency to endow words and letters with the concrete and specific solidity of signs. The tension and discrepancy between signs and meaning are consciously exploited in lines like

> Eyes and a mouth making three—
>
> (*CP*, p. 11)

There is an affinity between the young Oppen and Walter Benjamin, as he emerges in Hannah Arendt's discussion: "he understood language as an essentially poetic phenomenon" (i.e. in, and of, itself), and had what Arendt calls a "gift of thinking poetically" (or what Gertrude Stein called, "the realism of the composition of my thoughts," and she is not speaking of a mental naturalism that leads to such notions as stream-of-consciousness).

As constructs on a page the early poems of Zukofsky's *55 Poems* (1923-1935) sometimes seem tantalizingly close to Oppen's *Discrete Series*, but this is more an accident of shared technique than any actual affinity. Zukofsky, in fact, breaks away from these controlled, chiseled artifacts:

> Not much more than being
> Thoughts of isolate, beautiful
> Being at evening, to expect at a river-front:
>
> A shaft dims
> With a turning wheel;
>
> Men work on a jetty
> By a broken wagon;
>
> Leopard, glowing-spotted,
>   The summer river—
> Under: The Dragon:[4]

The opening line of number 17 in Zukofsky's *55 Poems* (*All*, p. 34)—"Cars once steel and green, now old"—has the linguistic sensibility of *Discrete Series* in the slight-off-balance of the matched adjectives, but Zukofsky's poem falls into fluid poetic speech once having weathered the excitement of the opening. The best measure of Oppen's technique of condensation, cutting, excision, ellipses, and elision, though, would be a comparison of the first version of Zukofsky's *"A"* in *AOA* with its final book publication. See, for instance, the original opening of the "Fifth Movement":

> An animate still-life—(night)
> In one hand, a leaf
> So that after a time
>
>   all's autumn
> Thread: middle down the brown leaf.
> In the next hand, a cigarette.
>   (*AOA*, p. 128)

which becomes:

>   Leaves, autumn
> Thread the middle.
>   A cigarette. . . .[5]

II. . . . *with postils to the same*

> — *Is Rashi home?*
> — *Our rabbi is in the vineyards.*
>   —Reznikoff (*AOA*, p. 87)

To restore the air, order and relationships of the original discrete

4. Louis Zukofsky, *All* (New York: Norton, 1965), p. 24. Hereafter this volume will be cited as *All*, and all such citations will be incorporated into the text.
5. Louis Zukofsky, *"A"* (Berkeley: Univ. of California Press, 1978), p. 17.

series of thirty-one short lyrics (note: the name of the book is both title and description), I will refer to the poems as stages, or pages, in a brief play.

Despite an error in pagination in "The Objectivist Press" edition, I will title the poems by their page referents of 1934.[6] The proem—page 7—faces a blank page with the watermark, "Utopian" and hanging scales in a circle, all but visible in the grain of the paper.

* * * * *

PAGE 7

The knowledge not of sorrow, you were
    saying, but of boredom
Is—aside from reading speaking
    smoking——
Of what, Maude Blessingbourne it was,
    wished to know when, having risen,
"approached the window as if to see
    what really was going on";
And saw rain falling, in the distance
    more slowly,
The road clear from her past the window-
    glass——
Of the world, weather-swept, with which
    one shares the century.

What can be said of the syntax of the lead-poem in *Discrete Series*? What is the mode of its syntax?—Involved? involuted? indirect? oblique? Jamesian?—The word is "Jamesian." ". . . what really was going on" is either clearly metaphysical in intent, or again, anti-metaphysical (i.e. clearly physical). The quotes in the poem of the misspelled heroine (the "error" is reproduced in *CP*) obviously relate to a line in James' story, "The Story In It." Where is the young Oppen's "I" in this proem? It is there, only insomuch as it relates to the "you" of the proem; it narrates what it was "you were/saying." But it is also there, "incognito," in the closure, "with which/one shares the century."

James' story, from *The Better Sort* (1903), initiates "the century"; but "my" or "our" seems carefully excised in the closure. The full Jamesian sentence from which the quotation is extracted reads: "She got up and stood by the fire, into which she looked a minute; then came round and approached the window as if to see

---

6. Hereafter I will also cite the various sections of *Discrete Series* by this same system, as, for example, *DS*7, *DS*8, etc.

what was really going on."7 In Oppen's text "what really was going on" (a shift of emphasis with the inversion) is an escape from the bafflement of abstraction ("The knowledge not of . . . but of . . .") to the intense concreteness of the image:

> And saw rain falling, in the distance
>   more slowly,
> The road clear from her past the window-
>   glass——

and then outward, via that which can be held (the instant of clear vision), in ever expanding circles—so that the local touches on the universal. The particular instant also merges with the great stream of measured (historical) time. The directional swing herein indicated will be typical of all Oppen's poems—following that austere twenty-five year silence.

The "window-/glass" image is not only central to Oppen in *Discrete Series*, as the fine boundary between "inner" and "outer," "here" and "there" (cf. "water in a glass" [*DS* 10]; "closed in glass" [*DS* 15]; "Between glasses" [*DS* 15]; "the round of a port-hole" [*DS* 17]; "window-box" [*DS* 36]; and countless later examples as "Some task beyond the window glass" [*CP*, p. 42]; "A thousand lives//Within that glass" [*CP*, p. 43] etc.), but also to James:

> The wind had risen and the storm gathered force; they gave from time to time a thump at the firm windows and dashed even against those protected by the verandah their vicious splotches of rain.
>
> *(Story*, p. 168)

> Mrs. Dyott, left alone, moved with an air of selection to the window, . . . gazing out at the wild weather. . . .
>
> *(Story*, p. 171)

Note how the self-conscious, reverberating grammar of James' "had risen" finds its way into the poem—"when, having risen,"—where James, himself, in the particular sentence, is much simpler: "She got up. . . ."

But the gorgeous phrase initiating the closure—"Of the world, weather-swept"—seems also to have been inspired by James (cf. the composite words, "weather-washed," "wind-battered"). The young Oppen, as is the case with most imitators, seems to have out Jamesed James—for James' "unhappy" the proem reads "sorrow," for James' "monotony" and "the bored reader" the proem reads "boredom" ("Nothing more real than boredom" [*CP*, p.186],

---

7. Henry James, "The Story In It," in *The Better Sort* (New York: Scribner's, 1903), p. 169. All subsequent references to this story will be to this edition, which will hereafter be cited as *Story*. All such citations will be incorporated into the text.

Oppen will write some thirty years later.) Even poor, lovely Maud Blessingbourne is given the additional ballast of Oppen's "e":

> Of what, Maude Blessingbourne it was,
> wished to know

Oppen, compounding his James with his Proust, is a master of the time-capsule. The essential simultaneity of the whole proem is astounding and impressive; a recounting of a bit of dialogue catapults the story-past ("The Story In It") into an ongoing present,

> And saw rain falling

and out, spiralling ahead into the gyres of "the century."

* * * * *

PAGE 8

1

> White. From the
> Under arm of T

> The red globe.

> Up
> Down. Round
> Shiny fixed
> Alternatives

> From the quiet

> Stone floor . . .

Originally titled "1930'S" (*sic*) in *AOA*, p. 43—hard to see why, unless because it has the "quiet" eroticism of a Bonnard "interior"—after the bath—with its specific angle of vision: the "eye" as director. Bonnard was painting these bathroom nudes in the late twenties and early thirties, and the Saint Tropez Museum houses quite a few. Concretely, on the page, it works that way moving up "From the quiet//Stone floor . . ." (foreground) to the "White." (of a breast seen?) "From the/Under arm of T" Even "T" (a woman's name?) is concrete and emblematic (without a period after the abbreviation)—reducing letters to signs—as in Williams' "T-beams" or more contemporary T-shirts.

The eye is exploratory and moves with the speed and concentration of shifting vision and changing focus. "The red globe" (a nipple?—in contour like a relief map; cf. "So Boldly tipped//With her intimate/Nerves—" [*CP*, p. 130]) is painterly, whereas

                    Up
                    Down. Round
                    Shiny fixed
                    Alternatives

sets the subject in movement. In any case, the "Parts" exposed
against the fixed ground sets up a pattern of shifting relationships.
Imagine the curves and angles created by these moving parts—the
target circle of a breast against "the quiet" (stable) ground.

Oppen will become the twentieth century master of camera-
eye vision—with its tricks of distension, enlargement, recession,
blur and high focus. Bonnard's key-hole compositions of the
mosaic-tile, unheated baths of the late twenties are its richer,
more-textured counterpart. As in Oppen, the identity of the
"anatomy" is less important—so that Bonnard can paint backs,
fronts, full-figure or cropped detail.

In so reading "1930'S" (former title), I am resisting the lure
of stanza three, which may induce us to play "Tender Buttons"
games and reduce the details to a riddle-like thing. The push-but-
ton elevator of the late twenties suggests itself "with its warning
red and its single track."[8] But how much richer the bending,
swivelling, self-occupied movements of the nude. Most of all, the
angle of attention (if it is an "elevator") is strangely dispersed,
unfocused, un-Oppenlike. Does the elevator have a "quiet//
Stone floor . . ."? Or is Oppen moving to the unseen base of the
shaft in this close-focus study? And even then, would it be
"Stone"? And what do we do with the opening "White."? This
Rashi feels that if Oppen were to write about an elevator, there
would be an "operator" in traditional stance before the familiar
arc of the operator's handle.

"The red globe" as seen "From the/Under arm of T" has the
same peculiarity as

                    Her ankles are watches
                    (Her arm-pits are causeways for water)
                                        (*DS* 11)

Lastly, the facing pages seem to establish a contrast of Interior
(anatomy), Intimate, Private—what I called exposed "Parts"—and
Exterior (machinery), Public, hidden "Parts." Of course, I could
be most convincing if I could locate the particular Bonnard; and
then again Tomlinson may have corroborated with Oppen.

                        * * * * *

8. Charles Tomlinson, "An Introductory Note on the Poetry of George Oppen," *Ironwood*, 5 (1975), 13.

PAGE 9

2

    Thus
Hides the

Parts—the prudery
Of Frigidaire, of
Soda-jerking——

Thus

Above the

Plane of lunch, of wives
Removes itself
(As soda-jerking from
the private act

Of
Cracking eggs);

    big-Business

The uncolloquial nature of "Thus": a tension between live speech patterns and formal dispositions of words that have little to do with spoken voice. "Thus" (1.1), "Thus" (1.6) function as arrows, road signs or mathematical symbols. Notice the uncanny relatedness of "Parts" (1.3) and "Plane" (1.8). Oppen's system of capitalization, we discover, is functional—not by rote. He has taken over the effective aspects of English Renaissance and Germanic capitalization. His deliberate capitalization of "Of" (1.4), "Of" (1.12) give them noun-like significance. What is more,

    Of Frigidaire, of

frames the brand name, like Williams' vertical, capitalized "SODA" /"ringed with/running lights." One thinks of Seitz's brilliant sentence (on Pollock): "the perceptual jolt by which one's impression of a visual field shifts." The closure, "big-Business," is a put on, with Oppen's unorthodox, though not arbitrary, minuscule for "big" and majuscule for "Business."

* * * * *

PAGE 10

The evening, water in a glass
Thru which our car runs on a higher road.

Over what has the air frozen?

Nothing can equal ip polish and obscured
     origin that dark instrument
A car
     (Which.
Ease; the hand on the sword-hilt

    How un-Eliotlike Oppen's "evening" ("water in a glass"), there, for specific density "Thru which our car runs on a higher road" introduces a personal pronoun—hardly an "I." The personal pronoun, "our," seems to work along the same lines as the adjective "higher"—"higher" than what?—and is just as indefinite. Stanza three—

Nothing can equal in polish and obscured
     origin that dark instrument
A car

—begins by sounding like Marianne Moore speaking of one of her rare or exotic animals (as she herself later, unsuccessfully, tried to speak of cars: "Edsel"). The closure, "Ease; the hand on the sword-hilt" suggests the rounded knob of the floor-stick shift (but, traditionally, also sexual)—cf. Crane on habitual acts: "the familiar gesture of a motorist in the modest act of shifting gears,"[9] and Mary Oppen's "taxi man . . . concerned about the mysteries of the gearshift" (*MAL*, p. 96), also Mary Oppen's "young taxi-driver . . . impressed with the difficult and different gear-shift of his Dodge" (*MAL*, p. 96).

* * * * *

PAGE 11

Her ankles are watches
(Her arm-pits are causeways for water)

When she steps
She walks on a sphere

Walks on the carpet, dressing.
Brushing her hair

Her movement accustomed, abstracted,
Declares this morning a woman's
"My hair, scalp——"

    To see what Oppen has eliminated, cf. the Lawrence of *Look!*

---

9. Hart Crane, "Modern Poetry," in *The Complete Poems and Selected Letters and Prose*, ed. Brom Weber (New York: Liveright, 1966), p. 262.

We Have Come Through writing in 1912:

> When she rises in the morning
> I linger to watch her;
> She spreads the bath-cloth underneath the window
> And the sunbeams catch her
> Glistening white on the shoulders,
> While down her sides the mellow
> Golden shadow glows as
> She stoops to the sponge, and her swung breasts
> Sway like full-blown yellow
> Gloire de Dijon roses.
>
> She drips herself with water, and her shoulders
> Glisten as silver, they crumple up
> Like wet and falling roses, and I listen
> For the sluicing of their rain-dishevelled petals....[10]

"(Her arm-pits are causeways for water)" is as much King James "Song of Solomon"—the patterned repetition, the oriental oddness ("Thy neck is like the tower of David builded for an armory, whereon . . .")—as it is like the Empson of "Camping Out" (1929)— "And now she cleans her teeth into the lake."[11] The verbal pattern (sometimes also visual) is in defiance of pattern. Patterns are inferred but broken before instigated. "Declares this morning a woman's/'My hair, scalp——' " is a paste-up. That cut-out snippet of would-be dialogue is collaged-in where it almost fits. It doesn't quite satisfy the demands of syntax and grammar, but sits there nevertheless.

Carl Rakosi said, "No. If you know George, that's simply the way he thinks. That's the way his mind works."

* * * * *

PAGE 12

1

> The three wide
> Funnels raked aft, and the masts slanted
>
>   the
> Deck-hand slung in a bosun's chair
> Works on this 20th century chic and
>   efficiency
> Not evident at "The Sailor's Rest."

---

10. D. H. Lawrence, "Gloire de Dijon," in *The Complete Poems*, ed. V. de Sola Pinto and F. Warren Roberts (New York: Viking, 1971), p. 217.
11. William Empson, "Camping Out," in *Collected Poems* (New York: Harvest Books, 1949), p. 18.

Steamship, or ocean liner: "parts" and "people." Precise parallelism presents the structure (embodies)—as in the paired, unusual verbs, "raked," "slung." Note that "the century" (proem) has been specified: "this 20th century chic and/efficiency."

* * * * *

PAGE 13

2

The lights, paving————
This important device
Of a race

Remains till morning.

        Burns
Against the wall.
He has chosen a place
With the usual considerations,
Without stating them.
Buildings.

Seemingly, "street lamp"—the subject unnamed, unspecified,

        This important device
Of a race

is the exact parallel of

        . . . that dark instrument
A car

"He" ("He has chosen a place/With the usual considerations"), without apparent referent, must relate back to "Of a race," i.e. *man*. "Buildings," the line of closure, are simply erected; installed alongside. But the "buildings," together with

        Burns
Against the wall.

give the specific, eerie effect of municipal lighting in peopleless streets.

Note: Parts of Ashbery's "Europe" (thirty years later) have a surface resemblance to some of Oppen's pages—superficial! There is no surrealism in *Discrete Series*. Still, that central section—

        Precise mechanisms
Love us[1][2]

—does recall Oppen.

12. John Ashbery, "Europe," in *The Tennis Court Oath* (Middletown: Wesleyan Univ. Press, 1962), p. 74.

* * * * *

PAGE 14

The mast
Inaudibly soars; bole-like, tapering:
Sail flattens from it beneath the wind.
The limp water holds the boat's round
                sides. Sun
Slants dry light on the deck.
                Beneath us glide
Rocks, sands, and unrimmed holes.

Already, the precise nautical usage, "raked" (*DS* 12), marked Oppen, the sailor. Here, "open" sailing is present in the disposition of the verbs:

             soars
        flattens
               holds
    Slants
                    glide

If you catch it at all, you catch it in movement. The careful excision of personal voice serves that effect. Keats said, "A poet is the least poetical of any thing in existence: it is for ever in, for, and fulfilling some other object." Oppen's verb "slants": the knowledge (physical) that a body tilted forward from the waist lends motion. The position indicates motion: "raked," "tapering."

Transference: two trains side by side at the station and the sensation of movement (in both) when one starts up, as in Oppen's lines:

          Beneath us glide
    Rocks, sand, and unrimmed holes.

The neologism, "unrimmed," is backed by such common terms as "unrigged," "unrippled" (cf. James' "unremoved mud, " [*Story*, p. 172]).

    The limp water holds the boat's round
              sides.

A perfect sentence, with the verb firmly in the center and the adjectives, on either end, flanking, and the sharp clarity of the nouns. Disposition, as pieces on a chessboard:

    CASTLE KNIGHT ... QUEEN ... KNIGHT CASTLE

Compare:

    Brilliant beneath the boat's round bilges
                   (*CP*, p. 245)

* * * * *

PAGE 15

> Closed car—closed in glass——
> At the curb,
> Unapplied and empty:
> A thing among others
> Over which clouds pass and the
>   alteration of lighting,
> An overstatement
> Hardly an exterior.
> Moving in traffic
> This thing is less strange——
> Tho the face, still within it,
> Between glasses——place, over which
>   time passes——a false light

"The closed car was no longer exclusively a rich man's posses-sion" (*Encyclopedia Brittanica*). "Closed car": can one date the expression?—Eliot has one in *The Waste Land* (l.136) as early as 1922 ("And if it rains, a closed car at four."). Oppen reduces it to semantics: "—closed in glass—" as a diagram in some manual reproducing only plate glass parts. "Unapplied and empty" is again Oppen the demographer, Oppen the social economist—one thinks of what "big-Business" called "money useless and unapplied." The thingness of the object, "empty," gives it a toylike supra-reality and palpability. Compare:

> On the water, solid——
> The singleness of a toy——
>
> A tug with two barges.
>   (*DS* 34)

Oppen places it as a figure in landscape—not so much domesti-cating it, as finding, for it, its habitation in the world:

> A thing among others
> Over which clouds pass and the
>   alteration of lighting,

One thinks of Nabokov's world-reflections on the painted steel and safety glass of a van; set in motion, the dance is multiple. But Oppen is less interested in effects of surface—he is more (Ponge-like) stalking his prey. Again,

> Moving in traffic
> This thing is less strange——

sounds "Marianne Moore." What Oppen is about in this second stanza is "Closed car" *applied*; just as "overstatement" is semantic description contiguous with meaning. "Between glasses" takes us back to Maude Blessingbourne at the window. Notice how the "Closed car" is activated into spatial dimensions of the universe—

> Over which clouds pass

—and into the dimension of time,

> ... over which
> time passes

Compare Zukofsky:

> Automobiles speed past the cemetery,
> No gage measures,
>
> No metre turns,
>
> (*AOA*, p. 121)

Later an uncorrected "typo" slips into the name "Ricky" (there, "Rickey") as that "e" appended to "poor lovely Maud." The contrast, on facing pages, between open sailing and cityscape with "Closed car" is maximum.

* * * * *

PAGE 16

> Who comes is occupied
> Toward the chest (in the crowd moving
> opposite
> Grasp of me)
> In firm overalls
> The middle-aged man sliding
> Levers in the steam-shovel cab,———
> Lift (running cable) and swung, back
> Remotely respond to the gesture before last
> Of his arms fingers continually———
> Turned with the cab. But if I (how goes
> it?)———
> The asphalt edge
> Loose on the plateau,
> Horse's classic height cartless
> See electric flash of streetcar,
> The fall is falling from electric burst.

"Who comes is occupied/Toward the chest"—an eloquent formality made awkward. But the oddness, here, is a result of the angle of vision, as foreshortening and uncanny proximities in photography. The subject is recognized by his habitual movements ("sliding/Levers")—hence, his occupation. The relationship between the smaller arena of bodily movement and the larger of the crane's response, is taken in at the level of sight. Note how the transitionless break initiates sudden (from down below), unpredictable, mechanical movement:

> Of his arms fingers continually——
> Turned with the cab.

The little preposition "with," here, does all the work.

>   But if I (how goes
>   it?)——

We are alert to the rareness of this "I" which makes its debut here; it no sooner pops in, but is run off—in favor of the succeeding subject—and disappears. The three lines of closure—

> Horse's classic height cartless
> See electric flash of streetcar,
> The fall is falling from electric burst.

—are pure Americana, U.S. cities of the twenties. First performances of Charles Ives' *Orchestral Sets* (e.g. "Three Places in New England") took place in the early thirties. "Horse's classic height cartless" is the carthorse un"cart"ed; it breaks a linguistic structure—"horse and cart"—in order to achieve its discrete, aplotomic portrait. See also the photograph of Oppen and Pom-Pon (*Ironwood*, 5, p. 58) for its perspectivist clarification of equine proportions.

* * * * *

PAGE 17

> Party on Shipboard
>
> Wave in the round of the port-hole
> Springs, passing,—arm waved,
> Shrieks, unbalanced by the motion——
> Like the sea incapable of contact
> Save in incidents (the sea is not
>   water)
> Homogeneously automatic—a green capped
>   white is momentarily a half mile
>   out——
> The shallow surface of the sea, this,
> Numerously—the first drinks——
> The sea is a constant weight
> In its bed. They pass, however, the sea
> Freely tumultuous.

"Party on Shipboard" is one of the two titles in *Discrete Series*. Set in the same typeface as the poem with only a line's space between, a tension is felt between title as title and title as adjunct of the poem (cf. Williams: "This Florida:1924/of which I am the sand——" [*AOA*, p. 101], and "DOWNTOWN/is a condition——" [*AOA*, p. 104]). Verb-noun play: a characteristic trait of late Zukofsky, an insistence that language be seen *as language*:

> Party on Shipboard
>
> Wave in the round of the port-hole
> Springs, passing,—arms waved,

"Wave" as noun; "waved" as verb—these shifts keep us on our toes, keep us language-conscious. Even the "Party" of the title keeps its tension of possible meanings—finally, insists on both.

Examine the opening line in terms of composition:

> Wave in the round of the port-hole

The three nouns are dropped one over the other like rope rings in a game of quoits. The still-life

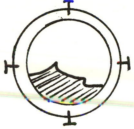

is exploded into a moving picture:

> Springs, passing,—arm waved,

The contiguity of "Wave . . ./Springs" and "—arm waved" is visual —the split-second in the life of a lens—both accidental and permanent.

Oppen is also a master at setting up pseudo-relationships between basically unlike words. The logic of grammar seems to argue for a false connection, as in "Homogeneously" (1.7) "Numerously" (1.11); also the system of capitalization and the placement of these words as line beginnings—

> ——a green capped
> white is momentarily a half mile
> out——

—is beautiful maritime (landless) observation. It is what Oppen defines as "The shape is a moment" (*DS* 27). Grammar is often probing in Oppen, as in the phrase "The shallow surface of the sea," where adjective is a test of the noun. The phrase, "—the first drinks—," is both descriptive and humorous in its relationship to "the sea" which establishes and incorporates metaphysical reverberations. The word, "unbalanced" (1.3), is like the gyroscope at the heart of a sophisticated mechanism, which set spinning continues determinate: What would a translation machine do with that word "drinks"?

* * * * *

PAGE 18

This land:
The hills, round under straw;
A house

With rigid trees

And flaunts
A family laundry,
And the glass of windows

Twenty-two words. The items of the landscape are the landscape; their enumeration is the composition. Analyze, for example, punctuation. Provincial landscape in post-impressionist painting (French); "flaunts" is the single non-painterly (non-imagistic, non-representational) item in the poem—the "I" of the poet. "And the glass of windows" continues Oppen's glazierly preoccupations. Note that "the glass of windows" as a verbal construct does not equal "window-glass." This seeming tautology is indicative of Oppen's method—the mode of *Discrete Series*.

* * * * *

PAGE 19

Semaphoring chorus,
The width of the stage. The usher from it:
Seats' curving rows two sides by distant
        phosphor. And those 'filled';
Man and wife, removing gloves
Or overcoat. Still faces already lunar.

A single semantic pattern becomes the spinal column of the poem—

Semaphoring

phosphor.

                    lunar.

The relationship: *sema*-phoring (bearing signals) to *phos*-phor (bearing light) to "lunar." The 2¢ plain of it is a Ziegfield Follies-like atmosphere—"chorus," "stage," "usher," "Seats' . . . rows." The accuracy of the detail-observed ("removing gloves") is undermined by the conjunction, "Or." What this does to what Oppen has called, "the quaintness of imagism"! A will towards precision (positionality) in language undermined by syntactical ambiguities:

> *Still* faces *already* lunar.
>
> (italics, mine)

What the abstract-expressionists called "push-pull" twenty years later. The sign-like quality of "filled" within Oppen's inverted commas—like Whitman's American "To Let" sign on the Parthenon.

* * * * *

PAGE 20

The edge of the ocean,	Beyond the lawn,
The shore: here	beyond the cliff,
Somebody's lawn,	the great wet brush of the sky
By the water.	dipped deep into the sea.

(*Story*, p. 168)

Comparing James' sentence from "The Story In It" to Oppen's word-structure is to underline the non-narrative, linguistic nature of his composition or construction. The shifting progression of a quarterback's zigzag speed; so that the tail of the sky can be one man's breath. The technique is mixed—both visual and semantic—with the kind of jolt as when activating the zoom, telescoping in or out. The two "marines" on facing pages: suburban ("small lawns of home" [*CP*, p. 29]), and urban ". . . until the small black tugs of England/Came to fetch us in" [*CP*, p. 48]). Notice how that one word, "lawn," (as in the "Newport" of Henry James, for example) humanizes the macro to micro to local progression, implying a particular civilization.

* * * * *

PAGE 21

Tug against the river——
Motor turning, lights
In the fast water off the bow-wave:
Passes slowly.

"Tug" for "Tugboat" is Oppen's preference, providing the

pull of the verbal form. Movement is perceived via visual effects: "Motor turning" and its direct (causal) relation to "lights/In the fast water." "Passes slowly" again shifts the focus (as seeing with the two ends of the telescope), with the flickering two-way tension ("fast"/"slowly") as in a deKooning overlay.

His fascinating tenacious structures—surely it was in this sense Crane used the phrase, "white buildings."

* * * * *

PAGE 22

> She lies, hip high,
> On a flat bed
> While the after-
> Sun passes.
>
> Plant, I breathe——
>   O Clearly,
> Eyes legs arms hands fingers,
> Simple legs in silk.

Note the shimmering connections between this poem and the next poem in the word, "silk":

"in silk"	"In silk"
(legs)	(Man)
bed	field

Note how "hip high,/On a flat bed" provides a topography of bedroom:

> While the after-
> Sun passes.

What kind of time sequence is involved here? The following lines suggest we may be in cinematic time:

> She lies, hip high,
> On a flat bed

(Lighting essential to both structures: page 22/page 23). The suggestive ambiguity of "hip high,"—either her hip high (female pelvis jutting) in the prone position, or, at the height of a hip (standard fucking position). "While the after-/Sun passes."—"noon?", we ask, as in reductive shorthand or . . . or, "after-/Sun," or . . . or, whatever. "Plant, I breathe—": here, the "I" is the (sensitive breathing) camera. "A Morality Play: Preface" (*CP*, p. 215) picks up this theme, consciously ("Again,"), many years later:

> Lying full length
> On the bed in the white room

Turns her eyes to me

Again,

Naked . .

* * * * *

PAGE 23

Civil war photo:
Grass near the lens;
Man in the field
In silk hat. Daylight.
The cannon of that day
In our parks.

Perhaps the most elegant, most economical, most perfect rendering of the miniature verbal structure (and unlike the tiny, voiced fragments of Sappho, which Hugh Kenner discusses in *The Pound Era*[13])—stunning in the relation of foreground to subject, if "a" subject can be determined. The "war" photo is soldierless; the middle lines effective in their slight discrepancy. Is the "cannon" in the photo? Or only metaphorical, being, in actuality, in the "parks" of to-day. What happens to time, here?—it is compounded (past/present). Simultaneity: a time structure:

Who shall say
How the Romantic stood in nature?
But I am sitting in an automobile
While Mary, lovely in a house dress, buys tomatoes from a
road side stand.
(*CP*, p. 62)

Or, foreground opening out onto background with time, "Again," compounded:

Mary in the noisy seascape
Of the whitecaps

Of another people's summer
(*CP*, p. 245)

But the splicing of 1932-1934 is sharper; more transitionless; condensed.

---

13. Hugh Kenner, *The Pound Era* (Berkeley: Univ. of California Press, 1971), pp. 5-6.

* * * * *

PAGE 24

As I saw
There
Year ago——
If there's a bird
On the cobbles;
One I've not seen

The most enigmatic of the series, with its dropped grammatical units, lost articles. What would remain of this structure in the grammar of another language?

> I do indeed know that my poems are difficult to translate. The line sense, the line breaks, and the syntax are intended to control the order of disclosure upon which the poem depends.[14]

The staccato, clipped, telegraphic language undermined by the formal, colloquial grammar:

As I saw
. . . I've not seen

The single, "individual" word in the poem: "cobbles," as in:

Sparrow in the cobbled street
(*CP*, p. 37)

* * * * *

PAGE 25

In itself, a series of three. Simultaneity—only in the physical structure of the poem or, more literally, juxtaposition. Three "material" views; three discrete states of physical being and disposition. From simple physical being (existence)—

Bolt
In the frame
Of the building——

to "change" through action or "occurrence" (cause and effect):

A ship
Grounds
Her immense keel
Chips
A stone
Under fifteen feet
Of harbor
Water——

---

14. George Oppen, letter to Serge Fauchereau, in *Ironwood*, 5 (1975), p. 81.

Here, the absence of punctuation between the "occurrence" and the "consequence" is in itself the mode. What happens between "keel" and "Chips" is the sensitive fulcrum. The secret of the "serious craftsman" that Ezra Pound saluted is visible also in the personal pronoun, "Her" (not "Its").

The final stage in the progression is to the metaphysical—the extensions beyond:

> The fiber of this tree
> Is live wood
> Running into the
> Branches and leaves
> In the air.

This is the "objectivist" version of Daphne's metamorphosis as presented definitively in Pound's early poem. It also embodies Oppen's characteristic movement from "inner" towards "outer"— the miniscule cells and "fiber" that breathe cosmic air.

* * * * *

PAGE 26

> From this distance thinking toward you,
> Time is recession
>
> Movement of no import
> Not encountering you
>
> Save the pulse cumulates a past
> And your pulse separate doubly.

"From this distance thinking toward you,/Time is recession."
Recession:

a. The action of receding from a place, or point;

b. Used with ref. to receding or distant parts of surfaces or out-lines;

c. A setting or going back in time. *rare*

(*OED*)

"Recession" as a poetic technique, in Oppen, which embodies all three meanings.

* * * * *

PAGE 27

> Town, a town,
> But location

> Over which the sun as it comes to it;
> Which cools, houses and lamp-posts,
>   during the night, with the roads——
> Inhabited partly by those
> Who have been born here,
> Houses built——. From a train one sees
>   him in the morning, his morning;
> Him in the afternoon, straightening——
> People everywhere, time and the work
>   pauseless:
> One moves between reading and re-reading,
> The shape is a moment.
> From a crowd a white powdered face,
> Eyes and mouth making three——
> Awaited——locally——a date.

"Town, a town," is already in the train; anticipates "From a train." It's as if the moving train breaks away from "time" in the sense—the town that awaited the sun's light and was passed now has the sun's light and the train is off and onward, and time and the sun-moon, day-night cycle will continue to operate in them, as we, moving, are nowhere but catch glimpses of places (location), people, operating within the calendar.

Page 26:   Time is recession//Movement . . .

Page 27:   The shape is a moment.

* * * * *

PAGE 28

> Near your eyes——
> Love at the pelvis
> Reaches the generic, gratuitous
>   (Your eyes like snail-tracks)
>
> Parallel emotions,
> We slide in separate hard grooves
> Bowstring to bent loins,
>   Self moving
> Moon, mid-air.

"Dover Beach" revisited. Compare James:

> . . . in their having drawn each other for a minute as close as possible—as possible, that is, with no help but the full clasp of hands. Thus they were mutually held, and the closeness was at any rate such that, for a little, though it took account of dangers, it did without words.   (*Story*, p. 172)

James' sentences are a paradigm of closeness, like that early Hockney ("Adhesiveness," 1960) with something going on down below though the eye fixes on the faces above.

> Near your eyes——
> Love at the pelvis

"(Your eyes like snail-tracks)" (l.4) continues the simultaneity—

> Up
> Down.

—in the cross-section study from "1930'S"—or, "Your eyes like snail-tracks" recording where we have been. "Parallel emotions," moves down to the anatomical horizontal:

> Parallel . . .
>   separate

recalling the closure (page 26), "separate doubly." Moving as close as possible, Oppen takes time to draw in the cosmic:

> Moon, mid-air.

tacking up that moon, giving it geography. One thinks of Williams' ". . . moon/noon/of night" ("Full Moon").

* * * * *

PAGE 29

> Fragonard,
> Your spiral women
> By a fountain
>
> '1732'
>
> Your picture lasts thru us
>
>   its air
> Thick with succession of civilizations;
> And the women.

Or again Williams ("Portrait of a Lady"):

> Agh! what
> sort of man was Fragonard?
>   (*AOA*, p. 181)

Oppen's objectivist, historical date in inverted commas

> '1732'

is used again as singular stanza:

> The great stone
> Above the river
> In the pylon of the bridge
>
> '1875'   (*CP*, p. 150)

His "Fragonard" is not static—the adjective "spiral" and the noun "fountain" see to that. "Your picture lasts thru us" is classical, Elizabethan, renegade-modern. Compare Mary Oppen's sentence: "The paintings carried deep sincerity, as though they expressed their times to me in a later time" (*MAL*, p. 125). Fragonard, and us:

> We slide in separate hard grooves
>
> (*DS* 28)

"And the women.", as closure, is witty, following closely upon:

> Thick with succession of civilizations;

* * * * *

PAGE 30 – PAGE 31

No interval of manner
Your body in the sun.
You? A solid, this that the dress
                    insisted,
Your face unaccented, your mouth a mouth?
                    Practical knees:
It is you who truly
Excel the vegetable,
The fitting of grasses—more bare than
                    that
Pointedly bent, your elbow on a car-edge
Incognito as summer
Among Mechanics.

'O city ladies'
Your coats wrapped,
Your hips a possession

Your shoes arched
Your walk is sharp

Your breasts
        Pertain to lingerie

The fields are road-sides,
Rooms outlast you.

The personal pronoun, "Your," directs both poems, on facing pages. Both are in "the ancient manner"—the hyperbole of the Shakespeare sonnet and the particularized orientalism of "Song of Songs" are updated, urbanized. Reznikoff must have been apportioning careful praise when he said of " 'O city ladies' " —"the only line that sings" (quoted in *MAL*, p. 146). There is also something of deKooning's 1950 women in

> your mouth a mouth?
> Practical knees:

and in

> Your hips a possession
>
> Your shoes arched
> Your walk is sharp
>
> Your breasts
>   Pertain to lingerie

Those personal pronouns partake of both city sidewalks and

advertising copy. Each of the five "Your" constructions (*DS* 31) is unlike in grammatical pattern but, serially, a continuation of "Your body," "Your face," "your mouth" (*DS* 30).

* * * * *

PAGE 32

> Bad times:
> The cars pass
> By the elevated posts
> And the movie sign.
> A man sells post-cards.

"Bad times:"—avoiding, "hard times." Prose vs. poetry. Compare Mary Oppen: ". . . the first stoplight rag in hand to wipe . . . our fathers impoverished" (*MAL*, p. 144), and George: ". . . shocked by seeing men one could recognize as carpenters, as masons, as small businessmen, asking us at the age of twenty, twenty-one, around there, for a dime."[15] But what is it in

> The cars pass
> By the elevated posts
> And the movie sign.
> A man sells post-cards.

that equals "Bad times:"? Except that saying it is so makes it so. Compare Reznikoff's poem from *Rhythms* (1919):

> Stubborn flies buzzing
> In the morning when she wakes.
>
> The flat roofs, higher, lower,
> Chimneys, water-tanks, cornices.[16]

* * * * *

PAGE 33

> It brightens up into the branches
> And against the same buildings
>
> A morning:
> His job is as regular.

Another version of "the sun as it comes to it" (page 27):

---

15. Charles Amirkhanian and David Gitin, "A Conversation with George Oppen," *Ironwood*, 5 (1975), 23.
16. Charles Reznikoff, *Rhythms II*, from *The Complete Poems*, Vol. 1, ed. Seamus Cooney (Santa Barbara: Black Sparrow, 1976), p. 22.

        It brightens up into the branches
        And against the same buildings

as,

        A morning:
        His job is as regular.

parallels:

           in the morning, his morning;
  . . .
                    and the work
pauseless:
                         (DS 27)

* * * * *

PAGE 34

On the water, solid——
The singleness of a toy——

A tug with two barges.

O what O what will
Bring us back to
Shore,
        the shore

Coiling a rope on the steel deck

The tug returns. "Coiling a rope on the steel deck" contains the action, the emotion.

* * * * *

PAGE 35

Drawing

Not by growth
    But the
Paper, turned, contains
This entire volume

Angle of vision—how? (from where?) you take it all in.

    Paper, turned, . . .

is the propelled image.

* * * * *

PAGE 36

Deaths everywhere——
The world too short for trend is land——
    In the mouths,
        Rims

    In this place, two geraniums
    In your window-box
    Are his life's eyes.

"In the mouths,/Rims" recalls the "unrimmed holes" over
which the boat glided (page 14). The poem is encompassed between "Deaths everywhere—" and "his life's eyes."

* * * * *

PAGE 37

Written structure,   discourse interminably
Shape of art,   uncontradicted
More formal
Than a field would be   level under the orchards
(existing in it)——   livid-drowsy green:[17]
Her pleasure's
Looser;
'O——.

        'Tomorrow?'—

Successive
Happenings
(the telephone)

But one would do well to follow the word, "field," through his
book.

---

17. Basil Bunting, "Ode 19," from *Collected Poems* (Oxford: Oxford Univ. Press, 1978),
p. 93.

THE CANON
II.
MIDDLE PERIOD

George Oppen & Charles Reznikoff. Photograph taken at a party in celebration of the publication of *The Materials*, 1962, courtesy of Mary Oppen.

BURTON HATLEN

"NOT ALTOGETHER LONE IN A LONE UNIVERSE":
GEORGE OPPEN'S THE MATERIALS

Two dramatic metamorphoses have punctuated George Oppen's adult life, transforming him first from an avant garde poet into a political activist—and then, over twenty years later, back into a poet. From the mid-1920s until 1935, Oppen and his wife Mary lived primarily within an avant garde artistic community. The search for such a community brought them from California to New York, and then to Europe. In New York the Oppens established close friendships with Louis Zukofsky and Charles Reznikoff, and in Europe they—or George at least—were welcomed as peers by Ezra Pound and Basil Bunting. During these years Oppen honed his poetic technique, as he assembled that most radical of modernist texts, *Discrete Series*. This slim volume was published, with a preface by Pound, in 1934, the year that the Oppens returned to New York. But even before *Discrete Series* appeared the Oppens were becoming concerned about the rise of Fascism in Europe and in America, and shortly after they returned to the United States they joined the Communist Party—but "not," says Mary Oppen, "as artist or writer because we did not find honesty or sincerity in the so-called arts of the left."[1] When George and Mary Oppen entered the Communist party, therefore, George also abandoned poetry—the beginning of a sabbatical that was to last over twenty years. For a time the Oppens worked as full-time party organizers, and for a considerably longer period they pursued a way of life shaped primarily by their political commitments. George joined the army in World War II to "fight fascism," and after the war he worked as a carpenter in Los Angeles for a few years. Then in 1950, he and Mary moved to Mexico to avoid

---

1. Mary Oppen, *Meaning A Life* (Santa Barbara: Black Sparrow, 1978), p. 151. Most of my information about the lives of George and Mary Oppen comes from this volume.

testifying before the McCarthy Committee. By this time the ties of the Oppens to the Communist Party had become tenuous, but even during their Mexican years they lived largely within a circle of fellow Communists or ex-Communists in exile. In 1958, however, George began to write the poems which were eventually collected in *The Materials*. Shortly thereafter the Oppens returned to the United States and set out to re-establish their long lapsed circle of artistic friendships, as George began once again to seek a career as a poet. This second metamorphosis initiated the third period of George Oppen's life—the period in which he established himself as a major poet, and which has not yet ended.

This brief summation of George Oppen's career confronts us with some fundamental questions: What is the relationship between poetry and politics? More specifically, what is the relationship, in the context of Twentieth Century America, between a radical poetics and a radical politics? The two key moments in George Oppen's career as a writer—the decision to abandon poetry for political work in the mid-1930s, and the decision to return to poetry in 1958—both dramatize these questions. However, I want to argue here that these two moments carry for us two quite different messages concerning the relationship between a radical politics and a radical poetics. In 1935, George and Mary Oppen saw the life of the *avant garde* artist and the life of the political activist as absolutely incompatible. They found unacceptable the political and social elitism of Pound and Eliot, the high priests of international literary modernism. And Dr. Williams's assertively "American" brand of modernism seemed equally unsatisfactory: for while Williams's instincts remained egalitarian, he refused to engage directly with economic and political questions. But if the Oppens rejected the social attitudes of the artistic *avant garde*, they also rejected the tendentious and doctrinaire approach to art characteristics of their new Communist comrades. For the party demanded an art accessible to the masses, and it insisted that artists must allow their art to become a "weapon in the class struggle." Rather than subjugate their artistic work to the demands of the party, however, the Oppens preferred to give up art itself. In 1935, then, the Oppens saw no possibility of a reconciliation between poetry and politics. But when George Oppen returned to poetry in the late 1950s, he did not, as I shall here try to demonstrate, leave his political commitments behind. Rather . Oppen's later poetry represents, I believe, a systematic attempt to body forth certain political commitments (Oppen today calls his political position "populism") in and through an uncompromisingly modernist poetic method. In the next section of this paper I shall describe in general terms Oppen's synthesis of a radically modernist poetic with a no less radical political vision. I shall then attempt to show how this synthesis shapes one specific text by Oppen, *The Materials*—the text which represents Oppen's return to poetry after his over twenty years as a Communist, and which therefore reveals with unusual clarity the conjunction of his political and poetic concerns.

I

From the beginning of his literary career, Oppen aligned himself with what Charles Altieri has called the "immanentist" (as opposed to the "symbolist") thrust in Twentieth Century poetry. Altieri finds in "Wordsworth's exploration of values immanent in the experience of secular, familiar objects" a paradigm of "what might be called the 'prose tradition' or the reliance on horizontal, rather than vertical, symbolic sources of value."[2] Wordsworth, Altieri further argues

> . . . works out several points that recur in subsequent aesthetics of immanent presence: the idea that experience has value without the artist intervening to rearrange and structure it; . . . a naturalistic theory of language opposing directness to creative artificiality; emphasis on the innate harmony between nature and the mind open to and actively participating in it; a theory of rhythm stressing its absolute qualities as a dimension of the experience, not its artificial functions; a consequent distrust of sophisticated culture and its mediated ways; and, finally, a morality of attention locating both moral and poetic values in one's capacity to look steadily at his object and to recover qualities inherent in it or in the act of perception. (Altieri, p. 36)

Altieri sees this immanentist poetic as standing over against a symbolist poetic:

> Symbolism in this sense is not the pursuit of spiritual correspondences or Platonic essences, but an attitude that emphasizes the creative role of human consciousness as a force that actively transforms the flux of human experiences into coherent perceptual and axiological structures. Symbolism, too, can be conceived as immanent in the sense that there need be no transcendental ground for the values it creates, but as a way of thinking it alters the idea of numinous presence. What matters is not what is there in immediate experience but what the mind can make of it.
> (Altieri, p. 36)

For all Twentieth Century poets, the primary source of an immanentist poetic practice has been the criticism and the poetry of

---

2. Charles Altieri, *Enlarging the Temple: New Directions in American Poetry During the 1960s* (Lewisburg: Bucknell Univ. Press, 1979), p. 35. Hereafter this volume will be cited as "Altieri," and all such citations will be incorporated into the text.

Ezra Pound. The first (and, I think, the most fundamental) of Pound's imagist principles sums up his immanentist commitments: "Direct treatment of the 'thing' whether subjective or objective."[3] In enunciating this principle, Pound implicitly repudiated the impulse to "privilege" the motions of the mind over the things of the world. Rather ideas too here become "things" *in* the world, rather than acts (as the symbolist would have it) that *make* the world. The insistence on "direct treatment" of the thing is no less significant, for it implies a repudiation of the ego. What the poet *makes* of things, what he/she "feels" about them—these are irrelevant. Rather the poet must give him/her self to the things of this world, and must trust the energies at work in and between these things to give form and meaning to his/her work.

What I have, following Altieri, here called "immanentist" poetry issues from an attitude that I would like to describe, borrowing a phrase from the psychologists, as "basic trust"—a trust, however, not in people but in *things*. For the symbolist poet (and I am here thinking of such representative texts as Coleridge's "Dejection" and most of Eliot's poetry) *things need me*. In the terminology of Husserl, the symbolist poet seeks to become the Transcendental Ego, the ego whose act of knowledge will be co-extensive with the world. For the symbolist poet (as to Husserl himself, at least in some of his moods) the very "worldness" of the world depends upon the existence of such an ego. But conversely, when the symbolist poet imagines a world from which spirit has been drained away, he can see only a shapeless, grey, nauseating mass. In contrast the immanentist poet can and does contentedly inhabit what Husserl called the "natural" viewpoint, simply because he/she begins with a sense that "things" can and do sustain themselves quite apart from "me."[4] Pound, looking out from his Pisan cage, knows that "things" don't need him—that, rather, *he* needs them:

> and as for the solidity of the white oxen in all this
> perhaps only Dr. Williams (Bill Carlos)
>   will understand its importance
> its benediction. He wd/have put in the cart.[5]

This sense of basic trust in things links Pound to Williams, and sets both of them over against Eliot, who lacks precisely this trust. In

---

3. Ezra Pound, "A Retrospect," in *Literary Essays of Ezra Pound*, ed. T. S. Eliot (New York: New Directions, 1968), p. 3.
4. In the course of his career, Husserl offered many different formulations of the relationship between the transcendental and the natural standpoints. See, for example, *Ideas: General Introduction to Pure Phenomenology*, trans. W. R. Royce Gibson (New York: Collier Books, 1962), pp. 91-167 and *Cartesian Meditations*, trans. Dorion Cairns (The Hague: Martinus Nijhoff, 1973), *passim*.
5. Ezra Pound, *The Cantos* (New York: New Directions, 1970), p. 483.

Twentieth Century American poetry, the Symbolist line runs from Eliot to Tate and Blackmur and Warren to Berryman, Roethke, Wilbur, Lowell, and all his epigones. As these Symbolists have struggled, often desperately, to *make* meaning, the immanentists (and this line runs from Pound and Williams to the Objectivists and Olson to Creeley, *et al.*) have been quietly *finding* meaning, in the simple given-ness of "things." "Things," for the immanentist poet, do not exclude the poet him/herself. The poet moves among things, touching them, naming them, above all *seeing* them. These actions are as "real" as the things themselves. But the poet's actions do not bring the things into being. Rather the poet greets things that exist prior to and independently of the poet's own perceptions. These very perceptions, and the words the poet uses to greet the things of the world, themselves also become, for the immanentist poet, things *in* the world. And the dance of the words in turn becomes, not a way of imposing a "human" order on the world, but rather a way of being joyously, angrily, sorrowfully *in* the world.

From the beginning, Oppen's poetry, like Pound's, sought a "direct treatment of the thing." As Oppen himself says in one of his few programmatic statements, "what 'modernism' restored to poetry [was] the sense of the poet's self among things. So much depends on the red wheelbarrow."[6] In this concern with "things" Oppen's entire oeuvre builds upon Pound's first principle of Imagism. But the early work of Oppen and the other Objectivists also implies a critique of Pound's work as in some measure failing in rigor. A still powerful impulse toward egoistic posturing, an at least sporadic hunger for some sort of transcendental "meaning" in experience, above all a residual taste for a richly rhetorical language—these lingering symbolist traits qualified the purity of the Poundian poetic enterprise. And so the Objectivists resolved to out-Pound Pound. Oppen in particular set out, in *Discrete Series*, to purge poetry of the interfering, order-demanding, meaning-making "subject," the ego that in symbolist poetry claims for itself the status of Creator—of the poem, and of the world. *Discrete Series* offers us a poetry of pure discontinuity. All the various links—logical relationship, narrative sequence, emotional association—through which we seek to find "meaning" in the world are here systematically deconstructed. Only pure contiguity remains:

---

6. George Oppen, "The Minds Own Place," *Kulchur*, 10 (1963); reprinted in *Montemora*, 1 (Fall 1975), 133. All subsequent references to this essay will be to the *Montemora* edition, which will hereafter be cited as *Mind*. All such citations will be incorporated into the text.

Civil war photo:
Grass near the lens;
Man in the field
In silk hat. Daylight.
The cannon of that day
In our parks.[7]

(An at least partial paradigm for this poetic enterprise may well be
once again Williams's red wheelbarrow, which is simply *there*,
"beside the white chickens.") If *Discrete Series* still seems one of
the most radical texts produced by an American modernist, however, the reason lies less in its deconstruction of the connectives
between things than in its deconstruction of syntax itself:

As I saw
There
Year ago——
If there's a bird
On the cobbles;
One I've not seen
(*CP*, p. 10)

The glue of syntax here dissolves, as phrases and even individual
words break loose to float in a kind of verbal vacuum. Syntax, the
young George Oppen seems to have concluded, constitutes the
most stubborn variety of mind-imposed order. Thus if we are to
preserve a fidelity to the thing as it actually offers itself to us, we
must be prepared to abandon syntax itself. What will we find
when we strip away all the false forms of "order" that our minds
impose upon the world? The young George Oppen doesn't know.
But like all immanentists he seems to be convinced that it will be
something wonderful—or at any rate better than the soggy ferment
of unanalyzed "feelings."

In the more than twenty years that elapsed between *Discrete
Series* and *The Materials*, Oppen complemented the already fully
developed linguistic radicalism of his first book with a coherent
and equally radical conception of the human life-world. Oppen
himself likes to describe his philosophic and political perspective
as "populist." In the 1962 programmatic essay from which I have
already quoted, Oppen distinguishes a "populist" tradition in
American culture, and he seems to align himself with this heritage:

... the search of the Beats, the thing which they have in common
with the Ash Can School of painting and the Chicago literary
renaissance of the twenties is an authentic American phenomenon,
a search for the common experience, for the ground under their
feet. I have strained matters considerably by using the word

---

7. George Oppen, *Collected Poems* (New York: New Directions, 1975), p. 9. All subsequent references to Oppen's poetry will be to this edition, which will be cited as *CP*. All
such citations will be incorporated into the text.

populist: certainly no *more* specifically political word could be used. The poet means to trust to his direct perceptions, and it is even possible that it might be useful for the country to listen, to hear evidence, to consider what indeed we have brought forth upon this continent. (*Mind*, pp. 135-6)

Populism, as Oppen uses the word here and elsewhere, implies a belief that the collective whole which radicals like to call "the people" does in fact exist, and can function as a locus of values. (*Of Being Numerous* is Oppen's most extended meditation on what might be called "the ontology of the human collectivity," but this theme is also important to *The Materials*.) We should of course respect Oppen's choice of the word "populist" over such possible alternatives as "Marxist" or "Communist." Yet we should also recognize that in calling himself a populist Oppen is decidedly *not* repudiating his Communist past, but is rather redefining in broader, less specifically partisan terms the commitments which originally led him and Mary into the CPUSA. Communists have always (in theory at least) sought guidance from "the people," and especially in the Popular Front era the CPUSA assiduously cultivated a "populist" image. That Oppen's populism owes something to his years in the Communist Party thus seems likely. But I would also argue that Oppen's poetic stance is not only "populist" but specifically Marxist in at least two ways. First, Oppen's is a "materialist" poetry in its rigorous refusal to surrender to what I would call the "transcendental temptation." The very title of *The Materials* testifies to Oppen's commitment to the physical world. But for Oppen as for Marx the material world is not simply a given. Rather it is "in process," as human labor reshapes the raw materials of nature. The *people* exerting their *labor* upon the *material* world—out of this matrix, Marx and Oppen agree, emerges the human life-world. That the concerns of Oppen's mature poetry are also shaped in part by specifically philosophic influences, especially Heidegger, seems to me indisputable. Yet at bottom, Oppen's vision of the world remains stubbornly political rather than philosophical, in one key respect: "truth" for him exists, if it exists at all, neither in "nature" nor in the splendid solitude of the reflective mind, but only in the collective, ongoing life of the people "*en masse*" (as Whitman liked to say), as they collectively make through their labor the only world we can know. By participating in this process, Oppen consistently affirms, poets can enter the "common experience," and can discover at the same moment "the ground under their feet." In this affirmation Oppen's poetry, even long after he and Mary left the Communist Party, represents, not a repudiation of or an alternative to the political commitments of Oppen's middle years, but rather an extension of these commitments back into poetry, thus making the third period of Oppen's life a synthesis of the first and second phases.

Some passages from Maritain's *Creative Intuition in Art and Poetry* may help us to understand the (still radical, if no longer specifically "Communist") ways in which the poet's self, the things of this world, and the collective labor of humankind come together in *The Materials*. George and Mary Oppen first read Maritain's book while they were still in Mexico, and both of them today still regard the book as an important way station in their journey from the hermetic world of the Communist Party back toward the world of the arts. Maritain's book provides one of the epigraphs of *The Materials*: "We awake in the same moment to ourselves and to things." Maritain's refusal to give the knowing "subject" priority over the "objects" of its apprehension clearly evoked a responsive echo in Oppen. Specifically, I would hypothesize, Maritain's epistemological principle suggested to Oppen a way in which he could at the same time preserve a "materialist" commitment to the concrete existence of human beings on this earth (i.e., could continue to eschew the "transcendental temptation"), while moving beyond the aridly mechanical variety of Marxian "materialism" that dominated the American Communist Party in the 1940s and 1950s. Maritain wants, for theological reasons, to avoid any "privileging" of the self. For similar reasons, he wants us to see all the things of the world as in some fashion numinous. The result is a rich (but not necessarily theological) sense of the mutual interpenetration of the poet's self and the things amid which the poet awakens to consciousness:

> I need to designate both the singularity and the infinite internal depths of this flesh-and-blood and spiritual existent, the artist; and I have only an abstract word: the Self. I need to designate the secretive depths and the implacable advance of that infinite host of beings, aspects, events, physical and moral tangles of horror and beauty—of that world, that undecipherable Other—with which Man the artist is faced; and I have no word for that except the poorest and tritest word of the human language; I shall say: the things of the world, the *Things*. But I would wish to invest this empty word with the feelings of primitive man looking at the all-pervading force of Nature, or of the old Ionian philosophers saying that "all things are full of gods."[8]

Maritain also argues that things speak to us most deeply if they are themselves already imbued with human labor:

> How is it that when coming from the ocean you pass the Pillars of Hercules and enter the Mediterranean, the beauty of the airy

---

8. Jacques Maritain, *Creative Intuition in Art and Poetry* (Cleveland: Meridian Books, 1954), p. 9. Hereafter this book will be cited as "Maritain," and such citations will be incorporated into the text.

shores and lifelike sea bursts into a song, a triumph? How is it
that the simple curves of the Campagna fill you with a plenitude
of emotion which seems inexhaustible? If not because of Vergil
and the Greek heroes (though you don't actually think of them),
and the impalpable breezes of memory which freshen your face.
These places on the earth have been impregnated with man's
intelligence and toil. It is through history that the union of
Nature and man is accomplished. As a result Nature radiates with
signs and significance, which make her beauty blossom forth.

(Maritain, p. 7)

"Things," both Maritain and Oppen recognize, can be simply,
inhumanely "other," but such "things" are the exception rather
than the rule. Normally the things to which we awaken, and which
awaken us to ourselves, offer themselves to us *already* impregnated with human labor. And Oppen's primary task as a poet will
be, neither to "give" meaning to things nor to break through to
some impossible "thing in itself." Rather he will seek to uncover
(or recover) the thing as it offers itself to us—that is, as it has been
shaped and reshaped within the matrix of history.

The social world, conceived not as a frozen "structure"
but as an historical process, becomes—and here I turn once again
to Altieri's useful system of terminology—Oppen's "creative
ground." The modern poet, Altieri argues, remains locked within
narcissism and a resultant existential nausea until he/she discovers
such a "creative ground":

The antithesis to nausea is a sense of what might be called a *creative ground*, a source of energy and value in the objective order
that otherwise mocks subjective consciousness. And once one can
imagine a creative ground, he then can oppose to narcissism a
sense of the *creative self* whose activity discloses or produces
aspects of that ground which have potential communal significance. Art becomes a social and cultural force and not some form
of individual therapy or self-regarding indulgence in the resources
of the individual's imagination. (Altieri, p. 33)

As Altieri notes, the symbolist poet finds a creative ground in "the
shaping spirit of the imagination," while most immanentist poets
(Wordsworth in the Nineteenth Century, Snyder and Duncan
among our contemporaries) find this ground in some version of
"nature." Oppen, as we have already seen, vigorously commits himself to immanentism. But unlike most other immanentists, Oppen
finds his creative ground, not in a trans-human "nature," but in the
human world of society and history. The poetry that results from
Oppen's infusion of a populist vision into an immanentist poetic
mode does not upon first inspection look very "political." Indeed,
Oppen has on occasion disavowed the very concept of "political
poetry"—as, for example, in the "Mind's Own Place" essay from

which I have already quoted: "the poet's business is not to use verse as an advanced form of rhetoric, nor to seek to give to political statements the aura of eternal truth" (*Mind*, p. 137). Oppen has in practice followed his own advice: unlike MacDiarmid and Zukofsky he has written no hymns to Lenin, and his poetry does not at any point propound a party line. Yet its very fidelity *both* to a rigorously modernist poetic *and* to a populist or even a Marxist sense of human possibility makes Oppen's poetry "political" in a deeper sense of this term: it charts out a new kind of relationship between the social order on the one side and poetry on the other. A radically immanentist poetic method, seeking a creative ground in the on-going life of the people, and dedicating itself to the faithful articulation of that life—this is, I believe, what George Oppen offers us in his mature work, including *The Materials*.

The poetic path that Oppen charted for himself has enabled him to avoid both the bombast characteristic of earlier "democratic" American poetry and the elitism of the "high" modernist tradition. There were populist poets before Oppen: Whitman in one of his incarnations, Sandburg, Lindsay. Oppen has on occasion confessed a lingering affection for some of this poetry, but he also recognizes and deplores its predilection for inflated and empty rhetorical gestures. "The People, Yes," Sandburg shouts, as if this verbal gesture alone could bring "the people" into being. The poetry of Williams largely eschews such windy rhetoric, but his populism seems at best fitful. And in his most assertively populist moods (I am thinking especially of *Paterson*) Williams retreats into symbolism, as the poet's ego projects (à la Hart Crane) its unifying myths upon the American landscape. On the other hand, the politics of the poet that the young Oppen most respected, Ezra Pound, became in the 1930s profoundly elitist and anti-democratic. (At the heart of Pound's work, as Oppen seems early to have sensed, lies a contradiction between an immanentist poetic method that seeks to open itself to the movement of the world as given, and a nostalgia for a closed, hierarchical political order. The clash between these two contrary impulses energizes Pound's poetry but it shattered his life.[9]) The poetic landscape of the 1930s thus seemed to offer only two alternatives, represented by Sandburg (noisy, sloppy, but democratic in spirit) on the one hand and by Pound (poetically rigorous, but profoundly elitist) on the other. Oppen refused both these alternatives, and from the late 1930s until the late 1950s he (albeit probably unconsciously) prepared

---

9. For a full and lucid discussion of this central contradiction in Pound's work, see Michael André Bernstein, *The Tale of the Tribe: Ezra Pound and the Modern Verse Epic* (Princeton: Princeton Univ. Press, 1980), pp. 29-187.

himself to create a new kind of poetry which would steer a path between the Scylla of vacuous populist rhetoric and the Charybdis of an arid elitism. Oppen was not the only poet of his generation to seek such an alternative path. Zukofsky, Reznikoff and Olson all found themselves facing the same alternatives that Oppen confronted; and like Oppen all three (although I cannot hope to document this assertion here[10]) found a way to ground their poetry in the collective life of the community, while rigorously refusing to retreat into that loosely sentimental rhetoric which the American "reading public" itself tends to equate with "poetry." Oppen learned much from Zukofsky and Reznikoff—and probably something from Olson as well. Yet in the end he had to find his own path to a poetic that would reconcile the claims of modernism and populism. In *The Materials*, we can see Oppen forging this revolutionary poetic. Let us therefore now examine in more detail the ways in which Oppen has, in the book that marks his return to poetry, sought to bridge the gap between poetry and politics, art and "the people," language and the things of our world.

II

The Materials is both a collection of poems and a unified whole, for the full implications of each individual poem emerge only as we allow these poems mutually to illuminate one another. In essence, Oppen here offers us a congery of "things," all treated "directly." These "things" fall into certain distinct categories, and the *energeia* of the book derives in large measure from certain patterns of interaction among the things of Oppen's world. These "things" include the space (sometimes air, but more often the sea, which represents, for Oppen as for Williams, the formless and so the anti-human—"I warn you," says Williams in *Paterson*, "the sea is *not* our home."[11]) which defines the limits of the human world; the various forms of solid matter (earth, wood, stone, and iron are especially important) on which people can and do live and which they can re-shape through the exercise of their labor—i.e., the "materials" of our world; the tools (hammers, saws, knives, lathes and other machines) which humans use to shape these "materials"; the flesh of human beings themselves and other living creatures (the repeated references to seeds, trees, and birds scattered through the poems fall into this category); the habitations (houses, sky-scrapers, boats) which human beings build for themselves; and the words which human beings use to tell one another about the world.

---

10. The case for including Olson in this group has been well argued by Don Byrd in *Charles Olson's "Maximus"* (Urbana: Univ. of Illinois Press, 1980), *passim*.
11. William Carlos Williams, *Paterson* (New York: New Directions, 1963), p. 235.

These images constitute the "materials" out of which Oppen makes his individual poems; and the recurrence of the same set of "materials" in one poem after another serves to unify the book. Obviously, it would be difficult for any poet to write a book of poems without once mentioning the sea or the earth. But when we note that twenty-one of the forty-one poems in the book contain references to the sea, and that sixteen of them contain references to rock, stone, or brick, then it seems fairly safe to assume that these patterns of recurrence are not happenstance. However, it seems important to re-iterate that the sea, for instance, is not here a symbol—at least not as I would use this term. Oppen does not want to project "meanings" onto the sea, etc., for he does not regard his consciousness as the "shaping spirit" of the world. And Oppen's things do not articulate their inherent meanings by entering individually into relationship with the poet's consciousness, as do the things in the world of a symbolist poet. Rather Oppen seeks to make his poems open fields in which things can "speak" to one another. For only as they speak to one another do the things of Oppen's world give up their meanings to the poet himself —and, through him, to us.

"Product" (*CP*, p. 40) offers an initial example of how, in Oppen's poetic method, "things" come together to create "meaning." The "things" of this poem include the sea, human hands, the tools they grip, etc. In themselves these things "mean" nothing in particular. But if the *hands* and the *tools* transform the *wood* into a *boat*, and if we then place the boat in the *sea*, suddenly the things of the world come together in a signifying pattern:

> There is no beauty in New England like the boats.
> Each itself, even the paint white
> Dipping to each wave each time
> At anchor, mast
> And rigging tightly part of it
> Fresh from the dry tools
> And the dry New England hands.
> The bow soars, finds the waves
> The hull accepts. Once someone
> Put a bowl afloat
> And there for all to see, for all the children,
> Even the New Englander
> Was boatness. What I've seen
> Is all I've found: myself.

The emergence of meaning out of the *conjunction* of things—this poem both tells us about this process and enacts the process itself, as "boatness," a new metaphysical essence, comes into being before us, out of the meeting between human intentionality and the sea. The meanings which this poem unfolds for us are not generated by the poet's consciousness, for this consciousness itself comes into existence only within the interaction among the worker (the boatbuilder), the worker's "materials" (i.e., the wood, paint, etc., of the boat), the sea that "holds" the boat but that is itself limitless, and the perceiving eye which registers the juxtaposition of all these "things." The fulcrum of the poem is the single word "boatness." When "boatness" comes into being, consciousness too comes into being—but *only* in this moment. And in this moment too the poet "finds" himself, as one among the things he has seen. We are not, that is, here dealing with the creation of order, as Steven's jar upon a hill orders the Tennessee wilderness. Rather Oppen's poem describes the *discovery* of an order, and the simultaneous discovery of the self as a part of this order. "Product," in other words, is an immanentist, not a symbolist, poem. "Product" also suggests that the key to Oppen's immanentism, the glue that for him brings the things of this world together into coherent patterns, is human labor. Here as throughout *The Materials* Oppen's basic poetic strategy is to illuminate for us the significance of human labor by focussing on the materials which are transformed by that labor, the tools through which human beings exercise their energy upon these materials, and the end products of this exercise of human labor upon the world. By means of this poetic strategy, Oppen is able to avoid the error of symbolism, which treats the "feelings" which an individual human being has toward the world as more important than the "being-and-becomingness" of the world itself. But equally important, this strategy enables Oppen to move beyond a mindless materialism which reduces human action to a meaningless commotion in an implacably determinist cosmos. By making work his central category, Oppen has succeeded in creating a poetry which transcends the objective-subjective dichotomy, and which (in the words of Robert Creeley) allows both "man and his objects" to be "presences in this field of force we call a poem."[1][2]

Certain patterns of inter-relationship among the "things" of Oppen's world recur often enough in *The Materials* to take on the status of "themes" (although I am using this word more in the musical than in the usual literary sense), and an examination of the most important of these recurrent patterns can help us to understand Oppen's poetic method. One such pattern we have already met in "Product": the encounter between the human world of work, especially the work of building the shelters within which we live our fragile lives, and the limitless, formless sea. By

---

12. Robert Creeley, "A Note on the Objective," in *A Quick Graph: Collected Notes and Essays* (San Francisco: Four Seasons, 1970), p. 19.

my count the sea asserts its presence in no less than twenty-one of the forty-one poems in *The Materials*, always in juxtaposition to some manifestation of the human community. The sea becomes for Oppen the embodiment of the not-human: it is what we, as humans, must live "on." We cannot shape the sea by our labor; and if we are to create a human world, it can only be in the sea's despite. Yet we must learn to live on the sea, for *here* (for better or for worse) "is where we are." This phrase comes from "Population" (*CP*, p. 22), a poem which makes clear Oppen's sense of the relationship between the human world and the formless but inescapable inhumanity of the sea:

> Like a flat sea,
> Here is where we are, the empty reaches
> Empty of ourselves
>
> Where dark, light, sound
> Shatter the mind born
> Alone to ocean
>
> Save we are
> A crowd, a population, those
> Born, those not yet dead, the moment's
>
> Populace, sea-borne and violent, finding
> Incredibly under the sense the rough deck
> Inhabited, and what it always was.

The absence of any principle of meaning and order in "nature" here seems clear. But we do not confront the "flat seas" alone. We are joined together in a community that includes not only the living but also the dead and the not-yet-born. The first two stanzas describe the sea; the last two describe the "crowd." Thus the entire poem pivots on the first word of the third stanza: "save." If we can find any sort of "salvation" in this world, we must look for it, it seems, in the human collectivity. This collectivity, born of the inhuman sea, retains some of the latent violence of that sea. Yet here we are, on the "rough deck," the habitation that we have collectively constructed for ourselves, and on which we must willy nilly live, *among* our fellow men and women, afloat *on* the inhuman sea. Such is our world, and it is, the poem affirms, habitable. For at the moment that we awaken to a consciousness both of the sea that we confront and of ourselves as members of a community, we also discover ("incredibly") the "rough deck/Inhabited," and this deck becomes what Oppen has called elsewhere "the ground under [our] feet" (*Mind*, p. 136).

In a few other poems in *The Materials* (for example, "Squall" and "California") the human collectivity directly confronts the

sea. But more often this relationship is mediated through the tools
that constitute the crystallized forms of human intentionality, and
which in turn serve as the means by which human intentionality
acts upon the world. An example is "Men of Sheepshead" (*CP*,
p. 50):

> Eric—we used to call him Eric—
> And Charlie Weber: I knew them well,
> Men of another century. And still at Sheepshead
> If a man carries pliers
> Or maul down these rambling piers he is a man who fetches
> Power into the afternoon
>   Speaking of things
>
> End-for-end, butted to each other,
> Dove-tailed, tenoned, doweled—Who is not at home
> Among these men? who make a home
> Of half truth, rules of thumb
> Of cam and lever and whose docks and piers
> Extend into the sea so self-contained.

Workmanship may seem an anachronism in our century. But the
shipbuilders of Sheepshead still carry their tools down to the sea,
and as they do so they "fetch/Power into the afternoon." These
tools, and this human power, serve(s) to join things together, and
thereby to "make a home" where we can all be "at home." The
home here at issue isn't "metaphysical"; it is made of wood, and
it is made by human hands (working by "rules of thumb"), with
the help of machines (cf. "cam and lever"). Yet the human world
so built, no less than the sea into which this human world extends,
is (and there is a crucial grammatical ambiguity here, for the last
phrase of the poem refers both to "sea" and to "docks and piers")
absolutely "self-contained," thus making for us an enclosed habitation that is both "on" and "in" a sea that is itself "self-contained," and therefore irreducibly "other."

A second, no less eloquent example of the sea/tool/commu-
nity conjunction is "Workman" (*CP*, p. 41):

> Leaving the house each dawn I see the hawk
> Flagrant over the driveway. In his claws
> That dot, that comma
> Is the broken animal: the dangling small beast knows
> The burden that he is: he has touched
> The hawk's drab feathers. But the carpenter's is a culture
> Of fitting, of firm dimensions,
> Of post and lintel. Quietly the roof lies
> That the carpenter has finished. The sea birds circle
> The beaches and cry in their own way,
> The innumerable sea birds, their beaks and their wings
> Over the beaches and the sea's glitter.

"Workman" draws together the human world of work, the limitless sea, and a third variable: the hawk and its "broken" prey. The "But" of line six underscores the contrast between the hawk's "flagrant" violence and the "firm," "quiet" world created by the carpenter. The poem does not, however, seek to create a simple "indifferent nature" vs. "ordering man" contrast. For the hawk's world has some oddly verbal overtones, as the "broken animal" becomes a "comma," and this "natural" world even contains some measure of consciousness: the beast "knows the burden that he is." Conversely, the carpenter's world is characterized not so much by the presence of a knowing subject as by the active *process* of fitting post and lintel together. The sea enters only in the ninth line, and the structure of the poem defines the sea as neither "flagrant" nor quietly "fitted." Rather the sea is here simply "other," beyond our human world, limitless. ("Unnumerable" suggests the endless otherness of the sea and everything associated with it.) If we do not wish to live with the hawk, neither can we live within the sea. But we can live on the sea. For between the hawk and the sea, there remains the carpenter's world—a human world, created by our collective labor. And it is there that this poem invites us to dwell.

A second recurrent pattern in *The Materials* juxtaposes the living creature and various hard, impervious substances—rocks, stones, bricks, etc.—which actively threaten our vulnerable flesh. "Beyond the window," we learn in the first poem of the book, "Flesh and rock and hunger" are "loose in the night sky." "Flesh" and "rock" have something in common: neither one "is" the world, but rather both are "in" the world, where they jostle (sometimes painfully) against each other. But rocks and brick, unlike our bodies, are unconscious, as Oppen recognizes in "Blood from a Stone" (*CP*, pp. 31-3):

> To a body anything can happen,
> Like a brick. Too obvious to say.
> But all horror came from it.

In the reduction of human flesh to a mere stone, Oppen discovers the supreme horror. Thus if the sea represents for Oppen the "encompassing inhuman," then the stone or brick represents the "imperviously inhuman": Being, not as Intentionality, but as mere matter-in-motion. Yet as Oppen declares in this same poem, whatever life we possess can and must be squeezed from the stones (here both the rubble of the city and the rocks of our fields) amid which we find ourselves:

> Blood from a stone, life
> From a stone dead dam. Mother

> Nature! because we find the others
> Deserted like ourselves and therefore brothers.

Mother nature may be a stone, and stone dead. But she becomes our "mother" nevertheless, she gives us the blood of life, when we come together as "brothers" (and sisters) in our solitude. The addition of sisters seems crucial, for "Blood from a Stone" is addressed, above all, to Mary:

> Everything I am is
> Us. Come home.

But in the poem this tiny community of George and Mary widens to encompass "the bequeathed pavements, the inherited lit streets." Even when separated from Mary by the war, Oppen can, carrying the "brick body as in one's hands" through the battlefields of France, suddenly meet "the smell of wood-smoke from the kitchen" and feel an "overwhelming sense of joy." The woodsmoke here becomes the tangible sign of the on-going human community, even amid the falling bricks of war. It is this community that allows us to "inherit" the streets, to make them our own. The stones that we stumble over as we make our way through the world are not, then, simply inhuman. Rather they are "materials," and what we make of them is, in large measure at least, up to us.

Indeed, most of the stones, etc., in *The Materials* are not "natural" phenomena at all. Rather they have been incorporated into the city, that supreme manifestation of the human will to erect an habitation in which we can, communally, dwell. In some ways this city is as "hard" as the rocks of France over which the soldier George Oppen found himself crawling. The "stone" of the city can be blatantly ostentious—"the absurd stone trimming of the building tops" (p. 22)—or blankly inhuman:

> We must look to Lever Brothers
>
> Based in a square block.
> A thousand lives
>
> Within that glass. What is the final meaning
> Of extravagance?
>
> *(CP,* p. 43)

On the one level the stone of the city permanently affronts and insults us, as the opening lines of "The Source" *(CP,* p. 55) suggest:

> If the city has roots, they are in filth.
> It is a slum. Even the sidewalk
> Rasps under the feet.

Yet within the hard, impervious city, there is a germ of radiant life that glows through the bricks of the city, as the concluding lines of "The Source" affirm:

> —In some black brick
> Tenement, a woman's body
>
> Glows. The gleam; the unimaginable
> Thin feet taper down
> The instep naked to the wooden floor!
>
> Hidden and disguised
> —and shy?
>
> The city's
> Secret warmth.

For Oppen, then, the city and the bricks and cut stone of which it is built are not simply "alien." There is here no fashionable "urban malaise," no sullen insistence that human beings deserve something better than this world we have made. Rather the city is simply the place where human flesh and the hard edges of the material world rasp against each other—and out of this friction, sometimes at least, a spark of life is born.

The encounter between human flesh and the hard edges of the city becomes particularly poignant when the human being in question is a child. But in these encounters, too, we see with special clarity the possibility that humankind can repossess the city, make it once again a fit habitation:

> PEDESTRIAN
>
> What generations could have dreamed
> This grandchild of the shopping streets, her eyes
>
> In the buyer's light, the store lights
> Brighter than the lighthouses, brighter than moonrise
>
> From the salt habor so rich
> So bright her city
>
> In a soil of pavement, a mesh of wires where she walks
> In the new winter among enormous buildings.
>
> (*CP*, p. 64)

There are no stones or bricks in this poem; but the "enormous buildings" dwarf the "grandchild," and both the "soil of pavement" and the "mesh of wires" threaten danger. Yet "her eyes" are "brighter than the lighthouses," brighter than the moonrise over the sea. Or is it the "store lights" that are "brighter than the lighthouses"? There is an apparently deliberate syntactic ambiguity here—and the implication seems to be that the eyes of the child borrow their glow at least in part from the lights of the stores. By thus underscoring the flagrantly commercial character of the city, with its "shopping streets" and "buyer's lights," Oppen avoids the potential sentimentality of the image of the child dwarfed by the city. Nevertheless, the shining eyes of the grandchild *do* take into themselves and transform the lights of the city, and the city itself thereby here becomes something (to isolate three adjectives from the last two stanzas) "rich," "bright," and "new."

One more recurrent pattern in *The Materials* deserves mention here: Oppen's emphasis on words both as an obstacle to clear perception and as the most powerful of all the tools which we use in making and remaking our world(s). In "To Memory" (*CP*, p. 66), Oppen invokes a familiar immanentist awareness of the limits of language (the "your" of the following poem is Memory herself):

> Words, there are words!
> But with your eyes
> We see. And so we possess the earth.
>
> Like an army of ants,
> A multiple dry carcass
> Of past selves
>
> Moving
> Thru a land dead behind us
> Of deeds, dates, documents . . .

Yet in an extraordinary moment in "Return" (*CP*, pp. 26-8), the word becomes the primary instrument through which we make the earth our own:

> And Linda five,
> Maybe six when the mare grazing
> In the meadow came to her.
> 'Horse,' she said, whispering
> By the roadside
> With the cars passing. Little girl welcomed,
> Learning welcome.

The world, in the person of the mare, offers itself freely and spontaneously to the child. In response the child, like Adam in the garden, offers the mare a name. In this intimate exchange, both mare and child come into the fulness of their being. Oppen's daughter here speaks what Buber would call the "primary word" which simultaneously brings into being both the "I" of the child itself and the "Thou" of the horse.[13] Rather than standing between us and the world, the word (but the word as *act*, not as object) here becomes the uniquely human way of being in the world, of welcoming and being welcomed by that world.

---

13. Martin Buber, *I and Thou* (New York: Scribner's, 1958), *passim*.

However, Oppen's fullest treatment of this process of *"in-habiting"* through language is the lovely "Sara in Her Father's Arms" (*CP*, p. 30):

Cell by cell the baby made herself, the cells
Made cells. That is to say
The baby is made largely of milk. Lying in her father's arms
        the little seed eyes
Moving, trying to see, smiling for us
To see, she will make a household
To her need of these rooms—Sara, little seed,
Little violent, diligent seed. Come let us look at the world
Glittering: this seed will speak,
Max, words! There will be no other words in the world
But those our children speak. What will she make of a world
Do you suppose, Max, of which she is made.

The poet here sees Sara first making herself "cell by cell" out of the raw materials provided by a world, and then making herself a world to inhabit— now with her "seed eyes," and later with the words she will someday speak. The poem then ends by envisioning a total interpenetration of self and world. The task at hand here is the same task that Oppen confronts in all his various "sea," "rock" and "city" poems: how to build a human habitation in a world in which even the creations of humankind confront us as alien, inhuman. Alienation is not, this poem promises us, our "natural," eternal condition. As we live, the world makes us and we in turn make it, not out of our minds, but out of the milk we drink and the words we speak. That is, speaking here becomes, not a "spiritual" or "mental" process of creating meaning in an otherwise meaningless world, but an act of "material" production —one among the many acts of production through which we constantly make and remake our world. And in a world thus endlessly, joyously made and remade within the very *act* of living, why should we trouble our hearts with the demand for a transcendent absolute?

III

Many individual poems in *The Materials* draw together the various motifs which I have catalogued above into patterns that are both subtle and beautiful. It would therefore seem proper to supplement the foregoing overview of recurrent patterns in *The Materials* with a more detailed examination of a few pivotal poems in the book. I shall begin with "Image of the Engine" (*CP*, pp. 18-21), the longest poem in *The Materials*. Before the poem is over, the engine of the title will become something rather like a "symbol." But in the first part of the poem Oppen offers us an image of the engine itself:

> Likely as not a ruined head gasket
> Spitting at every power stroke, if not a crank shaft
> Bearing knocking at the roots of the thing like a pile-driver:
> A machine involved with itself, a concentrated
> Hot lump of a machine
> Geared in the loose mechanics of the world with the valves
>   jumping
> And the heavy frenzy of the pistons. When the thing stops,
> Is stopped, with the last slow cough
> In the manifold, the flywheel blundering
> Against compression, stopping, finally
> Stopped, compression leaking
> From the idle cylinders will one imagine
> Then because he can imagine
> That squeezed from the cooling steel
> There hovers in that moment, wraith-like and like a plume
>   of steam, an aftermath,
> A still and quiet angel of knowledge and of comprehension.

The engine here described falls loosely into the category of "tool," insofar as it is an instrument which human beings have created; and tools, as we have already seen, generally have a positive meaning for Oppen. But this particular engine seems to be a tool gone wrong. First, it has no discernible function: at no point in the poem do we learn what kind of engine is here at issue or what purpose it serves. Second, this engine does not, as a proper tool should, mediate between human intentionality and inchoate matter. Rather this engine seems to have decided that it is an end in itself: it is "a machine involved with itself, a concentrated/Hot lump of a machine." Third, this engine is not only self obsessed but also, as words like "frenzy" and "blundering" imply, stupid; and in its stupidity it is knocking itself apart. This self-enclosed machine claims for itself the attributes of a living creature; and we may feel at least a momentary inclination to grant this claim as, watching the engine "die," we imagine something like a "soul" emerging from the machine at the moment of "death." But the syntactic twist in the last lines of this section remind us that any such meanings which we discover in the silence of the engine are projected by us upon the "cooling steel." Only by such an imaginative projection of our own intentionality into the machine can we find in the blind self-destruction of the machine some "spiritual" recompense, some kind "of knowledge and of comprehension." But the syntax of the lines, wavering as they do between the declarative and the interrogative, leave unresolved the question of in what way (if any) our imaginings are "true."

In Part Two we immediately learn the "meaning" of the

engine:

> Endlessly, endlessly,
> The definition of mortality
>
> The image of the engine
>
> That stops.

The engine, it would seem, represents human life as seen from the viewpoint of mechanistic materialism. From such a viewpoint, the body is no more than an engine that, eventually, stops. The inevitable counterpart of such a mechanistic materialism is a "spiritualism" which sees the machine as inhabited by a "soul"—a "ghost in the machine," in Gilbert Ryle's phrase.[14] But now Oppen rejects both mechanistic materialism and its "spiritualist" counterpart:

> We cannot live on that.
> I know that no one would live out
> Thirty years, fifty years if the world were ending
> With his life.

The alternative both to mechanistic materialism and to spiritualism, it here becomes clear, is what might be called a "collective humanism"—i.e., what Oppen would call "populism." We go on living only because we know that the "world"—here primarily the human community—will live on after us. And by rooting ourselves in this community, we make of ourselves something more than engines that stop. (But in paraphrasing Oppen's lives, I rob them of most of their power. For the simple psychological truth of Oppen's statement—none of us *would* "live out thirty years, fifty years" if we knew that the world would end with our lives—is at least as important as the philosophical and political overtones I have here emphasized.) After thus defining for us the inadequacies of mechanistic materialism, Oppen returns to the engine itself:

> The machine stares out,
> Stares out
> With all its eyes
>
> Thru the glass
> With the ripple in it, past the sill
> Which is dusty—If there is someone
> In the garden!
> Outside, and so beautiful.

---

14. I completed this discussion of "Image of the Engine" some months before reading the comments on this poem which Oppen made to L.S. Dembo in 1968, and which appear in the hitherto unpublished interview included in this volume, pp. 197-213. I was happy to discover that Oppen's comments seem to support my reading of this poem. Indeed, Oppen even quotes the same phrase from Gilbert Ryle that I mention in my discussion (cf. Gilbert Ryle, *The Concept of Mind* [New York: Barnes & Noble, 1949] *passim*).

Now for the first time we see the engine within a context: it seems
to be inside a building which is in turn in a garden. And the implacable, frenzied engine of part one now seems almost pathetic.
The "if" clause is deliberately ambiguous. On the one hand, the
machine seems to "stare out" in the hope of seeing someone
(someone *human* that is) in the garden outside. But at the same
time it is this very observer in the garden who seems to anthropo-
morphize the engine, ascribing to it "eyes" and the power to
"stare." Both meanings of the "if" clause, however, emphasize the
dependency of the engine on the human world. The machine, and
the individual human being as well, find their meaning, indeed
their very existence, only in and through the "other." Alone both
we as solitary human beings and the things into which we infuse
our intentions are mere machines that stop. But as we and our
tools enter into relationship with the "other," and implicitly with a
world that extends beyond our lives, the terms of our existence
begin to undergo a profound change, giving birth to a sudden
beauty.

In parts three and four, Oppen confronts the ultimate fragility of the human community itself:

> What ends
> Is that.
>   Even companionship
> Ending.

If we search for an antecedent for the "that" of the second line,
the most likely possibility would seem to be the meeting between
human and machine in the previous section. However, the "that"
in question seems designed to be as ambiguous as possible. In fact,
everything ends, including the "companionship" which alone
makes us something more than machines. But even as we confront
this bleak truth another voice intervenes:

> 'I want to ask if you remember
> When we were happy! As tho all travels
>
> Ended untold, all embarkations
> Foundered.

The single quotation mark suggests that someone else (Mary perhaps?) is here addressing the poet, with a poignant question that
simultaneously affirms human collectivity ("we" are united by our
memories) and implies that whatever was valuable in life has already ended. But the quotation remains unclosed, and thus the
voice of the other seems to dissolve back into the poet's own voice,
ruminating on the possibility of total failure, all tales untold and
all ships sunk. Part four extends this line of thinking by invoking

an image whose implications should be immediately clear to us, the image of shipwreck:

> On that water
> Grey with morning
> The gull will fold its wings
> And sit. And with its two eyes
> There as much as anything
> Can watch a ship and all its hallways
> And all companions sink.

The machine of part one which offends our humanity in its mindless, mechanical frenzy, here finds its counterpart in another kind of otherness: a nature no less mindless and inhuman than the machine. The sea, here as throughout *The Materials*, defines the irreducible, impassable boundaries of the human world. The sea personifies itself in the gull which stares on indifferent, wings folded, as both the human community (the "companions") and the things that humans create (the "ship and all its hallways") slip beneath the water. All voyages *do* ultimately "founder." The world may not end with our lives, but it *will* eventually end. What, then, can give purpose and value to human life?

In part four, Oppen finds in the very failure of our "embarkations" a new ground for human community, and thus a new way of postulating a "world": "*Also he has set the world/In their hearts*"—thus part four begins. The "world" here may have theological overtones—the "world and the flesh" as opposed to "heaven." But I suspect that "world" here carries no invidious inflection, and so we should consider another possible reading of the line. If the "world" is "set" in our "hearts," Oppen may here be implying, then world-making is an activity that will go on, even though all our embarkations "founder." Such, in any event, seems to be the point of the succeeding lines:

> From lumps, chunks,

> We are locked out: like children, seeking love
> At last among each other. With their first full strength
> The young go search for it,

> Native in the native air.

The "lumps" and "chunks" of the world—the rocks and bricks which we have encountered in other poems, the dumb and blind engine of this poem—drive us back upon our humanity, and force us to seek love "among each other." The love we thus create, Oppen proceeds to make clear, offers no permanent solution to our dilemma:

> But even in the beautiful bony children
> Who arise in the morning have left behind
> Them worn and squalid toys in the trash
>
> Which is a grimy death of love. The lost
> Glitter of the stores!
> The streets of stores!
> Crossed by the streets of stores
> And every crevice of the city leaking
> Rubble: concrete, conduit, pipe, a crumbling
> Rubble of our roots . . .

Our hunger for love enmeshes us among the things of the *human* world—the tawdry toys we learn as children to love, the stores where these stores are sold, the rubble (and here we are again among the lumps and chunks, the rocks and brick, on which our humanity runs aground) of the decaying city. The children who search for love seek to leave behind these toys, but in this very act they also experience the death of love. So in the very moment we "embark," we have *already* "foundered," and this will not be the last of our mishaps:

> But they will find
> In flood, storm, ultimate mishap:
> Earth, water, the tremendous
> Surface, the heart thundering
> Absolute desire.

Thus "Image of the Engine" concludes. The loss of our toys, the rubble in our streets, merely augur the ultimate shipwreck, death itself. But in the very moment of shipwreck, the hunger of the heart, a hunger for "the world," surges up. In these concluding lines of the poem, the engine returns, but now the alien machine into which we have projected our humanity is absorbed back into the human. No longer an image of the merely mechanical that stands over against the human community, the engine now becomes the symbol of the human heart itself, both "mechanical" and "natural," both "individual" and "collective," as it thunders out the beat that makes us all members one of another, and joins us to the sometimes inhuman world we have created, in the beat of "absolute desire."

For a second example of Oppen's poetic method working at its maximum complexity, let us turn to "Myself I Sing" (*CP*, pp. 35-6). The title alludes, obviously, to Whitman's "I celebrate myself and sing myself." Oppen here invokes the principal poetic spokesman for populism chiefly because he wants to raise a question about American populism itself. From Whitman's time to the present, American populism has celebrated "the individual." "The people," this brand of populism has assumed, will come into being only insofar as each one of us becomes an "individual." There is something decidedly Hegelian about this way of thinking —indeed, in the case of Whitman, consciously Hegelian. If each of us seeks to become the "concrete universal," "America" (the *collective* whole) will come into being. The opening lines of Oppen's poem subject this way of thinking to an ironic critique:

> Me! he says, hand on his chest.
> Actually, his shirt.
> > And there, perhaps,
> The question.

Everyman (Everyamerican? Perhaps Whitman himself, in the well-known photograph?) here strikes a comradely pose, and affirms his selfhood. But this "self" is not a purely natural creature. Does the "me" include the shirt or not? Does or does not the self include the things into which we project our humanity? That is the question. "Pioneers!" the poem goes on, again invoking Whitman's myth of the heroic American. "But trailer people?" Oppen wonders. Yes, "trailer people" too are "en route." But can they bear the burden of the mission which Whitman called them to?

> Wood box full of tools—
> > The most
> American. A sort of
> Shrinking
> > in themselves. A
> Less than adult: old.
>
> A pocket knife,
> A tool—

These Americans have apparently *become* their tools, and the tools themselves seem disorganized ("Wood box full of tools") and puny ("a pocket knife,/A tool"). And the men and women seem to have shrunk. Instead of growing "up," they have simply grown old. What hopes here of a "passage to India," a "passage to more than India"?

In the last half of "Myself I Sing," the poet adds himself to the picture:

> And I
> Here talking to the man?
> > The sky
>
> That dawned along the road
> And all I've been
> Is not myself? I think myself
> Is what I've seen and not myself

If the trailer people are hard-pressed to sustain the role of "pioneer," is the poet any more successful in sustaining the pose of

Whitmanesque bard? Like Whitman, this poet has travelled the open road, but he is not at all certain about the "self" that strode forward into the sunrise. The syntactically tangled questions in the last three lines of the quoted passage establish an opposition between being and seeing. Am I "all I've been" or am I "what I've seen"? Neither seems quite right; for to be at all is to be *in a world*, but if I am "what I've seen," then in a sense "I" don't exist at all. These musings on the problematics of selfhood lead the speaker back to a now familiar setting, the edge of the sea:

> A man marooned
> No longer looks for ships, imagines
> Anything on the horizon. On the beach
> The ocean ends in water. Finds a dune
> And on the beach sits near it. Two.
> He finds himself by two.
>
> Or more.
> 'Incapable of contact
> Save in incidents'

In one sense we are all marooned, and there is no prospect of rescue. But as we confront the limitless, alien sea, we find ourselves *not* alone. The "Two" here mentioned may be a man and the dune, or the poet and his trailer-park interlocutor, or even perhaps the man and the sea. But in any case "he finds himself by two." It is (only!) in relationship to the other that each of us comes into being as a self. The contact with the other may come only "in incidents," but we do (often all unknowingly) meet and so create one another, as we learn in the poignant conclusion of this poem:

> And yet at night
> Their weight is part of mine.
> For we are all housed now, all in our apartments,
> The world untended to, unwatched.
> And there is nothing left out there
> As night falls, but the rocks

A "we" has now come into existence which includes the man in the trailer, hand on his chest, and the poet, and all of us. Even in our solitary cells we bear the weight of one another's lives. Within this circle of mutual concern, we create for ourselves a tiny haven. Beyond, the world "untended to, unwatched," goes on its inhuman way. There remain out there only the (now familiar) rocks, emblems of the inhuman otherness of the world in which we find ourselves. But the very otherness of the rocks defines by contrast the human world which we have (all unconsciously) created, as we learn to bear the weight one of another.

My next example, "Vulcan" (*CP*, p. 46), brings sea and city, machine and child together into a disquieting pattern. "Vulcan" begins with a common Oppen juxtaposition—inside vs. outside, the human habitation vs. the natural world:

> The householder issuing to the street
> Is adrift a moment in that ice stiff
> Exterior.

The New York householder, issuing from his protecting shell, is momentarily startled to find himself in a harsh, frozen nature. To this image of the householder, Oppen juxtaposes a fragmentary quotation, apparently describing Manhattan as it might have appeared to John Smith or another earlier explorer:

> 'Peninsula
> Low lying in the bay
> And wooded—'

But the "wooded" Manhattan of the early explorers has given way to a Manhattan of the welder, a Manhattan of subways:

> Native now
> Are the welder and the welder's arc
> In the subway's iron circuits:

Still, Oppen goes on,

> We have not escaped each other,
> Not in the forest, not here.

These lines seem to imply that both in fleeing to the "new" world and in building houses for ourselves, our motive has been to find some sort of absolute solitude. Yet, as the next few lines suggest, we have failed in this effort:

> The crippled girl hobbles
> Painfully in the new depths
> Of the subway, and painfully
> We shift our eyes.

Our pain as we "shift our eyes" away from the crippled girl implicitly recognizes that we are one with her and her pain. The iron circuits of the subway seem to violate the aching flesh of the girl. But by moving beyond a sense of the subway simply as a dead "thing" to a perception of it as a product of human labor, we discover (and apparently she too discovers as well) a bond between the mother's labor that brought her into the world and the labor of the workman who built the subway:

> The bare rails
> And black walls contain
> Labor before her birth, her twisted
> Precarious birth and the men
> Laborious, burly—

Both the labor of childbirth and the labor of construction enter into the ongoing human project of world-production. And both types of labor also assume the symbolic form of Vulcan who gives his name to the poem. Vulcan, of course, was a blacksmith, like the welders of this poem, but he was also crippled like the girl, and he was cast out of Olympus—at least in some versions of the myth—to live in a cave beneath the sea, not only like the welders and the girl but also like the speaker of the poem. Insofar as we can "see" these various forms of labor (i.e., the labor of the mother and the labor of a welder) creating and re-creating our world, we enter into possession of our history. The poet, of course, has a capacity to see the processes in question—but more important, so does the girl:

> She sits
> Quiet, her eyes still. Slowly,
> Deliberately she sees
> An anchor's blunt fluke sink
> Thru coins and coin machines,
> The ancient iron and the voltage
> In the iron beneath us in the child's deep
> Harbors into harbor sand.

The anchor apparently belongs to an explorer's ship which, some centuries ago, hove to near the "wooded peninsula." The anchor and the "coins and coin machines" of the modern subway station and the electrified "iron circuits" of the subway tracks all come together in the "child's deep/Harbors"—these are, if I read the poem aright, her *eyes*. In her single act—not of "apprehension" and certainly not of symbolic projection, but simply of *sight*— her eyes "take in" the world. All history, and the lives of all the mute, inglorious Vulcans who make that history, are repossessed. The "child's deep harbors" and the "harbor sand" are here somehow one and the same. It is not "within" the child, then, that history is recovered. History, the coin machine, the anchor—all these are *really there*. But only as the eyes of the child "slowly, deliberately" *see* all these things do we as a race recover them. This labor of sight, this labor of recovery, is, it therefore seems, the tasks to which the crippled girl, and the poet, and we ourselves are all summoned.

I turn finally to the poem which has given me the title of this essay, "Birthplace: New Rochelle" (*CP*, p. 34):

> Returning to that house
> And the rounded rocks of childhood—They have lasted
> well.
>
> A world of things.

An aging man,
The knuckles of my hand
So jointed! I am this?

                    The house
My father's once, and the ground. There is a color of his
        times
In the sun's light.

A generation's mark.
It intervenes. My child,
Not now a child, our child
Not altogether lone in a lone universe that suffers time
Like stones in sun. For we do not.

This poem begins by linking together the house in which Oppen lived as a child and the "rounded rocks" around the house. Both have "lasted well"— i.e., have changed little with the passing years. The phrase "A world of things," isolated between the first and second stanzas, points both forward and backward. The house and the rocks are clearly "things"—objects whose existence depends not at all upon the presence of an observer. By applying this label to the house and the rocks, Oppen emphasizes the distance between such objects and the perceiving subject. But as the focus of the poet's consciousness moves from these inanimate objects to his own body, he experiences a startling discovery. His own hand manifests itself to him as yet another object, a thing in a world of things. Thus the startled exclamation point after "so jointed." Thus too the puzzled, rather pained query, "I am this?" "Is it possible," Oppen here seems to wonder, "that this oddly mechanical ('the knuckles . . ./So jointed'), somewhat grotesque 'thing' is *me*?" Yet even as the poet discovers his own hand as an object among objects, he also singles out the quality that distinguishes human flesh from the other objects of this world. He is "an aging man," and the hand itself, unlike the house and the rocks, has also aged: it has been weathered by the world's work. The poet thus here perceives his hand, not simple as a "thing," but as a unique kind of "thing," insofar as it exists within time as well as within space. This sense of the body's distinctive mode of existence in turn impells the poet's attention away from the world of "objective" "things" toward the human world, and specifically toward the bonds between generations. The poet has come to this place because it was "my father's once." Clearly, any claims we make to possess the earth are transitory. Yet something of the father remains here, in the "color of the sun's light," if not in the rocks or even in the house itself. The recognition that this place bears the "mark" of a specific generation, a specific moment in history, "intervenes" between the poet and the objects of his perception.

No longer does he perceive the house, the rocks, or his own hand simply as material "things," objects existing in an "external" space into which his consciousness can enter only as an alien presence. Rather he now recognizes that these "things" exist *only* as objects of human intentionality, and thus only as elements within an ongoing historical world. In the poetry of William Carlos Williams, the dissolution of "the world of things" would be experienced as a tragic loss. But the "intervention" that occurs at this decisive moment in Oppen's poem, and which forces upon the poet a recognition of the ultimate unknowability of the "thing in itself," does not issue in a despairing retreat into the self. Rather (and this shift offers, I think, decisive evidence that for Oppen the ultimate "creative ground" is indeed the human community itself) the poet turns at this moment to his companions in this pilgrimage to his childhood home: first to his daughter Linda, already herself an adult ("My child,/Not now a child"), and then, by implication at least, to Mary as well ("our child"). The child is invoked, but after the opening phrases in direct address, the penultimate sentence of the poem seems to disintegrate, as the poet resists the Wordsworthian temptation to emote eloquently to his companion. Rather her mere presence is enough to demonstrate (to the poet, to his absent father, and to the child herself, as she here comes into the presence of her long departed grandfather) that we are "Not altogether lone in a lone universe." The recognition of the bonds that join us together into a community defines by contrast the ways in which the "world of things" is truly "other." These "things" are not epistemologically "other"; as we have already discovered, we are wrong to see them as "material" objects perceived by a "spiritual" consciousness. But the rocks, etc., are *morally* other, for they (and by extension the entire non-human universe that they represent) are "lone," and we are not—anyway, not *entirely*. The difference is simple: the "lone universe" "suffers time/Like stones in sun"—i.e., this universe doesn't actually *suffer* time at all. But we are not thus immune. We *do* suffer time, as the poet's aging hand, and his absent father, and his full-grown daughter all remind him. And yet, here as throughout *The Materials*, it is out of this suffering itself that the human community is born.

* * * * *

In the years since the publication of *The Materials*, Oppen has extended and elaborated the thematic concerns first enunciated and the poetic methods first developed in this book. Yet none of his late volumes brings together all of his characteristic concerns so completely as does *The Materials*. Furthermore, this book is accessible in ways that the later poetry, with its systematic deconstruction of syntax, often is not. *The Materials* thus remains an essential point of entry into Oppen's *oeuvre*. *The Materials* is also in itself, as I have here attempted to show, a rich and subtle poetic achievement. But the importance of *The Materials* lies, I think, not only in the author's personal integrity and rhythmic grace, but also in what his work represents. For *The Materials* implicitly challenges a cluster of assumptions that has since the 1930s dominated the discussion of poetry—and, to a large extent, the practice of poetry also—in this country. In the years before World War II, everyone (everyone in Paris anyway, and no-one else *really* counted) knew that two revolutions were going on in the world: the social revolution, conducted under the aegis of Marx and (usually) Lenin, and the revolution of the word, which found its high priests in James Joyce, Gertrude Stein, and Ezra Pound. According to the version of literary history that is still generally promulgated in American universities, these two revolutions were independent, even antithetical, movements. In defending this assumption, our literary historians can point to the ostentatiously apolitical stances assumed by Joyce and Stein, and to the assertively conservative positions of certain well-known members of the *avant garde* (Pound, Yeats, Eliot, the Southern Agrarians) who did publically affirm a political commitment. Furthermore, during the same years in which the aforementioned members of the English and American literary *avant garde* were moving toward apolitical or reactionary positions, the art of the major socialist country, the Soviet Union, retreated, under the banner of "Socialist Realism," into a sterile scholasticism. These developments have nurtured among American writers and critics a widespread assumption that there is some sort of natural antipathy between artistic and political radicalism. But, this assumption is, I believe, quite false, as we quickly perceive if we look beyond the boundaries of the United States. In France the major revolutionaries of the word were the Surrealists; and the leaders of this movement—Breton, Aragon, Eluard—were all Communists for extended periods. France had its own Mandarin *avant garde*: Valéry is a representative example. It also had an indigenous Fascist *avant garde*, as the case of Céline demonstrates. But the work of Eluard in particular reveals that in the France of the 1930s and 1940s there also existed a poetry which sought to reconcile the social revolution and the revolution of the word. Among Spanish and Latin American poets of this period, furthermore, a fusion of artistic and political radicalism is the rule rather than the exception. The Communists Neruda, Vallejo, and Alberti all offer evidence in support of this generalization; and the most important Spanish poet of the century, Lorca, while not a Communist, was at least (in Oppen's terminology) a populist. Even in the British Isles, at least one major poet also examplifies a similar combination of a poetic and political radicalism: Hugh MacDiarmid. That the United States has had its own counterparts to Eluard and Vallejo and MacDiarmid, the work of Oppen (and in different ways, the work of Rakosi, Zukofsky, and Reznikoff as well) demonstrates. The existence of such an indigenous alternative to the mandarinism of Eliot and his various scions has long been one of the best kept secrets of American literary culture. Thus as we struggle to come to terms with *The Materials*, we are also learning to come to terms with a repressed—perhaps even suppressed— portion of our own history. In his refusal to allow the mandarins to pre-empt our heritage, George Oppen is, in his self-effacing way, a hero. And it is time, I think, to recognize him as such.

NORMAN M. FINKELSTEIN

THE DIALECTIC OF THIS IN WHICH

George Oppen's doubtful statements concerning the efficacy of political poetry have always been problematic to some extent, given the frequently political context of his verse. Although his empirically-oriented objectivist techniques and his profoundly ethical motivations seem to merge when he calls poetry "a test of truth," one is still moved to wonder at an ideology that questions all partisanship within the field of the poem.[1] Certainly, Oppen is accurate in his condemnation of the self-congratulatory "political" poet who contributes to the cause by writing poems about it.[2] Overt propaganda usually plays a small role in the making of art *or* revolution, and it seems almost a commonplace of Marxist criticism to note that genuinely revolutionary works are those that call existing circumstance into question before allowing for an espousal of a given cause or even an affirmation of faith. But Oppen's case has always been more complex. Those of us who have seen in Oppen one of the most important poets of our time have often linked our admiration to his ability to embody difficult political issues in a poetry of startling clarity, a discourse that itself forbids answers while continually insisting that questions be asked. As such, Oppen's poetry is an astonishingly fruitful out-growth of Modernism, in which that movement's almost obsessive concern with "process" and its resistance to "closure" result in a body of work in which those traits bear both aesthetic and political impact. The dialectical force of Oppen's work is such that the object of the poem allows for subjective statements while simultaneously calling for a scrupulous interrogation of the subject that deigns to speak. It is in this way that poetry indeed becomes a test of truth, because it acknowledges material circumstance, the desire

---

1. "The Mind's Own Place," *Kulchur* 3, 10 (1963), 4.
2. "The 'Objectivist' Poet: Four Interviews," *Contemporary Literature* 10 (1969), 174. Cited hereafter in the text, as "Interviews."

to change that circumstance and the questioning that always must temper that desire. Thus Oppen's poetry is resolved and not resolved, a condition that is itself necessary for the continuance of poetry at higher and higher levels of consciousness.

The volume in which this process most clearly may be seen as taking place is *This in Which* (1965); hence it may be regarded as Oppen's most explicitly politicized work. It is a more public book than *The Materials* (1962), which places Oppen's personal integrity against the unique circumstances that shaped his own life after he "gave up" poetry in the Thirties to join the Communist Party. And it is a more wide-ranging book than his masterpiece, *Of Being Numerous* (1968), which concentrates Oppen's meditative powers upon the single crucial relationship of the self to community. In *This in Which*, the poet examines the limits of bourgeois ideology in contrast to his own sense of ethics, based upon long years of political praxis. The poems touch upon all of Oppen's most important concerns, from the ontological and epistemological questions raised by objectivist techniques (and the act of writing poetry itself) to the more overt expressions of consciousness at odds with undeniable political facts. Although they follow no set program, the poems may all be regarded as occasions that test, at times almost empirically, the way in which consciousness may regard itself in the context of a given political or philosophical problem. At times such examinations yield identifiable solutions, at times not; but regardless of the outcome, the act of questioning is crucial to self-consciousness and personal ethical integrity.[3]

"Guest Room," so obviously full of questions, is a good example. Oppen begins by asserting that it is in age that one's capacity for interrogation becomes greatest, so much so that the questioner runs the risk of "homelessness."[4] Homelessness means the loss of the ground of philosophical belief, the loss of a spiritual home that may result when "The maxims//Expose themselves." Always quick to challenge any preconceived code of behavior (and the particular economic and social conditions upon which it rests), Oppen realizes that in the guest room of the rich home, the "happy ending" of wealth and its attendant moral certainly expose themselves. Thus "The clamor of wealth" is "the voice//Of Hell," and Oppen is almost self-congratulatory when he observes that "The virtue of the mind//Is that emotion//Which causes/To see." But this is too quick, too easy. The poet is himself a guest

---

3. *This in Which* may in this respect be seen as a preliminary to *Of Being Numerous*, in which the individual consciousness, having come to terms with itself, may in turn question the nature of its relationship to the masses.
4. *This in Which* (New York: New Directions, 1965), p. 29. Cited hereafter in the text as *TIW*.

here, and in order to keep from becoming too comfortable in his "radicalism," he proceeds to question his own discourse as well: "Virtue . . . // Virtue . . . ?" Such vacillation and doubt seem to free Oppen, and with sudden sureness he declares:

> . . . The great house
> With its servants,
>
> The great utensiled
> House
>
> Of air conditioners, safe harbor
>
> In which the heart sinks, closes
> Now like a fortress
>
> In daylight, setting its weight
> Against the bare blank paper.
>
> (*TIW*, pp. 29-30)

The over-protected life of the rich imposes itself on the poet, cutting him off from his emotional responses and stultifying his ability to write. He realizes this only after voicing his initial concerns about homelessness, a condition, it is implied, that has become preferable to the all too insulated home in which he finds himself a guest.

Oppen's next step is to probe further into his situation by questioning its historical dimension. Evoking a world of secure gentility, the poet simply demands a justification for such privilege:

> The purpose
> Of their days.
>
> And their nights?
> Their evenings
> And the candle light?
>
> What could they mean by that?
> Because the hard light dims
>
> Outside, what ancient
> Privilege? What gleaming
> Mandate
>
> From what past?
>
> (*TIW*, p. 30)

The tone here is deceptive, seemingly innocent but actually critical. The "hard light" outside the enclave of wealth stands in contrast to the candlelight within, reminding us of a time when anything but natural light was a luxury. The ancient privilege and gleaming mandate seem incapable of justification in such a stark, almost impoverished syntactic structure, and the last phrase, "From what past?," calls to mind the fact that those who control the present shape history. And to challenge the present's configuration of the past is to challenge any assumed mandate of power.

Finally, however, Oppen cannot be too severe with his rich hosts because "one has only his ability//To arrange/Matters" and death always "Looms as the horror/Which will arrive//When one is most without defenses" (*TIW*, p. 31). Moving from the political to the existential, Oppen must admit that the wealthy, "Embattled and despairing," are "an *avant garde*//Near the limits of life" (*TIW*, p. 32). The term *avant garde* is full of Oppen's typical ambiguity, for it at once represents a serious challenge to that which is, and a pretentious false front of idle "radicalism."[5] Wealth is power, and power holds the potential to further the boundaries of human existence. So too does the poet; and so, though they are vastly different, both may be viewed as "ridiculous" if their potential remains unfilfilled. In accordance with his ideals, Oppen then has no choice but to go "unarmored, to return//Now to the old questions—."

But rather than indicate a never-ending series of questions and doubts, the poet concludes by shifting to a natural scene and a sense of confidence that is elsewhere lacking:

> . . . and we
> Perched in the dawn wind
> Of that coast like leaves
> Of the most recent weed—And yet the things
>
> That happen! Signs,
> Promises—we took it
> As sign, as promise
>
> Still for nothing wavered,
> Nothing begged or was unreal, the thing
> Happening, filling our eyesight
> Out to the horizon—I remember the sky
> And the moving sea.
>
>   (*TIW*, p. 32)

The certainty of nature's immediacy, "the thing/Happening," is seen as a sign or promise because it is a direct contrast to the wavering of consciousness in the face of social vicissitudes. Oppen can offer us no more in this poem, for in a sense he has exhausted his poetic capability of examining himself examining circumstance. Having raised the questions and provided a range of

---

5. See Oppen's remarks on the subject of Bohemia in "The Mind's Own Place," p. 2.

answers, he has acted responsibly, as he contemplates the moving—the constantly changing—sea.

† † † † †

The typical movement of the poems in *This in Which*, which has been adumbrated in the above reading, manifests itself in a number of different poetic modes throughout the volume. Essential to an understanding of Oppen's intentions are those pieces that present themselves as questions of epistemology and ontology, questions of knowing and being that demand the poet's attention before he can determine a more complex ethical position. What can one know, what can one determine to be a given? For one on Heidegger's "arduous path of appearance," the answer, initially, is very little. But as in the other epigraph to *This in Which*, one learns quickly that an explanation of personal existence leads inevitably to an explanation of all Being. How one can rest secure in such explanations, and how one can write of them, are the challenges that these poems offer both the poet and the reader.

Thus, in "The Forms of Love," Oppen looks back at the young George and Mary, who, caught up in their love for the first time, question what they see before them against what they believe to be true. Much of the poem unfolds as a series of factual statements:

> We saw
> A lake beside us
> When the moon rose.
> I remember
>
> Leaving that ancient car
> Together. I remember
> Standing in the white grass
> Beside it.

(TIW, p. 28)

But the lake is really fog; it is the wonder of the young lovers, their heads "Ringing under the stars," that has made them believe otherwise. Subjectivity can alter perception; the forms of the world become the forms of love, and what one *knows* is contingent upon what one *is*. The lovers see what they believe to be true. The older Oppen, recounting the event, understands how love literally changed the world at that moment; he is aware of who he is now as well as what he learned then. Self-consciousness, therefore, is that quality of mind that understands its capacity for understanding and can articulate this. Simple as this seems, it is a moment of insight to which Oppen continually returns.

The deer in "Psalm," for instance, serve in much the same way as does the fog in "The Forms of Love," though here the process of knowing and recording takes place immediately rather than over a long span of time, and with far greater clarity. The poem alternates between descriptions of the deer and assertions of their presence. Consciousness understands that it *can* ascertain identifiable qualities of Being; it can question perception, receive a sure answer, and record that experience as a testimony to itself and the world. The poet's ability to express a given truth in language is celebrated at the end of the poem ("The small nouns/ Crying faith/In this in which the wild deer/Startle, and stare out." [*TIW*, p. 20]), and it is this faith that Oppen has named as a foundation of his work:

> Q. What exactly is the faith. Is it in the world as world or is it in man's ability to know the world?
>
> A. Well, that the nouns do refer to something; that it's there, that it's true, the whole implication of these nouns; that appearances represent reality, whether or not they misrepresent it: that this in which the thing takes place, this thing is here, and that these things do take place.
>
> ("Interviews," p. 163)

On the other hand, a poem like "The Occurrences" calls attention to the distance between reality and language, and therefore emphasizes the disparity between *what is* and *what is known*:

> The simplest
> Words say the grass blade
> Hides the blaze
> Of a sun
> To throw a shadow
> In which the bugs crawl
> At the roots of the grass;
>
> Father, father
> Of fatherhood
> Who haunts me, shivering
> Man most naked
> Of us all, O father
>
>   watch
> At the roots
> Of the grass the creating
> *Now*   that tremendous
> plunge
>
> (*TIW*, p. 68)

The poem's ambiguous syntax and quantum leaps between stanzas work against any attempt at a definitive reading, but Oppen's use of the verb "Hides" in the third line seems to indicate that simple words obscure the complex natural relationships that they supposedly represent. Even as the grass blade casts a shadow that falls between the sun and the bugs, so too does language prevent light from being shed on the "roots" of reality. Given this condition, Oppen appeals to the "father," the "Man most naked," a primordial, Adamic figure who appears to be directly in touch with the immediate world. He is the poet's guardian as Oppen experiences "the creating/*Now* that tremendous/plunge" which brings him in touch with "the occurences" but ironically ends the poem. To experience immediate events direction is to preclude the possibility of language, which by its very nature is a mediating power.

The philosophical impasse that Oppen encounters again and again is built then on the contradictory experiences of language and of immediate reality. Although Oppen's faith is predicated upon what he conceives to be ontological and epistemological verities, it is still merely a matter of faith, of the belief that the ways in which we know and describe the world correspond to what actually is. This is the condition of "The inelegant heart/ Which cannot grasp/The world/And makes art" (*TIW*, p. 13). Despite the obvious inadequacies of language (as well as his own skepticism), the poet must still go about his work. Caught up in immediate circumstance, he still recognizes the necessity of poetry, and so proceeds in the same way as does the steel worker in "The Building of the Skyscraper." The only way in which the poet may continue is through an especially careful mode of discourse:

> There are words that mean nothing
> But there is something to mean.
> Not a declaration which is truth
> But a thing
> Which is. It is the business of the poet
> 'To suffer the things of the world
> And to speak them and himself out.'
> (*TIW*, p. 73)

The distinction between "a declaration which is truth" and "a thing/Which is" is difficult but obviously crucial. It is, I believe, a distinction between accepting a preconceived view of the world and formulating one's own view after suffering the things of the world, i.e., taking the measure of things as they are to the best of one's abilities. Always in doubt, or in the words of the poem, "on

the verge/Of vertigo," the poet is left with no ethical choice but
to speak out concerning what he believes to be true.

† † † † †

Such being the case, many of the more overtly politicized
poems in *This in Which* take the form of brief statements in which
observation and comment merge and lead to a political insight.
These poems are not strictly objectivist pieces, for they are tempered by the mature subjectivity of Oppen's ethical concerns.
However, their deliberately limited scope and careful attention to
detail are often reminiscent of Williams' work in the Twenties and
Thirties. "Street," for example, addresses the same subject as that
of many Williams pieces, working-class life in the streets of urban
New Jersey:

> Ah these are the poor,
> These are the poor—
>
> Bergen street.
>
> Humiliation,
> Hardship . . .
>
> Nor are they very good to each other;
> It is not that. I want
>
> An end of poverty
> As much as anyone
>
> For the sake of intelligence,
> 'The conquest of existence'—
>
> It has been said, and is true—
>
> And this is real pain,
> Moreover. It is terrible to see the children,
>
> The righteous little girls;
> So good, they expect to be so good . . .
>
> > (*TIW*, p. 51)

With gentle grace, Oppen leads us from a generalized observation of poverty to an idea that pierces the rhetoric of mere
social reform. Poverty is terrible because it stifles the growth of
the mind; it cuts off the human potential to shape the material
conditions of existence, which in turn shape consciousness itself.
Hence the pathetic expectations of the "righteous little girls,"
whose innocent desire "to be so good," probably inspired by

religion, is doomed by what poverty will compell them to make of their lives. Ending the poem with such suggestive detail balances the abstract movement of its middle stanzas. The total effect is one of determined understatement, in which the syntactic fragmentation of the ellipsis and the dash brings us to the beginning of insight and allows us to draw our own inevitable conclusions. Likewise, the poem resists the potential sentimentality of its subject by upsetting reader expectations of gritty "realism" with passages drawn from philosophical discourse. The poem is thus a vehicle for the development of political awareness, although it offers neither encouragement nor resignation. Instead, we hear the poet's own attempt to come to terms with the problem raised by a single poverty-ridden scene, the implications of which move us far beyond its localized particulars.

This very insufficiency of one's particular surroundings at a given point in time, when compared to the immense and often horrible potential of political realities, is the theme of "Seated Man." The place where the old man presently lives, the city that Oppen calls "The machine which has so long sustained him" (*TIW*, p. 50), can do nothing for him when memories of brutality and heroism in Nazi Germany return. The incongruity between the old man's secure present and his tortured past leads the poet to state that "The fact is/It is not his world." (*TIW*, p. 50) Indeed, the man's position is such that he is bereft of any world; he cannot consider himself a part of either his present or his past, and to some extent this accounts for the remarkably muted tone in which Oppen has voiced his dilemma. The diction throughout is thoroughly prosaic; and, as in "Street," fragmented syntax carries the burden of the verse. The structure of the poem seems to deliberately create anti-climax, as in its first stanzas:

> The man is old and—
> Out of scale
>
> Sitting in the rank grass. The fact is
> It is not his world. . . .
>
> (*TIW*, p. 50)

"Out of scale" does not meet up to the drama of the dash that precedes it, and "Sitting in the rank grass," the phrase that completes the sentence in the second stanza, appears almost as an afterthought. The same is true for the crucial statement that follows, for "The fact is" is so understated and conversational that it defuses the potential force of "It is not his world." Even the end of the poem is stated in a matter-of-fact way, despite the horror of which it speaks. The entire piece, however, movingly embodies the condition of exile: in the simultaneous experience of loss and security, one may regard the past and present dispassionately, and learn what one can. There is much of Oppen himself in this "Seated Man," for the poet has always portrayed himself as something of an exile, whose own experiences have taught him the relative values of homelessness and home.

The harsh lessons that Oppen offers throughout *This in Which* are often modulated into different keys, as it were, although their political impact is always discernible. In "Boy's Room," the politics of sexuality emerge from a discussion of "the rooms/Of Keats and Shelley" (*TIW*, p. 46), which, because they were the rooms of naive, inexperienced boys, offer less excitement than the presence of "the unbeautiful banker." In "A Language of New York" Oppen has already castigated banks, relating them to "Ghosts/Which have run mad," (*TIW*, p. 39) yet here the individual banker is a far more ambiguous figure. Shelley and Keats, and by extension all poets, are seen on one level as perennial boys, who lack those qualities that the mundane, potentially evil banker possesses. What a banker has that a poet lacks is power, the command of material circumstance through his economic position. Oppen transfers that power to the realm of sex, so that the banker "Is exciting to a woman, a man/Not a boy gasping/For breath over a girl's body." (*TIW*, p. 46) Unpleasant as this may seem to those who would romanticize the lives of the poets, its truth is undeniable. As Marx says,

> The stronger the power of my money, the stronger am I. The properties of money are my, the possessor's, properties and essential powers. Therefore what I *am* and what I *can do* is by no means determined by my individuality. I *am* ugly, but I can buy the *most beautiful* woman. Which means to say that I am not *ugly*, for the effect of *ugliness*, its repelling power, is destroyed by money.[6]

Oppen acknowledges this situation, but he also understands the power of the poet, which is of an entirely different order. It is no accident that Oppen invokes Shelley and Keats here, for we think of these poets as figures against whom the accumulated woes of what would become modern society were brought to bear. Both were frustrated in love. Keats suffered from an illness exacerbated by poverty, which also kept him from marriage to Fanny Brawne. Shelley's turbulent love life always moved in counterpoint to his changing philosophical and political beliefs, which grew progressively darker throughout his life. Yet in each case, the poet was

---

6. Karl Marx, "Economic and Philosophical Manuscripts," trans. Gregor Benton, *Early Writings*, ed. Quinton Hoare (New York: Vintage Books, 1974), p. 377.

able to resist "the sterile power of the merely existent" (the phrase is Georg Lukács's) and create a body of work that magnificently subsumes the struggle of unfulfilled desire. The state of perpetual desire that is the hallmark of poetry's heroic tradition is the antithesis of the banker's material triumph. Below the unassuming surface of "Boy's Room" is the understanding that from what the banker possesses, what the poet is denied, comes the tragic dialectic of culture since the Romantics. And as Oppen, the implacable realist, says of this understanding in "Giovanni's *Rape of the Sabine Women* at Wildenstein's":

> . . . If this is treason
> To the artists, make the most of it; one needs such faith,
>
> Such faith in it
> In the whole thing, more than I,
> Or they, have had in songs.
>
> (*TIW*, p. 35)

The pervasive dialectic of doubt and commitment that I believe informs all of Oppen's poetry is clearly articulated in the most ambitious poem of *This in Which*, "A Narrative." ("A Language of New York," as fine as it is, now seems sketchy and pale in comparison to the expanded "Of Being Numerous"). Like Eliot, Oppen has always sought "to construct something/Upon which to rejoice," but has also sought for a more complex social understanding of those forces that make our lives genuinely livable, and to what extent. The magnificent hymn to "happiness, rising//Into what is there" (*TIW*, p. 82) that concludes "A Narrative," therefore, comes only after a struggle to comprehend the limits of personal satisfaction when faced with a world in which people "lose connection/With themselves" (*TIW*, p. 77) and the subsequent existential doubt that such a world creates. As should be clear by now, Oppen is *not* a poet like William Bronk, whose skepticism is so profound that it generates a terrifically powerful, self-negating rhetoric which at its best creates a "made world" despite the void to which it always refers. When Oppen invokes Bronk in "A Narrative," he does so in order to confirm the validity of the proposition that "Perhaps the world/Is horror," (*TIW*, p. 80) a proposition that represents only one side of an argument he has never resolved. Typically, Oppen asserts immediately after the section on Bronk that "one may cherish/Invention and the invented terms/We act on." (*TIW*, p. 80) This is the conflict we have encountered in the shorter poems of *This in Which*, only here it is expanded and vacillates even more violently through the medium of the series poem. As in *Of Being Numerous*, the disjunctive structure of "A Narrative" (which parallels Oppen's use of fragmentation on the syntactic level) allows the poet to pursue the differing strands of his argument at some length. In this way, the poem may be regarded as the thematic center of *This in Which*, in which the volume's most important ideas coalesce to form not a unified whole, but a field in which themes may inform each other to a much greater extent than in any single lyric. It is only by bringing his differing, even contradictory concerns into such close proximity with each other that Oppen can hope to achieve a clearer understanding of what social forces inform his dialectical insights.

Given the way in which the poem functions, one of its most striking features is its discourse, which simultaneously contains political and philosophical implications. Appropriately, it is much more difficult in "A Narrative" than it is in the shorter poems to distinguish a rhetoric of thought from a rhetoric of action: Oppen at his most complex (and most eloquent) sweeps such distinctions aside. Works such as "A Narrative" and *Of Being Numerous* may be considered poetic embodiments of the Marxist conception of praxis, for they do away with separate notions of contemplative philosophy and objective action in the material world. The poem unfolds self-consciously out of the realization that language may give form simultaneously to movements of thought and to objective actions that are crucially linked to them. "Thought leaped on us" (*TIW*, p. 82) Oppen exclaims, the phrase itself a paradigm for the operations of language throughout the poem.

The first two sections are representative of the way in which this notion of praxis controls the entire work:

1

I am the father of no country
And can lie.

But whether mendacity
Is really the best policy. And whether

One is not afraid
To lie.

2

And truth? O,
Truth!

Attack
On the innocent

> If all we have
> Is time.
>
> (*TIW*, pp. 74-75)

Oppen begins with the idea that speech affects policy, and vice versa. One's linguistic responsibilities, the articulation of what one takes to be true, can have direct political consequences, but cannot be considered directly because the very idea of truth has become abused by the most vulgar kinds of ideology. If the "truth" of Washington's official heirs results in an "Attack/On the innocent," then perhaps "mendacity/Is really the best policy." No preconceived ethical philosophy, no single mode of discourse, is therefore sufficient in dealing with the complexities of contemporary social realities. What is needed instead is the courage to examine and judge those conditions that not only militate against ethically-based political action, but even against the linguistic powers necessary to conceive and give form to such action. This is what much of "A Narrative" does: it judges, balances what Oppen sees as "horror" against those few articles of faith, those few words and experiences upon which he can always rely.

When Oppen launches out against the institutions that cause us to lose our humanity, he finds himself in a world "In which things explain each other,/Not themselves" (*TIW*, p. 76), a world that appears coherent but is actually

> An enclave
> Filled with their own
> Lives, they said, but they disperse
>
> Into their jobs,
> Their 'circles,' lose connection
> With themselves . . .
>
> (*TIW*, p. 77)

The atomized social structure that Oppen examines in detail in "Of Being Numerous" is here only briefly acknowledged before the sterility it causes begins to torture him:

> 5
>
> It is a place.
> Nothing has entered it.
> Nothing has left it.
> People are born
>
> From those who are there. How have I forgotten . .

> How have we forgotten
> That which is clear, we
> Dwindle, but that I have forgotten
> Tortures me.
>
> (*TIW*, p. 78)

What seems to plague the poet most is the *constancy* of this dehumanizing process, its omnipresence that dulls one into forgetfulness. This accounts for the references to ongoing, unrelieved time throughout the poem, beginning with the ironic "If all we have/Is time" in section 2, followed by "The constant singing/Of the radios" in section 3, the empty cycle of life in section 5, and culminating in the image of "Serpent, Ouroboros/Whose tail is in his mouth" in section 7. Ouroboros, the symbol of eternity, here is related to the traditional serpent of evil, for as Pound says in Canto XXX, "Time is the evil." What both poets mean is that mere duration, what appears to us as the inexorable, linear movement of the days and years, actually destroys our sense of past and future. Trapped in the present moment, which assumes the appearance of eternity, we lose our ability to conceive of the world as different from what it is. Thus the world is certainly a horror, and "The eye/It happens/Registers/But it is dark" (*TIW*, p. 80). The eye is dark, metaphorically speaking, because we cannot *see* what happens. All we perceive are random events that seem to have lost all spatial or temporal coherence.

Two potential solutions are offered to this problem in *This in Which*, and Oppen makes use of both of them in "A Narrative." The first, as we have seen in such poems as "Psalm," is the idea that language, as unreliable as it may be, can correspond to our perceptions of reality, "and there is a moment, an actual time, when you believe something to be true, and you construct a meaning from these moments of conviction" ("Interviews," p. 161). The world, at such moments, becomes comprehensible; a potential for understanding comes into being that encompasses and transcends the immediate moment. In Oppen's work, this realization frequently occurs when consciousness comes into contact with nature and a cyclical conception of time, but Oppen always extends his insight to include the abstract, universal world of the mind. As he says at the end of "A Narrative,"

> . . . The marvel of the wave
> Even here is its noise seething
> In the world; I thought that even if there were nothing
>
> The possibility of being would exist;
> I thought I had encountered

Permanence; thought leaped on us in that sea
For in that sea we breathe the open
Miracle

Of place, and speak
If we would rescue
Love to the ice-lit

Upper World a substantial language
Of clarity, and of respect.
                    (*TIW*, p. 82)

We maintain a sense of being, of coherence, even "if there were nothing," and bring from this experience "a substantial language/Of clarity, and of respect."

This leads us to the second solution to the problems of dehumanization and stasis, an understanding of the workings of history as the ongoing struggle of humanity to perfect itself. Oppen is too much the doubter to ever name this struggle as such, but he comes close in such poems as "Eros," in which he terms it "A devoutness//Toward the future" (*TIW*, pp. 44-45) or in "World, World," in which it appears as "the act of being/More than oneself" (*TIW*, p. 85). In "A Narrative" it takes the form of an Indian ritual, the memory of which recurs in Oppen's more recent poems:

And because they were also a people in danger,
Because they feared also the thing might end,
I think of the Indian songs . . .
'There was no question what the old men were singing'
The anthropologist wrote,

Aware that the old men sang
On those prairies,
Return, the return of the sun.
                    (*TIW*, p. 81)

We yearn to secure what we always have, and yet are always losing. This Utopian desire, which survives despite and because of the violent flux of history, is the last resting place of Oppen's dialectic; it is the visionary point to which all the unresolved doubts in *This in Which* must at last return.

HENRY WEINFIELD

"OF BEING NUMEROUS" BY GEORGE OPPEN

"Of Being Numerous," George Oppen's masterpiece, is a poem of the highest ambition, with a serious claim on our attention for the importance of its theme, the depth of its thought, and the beauty of its diction. A sequence poem, perhaps the most successful in that mode to have yet been written, it accumulates tremendous power and resonance as it moves through its forty sections. Although its method is disjunctive and associational, this is always in the service of a clarity and a cohesion which could not otherwise have been attained.

In its title, "Of Being Numerous" recalls the ancient paradox of the One and the Many, which for Oppen is extended to the problem of the continued existence of poetry in the modern world. With respect to the poetic process in general, the paradox of the One and the Many might be stated as follows: The poet *qua* poet must exist both as a separate consciousness, with the capacity to impose his signature on the world, and as a spokesman for humanity as a whole. Thus, he can neither be isolated from the masses, nor can he merge with them fully: If the former, he risks forfeiting his humanity; if the latter, his originality; in both cases, his poetic identity.

The burden of the poem, however, is that under the conditions of modernity, which the conditions of poetry must somehow reflect, this classical balance between subjectivity and objectivity seems no longer to hold. Consequently, the danger of falling into one or the other abstraction—of being stranded in the state of solipsism, on the one hand, or being pulled back into an undifferentiated morass, on the other—is very great:

6

We are pressed, pressed on each other,
We will be told at once
Of anything that happens

And the discovery of fact bursts
In a paroxysm of emotion
Now as always. Crusoe

We say was
'Rescued'.
So we have chosen.[1]

Because the danger of isolation and the danger of merging
exist simultaneously, and because they are equal sources of anxiety, the image turns in upon itself. Hence the next section of the
poem, where the theme is stated openly:

7

Obsessed, bewildered

By the shipwreck
Of the singular

We have chosen the meaning
Of being numerous.
                              (*CP*, p. 151)

"Crusoe/We say was/'Rescued'"—but only to experience the "ship-
wreck/Of the singular"; for between this Scylla and Charybdis
there is no relief. One thinks of Prufrock's lament: "Till human
voices wake us and we drown"; or of the line from Petronius
Arbiter that was used as the epigraph to the volume in which
"Lycidas" originally appeared: *"Si recte calculum ponas, ubique
naufragium est"* ("If you calculate matters correctly, there is shipwreck everywhere").

The Crusoe motif, which is repeated several times and in different contexts during the course of the poem, brings to mind the
famous passage in *Capital*, where Marx inveighs against those
"Robinsonades," in which the pastoral illusion of being able to
step outside of the world economy is projected. It was this that
led Pound to suppose that it was possible to circumvent capitalism without changing underlying social relations, simply by
issuing scrip money as credits against production. And with reference to Oppen's personal experience, we know that he was a
member of the Pound circle in Paris during the early 'thirties;
that he witnessed Pound's disintegration under the aegis of fascism; and that he subsequently spent many years in the Communist Party, during which he wrote no poetry.

---

1. George Oppen, *Collected Poems* (New York: New Directions, 1975), p. 150. All subsequent references to "Of Being Numerous" will be to this edition, which will be cited
as *CP* in the text.

For Oppen, therefore, the pastoral is not a viable option—neither in its aristocratic form, in which the solitary poet stands above the masses, nor in its populist manifestation, as with the CP's cult of "proletarian literature." "Of Being Numerous" is a poem of maturity, in which Oppen has come into the full extent of his powers. But this brings with it the responsibility to face difficult truths, both in the realm of aesthetics and in that of ethics:

9

'Whether, as the intensity of seeing increases, one's distance
     from Them, the people, does not also increase'
I know, of course I know, I can enter no other place

Yet I am one of those who from nothing but man's way of
     thought and one of his dialects and what has happened
     to me
Have made poetry

To dream of that beach
For the sake of an instant in the eyes,

The absolute singular

The unearthly bonds
Of the singular

Which is the bright light of shipwreck
                              (*CP*, p. 152)

It is a painful affirmation of poetry, though an affirmation nonetheless. For if the only focus for poetry can be "the bright light of shipwreck," then that light, which enters in as "an instant in the eyes," must also be ambiguous:

10

Or, in that light, New Arts! Dithyrambic, audience-as-artists!
But I will listen to a man, I will listen to a man, and when I
speak I will speak, tho he will fail and I will fail. But I will
listen to him speak. The shuffling of a crowd is nothing—
well, nothing but the many that we are, but nothing.

Urban art, art of the cities, art of the young in the cities—
The isolated man is dead, his world around him exhausted

And he fails! He fails, that meditative man! And indeed they
cannot 'bear' it.
                              (*CP*, p. 152)

Thus, from section to section, there is a counterpoint between the movement toward the "absolute singular" and the pull of the crowd, which, if it is nothing, is also the "many that we are." The crowd at the baseball game, in the thirteenth section, consists of "ghosts that endanger/One's soul" from whom "one may honorably keep/His distance/If he can" (*CP*, p. 156). Yet the fourteenth section begins: "I cannot even now/Altogether disengage myself/From those men/With whom I stood in emplacements, in mess tents" (*CP*, p. 157); and from this memory of an experience of solidarity with others, a question emerges: "How talk distantly of 'The People'?" And yet this is no resting-place; for 'The People' are "that force/Within the walls/Of cities//Wherein their cars//Echo like history/Down walled avenues/In which one cannot speak" (*CP*, p. 157).

* * * * *

For Oppen, the problem of the continued existence of poetry is primary—not because it is separable from other concerns, but because it is ultimately synonymous with the problem of the continued existence of the species. Thus, in sections 18 through 20, when the poem shifts to take an explicitly political focus, there is not the slightest discontinuity:

18

It is the air of atrocity,
An event as ordinary
As a President.

A plume of smoke, visible at a distance
In which people burn.

19

Now in the helicopters the casual will
Is atrocious

Insanity in high places,
If it is true we must do these things
We must cut our throats

The fly in the bottle

Insane, the insane fly

Which, over the city
Is the bright light of shipwreck
(*CP*, p. 160)

The atrocity stems from the failure to connect to humanity; its banality stems from the fact that we are inured to it as part of our ordinary, fragmented experience. The task of the poet is thus to "make it cohere," but without sacrificing any of its complexity:

27

It is difficult now to speak of poetry—

about those who have recognized the range of choice or those
who have lived within the life they were born to—. It is not
precisely a question of profundity but a different order of
experience. One would have to tell what happens in a life,
what choices present themselves, what the world is for us,
what happens in time, what thought is in the course of a life
and therefore what art is, and the isolation of the actual

I would want to talk of rooms and what they look out on
and of basements, the rough walls bearing the marks of the
forms, the old marks of wood in the concrete, such solitude
as we know—

and the swept floors. Someone, a workman bearing about
him, feeling about him that peculiar word like a dishonored
fatherhood has swept this solitary floor, this profoundly hidden floor—such solitude as we know.

One must not come to feel that he has a thousand threads
        in his hands,
He must somehow see the one thing;
This is the level of art
There are other levels
But there is no other level of art
                    (CP, p. 168)

It is, indeed, difficult to speak now of poetry. Most of the
poetry that has been written since the second World War fails
precisely because the order of difficulty it assumes is so minimal.
Most poets today "lead their lives/Among poets,//They have lost
the metaphysical sense/Of the future" (*CP*, p. 165), as the poet
tells us. "Of Being Numerous," however, is a poem that "includes
history" with greater depth than any we have had in recent years.
Thus, although it makes no such claim for itself but even questions the validity of such a claim for poetry in the present, it
carries the burden of the modernist version of epic, serving as both
a continuation and a corrective to that tradition.

DAVID McALEAVEY

CLARITY AND PROCESS: OPPEN'S OF BEING NUMEROUS

Oppen's two long poems included in his Pulitzer-winning fourth book are, like much of his work, difficult even though he values clarity. He expresses it as an ideal in one section of "Of Being Numerous":

> Clarity
>
> In the sense of *transparence*,
> I don't mean that much can be explained.
>
> Clarity in the sense of silence.[1]

But when he listens to silence he hears noise, and consequently his poetry turns and turns through itself as each stage of thought concludes by producing another:

> It is true the great mineral silence
> Vibrates, hums, a process
> Completing itself. . . .
>
> (#26)

"Of Being Numerous" can be seen as a complicated analysis of the relation between clarity and process. What follows is a presentation of that analysis in an order which, without being Oppen's, permits a revelation of the dynamics of his thought. The fundamental situation resembles that described by the Heisenberg Uncertainty Principle, that the location and the momentum of an elementary particle cannot both be known at the same time. The rational mind's desire for a clear understanding is defeated and replaced by, though also brought about by, the continually

---

1. George Oppen, "Of Being Numerous," *Of Being Numerous* (New York: New Directions, 1968), p. 24. All subsequent references to this poem and to the other long poem, "Route," from this book will be indicated parenthetically in the text, by section number. Other books by George Oppen are often referred to by abbreviations, as follows: *The Materials* (*M*) and *This in Which* (*TW*).

proceeding world. Successive movements toward that "dark" world by the imagination, by intuition, and by emotion lead Oppen to affirm a fundamental but only partially knowable "real" world, which is not the "true" world. The terms "true" and "false" no longer apply to this "real" world.

The intellect, however, *needs* clarity. Desirous of knowing all that it can, it carefully avoids an all-out affirmation of nothing but an "objective" world. Oppen in "Of Being Numerous" tries a series of strategies on behalf of the mind. In one, the mind claims autonomy, though that immediately turns out to be unsatisfactory. The mind, however, can at least assert that it is the source of artistic unity; it also claims that awareness can remove guilt. Furthermore, it is the mind alone which needs social and religious covenants, which can develop a metaphysic of hope, and which can locate what Oppen calls "lyric valuables"; perhaps most importantly the mind is the arena of truthfulness. Oppen concludes his treatment of these various strategies, all of which are ways of structuring the tension between subject and object, with the assertion that the known and the unknown touch.

If that is intelligible, however, it means that whatever boundary there might be between the unknown and the known cannot be stable, in part because Oppen affirms no single intellectual strategy. But when he says, at the beginning of one section of this title poem, "It is difficult now to speak of poetry," he is not being melodramatic. At the deepest level, it is Oppen's very unwillingness to valorize any set of assumptions about the mind and the process of the world which informs his work. Because his skepticism is immense, conclusive speech is difficult for him. That he speaks at all, it often seems to me, is the precise measure of his intellect's need for survival. He overcomes tension, but never escapes it—and perhaps never really wishes to.

One strategy Oppen tests, I have suggested, is that the mind is autonomous; in the fifth section of "Of Being Numerous," he puts it this way:

> The great stone
> Above the river
> In the pylon of the bridge
>
> '1875'
>
> Frozen in the moonlight
> On the frozen air over the footpath, consciousness
>
> Which has nothing to gain, which awaits nothing,
> Which loves itself.
>
> (#5)

This passage resembles Williams's entry of 9/29 in "The Descent of Winter":

> only the number
> remains
> .2.
>
> on an oval disc
> of celluloid
> tacked
>
> to the whiteenameled
> woodwork
> with
>
> two bright nails
> like stars
> beside
>
> the moon[2]

But where Williams states an idiosyncratic reality, drawing from it the possibility of physical analogy—a simple form of metaphor, and delightful in its own way—Oppen works his observation of reality, more ponderous and public, into an explicit statement about the mind. At any rate Oppen gives the appearance of plumbing deeper into the significance of the image before him. His use of "frozen air," for instance, almost inconspicuous in the flow of the poem, goes back to a similar image in *Discrete Series* (in the poem "The evening, water in a glass"), and the connection both poems offer is with Stevens's "Snow Man" and similar poems on winter vision, including one by Henry Zolinsky in the Objectivism issue of *Poetry*. All these poems affirm that winter reveals that the mind is at home, not in nature, but only when it dwells in itself, in consciousness, and has an internal sense of place.

Yet as Oppen sees it, such a sense of place would be a sort of narcissism. The mind must provide unity, he argues, but not wholly on its own terms, not in the "mathematical" mode Pound had deplored, for good reason, in the closing pages of his 1933 *The Active Anthology*. Admitting the difficulty of talking about poetry, Oppen goes on to assert that one must find in art a unified vision. Art's wholeness is not that of the total process of chaotic experience; thought alone can provide its unity:

> One must not come to feel that he has a thousand threads
>   in his hands,

---

2. William Carlos Williams, "The Descent of Winter," in *Imaginations*, ed. Webster Schott (New York: New Directions, 1970), pp. 234-5.

> He must somehow see the one thing;
> This is the level of art
> There are other levels
> But there is no other level of art
>   (#27)

To feel that one "has a thousand threads in his hands" is to be in a condition of anxiety, to diverge from the on-going process revealed by the attempt to approach silence. Intellectual scatteredness comes from having abandoned the attempt to approach silence, and anxiety is a result.

Since mind must look into process if it is to be at "the level of art," Oppen begins "Of Being Numerous" with a new phrasing of the quote from Maritain he had used to initiate *The Materials*:

> There are things
> We live among 'and to see them
> Is to know ourselves'.
>   (#1)

The "Occurrence" of these things, each "a part/Of an infinite series," goes on without us. What we know at any one time is such a slight fraction of occurrence (*"Now* that tremendous/ Plunge" he can be taken to have urged in "The Occurrences," in *This in Which*) that all the things we do see are "sad marvels." To see at "the level of art" is to miss much, and to know it.

The sadness is a quality Oppen does not spend much time agonizing about. It is better to see at the artistic level than to feel anxiety. He uses the phrase "sad marvels" to register the discrepancy inherent in the discovery that "the level of art" is not possible without the attempt to approach silence. Consequently art is a way of recovering from being out of touch with or skew to the "infinite" series, which is a linear extension of the "discrete" series of his first book. The series in either case consists of non-continuous events, and hence of gaps. Like Stevens, Oppen believes in the renewing power of art and the imagination which is able to see across gaps. To call the largest gap of all, between the known and the unknown, a "discrepancy" as I have done, is like calling the infinite "discrete"—in both cases a deliberate blindness may appear to have been invited. Yet Oppen goes on in this first section to acknowledge that one of the oldest myths, that of the Fall, is his subject:

> Of this was told
> A tale of our wickedness.
> It is not our wickedness.
>   (#1)

The Fall is not an occasion for guilt. Our response resembles, like

Oppen's, N. O. Brown's: "If, as Blake said, the Fall is into Division /the vocation of the intellectual is to overcome the consequences of the Fall."[3] The Fall is a lamentable situation we find ourselves in; Oppen looks for a way to dispense with needless agony, and works toward enlightenment. In this book, Oppen moves away from the judgments of his earlier books as he comes to accept his situation—or to situate himself—in the New York City of his return. To see the things he lives among is to come to know himself, to establish identity in unity with the occurrence of existence. But the Fall is the nature of things, not due to human error. To grow conscious, to come to have vision, is to recover from error. One of the best descriptions of the development of vision, or the kindling of an inner light is this by Olson—and is relevant here because Olson, like Oppen, finds the Fall remediable:

> But the three of us were sitting there and suddenly we were talking about—the word was photo-copic, which I thought was marvelous in terms of all this shit of McLuhan's (excuse me) and today, like, as of literally what I'm here to, in that sense, both mis-represent and represent otherwise. And this word was suddenly the whole meaning of all of our experience with photo— how can I say it—photo-copic: that we *are* darkness. That our, like, condition inside is dark. In other words, if you stop to think of yourself as an impediment of creation, I mean you . . . I think you follow me, that the unknown is rather your self's insides. And I suddenly was talking to these two men on the basis of the fact that that's exactly the whole meaning: that we become sure in the dark, that we move wherever we wish in the six directions with *that* light. I mean literally, that to *light that dark* is to have come to whatever it is any of us seeks.[4]

Oppen goes further than Olson by supposing an intimate relation between the inner light and the natural world. Man may not have fallen as far from understanding in his view, consequently, as in Olson's.

"Recover" after all suggests that consciousness tends toward a state previously achieved. Consciousness attempts to counteract "homesickness." This is consistent with the history of Oppen's opinions since *Discrete Series*, and he concludes the first section of this 40-part poem with a reaffirming narration:

> 'You remember that old town we went to, and we sat in the ruined window, and we tried to imagine that we belonged to those times—It is dead and it is not dead, and you cannot imagine either its life or its death; the earth speaks and the salamander speaks, the Spring comes and only obscures it—' (#1)

---

3. Norman O. Brown, "From Politics to Metapoetics," (1967), in Clayton Eshleman (ed.), *Caterpillar Anthology* (Garden City, New York: Doubleday, 1971), p. 8.
4. Charles Olson, *Poetry and Truth* (the Beloit lectures, 1968), *Writing* 27 (San Francisco, 1971), pp. 43-4.

That timelessness might come from belonging imaginatively to a particular historical place and time is a theme common to Olson's *Maximus*, Pound's *Cantos*, Eliot's *Quartets*. In Oppen the imagination succeeds and fails simultaneously. He sits in a ruined window, emblem of the imagination's ambiguity. The effort ("we tried to imagine that we belonged") succeeds, if "It is dead and it is not dead" can be believed; but it succeeds at the expense of discovering its own limitations: "you cannot imagine. . . ." Oppen reaffirms his "thought" from the final section of "A Narrative":

> I thought that even if there were nothing
>
> The possibility of being would exist;
> I thought I had encountered
>
> Permanence. . . .
> (*TW*, p. 82)

The capitalized "spring" which "obscures" existence loops us back to "Technologies" and "Rationality" (from *TW*) with their sense of the triviality of the mundane seasons. It is as if to be aware of a season is too ordinary; if the salamander is to speak, existence itself, not mutability, must be the subject of imagination. "So," continues Oppen in the second section of "Of Being Numerous,"

> So spoke of the existence of things,
> An unmanageable pantheon
>
> Absolute, but they say
> Arid.
> (#2)

Oppen does not care that his poetry seems flat, dry, infertile to some. He intuits that there are connections between capitalist society and bourgeois art:

> A city of the corporations
>
> Glassed
> In dreams
>
> And images—
>
> And the pure joy
> Of the mineral fact
> (#2)

But he is not in this poem as antagonistic to the city as he has been in earlier poems; he has situated his home in the city, and is able to recognize that

> We are not coeval
> With a locality
> But we imagine others are,
>
> We encounter them. Actually
> A populace flows
> Thru the city.
>
> This is a language, therefore, of New York
> (#3)

The personal dissolves in the multitudinous flow of language through place—the place a city, a system of walls and systems; in this flow the poet becomes a user of the language of a place. A later section discusses the issue of "urban art": for one consequence of the view that the poet is merely custodian of the tribe's language is that the poet cannot function *as* an individual. But this view Oppen attacks:

> Or, in that light, New arts! Dithyrambic, audience-as-artists!
> But I will listen to a man, I will listen to a man, and when I
> speak I will speak, tho he will fail and I will fail. But I will
> listen to him speak. The shuffling of a crowd is nothing—
> well, nothing but the many that we are, but nothing.
>
> Urban art, art of the cities, art of the young in the cities—
> The isolated man is dead, his world around him exhausted
>
> And he fails! He fails, that meditative man! And indeed they
> cannot 'bear' it.
> (#10)

The failure of the "meditative man" is inevitable but it is not due to the increase in noise levels in the cities. The "light" in which "Dithyrambic," Dionysiac art appears valid is itself a "false light" (to use a phrase from *Discrete Series*), one of the two lights Oppen calls "the bright light of shipwreck" (#9). To understand the significance of shipwreck we must look at sections #6 and #7, the latter of which contains the phrase which is the title of both poem and book:

> We are pressed, pressed on each other,
> We will be told at once
> Of anything that happens
>
> And the discovery of fact bursts
> In a paroxysm of emotion
> Now as always.   Crusoe
>
> We say was
> 'Rescued'.
> So we have chosen.
> (#6)

Obsessed, bewildered

By the shipwreck
Of the singular

We have chosen the meaning
Of being numerous.

(#7)

At one point in *Call Me Ishmael* Olson declares that *Moby Dick* marks the end of the self-sufficient ego; Oppen pushes the literary mark back a century to Defoe's novel. Crusoe's story, addressing the value of existence in terms of the potential self-sufficiency of the individual, is the story finally of our terrifying need for society, Crusoe's discovery of the solitary human footprint being therefore curiously parallel to section #28 of *Song of Myself* ("Is this then a touch?"), with all its excitement at overcoming the fear of contact.

The contact Oppen, Defoe and Melville all distrust is the closeness of *news*: the "paroxysm of emotion" to which the populace becomes addicted. A later section of Oppen's poem analyzes the need for this emotional excitement as a mad craving for the appearance of life:

——They await

War, and the news
Is war

As always

That the juices may flow in them
Tho the juices lie.

(#20)

The problem of "numerosity" is *how* to be social since one *must* be. Oppen's irony in section #6, our saying Crusoe was "Rescued," indicates that an apparently happy self-sufficient man was brought back to a civilization which was practically insane. He had rescued himself from shipwreck in the first place, and now he must be rescued from that self-rescue, which we call "shipwreck." Poetry resists the encroachment of society:

Yet I am one of those who from nothing but man's way of
    thought and one of his dialects and what has happened
    to me
Have made poetry

To dream of that beach
For the sake of an instant in the eyes,

The absolute singular

The unearthly bonds
Of the singular

Which is the bright light of shipwreck
                                        (#9)

The failure of the meditative man resembles Crusoe's. Both find
light and peace in solitude, which the city or society destroys.

"Pro Nobis" (*TW*) had lamented Oppen's failure "to arrive/
At an actuality/In the mere number of us." Even in *Of Being
Numerous*, Oppen has said, he "tries to say that there is a concept
of humanity, there is something we want humanity to be or to
become." But he paradoxically wonders if value can *survive* number. For evidence that it can, he turns to a story of Phyllis—"not
neo-classic" (that is, unlike Williams's mock-pastoral in *Paterson
IV*):

Phyllis—not neo-classic,
The girl's name is Phyllis—

Coming home from her first job
On the bus in the bare civic interior
Among those people, the small doors
Opening on the night at the curb
Her heart, she told me, suddenly tight with happiness—

So small a picture,
A spot of light on the curb, it cannot demean us
                                                (#11)

The city itself can inspire ecstasy, and consequently is not irre-
deemable. The danger with the city as "Dithyrambic" frenzy is
not that it is ignoble but that it is "abstracted." The chief qualification of the realistic impulse that Oppen has always made is that
private ecstatic experience has priceless value. When he cannot
accept the particulars he sees *with* his eyes as absolute, it is because they are too removed from primitive or basal realities which
he can imagine or see *through* his eyes and which lead him more
easily to the state of awe. Oppen is enough of a realist to see however that primitivism is untenable. Section #12 tests an imaginary
primitiveness:

They made small objects
Of wood and the bones of fish
And of stone. They talked,
Families talked,
They gathered in council
And spoke, carrying objects.
They were credulous,
Their things shone in the forest.

> They were patient
> With the world.
> This will never return, never,
> Unless having reached their limits
>
> They will begin over, that is,
> Over and over
>   (#12)

"That which is clear/We dwindle," Oppen has said in "A Narrative" (*TW*), and as here, the dwindling is not in the physical place
but in a mental state. Social organization is not at fault: generations occur in families, and "they" and "their" can refer to
"credulous" persons as well as anxious ones. Cyclical return to the
origin of society is only offered here in hopeless self-mockery.
Elsewhere Oppen repudiates such a possibility, as in "A Narrative,"
for instance, where he rejects Ouroboros, the river/snake with its
tail in its mouth with which Williams had hoped to conclude
Paterson. Any cyclical possibility is flatly denied in section #13
of "Of Being Numerous," where Oppen asserts that we are "unable
to begin/At the beginning." He cannot however bring himself to
approve of "the fortunate" ones who

> Find everything already here. They are shoppers,
> Choosers, judges; . . . And here the brutal
> is without issue, a dead end.
>   They develop
> Argument in order to speak, they become
> unreal, unreal, life loses
> solidity, loses extent, baseball's their game
> because baseball is not a game
> but an argument and difference of opinion
> makes the horse races. They are ghosts that endanger
>
> One's soul. There is change
> In an air
> That smells stale, they will come to the end
> Of an era
> First of all peoples
> And one may honorably keep
>
> His distance
> If he can.
>   (#13)

The greater resoluteness indicated by the period's presence (only
22 of the poem's sections end with a punctuated full stop), the
finality it indicates, also indicates that the speaking voice intends
to be less provisional and more authentic. Argument makes Oppen
aware that existence is not in focus, as he says in his interview
with Dembo:

> A statement can be made in which the subject plays a very little part, except for argumentation; one hangs a predicate on it that is one's comment about it. This is an approximate quotation from Hegel, who added (I like the quote very much): "Disagreement marks where the subject-matter ends. It is what the subject-matter is not." The important thing is that if we are talking about the nature of reality, then we are not really talking about our *comment about it*; we are talking about the apprehension of some *thing*, whether it is or not, whether one can make a thing of it or not. *Of Being Numerous* asks the question whether or not we can deal with humanity as something which actually does exist.[5]

Many of Oppen's own claims appear contradictory, however, and though consistency may be an unnecessary god in the pantheon, oftentimes merely apparent contradictions yield to a greater coherence. To sort them out it is necessary to recall his praise for Giovanni's spiralling statue (in *TW*).

For Oppen does not want to "keep//His distance/If he can" but wants people to speak of what is. His is a guarded love. The fourteenth section thus denies the thirteenth, remembering "those men//With whom I stood in emplacements," who are fellow Americans from whom he cannot withhold himself—Among them "many men/More capable than I." To withhold himself becomes for Oppen the same as inducing a blindness to his own experience. "How talk/Distantly of 'The People'" he asks, knowing very well that they are inarticulate and not honorable:

> their cars
>
> Echo like history
> Down walled avenues
> In which one cannot speak.
> (#14)

The need to speak is not an absolute for Oppen. He presents one motive behind speech, but does not altogether approve of it: "Find me/So that I will exist" he has an "androgynous" chorus entreat, "find every hair/Of my belly." Language can create, can bring things into existence. In a subsequent section the middle American voice Oppen argued against in "Myself I Sing" (*M*) reiterates the choric complaint:

> There is nobody here but us chickens
>
> Anti-ontology——

---

5. George Oppen, interviewed by L. S. Dembo, 25 April 1968. In L. S. Dembo and B. N. Pondrom (eds.), *The Contemporary Writer: Interviews with Sixteen Novelists and Poets* (Madison: University of Wisconsin Press, 1972), p. 175.

> He wants to say
> His life is real,
> No one can say why .
>
> It is not easy to speak
>
> A ferocious mumbling, in public
> Of rootless speech
>   (#17)

"Roots" of course ties in with a series of the most central images in Oppen's poetry, and especially in this context; "The roots of words/Dim in the subways" invite comparisons to "Vulcan," "Return," "Workman" (all in *M*), and innumerable other poems. "Rootless speech" terrifies Oppen, because it is symptomatic of what he calls in section #18 "the air of atrocity":

> An event as ordinary
> As a President.
>
> A plume of smoke, visible at a distance
> In which people burn.
>   (#18)

The Vietnam war is the focus. His is one of the few politically motivated poetries—Brecht's is another—to manage outright condemnation by maintaining a continual and rigorous pressure toward understatement:

> Now in the helicopters the casual will
> Is atrocious
>
> Insanity in high places,
> If it is true we must do these things
> We must cut our throats
>
> The fly in the bottle
>
> Insane, the insane fly
>
> Which, over the city
> Is the bright light of shipwreck
>   (#19)

This particular "light of shipwreck" does not stand for the solitary job or a deserted beach, but instead parallels the "ferocious mumbling in public/Of rootless speech" characteristic of the society which Crusoe returns to. In fact this insane or false "light of shipwreck" has the same relation to the other, illuminative light of shipwreck that "Ferocious mumbling" has to the noise of mineral process already referred to and which plays a part in the long central section #26. At this point in the poem, however, what is essential is the need to find a way to avoid the implication of the image of the bottled fly: that destiny has decreed the insanity of the atrocious "casual will" and that consequently self-destruction is the only acceptable moral consequence of life. (Wittgenstein: "What is your aim in philosophy?—To shew the fly the way out of the fly-bottle."[6])

Another way to say this is that Oppen is struggling to externalize death. He does not accept Freud's pessimistic view that the death instinct inheres in the personality. In fact Oppen's poetry is throughout a message of hope, its privations, as I began by saying, testifying to his conviction of the scariness of the human predicament. To eliminate guilt associated with death would clearly make it possible for men to hope more easily. He will not take responsibility for death. He turns to the most minimal and indisputable of philosophies:

> I do believe that consciousness exists and that it is consciousness of something, and that is a fairly complete but not very detailed theology, as a matter of fact.[7]

Certainly it is hard to fault Oppen with an eagerness to prove his superiority over the metaphysical problems he confronts. Bolstered with Sartrian modes of thought, he can say "we have chosen" to say "Rescued," or "We have chosen the meaning/Of being numerous," in effect repudiating his earlier ironic position (in "The Crowded Countries of the Bomb," from *M*) that "chance . . . has spared us/Choice." In "Of Being Numerous" he faces the issue of choice and determinism more squarely than that. He will not yield to chance or any destiny which he does not have to accept. He does not look away from either history or his own weakness, and still he can find room for hope in the most unlikely places:

> Great things have happened
> On the earth and given it history, armies
> And the ragged hordes moving and the passions
> Of that death. But who escapes
> Death
>
> Among these riders
> Of the subway,
>
> They know
> By now as I know

---

6. Ludwig Wittgenstein, *Philosophical Investigations* (New York: Macmillan, 1953), p. 103e.
7. Oppen, Dembo interview, p. 176.

> Failure and the guilt
> Of failure.
> As in Hardy's poem of Christmas
>
> We might half-hope to find the animals
> In the sheds of a nation
> Kneeling at midnight,
>
> Farm animals,
> Draft animals, beasts for slaughter
> Because it would mean they have forgiven us,
> Or which is the same thing,
> That we do not altogether matter.
>   (#20)

Hardy's poem ("The Oxen") is intensely aware of the immensity of the wish for things to be all right, and the reader senses Hardy's lack of faith, his pessimism: "So fair a fancy few would weave/In these years!" Oppen's final line here of course carries the meaning that the animals kneel to some other source or repository of value, not perhaps far removed from Hardy's poem but actually more complete in its imagination of the significance of the animals' kneeling. The next two sections search for evidence that the beasts might kneel, one in encountering the ongoing existence of a brick, the other in the principle of clarity "in the sense of silence"; but the poem rides its energy beyond those possible stays, since, as the following section (#23) declares,

> Under the soil
> In the blind pressure
> The lump,
> Entity
> Of substance
> Changes also.
>   (#23)

To ask whether "entities" change or not, or what "substance" might be, is to quibble. It is the blindness of the pressure from above which Oppen distrusts:

> In two dozen rooms,
> Two dozen apartments
> After the party
> The girls
> Stare at the ceilings
> Blindly as they are filled
> And then they sleep.
>   (#23)

The bitterness expressed by the distance and understatement of these lines modulates, in the following section, to outraged sarcasm:

> In this nation
> Which is in some sense
> Our home. Covenant!
>
> The covenant is:
> There shall be peoples.
>   (#24)

Oppen's sexual morality, clearly, is as traditional as Williams's was most of his life, and in fact section #24 cites the line "The pure products of America" in testimony to the two poets' closeness here.

Section #26 effects a crucial switch of emphasis in "Of Being Numerous." The subject of suicide resurfaces, now seen as the logical conclusion of a "nativeness" which cannot recognize significance beyond the passage of one's own life. Generation, for Oppen, depends on faith in some sort of covenant, and cannot be supported without the "Limitation" of

> The metaphysic
> On which rest
>
> The boundaries
> Of our distances.
> We want to say
>
> 'Common sense'
> And cannot. We stand on
>
> That denial
> Of death that paved the cities,
> Paved the cities
>
> Generation
> For generation and the pavement
>
> Is filthy as the corridors
> Of the police.
>   (#26)

Oppen's sympathies are still politically radical, and he turns for hope to the youth of a new generation:

> Where the earth is most torn
> And the wounds untended and the voices confused,
> There is the head of the moving column
>
> Who if they cannot find
> Their generation
> Wither in the infirmaries
>   (#26)

This is once again the message of "Eros" (*TW*), re-enacted by Paris

in the student-labor revolt of 1968, the year *Of Being Numerous*
appeared. Life is more powerful than death, and considerably
more vociferous. The defense of this position rests, as it did for
the Paris Commune of 1871, on metaphysic, and so Oppen returns
to *Moby Dick*:

> The power of the mind, the
> Power and weight
> Of the mind which
> Is not enough, it is nothing
> And does nothing
>
> Against the natural world,
> Behemoth, white whale, beast
> They will say and less than beast,
> The fatal rock
>
> Which is the world——
>   (#26)

"Fatal" carries a special charge, pointing back to the "love of fate
//For which the city alone/Is audience//Perhaps blasphemous"
(#8). It would therefore be blasphemous to suppose the mind has
no "weight" and can know nothing. To justify his faith Oppen
turns (as he declares in his Dembo interview) to the "lyric valuables" (a phrase which appears in "From Disaster," in *M*). One of
two "valuables" he appeals to here is the imagist virtue of clear
sight, the ability to see pebbles clearly through water. The other
is an illuminated model of habitation:

> O if the streets
> Seem bright enough,
> Fold within fold
> Of residence . . .
>   (#26)

These cerebral folds, like the shifting contexts of this long poem,
are a place or home (the City of Light) to exist in. Each person in
his residence enacts a similar drama or dilemma, and Oppen, as
the next section shows, is enabled by this calming realization to
disclose what he himself wants to say about the experience provided by poetry:

> I would want to talk of rooms and of what they look out on
> and of basements, the rough walls bearing the marks of the
> forms, the old marks of wood in the concrete, such solitude
> as we know——
>
> and the swept floors. Someone, a workman bearing about
> him, feeling about him that peculiar word like a dishonored
> fatherhood has swept this solitary floor, this profoundly hid-
> den floor—such solitude as we know.   (#27)

"Profoundly hidden" in its separate "fold," this passage of prose is moving as few poems are. What it signifies is that Oppen has stopped trying to declare an absolute value for existence: "What can I say/Of living?" he asks later in the poem, and answers, "I cannot judge it." He returns to the *feeling* of solitude, the pain of its loneliness. The poem connects with other poems about mortality, "Alpine" (*TW*), "Return" (*M*), and "Stranger's Child" (*M*):

> The baffling hierarchies
> Of father and child
>
> As of leaves on their high
> Thin twigs to shield us
>
> From time, from open
> Time
>   (#29)

These lines do not simply repeat thought developed in those earlier poems; for they invest greater emotional energy in visual imagery. Once feeling is introduced, Oppen's strategies shift again, for soon he comes to argue that desire is beauty:

>   the wet lips
> Laughing
>
> Or the curl of the white shell
>
> And the beauty of women, the perfect tendons
> Under the skin, the perfect life
>
> That can twist in a flood
> Of desire
>
> Not truth but each other
>
> The bright, bright skin, her hands wavering
> In her incredible need
>   (#32)

The equation of need and beauty leads to self-recognition, as the subsequent section shows:

> Which is ours, which is ourselves,
> This is our jubilation
> Exalted and as old as that truthfulness
> Which illumines speech.
>   (#33)

"Truthfulness which illumines speech" is a precise expression of the virtue Oppen's poetry both seeks and grows out of. That his desire should be "not for truth but each other" may be a hard pill to swallow, even though in the penultimate section he points

out that the "sad marvels" of occurrence happen "neither for self/
Nor for truth." He hopes to engage a reality larger than the *true*,
namely the *real*, but he means to keep the intellectual manner of
truth-telling. If he can, then he feels he may have a basis for speaking and asserting in the first place, and then he could be confident
of his ability to write poems—to establish communication with
others.

"Surely infiniteness is the most evident thing in the world,"
he says in section #34, heading into that more fundamental but
still endangered place,

> Tho the world
> Is the obvious, the seen
> And unforeseeable,
> That which one cannot
> Not see
>
> Which the first eyes
> Saw—
>
> For us
> Also each
> Man or woman
> Near is
> Knowledge
>
> Tho it may be of the noon's
> Own vacuity
>
> ——and the mad, too, speak only of conspiracy
> and people talking——
>
> And if those paths
> Of the mind
> Cannot break
>
> It is not the wild glare
> Of the world even that one dies in.
>   (#36)

We recall the burden of "A Narrative" (*TW*), that one must speak
a "substantial language" in order to "rescue love," like Orpheus
carrying Eurydice out of Hades. Oppen is not convinced the battle
can be won; what he can grant is that

> One witnesses——
> It is ennobling
> If one thinks so.
>
> If to know is noble
>
> It is ennobling.   (#31)

There can be no *final* source of value, because knowledge is surrounded by ignorance. Oppen introduced these lines by saying that "the known and the unknown/Touch," which resembles his Valéryesque statment in the Dembo interview: "At any given time the explanation for something will be the name of something unknown."[8]

In an earlier fold of his thought he had tried to talk more simply of the known in a passage reminiscent of both Whitman and Williams:

> Tho the house on the low land
> Of the city
>
> Catches the dawn light
>
> I can tell myself, and I tell myself
> Only what we all believe
> True
>
> And in the sudden vacuum
> Of time . . .
>
> . . . is it not
> In fear the roots grip
>
> Downward
>
> (#29)

As we are often made aware in Oppen's poetry, this is the work of an older man, for whom "sad marvels" occur in "the last credible circumstance . . . the room of a very old man" (#39). This old man however makes use of others who have also uncovered some marvels themselves: the concluding, fortieth section is from Whitman's diaries just as the sixteenth was taken from Kierkegaard's *Fear and Trembling*; the one testifies to the miraculous, "curious," absurd interaction between man, art, and nature, the other to the possible imaginative rewards of endeavor:

> . . . only he who unsheathes his knife shall be given
> Isaac again. He who will not work shall not eat . . .
> but he who will work shall give birth to his own father.
>
> (#16)

* * * * *

The other long poem in *Of Being Numerous*, the fourteen-sectioned "Route," with its epigraph "the void eternally regenerative," grounds the many concerns of the title poem in a repeated

---

8. Oppen, Dembo interview, p. 176.

call "to achieve clarity" (#1). Since process or flux is inescapable, it can seem a tyranny of change, and mere fear of process may motivate the desire to be clear, fear that "Things alter. . . ." "Route," however, and the final poem of the book, "Ballad," reach beyond fear, to affirm the objective world. Oppen aims for a heightened consciousness which is non-reflexive. To achieve that requires heroism, as he sees (considering that "failure" is inevitable). Heroism, however, is possible, and can lead to affirmation—of "visiting," of curiosity, of the objective world—and can ultimately result in a condition which must be called salvation, the state of the "native/Native." The fluxional regenerative void, paradoxically, offers hope. But first the fear of process must be defeated.

Evidence of process is evidence also of "what is not autonomous in us," of the existence of an exterior reality ("blind eye/ Which has taught us to stare") which opposes our own sense of belonging and owning:

> The unreality of our house in moonlight
> Is that if the moonlight strikes it
> It is truly there tho it is ours
>
> (#2)

The drive here is to meet permanence, and the poet's complaint is that clarity can be achieved neither by silence nor by transparence: "Words cannot be wholly transparent" (#4), and cannot therefore satisfy the poet's need to reveal the reality of the world. The "claiming sweep" and the "mineral hum" are in a perpetual dialectic. The failure of every attempt to gain clarity means that the "meditative man" will fail; and if that weren't enough, there is the further complicating fact that no experiences can be the same: "Neither friends nor lovers are coeval . . ." and consequently, the meditative man fails,

> as for a long time we have abandoned those in
>   extremity and we find it unbearable that we should
>   do so . . .
>
> The sea anemone dreamed of something, filtering the sea
>   water thru its body,
>
> Nothing more real than boredom—dreamlessness, the
>   experience of time, never felt by the new arrival,
>   never at the doors, the thresholds, it is the native
>
> Native in native time . . .
>
> The purity of the materials, not theology, but to present
>   the circumstances
>
> (#4)

Oppen's goal is an awareness without alienation, without self-
awareness, the awareness of the wild deer ("Psalm," in *TW*) before
they "startle, and stare out." The force of the long prose section
(#5) of "Route," detailing the sufferings of resistance fighters in
Alsace, which culminates with a story of suicide, comes from just
such a non-reflexive consciousness, although in this case the
imagined absence of self-awareness is a result of a heightened consciousness rather than of a reduction into a sea-anemone's dream-
life. This is to say, the experience of awareness remains a form of
consciousness. But the heightened consciousness Oppen looks for
is not limited by the endless game of involuted rationality. Oppen's
prose is spare and emotional, void of repetition or extravagance; it
seems almost unfair to excerpt from it. Nonetheless the following
paragraphs tell of the route one Alsatian chose instead of going
into hiding, which might have resulted in the destruction of his
family:

> There was an escape from that dilemma, as, in a way,
> there always is. Pierre told me of a man who, receiving the
> notification that he was to report to the German army, called
> a celebration and farewell at his home. Nothing was said at
> that party that was not jovial. They drank and sang. At the
> proper time, the host got his bicycle and waved goodbye. The
> house stood at the top of a hill and, still waving and calling
> farewells, he rode with great energy and as fast as he could
> down the hill, and, at the bottom, drove into a tree.

> It must be hard to do. Probably easier in an automobile.
> There is, in an automobile, a considerable time during which
> you cannot change you mind. Riding a bicycle, since in those
> woods it is impossible that the tree should be a redwood, it
> must be necessary to continue aiming at the tree right up to
> the moment of impact. Undoubtedly difficult to do. And, of
> course, the children had no father. Thereafter.

                                                        (#5)

The act of courage—which is another way of talking about the
issues Oppen has been dealing with—is an act in which self is put
out of consideration. But what gives it courage is not its selflessness but its devotion to an ideal. Even more to the point, perhaps,
is the fact that Oppen too fears not-being. This passage has especial
significance for him because it manifests that fear and dramatizes circumstances under which at least one man was able to free
himself from it. Whenever possible Oppen sees his job as poet to
be to loosen the hold of fear and guilt. The poet, and this is fundamental for Oppen, must be heroic:

> Cars on the highway filled with speech,
> People talk, they talk to each other;

Imagine a man in the ditch,
The wheels of the overturned wreck
Still spinning—

I don't mean he despairs, I mean if he does not
He sees in the manner of poetry
                                        (#8)

Opposed to this idealism is Oppen's knowledge that not just the imagination but all the mind's faculties are imperfect:

I was saying: there is a mountain, there is a lake

A picture seen from within. The picture is unstable, a
moving picture, unlimited drift. Still, the picture
exists.
              (#6)

Along the path of Oppen's tortuous route run "in a void of utensils" lies the countryside, the "context" which is "history/Moving toward the light of the conscious" (#9). "Reportage" emerges as the half-ironic, half precious (in both its senses) end of poetry:

Not the symbol but the scene this pavement leads
To roadsides—the finite

Losing its purposes
Is estranged

All this reportage.
                          (#10)

The road the car travels, the route, is also the context, the "thousands of days" (#9), the "void eternally regenerative" and also the Tao on which "what was there to be thought" is met, "Virgin" (#10). A life which has lost its direction or purpose loses touch with the finite quality of the roadsides and the "appalling fields" beyond, where one's encounters with one's parents occur (#9). The "stumbling" of estrangement is a kind of punishment:

All punishes him. I stumble over these stories—
Progeny, the possibility of progeny, continuity

Or love that tempted him

He is punished by place, by scene, by all that holds
all he has found, this pavement, the silent symbols

Of it, the word it, never more powerful than in this
moment. Well, hardly an epiphany, but there the thing
is all the same

All this is reportage
                          (#11)

Oppen's poetry moves toward a monotheism of principle, as the word "reportage" might indicate. In section #12 he casts a cold eye on Milton and *Genesis*:

> To insist that what is true is good, no matter, no matter,
>   a definition——?
>
> That tree
>   whose fruit . . .
>   (#12)

The suspicion Oppen seems to have formulated here is that his own quest for truth is if not satanic at least rebellious. He is fully aware that his countrymen are not concerned with truth but pursue their own pleasures "unmarred by indifference," by the "hard edge of concrete continually crumbling//into gravel in the gravel of the shoulders" (#12). Oppen goes on, however, with whatever defiance is involved, reasoning that he is closer to harmony than defiance, nearer unity than indifference. He has sought

> To owe nothing to fortune, to chance, nor by the power of
>   his heart
> Or her heart to have made these things sing
> But the benevolence of the real
>   (#13)

And though Oppen does believe the millenialist's supposition that "we are at the beginning of a radical depopulation of the earth," he also declares the key to his method of thinking:

> These things at the limits of reason, nothing at the limits
> of dream, the dream merely ends, by this we know it is the
> real
>
> That we confront
>   (#14)

The final poem of the book offers us "the real" itself in opening to us a possibility of humane sharing. If each solitary person is imaginatively active and accurately observant, then we can arrive at the condition of the lobsterman's wife that Oppen met on a small island in Maine:

> An island
> Has a public quality
>
> His wife in the front seat
>
> In a soft dress
> Such as poor women wear
>
> She took it that we came——
> I don't know how to say, she said——

Not for anything we did, she said,
Mildly, 'from God'. She said

What I like more than anything
Is to visit other islands . . .
(p. 64)

Of Being Numerous, with its concern for social and historical
otherness, affirms the reality of the shifting world which opens
before us. "I might at the top of my ability," Oppen says, "stand
at a window/and say, look out; out there is the world" ("Route,"
#3). *Of Being Numerous*, besides affirming the reality of the exis-
tent world (an intellectual gesture much like the dropping of the
anchor in "Vulcan," in *The Materials*), confronts that world.
Opposed to homesickness is curiosity, and the fisherwife's desire
to go visiting is motivated by curiosity—as well as the yearning of
"homesickness." But "visiting" is a guilt-free encounter with the
real, a painless way of accepting the world, but also one that
demands confidence. The self must be free enough to move. Once
it is free enough to move it can experience itself as "native."
Intellectually, the "native" sojourner can travel from fold to fold
of thought, striving to become the "native//Native in time." Which
is the condition one is born to.

THE CANON
III.
RECENT WORK

George Oppen. Photograph 1970, courtesy of Mary Oppen.

DONALD DAVIE

NOTES ON GEORGE OPPEN'S
SEASCAPE: NEEDLE'S EYE[1]

For us to come to terms with Oppen, the time has long gone by—if it ever existed—when it was useful to start plotting his place in a scheme of alternative or successive poetic "schools" or "traditions." Imagism, objectivism, constructivism, objectism: if there was ever any point in shoving those counters about, that time is long gone by. At present, that sort of categorizing only ducks the challenge that the poems throw down: the way of living, and of thinking about living, which they propose to us.

Oppen is not at all a representative American poet. Not only is he in earnest as few poets are, but the nature of his earnestness is not of a sort we think of as "American." In his background and his past there is a good deal of Marxism, and so his attempts to understand the moment in which he writes are a historian's attempts, not (as with most American poets of comparable seriousness) psychological and/or mythopoeic. Not for him, for instance, the naive pastoralism, the harking back to a pre-industrial economy, which is the stock-in-trade of the American poets currently most popular with the American public. And so it is ironical that when Charles Olson responded to Oppen's review of him he should have protested, "I wanted to open mr Oppen to history"; being open to history is one thing, being open to the recorded and unrecorded past is something else. And one may stay closed to that past not because of ignorance or limited imagination, but as an act of willed choice. This is the choice that Oppen seems to make in a recent poem called, "The Taste":

---

1. Reprinted from *The Grosseteste Review*, 6, 1-4 (1973), pp. 233-9).

> Old ships are preserved
> For their queer silence of obedient seas
> Their cutwaters floating in the still water
> With their cozy black'iron work
> And Swedish seamen dead   the cabins
> Hold the spaces of their deaths
> And the hammered nails of necessity
> Carried thru the oceans
> Where the moon rises grandly
> In the grandeur of cause
> We have a taste for bedrock
> Beneath this spectacle
> To gawk at
> Something is wrong with the antiques, a black fluid
> Has covered them, a black splintering
> Under the eyes of young wives
> People talk wildly, we are beginning to talk wildly, the wind
> At every summit
> Our overcoats trip us
> Running for the bus
> Our arms stretched out
> In a wind from what were sand dunes[2]

Those who know San Francisco know that wind, they know also the ships that Oppen means, and they will share his sense that in the California scene such attempts at historical *pietas* have an air of irrelevant connoisseurship. The poem comes in fact in a sequence with the deceptively modest title, "Some San Francisco Poems." But then. . . . Oppen is a San Franciscan, once again voluntarily, by choice. He moves about the city and its hinterland seeing it through eyes that have been conditioned elsewhere. It is an Atlantic eye that looks out over the edge of a continent and a cultural epoch, at the Pacific. The beautiful and precarious shallowness of coastal California, treacherously gummed on to the continent across the San Andreas fault, is caught by him as by no native or thoroughly assimilated Californian. He is as much a foreigner there as we might be, and therefore as incredulous, as dubious, above all as apprehensive.

It is possible to think that poetry should be responsible for giving to Californian youth that ballast which we feel that it so perilously lacks—"You were *not* born yesterday!" That was the response of a thoroughly assimilated Californian, Yvor Winters, in poems like "California Oaks." Oppen will have none of it. For him on the contrary sanity is in holding on to

---

2. George Oppen, *Collected Poems* (New York: New Directions, 1975), p. 225. Hereafter all references to Oppen's work will be to this edition, and such citations will be incorporated into the text.

'the picturesque
common lot' the unwarranted light

Where everyone has been

(*CP*, p. 219)

And so "the courageous and precarious children" (*CP*, p. 226), as he calls them, are to be—have to be—trusted, with whatever misgivings. The past will not help them; and perhaps we only thought that it helped us.

That goes also for the past of Art, of poetic art for instance:

O withering seas
Of the doorstep and local winds unveil

The face of art

Carpenter, plunge and drip in the sea   Art's face
We know that face

More blinding than the sea   a haunted house   a limited

Consensus unwinding

Its powers
Toward the thread's end

In the record of great blows   shocks
Ravishment   devastation   the wood splintered

The keyboard gone in the rank grass swept her hand
Over the strings and the thing rang out

Over the rocks and the ocean
Not my poem   Mr Steinway's

Poem   Not mine   A 'marvelous' object
Is not the marvel of things

        twisting the new
Mouth   forcing the new
Tongue   But it rang

(*CP*, p. 224)

We have heard something like this before, from William Carlos Williams. The resemblance is real, and Oppen no doubt would acknowledge it. But the differences are striking too. Williams after all was a mythopoeic poet (*Paterson*) and a historian only so far as he could turn history into myth. He was even a systematizer, and in his last years a master or a prophet looking for (and thinking he found) disciples. Oppen has no such hopes or intentions; his tone is ruminative, intimate, domestic. There is no writer to whom a tag like "American expansiveness" is less appropriate. And indeed this goes beyond "tone"; in a very unAmerican way Oppen seems to offer us, as Hardy did, only "disconnected observations." The claims that he makes on us, for himself and his art, are disarmingly modest.

All the same, and in fact even less avoidably than with Williams, the challenge is thrown down to us: the past is irrelevant, a dangerous distraction. Well, *is* it? For instance, the past of our art. . . . Much as we may agree that "a 'marvelous' object Is not the marvel of things," or that the commonplace is fruitfully mysterious in ways that only this sort of poetry can make us see, still, are we Marxist enough, historical determinists enough, to agree that the time is past for so many of the traditional splendours and clarities as this poetry wants us to dispense with? Outside of the San Francisco sequence there is a poem called (and the title is important) "West":

> Elephant, say, scraping its dry sides
> In a narrow place as he passes says yes
>
> This is true
>
> So one knows?   and the ferns unfurling   leaves
>
> In the wind
>
> . . . sea   from which . .
>
> 'We address the future?   '
>
> Unsure of the times
> Unsure I can answer
>
> To myself   We have been ignited
> Blazing
>
> In wrath we await
>
> The rare poetic
> Of veracity that huge art whose geometric
> Light seems not its own in that most dense world West
>   and East
> Have denied have hated have wandered in   *precariousness*
>   (*CP*, p. 208)

(I break off at mid-point.) "Splendours"—is that the word for what an old-fashioned reader would feel the lack of, in these verses? Hardly; that elephant, so abruptly huge and patient before

us, is himself a splendour. "Clarities," then? Well, yes; the sup-
pression of so much punctuation certainly makes for obscurity
(though the most obscure poem is one called "The Occurrences,"
which has no punctuation-stops at all). But the right word, to
point for instance to the melodiousness which it seems plain we
must not look for in this writing, is still to seek. I suggest: "*braveries.*" This writing denies itself certain traditional braveries
(rhyme, assonance, determinable auditory rhythm) precisely
because they would testify in the poet to a bravery (in the other
sense) about his vocation and the art he practises, a bravery that
we cannot afford once we have acknowledged that our condition,
obscured from us by Western and Eastern cultures alike, is above
all "precarious."

Can we agree? I submit that we cannot. For what we are
faced with is a sort of illusionism after all. The poem *has* its own
splendours, its own clarities, certainly its own audacities. (Consider only the imperious rapidity of the transitions it manages.) It
has all the braveries; even the melody that it seems to lack may
have been merely lost in the passage from a Jewish-American
mouth to a British ear. The object, willy-nilly, *is* "marvelous." It
has to be; since it is an articulation in and of the marvel that is
human language. That lack-lustre phrase is certainly a shabby
rabbit out of any conjuror's hat. But the shabbiness is appropriate
as the response to a shabby argument. If we truly want or need to
cut loose from our inherited past, then we should discard not just
poetic figurations of language but any figurations whatever,
including those which make it possible to communicate at all,
except by grunts and yelps. Rhetoric is inseparable from language,
including language at its most demotically "spoken." And thus, let
language be never so fractured and disjointed in order that the
saving commonplaceness of common things shine through it, all
that is happening is that a new rhetoric is being preferred before
an old one. To put it another way, no Mr Steinway manufactured
the instrument, language, on which Oppen performs. And, like it
or not, a performance is what each of his poems is—as certainly as
a sonnet by Philip Sidney.

This is not in the first place an argument with Oppen or with
Oppen's poems. It is a quarrel with those of his admirers—I have
met some among "the courageous and precarious children"—who
would explain their admiration by appeal to the untenable positions that Williams's obtuseness trapped him into (from which he
later tried to extricate himself by such manifest absurdities as his
"variable foot"). Granted that Oppen does not discard rhetoric for
non-rhetoric (which last is an impossibility), but rejects an old

rhetoric for a newer one, we have to admire what the new rhetoric
permits him to do. In the first place it opens up for him, as it
sometimes did for Williams, an extraordinary directness and gentleness in intimacy, as at the end of "Anniversary Poem":

> To find now depth, not time, since we cannot, but depth
>
> To come out safe,   to end well
>
> We have begun to say good bye
> To each other
> And cannot say it
>
> (*CP*, p. 220)

Indeed, in the world that Oppen charts about him as he thinks of
approaching his end, so hedged about as it is with apprehension
and misgivings, this particular tone embodies so much of what he
can still feel grateful for and sanguine about, that the newer rhetoric justifies itself on this count alone. And it is quite true that
the older rhetoric cannot compass this tone of voice. It speaks
again on the last page of this slim but substantial collection, in a
poem called "Exodus":

> Miracle of the children   the brilliant
> Children   the word
> Liquid as woodlands   Children?
>
> When she was a child I read Exodus
> To my daughter   'The children of Israel . . .'
>
> Pillar of fire
> Pillar of cloud
>
> We stared at the end
> Into each other's eyes   Where
> She said hushed
>
> Were the adults   We dreamed to each other
> Miracle of the children
> The brilliant children   Miracle
>
> Of their brilliance   Miracle
> of
>
> (*CP*, p. 229)

I would call that (though the word may give offence) elegant as
well as touching. And I would say indeed that the elegance and the
touchingness depend upon each other.

MICHAEL HAMBURGER

GEORGE OPPEN'S COLLECTED POEMS[1]

Though George Oppen's first book, *Discrete Series*, appeared nearly forty years ago, with a preface by Ezra Pound, his work has received little attention in this country; or in America, for that matter, at least until he received the Pulitzer Prize in 1969. Very few of the would-be representative anthologies include it at all, and the same is true of critical surveys. Specialists and students may know of Oppen as a member of the Objectivist group, but that group itself remained obscure for several decades, until the recent revival of interest in the work of Oppen, Charles Reznikoff, Carl Rakosi and, of course, Louis Zukofsky. Even now it is difficult for a non-specialist to find any critical comment on the practice of the group or movement as such, though William Carlos Williams's association with it has been fairly well documented.

Williams's "No idea/but in things" might serve as a motto, but it could easily be a misleading one, if taken too literally as a programme or prescription. Carl Rakosi has written that the aim of Objectivism was

> to present objects in their essential reality and to make of each poem an object . . . meaning by this, obviously, the opposite of a subject; the opposite, that is, of all forms of *personal vagueness*, of loose bowels and streaming, sometimes screaming, consciousness. And how does one make into an object the subjective experience from which a poem issues? By feeling the experience sincerely, by discriminating particularity, by honesty and intelligence, by imagination and craftsmanship . . . qualities not belonging to Objectivists alone.

This definition is so close to many other prescriptions for good writing in our century that one is tempted to forget all about Objectivism in approaching the work of George Oppen, quite

1. Reprinted from *Art as Second Nature* (Manchester: Carcanet Press, 1975), pp. 153-156.

especially in view of the philosophical and psychological complexities inherent in Rakosi's object/subject antinomy.

Yet those very complexities are a real clue to George Oppen's constant preoccupations, and to the distinction of his work. The poems from his first collection—not followed by another until nearly thirty years later, in 1962—are difficult precisely because they present objects, clusters of objects, situations, complex perceptions not linked by argument, narrative, or an easily recognizable subjective correlative. It is not till the second collection, *The Materials*, that what seemed like an alienation of subject from object is shown to have been a reciprocity, the process of perceiving a mode of self-discovery:

> What I've seen
> Is all I've found: myself.[2]

or:

> And all I've been
> Is not myself? I think myself
> Is what I've seen and not myself
>
> (*CP*, p. 35)

As this process of self-discovery continues, the manner becomes less elliptical, though Oppen's art remains one of extreme spareness. Paradoxically, this poet of clearly denoted phenomena—mechanical or architectural as often as natural or human—turns out to be a rigorous thinker about the relations between individuals and society, between consciousness and environment—about "the world, weather-swept, with which one shares the century" (*CP*, p. 3), to quote from the very first poem in the book. Complex interactions and relationships are his theme; whether between father and child, as in "From a Photograph" (*CP*, p. 47), or between a man and a particular urban scene, which in turn becomes "the realm of nations," as in "Time of the Missile" (*CP*, p. 49). If this suggests only austerity and tough-mindedness, at which Oppen does excel, readers should turn to the poem "Psalm" (*CP*, p. 78), a celebration of seeing deer, or of the tenderness and wonderment of the seeing ("That they are there!"). "The Bicycles and the Apex," from the same collection of 1965, enacts a response quite as intense to the "mechanisms . . . Light/And miraculous" that have become

> Part of the platitude
> Of our discontent.
>
> (*CP*, p. 125)

---

2. George Oppen, *Collected Poems* (New York: New Directions, 1975), p. 40. Most subsequent references to Oppen's poetry will be to this edition, which will hereafter be cited as *CP*. Such citations will be incorporated into the text.

One thing that Oppen owes to his early objectivist discipline is that in his poems social criticism of America is inseparable from personal or confessional lyricism. He does not need to protest, rant, howl or ironize. The social criticism is as completely merged in the objects he presents as any other element of experience or response:

> I have not and never did have any motive of poetry
> But to achieve clarity
>
> (*CP*, p. 185)

he writes in a late poem sequence, "Route," but the clarity he achieves is never simplistic or banal, because of the subtlety of his thought and sensibility, his concern with the discrepancies between individual and collective awareness. ("There is madness in the number/Of the living"), and his grappling with the metaphysical complexities already mentioned:

> Reality, blind eye
> Which has taught us to stare—
>
> (*CP*, p. 184)

As an instance of the spareness, clarity, and the increasing directness with which Oppen has rendered delicate perceptions (no longer necessarily visual) I want to quote one complete poem, "A Barbarity":

> We lead our real lives
> in dreams
> one said meaning
> because he was awake
> we are locked in ourselves
> That was not what he dreamed
> in any dream
> he dreamed the weird morning
> of the bird waking.[3]

George Oppen strikes me as a poet who has come through by the hardest way, resisting facile effects and comfortable epiphanies. Every line in his book has been wrung from recalcitrant realities, by outstaring the "blind eye." In "To C. T.", originally part of a letter to Charles Tomlinson, divided into lines at his suggestion, Oppen writes: "One imagines himself/addressing his peers/I suppose. Surely/that might be the definition/of 'seriousness'?" (*CP*, p. 142). It is; but it is also the definition of work that is worth reading and re-reading by persons who don't think of themselves as the poet's peers.

---

3. George Oppen, *Alpine*, (Mount Horeb, Wisc.: The Perishable Press, 1969), no pagination. This poem was not reprinted in *CP*.

MICHAEL HELLER

CONVICTION'S NET OF BRANCHES[1]

I

The poetry of George Oppen is one of our most sustained examinations of the characteristic themes of poetry (themes of love and of death, and of a sense of history), an attempt to determine if the very meaning of such words as "love" or "humanity" can be retained in the light of what we have come to know and of what we have become. Indeed, Oppen's work has been to show forth the meanings of these terms by exploring in the deepest sense our need to resort to them.

Oppen sees the poet involved in a task which is as much question and inquiry as it is an order of expression, a task which asks whether the moral, religious and philosophical notions by which we live, and which have informed our common heritage, are any longer possibilities. His is a poetry which arises from our own ambivalence toward what we know and have come to rely on, a poetry very much aware of the human effort to remain in predictive and utilitarian certainties (aware also of the religious attractiveness they engender). Yet the power of his poems is that they do deliver us by a process of skeptical homage into a world seen afresh, vivified by an emergence from inauthentic and outworn sentiment.

There are certain pressures and attitudes in what we might call the Western mind with which Oppen has been struggling throughout his career. There is that impulse which for better or worse is labelled "metaphysical," that taste

1. Reprinted with the permission of the author from *The American Poetry Review*, 4,2 (March/April, 1975), pp. 1-4.

for bedrock
Beneath this spectacle
To gawk at . . .[2]

And there is the contrary of that taste: the hardening of what is intellectually and emotionally grasped into conceptions, into a "Solution," as Oppen ironically entitled an earlier poem about a jigsaw puzzle "assembled at last" which curiously apes our flawed science and technology:

The jigsaw of cracks
Crazes the landscape but there is no gap,
No actual edged hole
Nowhere the wooden texture of the table top
Glares out of scale in the picture,
Sordid as cellars, as bare foundations:
There is no piece missing. The puzzle is complete
Now in its red and green and brown.
(*CP*, p. 24)

The irony here of course is that in addition to its freight of misused benefits and dangling hopes, this solution too, by virtue of that metaphysical impulse, begins to look like (to use a recurrent and important expression of Oppen's) "mechanics." And like mechanics ("remote mechanics," Oppen says in one place), distanced from the human world. Thus, the poet feels that ever-modern estrangement, where

Perhaps one is himself
Beyond the heart, the center of the thing

And cannot praise it

As he would want to . . .
(*CP*, p. 93)

In this, poet, thinker, contemporary man are co-joined in a time when, as the critic Erich Heller has noted, "uncertainty alone is ineluctably real."

Oppen is among our most profound and eloquent explorers of this theme, profound because he comes without illusion into the act of writing poetry, eloquent because the order of his craft cannot be separated from the order of his perception. In *Seascape: Needle'e Eye* he continues an interrogation of reality in language which has always been at the very center of his work, continues it, as Wittgenstein warned, against the bewitchment of language itself:

2. George Oppen, *Collected Poems* (New York: New Directions, 1975), p. 225. All subsequent references to Oppen's poetry will be to this edition; such citations will be incorporated into my text.

'out of poverty
to begin

again'   impoverished

of tone of pose that common
wealth

of parlance

(*CP*, p. 213)

The word "poverty" provides a peculiarly modern test of articulation, a form of resolve against certain historical and elegaic associations of words or of the convenient knowingness of slang. (Kenner, in *The Pound Era*, speaking of the yet to be written history of the Objectivists, among them Oppen, Williams and Zukofsky, puts it this way: "In that machine [the poem] made out of words ... [the word] is a term, not a focus for sentiment; simply a word, the exact and plausible word, not inviting the imagination to linger: an element in the economy of a sentence").[3] In Oppen, this is a principle raised to a very high degree of thoughtfulness and choice. Indeed, in reading him, it often seems that one is confronting not so much an innovation but a search for the adequation of means and ends, an intuitive feel for what is necessary rather than any sense of experimentation. What is given up (or in Oppen's case, better to say rarely taken up) is the analogical mode in language where image and symbol stand as metaphors for *another* reality. Because of this, Oppen's work seems like a kind of first poetry, not by virtue of any crudeness since it is both a subtle and sophisticated body of verse, but by virtue of the sheer unaccountability of its construction. Its beauty and power derive from the simultaneous apperception of its radical construction and the depth at which it seeks to cohere in sense.

Throughout *Seascape: Needle's Eye*, more so than in his earlier work, there is a heightened sense of the struggle to articulate; the language is starker, more primordial, as is the use of spacing, so that the poems have a feeling of resolution arrived at only *in extremis*. Against the "mechanics" of thought, Oppen poses the world of temporality and fragility, the tragic dimension of which is stasis and death. This encounter is experienced through sight and emotions, that "emotion which causes to see" he terms it in an earlier poem, and it is not the unusual or the novel which

---

3. Hugh Kenner, *The Pound Era* (Berkeley: University of California Press, 1971), p. 404.

one sees, but that one sees attentively, with an intensity of
sight[4] that moves

> With all one's force
> Into the commonplace that pierces or erodes
> (CP, p. 206)

or becomes

> Ob via   the obvious . . .

> Place
>
> Place where   desire
> Lust of the eyes the pride of life . . .
> (CP, p. 205)

These last phrases hark back to that epigram of Heidegger's which
Oppen has quoted, and which might well be the rubric of Oppen's
poetics: "the arduous path of appearance."

II

The world of appearance and the commonality of words
(their intersubjective meanings) form the twin aspects of Oppen's
poetry. The poems move as dialectical occasions between sight and
naming, and the poet's truth—no one else's perhaps—is established
in the encounter between what is seen and words, with the poet as
mediating agency of the process. To this extent, the encounter is
seen by Oppen as one which is extreme in its selflessness. Yet it
is not impersonal, not a negation of personality as the word
objective might imply; rather, it is a *going through* personality, a
testing of the ego:

> Liquid
> Pride of the living life's liquid
> Pride in the sandspit wind this ether this
> other this element all
> It is I or I believe
>
> . . . no other way
> To come here the outer
> Limit of the ego
> (CP, p. 205)

This is perhaps Oppen's most important working principle
in that, as he grasps for adequate language, a sense of existence,

---

4. For further discussion of the importance of sight and clarity in Oppen's work, see
L. S. Dembo, "The Existential World of George Oppen," *Iowa Review*, 3, 1 (Winter,
1972), pp. 64-91.

of personal and social drama, is defined against the counter-foil of conventional or unthoughtful language which may offer solace or benumb, yet which in effect distances one from what is actually going on. In the main sequence of *Seascape: Needle's Eye* entitled "Some San Francisco Poems" there is a constant play between these modes of language. The first poem in the series describes the mass migration of young people to a rock concert, even though:

> the songs they go to hear on
> this occasion are no one's own
>
> (*CP*, p. 214)

Here "no one's own" implies a sort of mystical and ephemeral feeling of togetherness, a *mystique* which Oppen does not regard as the sole property of the young (though it may be of special importance to him there). Rather, for Oppen, the emotional reality of human longings, feelings of isolation, etc., which are easily exploitable (one thinks of nationalistic and cultural versions of such exploitation) must be understood and exposed if history is not to be the series of mistaken movements that it has been.

On the level of language, it is the entire enterprise of symbol-making which Oppen attempts to call into question, taking it from childhood roots where

> Night hums like the telephone dial tone blue gauze
> Of the forge flames the pulse
> Of infant
> Sorrows at the crux
>
> (*CP*, p. 206)

The "crux" is an intersection of emotion and the imaginary object it creates to bind it. Thus, in the same poem, "the elves the/Magic people in their world/Among the plant roots," the latent content, as Freud might say, of superstitions and mystiques, are

> hopes
> Which are the hopes
> Of small self interest called
>
> Superstition chitinous
> Toys of the children wings
> Of the wasp
>
> (*CP*, p. 206)

That these are, to Oppen, subtly dangerous creations seems implied in that final image of the wasp wings. To live by them leads again to recurrent social failure. Hence, returning to the first poem of the San Francisco series,

> *as the tremendous volume of the music takes*
> *over obscured by their long hair they seem*
> *to be mourning*

(CP, p. 214)

What is manifest here, as in Oppen's earlier work, is a rather important and profound ambivalence toward the creative faculty itself, a faculty which in its power to symbolize and to create empathy towards various conceptions of reality is not without its formal, social and political dangers. For while it may be true that imagination itself cannot be denied, it can be, in Oppen's opinion, frustrated and misapplied. Oppen would have us believe that there is no morality *per se* in the creative life—this perhaps goes against the notion of the artist as savant or *enfant terrible* leading us on to spiritual heights—there is only a curious kind of moral possibility within the creative act. He puts this quite bluntly in "Five Poems about Poetry" in *This In Which* (1965):

Art

Also is not good

For us
Unless like the fool

Persisting
In his folly

It may rescue us
As only the true

Might rescue us . . .

(CP, p. 84)

For Oppen, this moral possibility lies in the artist's fidelity to that Heideggerian world of appearance and to a language which seeks to make (as he said in his essay "The Mind's Own Place,") "clear pictures of the world in verse which means only to be clear, to be honest, to produce the realization of reality and to construct a form out of no desire for the trick of gracefulness, but in order to make it possible to grasp, to hold the insight which is the content of the poem."[5]

We have in Oppen's *oeuvre* a body of work then whose protagonist is language struggling with the clichéd and unthoughtful language of mass mind and mass fantasy, where the artist's attempt to give voice to the visible world becomes a form of *claritas* by at least offering out the possibility of an intersubjective

---

5. George Oppen, "The Mind's Own Place," *Kulchur* 3, 10 (1963), p. 4.

reality—i.e., one in which there will be some occasions in which human beings agree, thus making "truth" provisionally possible. If in Oppen's poetry language is transformed, it would seem to be from individuated literal words into a kind of *supra*literalism consisting of statements which, as Oppen puts it, "cannot not be understood." The mystery of such statements would lie not in their need to be explained, but in the sheer substance of their existence. They would be that "other miracle" which the French philosopher Merleau-Ponty refers to in saying: "it is easy to strip language and action of all meaning and make them seem absurd. . . But that other miracle, the fact that in an absurd world language and behavior do have meaning for those who speak and act, remains to be understood."

III

Intensity of sight, its literal counterpart in language, the clarity in effect which these become are the essential modes in Oppen's work by which reality is grasped. An attitude, an impression, even the deepest expression of an emotion are rendered in terms of the visible. As a modality, sight and transformation via the offices of vision, almost in the manner of Donne and the Metaphysicals, are the agency of a singular and personal love. Thus, in "A Morality Play: Preface," light is played upon, a sort of metaphor of interanimation, like the function of sight in "The Exstasy":

> Never to forget her naked eyes
>
> Beautiful and brave
> Her naked eyes
>
> Turn inward
>
> Feminine light
>
> The unimagined
> Feminine light
>
> Feminine ardor
>
> Pierced and touched

(*CP*, p. 215)

Here, as with "the commonplace that pierces or erodes," love and the visible are intertwined, bridging individual lives. The morality play of the title lies in the distinction between this personal sense of love and the abstract uses of the word, a juxtaposition which is the development of a theme previously elaborated in Oppen's important long poem "Of Being Numerous" (1968), where the individual in his isolation both mental and physical, the "shipwreck of the singular," is transcended not in any abstraction of "humanity," but by attentiveness and curiosity, a form of love of the visible. Without this attentiveness, "Morality Play" goes on, "Tho all say/Huddled among each other/Love," there is only the implicit continuous failure of mankind *en mass*, the apocalyptic image of

> This city died young
>
> You too will be shown this
>
> You will see the young couples
>
> Leaving again in rags
>
> (*CP*, p. 216)

As Dembo's essay suggests, this love *within* clarity or as a form of clarity is, for Oppen, the central impulse which resolves the dialectic of seeing and naming, an experience very much akin to the philosopher's sense of wonder:

> It is impossible the world should be either
>   good or bad
> If its colors are beautiful or if they are not
>   beautiful
> If parts of it taste good or if no parts of it
>   taste good
> It is as remarkable in one case as the other
>   (*CP*, p. 217)

Taken this way, clarity itself is a good which transcends *and thereby tests* our ordinary systems of value. As Oppen tellingly puts it in "Route" (one of the poems in *Of Being Numerous*),

> Imagine a man in the ditch,
> The wheels of the overturned wreck
> Still spinning—
>
> I don't mean he despairs, I mean if he does not
> He sees in the manner of poetry
>   (*CP*, p. 191)

Recalling that the poet's truth is encountered at the "outer limits of the ego," such clarity becomes a way of bearing witness that is neither academic nor detached; for all of its relation to philosophy, Oppen's poetry has left the ivory tower and gone among men and things both intellectually and emotionally. Thus, in "And Their Winter and Night in Disguise" the world's remarkableness is tempered by the suffering of man, as in war:

> As against this

> We have suffered fear, we know something of fear
> And of humiliation mounting to horror
>
> (*CP*, p. 217)

Yet, it is the uniqueness and power of Oppen's work that he does not leave the matter resting there as yet another image of social horror. Rather, he explores further the ambiguity of bearing witness (another dimension of his ambivalent relation to creativity), suggesting that in seeking out the truth it is also the poet's task to forbear the schizophrenic and vicarious glorifications of both terrors and heroics. Thus the foxholes are *These little dumps*/The poem is about them," their fascination lying in the fact that "Our hearts are twisted/In dead men's pride" (*CP*, p. 218). As with other images of mass mind and fantasy, it is not truth but falseness, mystical falseness, which makes an adventure out of these horrors, which makes them both endangering and attractive to the imagination:

> Minds may crack

> But not for what is discovered

> Unless that everyone knew
> And kept silent

> Our minds are split
> To seek the danger out

> From among the miserable soldiers
>
> (*CP*, p. 218)

If, through recognition of such ambivalence, the truths that Oppen discovers and gives voice to remain partial and speculative, fragile as the shifts of sight and life itself, it is the depth of Oppen's work, the level at which he seeks for answers, that make his skepticism never an exercise, never the *hubris* of a sophist. Indeed, the poet's search for clarity, the needle's eye of the title, becomes for the poet finally a way into praise of the world:

> conviction's

> Net of branches
> In the horde of events the sacred swarm avalanche
> Masked in the sunset

Needle after needle more numerous than planets

Or the liquid waves
In the tide rips

We believe   we believe

                                        (*CP*, p. 223)

IV

Oppen is unique in American poetry. While he has marked
out for himself the burden of the singular, the isolate man, that
both more than and less than Romantic hero of the Western drama
of the mind, the one who in rending the veil finds another and yet
another before him, he has never taken the fashionable position of
being "alienated" or messianic. The few commentators on his
work have noted his capacity to remain free of redemptive and
prescriptive attitudes, to remain at once free and skeptical even
with regard to his own efforts (note the question mark in the first
line below):

'We address the future? '

Unsure of the times
Unsure I can answer

To myself   We have been ignited
Blazing

In wrath we await

The rare poetic
Of veracity . . .

                                        (*CP*, p. 208)

Yet, there is an aspect of Oppen's work which keeps it continually
positive and human—human in the sense that it aligns itself with a
belief in the value of that exploration of reality by creative effort.
There is, for example, the recognition of that impulse which transcends one's personal death, as in this passage from the earliest of
his mature work ("Image of the Engine," in *The Materials*, 1962):

Endlessly, endlessly,
The definition of mortality

The image of the engine

> That stops.
> We cannot live on that.
> I know that no one would live out
> Thirty years, fifty years if the world were ending
> With his life.
>
> (*CP*, p. 19)

Oppen here implicitly acknowledges the existence of a community in which the poet's labor both weighs and joins through language the feeling of shared experience, (perhaps in Oppen's case only at that point where "it cannot be understood"). In *Seascape: Needle's Eye*, there is an almost elegaic sense of the transmittal of the poet's burden, a transmittal to the young, to the children who will become

> New skilled fishermen
> In the great bays and the narrow bights
>
> (*CP*, p. 209)

and who will find, he says,

> In the continual sound
> Are chords
> Not yet struck
> Which will be struck
> Nevertheless yes
>
> (*CP*, p. 223)

Against the songs which are "no one's own" is the prospective of a life realized in language, in language bearing the weight of the visible as evidence of its attempt to be clearly understood. Its recurrence possibly in the young is for Oppen *the* compensatory value:

> We dreamed to each other
> Miracle of the children
> The brilliant children   Miracle
>
> Of their brilliance   Miracle
> of
>
> (*CP*, p. 229)

In an age of false gods and false certainties, Oppen's intention to mean, to seek clarity, transcends our notions of a poetics; it becomes the voice of our deepest feelings and our deepest doubts, holding, in the face of death and aging, that the voice itself is valuable, perhaps no more so than at its most unbearably beautiful and poignant moments:

> How shall we say this happened, these stories, our
>   stories
>
> Scope, mere size, a kind of redemption

Exposed still and jagged on the San Francisco hills

Time and depth before us, paradise of the real, we
              know what it is

To find now depth, not time, since we cannot, but depth

To come out safe,   to end well

We have begun to say good bye
To each other
And cannot say it
                              (*CP*, pp. 219-220)

I think that Oppen has tried to do nothing more than make this, our condition, absolutely clear. It is a major achievement. Oppen stands alone in this regard: that his poetry is not composed of the effects of modern life upon the self, but is rather our most profound investigation of it.

NORMAN M. FINKELSTEIN

SYNTAX AND TRADITION:
GEORGE OPPEN'S PRIMITIVE

George Oppen, erstwhile Objectivist, begins his career with *Discrete Series* (1934), a book that pushes the Modernist tendency to isolate and examine discrete objects within the field of experience to its furthest limit. Grounded in the tenets of Imagism and Objectivism, Oppen rapidly brings his verse to a point at which the empiricism of those poetics proves insufficient to meet the moral and political imperatives that the poet feels he is obliged to confront. Thus begins a life-long process of retrenchment, through which the original concerns that led Oppen to poetry are gradually made manifest in a re-subjectivized verse which still serves, as Oppen would say, as "a test of truth."[1] From his long hiatus from poetry, which includes periods of political organizing and self-imposed exile, through his return to literature that culminates in his masterpiece *Of Being Numerous*, Oppen continually seeks the proper balance between artistic and moral commitment, developing a philosophy that places the individual's sense of truth and sincerity in direct confrontation with increasingly more complex ethical dilemmas. Consciousness, rather than mere perception, grows in importance: "Tell the life of the mind, the mind creates the finite."[2] As the poetry comes into full maturity, the objects of experience are subsumed into the subjective consciousness, even as consciousness, at the beginning, seems lost among objects. A process has come full circle.[3]

Primitive (1978), Oppen's latest collection, is the culmination of this exploration of consciousness that began nearly fifty years ago. It consists of poetry as radical as that of *Discrete*

---

1. George Oppen, "The Mind's Own Place," *Kulchur*, 3, 10 (1963), 4.
2. *The Collected Poems of George Oppen* (New York: New Directions, 1975), p. 193. Cited in the text as *CP*. Also cited in the text, as *P*, is *Primitive* (Santa Barbara: Black Sparrow Press, 1978).
3. For a complete version of this summary of Oppen's philosophical development, I refer the reader to my essay "Political Commitment and Poetic Subjectification: George Oppen's Test of Truth," *Contemporary Literature*, Winter 1981, pp. 24-41.

Series, its philosophical antithesis, for it asserts the primacy of the mind, through which all objects are filtered. But the mind itself seems lost in *Primitive*, too frequently buffeted by historical exigencies, by the welter of political events beyond the control of even the morally responsible individual. It is only when deep emotion sways consciousness that it is capable of the lyric expressions and sudden outpourings of truth that highlight the volume. Then, and only then, do we encounter the synthesizing power of the mind. Consider, for example, "Waking Who Knows":

> Waking Who Knows
>
> the great
>
> doors of the tall
>
> buildings and the grid
>
> of the streets the seed
>
> is a place the stone
> is a place mind
>
> will burn the world down alone
> and transparent
>
> will burn the world down tho the starlight is
> part of ourselves
>
> (*P*, p. 17)

Beneath the meticulously placed words, one senses enormous mental effort, as if consciousness were literally wrestling with the buildings, streets and stones. And consciousness, in its own terms, wins in this struggle; its synthesizing capabilities are asserted with such certainty that for a moment we believe that mind can "burn the world down alone." The last lines of the poem convince us through their sudden, simple insight: the dialectic of self and world has not been abandoned to mere solipsism, but has been internalized to such an extent that even the stars have become man's intimates.

For Oppen, however, such a poetic fate by now seems inevitable, as he explains in "The Tongues":

> The Tongues
>
> of appearance
> speak in the unchosen
> journey immense
> journey there is loss in denying
> that force the moments the years

> even of death lost
> in denying
> that force   the words
> out of that whirlwind his
> and not his strange
> words surround him
>
> (*P*, p. 19)

The poet has no choice at the beginning of his phenomenology of mind: as his journey commences, objects speak directly, become a language out of which a poetry is built. It is only from the mind's first simple contacts that a more complex philosophical understanding of the world can develop. As Oppen has said, refering to his poem "Psalm," "I do believe that consciousness exists and that it is conscious of something, and that is a fairly complete but not very detailed theology, as a matter of fact."[4] By now, we may say that Oppen has moved through the details of his "theology" to a point at which the voices of objects return to him again, but in a less concrete, more ghostly form. Thus the words that come to him in *Primitive* are "his/and not his"; they represent a lifetime and more of intellectual refinement, but always hold the possibility of sudden, direct contact with raw experience.

As should be clear from "Waking Who Knows" and "The Tongues," Oppen has developed certain highly sophisticated poetic strategies for embodying those moments of insight when the mind breaks free of its purely subjective cast to unite with the objects of experience. The use of a complex syntax, sometimes troubling but always accurate and provocative, ably reflects the exact conditions of consciousness at the moment of composition. An understanding of the workings of *Primitive*'s syntax is an important key to the understanding of Oppen's philosophical stance and ethical intentions in his latest poems. The sense of sudden linguistic concentration we experience in "Waking Who Knows" is a function of a passionate but ambiguous poetic honed by years of reflection on essential issues of commitment and doubt. This sense of concentrated presence amidst loss, of meaning arising out of inchoate language and experience, is bolstered by the subtle use of allusion throughout the poems. The whirlwind which brings strange words to the poet in "The Tongues" is the whirlwind that spoke to Job, archetypal man of faith beset by the trials of doubt. The series of allusions we encounter in *Primitive* (and Oppen has made spare use of this self-consciously literary technique up until now), suspended, as it were, amidst

---

4. "The 'Objectivist' Poet: Four Interviews," *Contemporary Literature*, 10, 2 (1969), 163.

less mediated objects of experience, betokens a lasting tradition
of which Oppen has unquestionably become a part. This tradition,
heroic in its outlook on life and capable of both profound philosophical insights and magnificent lyric flights, seeks the continuance of what Oppen calls *"that light within/and without,"* the
·illumination of the self and the world through their continued
dialectical encounters.

Oppen achieves such illumination, however, only through
extraordinary difficulties, which appear formally in the poem as
fragmented syntax, ambiguous phrasing, unexpected repetition
and ellipsis, and an overall sense of linguistic abstraction. As I
have implied, Oppen's syntax works both for and against him in
Primitive. On the one hand, its flexibility allows him to report
the mental occasions of the poems with great precision, and as
we know from the poem "Route," "reportage" is always an important aspect of his work. But we also know that "clarity" is
Oppen's greatest goal in writing poetry, and even his most devoted readers would have to admit that *Primitive* contains some of
the least accessible poetry he has ever written. The fine, meditative balance of *Of Being Numerous* has become lost to Oppen in
the last ten years, and a new mode of discourse has supplanted it.
The rewards of this discourse do not come as easily and do not
move us in the ways that Oppen's more confidently voiced poetry
has done. What remains is Oppen's unswerving measure of truth, as
in "A Political Poem":

> for sometimes over the fields astride
> of love? begin with
>
> nothing or
>
> everything   the nerve
>
> the thread
> reverberates
>
> in the unfinished
>
> voyage loneliness
>
> of becalmed ships and the violent men
>
> and women of the cities'
> doorsteps unexpected
>
> this sad and hungry
>
> wolf walks in my footprints fear fear
> birds, stones, and the sun-lit

earth turning, that great

loneliness all

or nothing
confronts us
the image

the day

dawns on the doorsteps its sharpness
dazes and nearly blinds us

(*P*, pp. 9-10)

The ambiguity of this poem, its doubts about the fate of society and the individual within society, can be traced in the way its structure mirrors the poet's thought. It begins with the fragment of a question that casts doubt on love, traditionally considered the prime mover of man's enterprise. From there, as if to answer the question, Oppen states one of his most important themes: consciousness encounters the world with nothing, no mediation, and in this encounter everything remains in frightening potential. To state this philosophical condition so baldly, placing "nothing or// everything" on their own in the space of the page, reminds Oppen of the loneliness of consciousness, due in part to its vulnerability in the face of experience, which is open to numerous subjective interpretations. Thus we may read that "the thread/ reverberates// in the unfinished," that "the thread/reverberates//in the unfinished//voyage," or that "the thread/reverberates//in the unfinished//voyage loneliness." The first phrasing presents "the unfinished" as a direct object, a noun; the second presents "unfinished" as an adjective modifying "voyage"; the third, the most unusual but still possible, presents both "unfinished" and "voyage" as adjectives modifying "loneliness." Spacing, enjambment and lack of punctuation heighten the ambiguity of meaning, and foster the original feeling of loneliness, making it into a sensuous experience. That the word "loneliness" can also be read as the beginning of the next phrase (loneliness//of becalmed ships, etc.) continues the sense of expanding potential, and of expanding confusion as well.

But while the poem has been moving outward through its shifting syntax, it has become more concentrated and specific in terms of its diction. The "becalmed ships and the violent men// and women of the cities'/doorsteps" trigger an emotional response in the hitherto abstract poetic consciousness, and Oppen is able to voice the central problem of the poem: "this sad and hungry// wolf walks in my footprints fear fear//birds, stones, and the sun-lit//earth turning, that great//loneliness." Fear lies at the heart of the individual's confusion, and the repetition of the word creates further ambiguity, for it can act either as a noun beginning a list (fear/birds, stones, and the sun-lit//earth) or as an imperative verb, a command. In either case, the emphasis is on the individual's inability to deal with objects of experience, implying a never-ending cycle of fear and isolation, as the choice of "all/or nothing" is repeated as well. The asymmetrical rhythms of the long and short lines, as well as their spacing, lend a feeling of panicked speed. Suddenly "the image//the day//dawn on the doorsteps its sharpness/dazes and nearly blinds us." The verse stops short at the word "image"; day dawns; its light is almost overwhelming. The image in the light of day, while maintaining threatening implications, rescues the poem (and the poet) from complete isolation, as the potential for clarity and linguistic control asserts itself for the first time. While the fear that permeates the poem is not driven off, we sense the alternatives that may be open to us in the light of day. Hence the title, "A Political Poem"—for the poem is political in the broadest, universally applicable sense of the term, as society's violence, isolation and fear are brought to bear in the abstract upon the poetic consciousness.

Oppen's ambivalence in the face of imposing objective reality may be observed again in the syntax of "*Gold On Oak Leaves*," a more personal lyric, but as philosophically dense as "A Political Poem." The fragmentation and scintillating imagery of this and a number of other recent pieces is reminiscent of Pound's last Cantos, in which "the great acorn of light" that occasionally appears represents a lost visionary totality upon which the mind can never fasten. For Oppen, that totality was to be found in objective experience itself, but by now the poet has grave doubts as to the feasibility of such a course:

> *gold* said her golden
>
> young poem for she sleeps and impossible
> truths move
>
> brave thru the gold the living
> veins but for the gold
>
> light I am lost
>
> in the gold
>
> light on this salt and sleepless
>
> sea

(*P*, p. 23)

The "young poem" with its truths that move through "the living/ veins" challenges Oppen, and his syntax vacillates as he considers the problem. How does the poet regard the gold light of the immediate? He says that "but for the gold//light I am lost" *and* that "I am lost//in the gold//light on this salt and sleepless//sea." Unable to determine whether immediacy (which has begun to take on an almost mythic dimension through the synechdochic use of light) remains a virtue, Oppen suspends judgment through the lines' enjambment and incomplete syntax. Apparently, the teeming world of experience continues to cause the "bright light of ship-wreak" of *Of Being Numerous*, and Oppen has yet to resolve the problem of the isolated consciousness forced to confront the numerosity of that world. Arguably, no single man can ever resolve such a problem, even for himself: the answer lies in the continuing attempt to perfect the social order in which the individual dwells, a dialectic that is always struggling to complete itself. But for Oppen, this insight is now denied as sensuous poetic content, and thus he must declare that

> I haunt an old
>
> ship the sun
>
> glints thru ragged
> caulking I would go out
> past the axioms
>
> of wandering
>
> timbers garboards keelson the keel full
>
> depth
>
> of the ship in that
> light into all
>
> that never
> knew me

(*P*, pp. 23-24)

Moved by his dilemma, Oppen again gathers the necessary emotional force to make his language cohere. As in "A Political Poem," the concrete diction of "ragged/caulking" and "timber garboards keelson the keel" aids in focusing the problem stated in the first lines of the poem. Beyond the "axioms//of wandering" and the mere details of the immediate situation lies a renewed freedom in which consciousness may face the unknown, the future, and accept its fate. Because objective experience has, in a sense, completely dazzled consciousness, Oppen can rely only on all that never knew him to complete what his own efforts have begun. This is, perhaps, what is implied by all the luminous, indefinite fragments of *Primitive,* which point to the meaning and linguistic fulfillment that they cannot in themselves achieve. Thus Oppen's faith in natural processes, of which poetry itself has become a part, allows his voice to fade into mythic, elemental quiet as the poem concludes:

> alone
>
> in the sea fellow
> me feminine
>
> winds as you pass

In such a poem as "*Gold On Oak Leaves,*" language and the individual consciousness seem to have extended themselves as far as they can go before they must grow silent in the presence of the objective natural order, or be renewed by a power beyond that of the individual.

Many of the poems in *Primitive* do embody that renewal, and despite their tenuous form achieve a remarkable vitality of utterance. The source of this strength lies not in the individual consciousness, but in what Marx would call *species being*, which is manifested in the poem through an engagement with the heroic tradition from which Oppen as a poet springs. For even as man posits his truest identity as part of a universal species creating itself through its own labor, so too does the poet find his greatest strength in his identification with a tradition of self-subsisting creativity and desire. The allusions to the poetic tradition we find in *Primitive* indicate Oppen's awareness that the truest sources of of his art are not to be found in the immediate contacts of consciousness with empirical reality, but in the emotionally-charged, chastening encounters with previous bearers of his poetic standards. The broken grandeur of *Primitive* lies in the fact that Oppen can *only* allude to this tradition: just as his syntax too often remains incomplete, his relationship to the tradition is not fully subsumed in the resonant voice of the poem. Nevertheless, the poignancy of these references, indications of Oppen's continued faith in poetry's capacity for heroic emotions in the face of spiritually impoverished circumstance, in itself becomes a stirring poetic gesture.

"Disasters," for example, begins with a series of references to Shelley's poetry and prose, gesturing towards the Romantic sublime in a way that is completely appropriate to the poem's political content:

> Disasters
>
> of war o western
> wind and storm
>
> of politics I am sick with a poet's
> vanity   legislators
>
> of the unacknowledged
>
> world *it is   dreary*
> *to descend*
>
> *and be a stranger* how
> shall we descend
>
> who have become strangers in this wind that
>
> rises like a gift
> in the disorder
>
> (*P*, p. 11)

The "vanity" of the poet, that is, his revolutionary sense of justice, is appalled in the same way Shelley's was when he wrote "Ode to the West Wind" following the agitation for social reform in England in 1819. But the historical conditions under which a poet writes have changed drastically since then, and it is unlikely that Oppen can state as surely as does Shelley that "The most unfailing herald, companion, and follower of the awakening of a great people to work a beneficial change in opinion or institution is poetry."[5] This is why Oppen inverts Shelley's claim that "Poets are the unacknowledged legislators of the world," naming them instead the "legislators//of the unacknowledged//world." Shelley believes that poets bring to light essential truths that have previously lain inchoate and inarticulate. Just before his famous conclusion to *A Defense of Poetry*, he declares that "Poets are the hierophants of an unapprehended inspiration; the mirrors of the gigantic shadows which futurity casts upon the present."[6] For Oppen, however, the world itself is no longer acknowledged; poets legislate a value system whose existence is no longer even suspected; and the mode of discourse out of which Shelley was able to speak is no more. As Oppen says of the poets in *Of Being Numerous*, "They have lost the metaphysical sense/Of the future, they feel themselves/The end of a chain" (*CP*, p. 165). Such being the case, it is no wonder that Oppen feels a stranger to Shelley's

---

5. *Shelley's Prose or The Trumpet of a Prophecy*, ed. David Lee Clark (Albuquerque: Univ. of New Mexico Press, 1954), p. 297.
6. Ibid.

visionary wind, which, while still rising like "a gift/in the disorder," cannot speak through the poet with its former resonance and rhetorical power.

Tragically then, the conclusion of "Disasters" better describes the present circumstances:

> Sarah Sarah I see the tent
> in the desert my life
> narrows my life
> is another I see
> him in the desert I watch
> him he is clumsy
> and alone my young
> brother he is my lost
> sister her small
>
> voice among the people the salt
>
> and terrible hills whose armies
>
> have marched and the caves
> of the hidden
> people
>   (*P*, pp. 12-13)

Like a lost Abraham bereft of his people, Oppen is compelled to watch the possibilities of his life "narrow." He can only sadly identify with those adrift about him, victims in a violent desert of culture, over which armies march and under which is hidden the true populace. This is certainly the unacknowledged world, where poetic values, like suppressed peoples, go underground in bitter exile.

Despite the fact of the poet's seeming exile, his desire, from which always comes inspiration, has not been extinguished. In "The Poem," Oppen marvels that this is so, again evoking the Romantic tradition as if to assure himself that the art he practices after a lifetime remains vital:

> how shall I light
> this room that measures years
>
> and years not miracles nor were we
> judged but a direction
>
> of things in us burning burning for we are not
> still nor is the place a wind
> utterly outside ourselves and yet it is
> unknown and all the sails full to the last
>
> rug of the topgallant, royal
> tops'l, the least rags
> at the mast-heads   (*P*, p. 14)

Even as he questions his ability to "light/this room that measures years," to meet the rigorous ideals of the tradition, Oppen finds his boat under full sail—always a metaphor, for the old sailor of Penobscot Bay, for the continuance of creative freedom. Everything in the poet's world, from the least sail of his craft to the sky above, suddenly is filled with the power of Blake's Tyger, called into being again through the heroism of Oppen's experiences:

> Tyger still burning in me burning
> in the night sky burning
> in us the light
>
> in the room it was all
> part of the wars
> of things brilliance
> of things
>
> in the appalling
> seas

The result is a pattern of language, a form that rises out of the depths of the emotions and in turn wakes the poet to give voice to his faith:

> language
>
> lives and wakes us together
> out of sleep the poem
> opens its dazzling whispering hands

Oppen's sense of his own life thus finds a correlative within the poetic tradition, and through that correlative re-asserts itself with a force that calls poetry into being again and again.

Because of such moments of identification, in which Oppen's skepticism is abruptly silenced, many of the poems in *Primitive* allude to Oppen's own earlier work, as if the poet now regards his past achievements as sources of inspiration planted firmly in the tradition which gives him strength. And this is really an appropriate attitude for him to take, for his self-consciousness of his own historical importance is thereby freed. Like other Modernists in the latter parts of their careers (one thinks again of Pound's last Cantos or the "familiar composite ghost" Eliot meets in "Little Gidding"), Oppen can write about the self as Other, opening doorways in the past so that the future may be summoned into being.

This is the theme of "To Make Much," an uncanny poem made up for the most part of the earlier "To The Poets: To Make Much Of Life" (from *Myth of the Blaze*), placed in the new poem almost verbatim. The first piece is a celebration of old age, particularly the old age of poets, and the means by which the

antinomies of political action and contemplative art can be, if not
resolved, at least memorialized in the poem:

no need to light

lamps in daylight working year
after
year the poem

discovered

in the crystal
center of the rock image

and image the transparent

present tho we speak of the abyss
of the hungry we see their feet their tired

feet in the news and mountain and valley
and sea as in universal

storm
the fathers said we are old
we are shrivelled

come.

(*CP*, p. 254)

"To Make Much" condenses these lines to a certain extent and
then seems to conclude. One must literally turn the page to see
that a coda has now been added:

to the shining
of rails in the night
the shining way the way away
from home arrow in the air
hat-brim fluttered in the air as she ran
forward and it seemed so beautiful so beautiful
the sun-lit air it was no dream all's wild
out there as we unlikely
image of love found the way
away from home

(*P*, p. 16)

A renewed vision of youth and love breaks the hushed calm of the
previous lines. Both the syntax and spacing become more concentrated, more concrete. Beyond any mere memory, Oppen throws
off his nostalgia to take full, sensuous delight in the wild freedom
of youth discovering the world for the first time. The poet makes
much of life in a way that he could not in the first poem, which,
while complete in itself, was also the necessary antecedent to the

more vigorous new lines.

Yet these lines in all probability refer to the trip that Oppen made with Mary Colby nearly fifty years ago, a trip across the country that secured the freedom from middle-class propriety that the young couple so desired.[7] Such memories as these, which usually have already been preserved in other poems, paradoxically inspire some of *Primitive*'s most poignant verse. These memories echo and re-echo in the book until *Primitive* memorializes not only Oppen's earlier work, but the work's very capacity to remember. *"If It All Went Up In Smoke"* and "The Natural" continue the process of quoting from earlier work, for the latter poem quotes the former, which precedes it by just a few pages in the volume. *"If It All Went Up In Smoke"* is a hesitant meditation on the sources of poetry, which

> begins
>
> neither in word
>
> nor meaning but the small
> selves haunting
>
> us in the stones and is less
>
> always than that help me I am
> of that people the grass
>
> blades touch
>
> and touch in their small
>
> distances the poem
> begins
>
> (*P*, p. 18)

This is the ending of the poem, which we may compare to "The Natural" in its entirety:

> The Natural
>
> world *the fog*
> *coming up in the fields* we learned those
> rural words later we thought it was ocean the flood
> of the ocean the light
> of the world help me I am
>
> of that people the grass
> blades touch

---

7. See Mary Oppen, *Meaning A Life* (Santa Barbara: Black Sparrow Press, 1978), pp. 61-76.

and touch the small

distances the poem
begins
(*P*, p. 25)

    Both poems end on the same lines and the same idea: that Oppen is compelled to write when in the presence of his most vital memories, "the small/selves haunting//us in the stones." The particular event at the root of these poems is the first evening Oppen and Mary spent together, an evening that Mary describes in *Meaning A Life* and about which Oppen has written in "The Forms of Love," from *This in Which*:

We groped
Our way together
Downhill in the bright
Incredible light

Beginning to wonder
Whether it could be lake
Or fog
We saw, our heads
Ringing under the stars we walked
To where it would have wet our feet
Had it been water
(*CP*, p. 86)

The light of the fog and its mystery have remained with Oppen throughout his life, always to inspire his poetry and give form to his desire. Oppen is "of that people" for whom personal events resonate through time, taking on greater and greater significance. In the course of his turbulent life, one moment marks the beginning of love, a first vision of "the light/of the world." To perceive that light is to write poetry; thus "the poem/begins" each time Oppen returns to that scene.

    Oppen's self-conscious use of his own life as the traditional *matter* of poetry argues for his heroism in a time when such a poetic stance seems historically untenable. But as we have seen in Oppen's relation to the past, his heroism is, in its greatest significance, more than that of the individual consciousness: it is supported and made lawful by an enduring sense of poetic and social creativity. Even when his syntax is at its most tenuous and his meaning at its most ambiguous, Oppen implicitly understands what Northrop Frye so beautifully articulates:

Desire in this sense is the social aspect of what we met on the literal level as emotion, an impulse toward expression which would have remained amorphous if the poem had not liberated it by providing the form of its expression. The form of desire, similarly, is liberated and made apparent by civilization. The efficient cause of civilization is work, and poetry in its social aspect has the function of expressing, as a verbal hypothesis, a vision of the goal of work and the forms of desire.[8]

This concept goes far in explaining the depth of Oppen's political commitment, which is inextricably bound up in his dedication to poetry as well. Oppen has always conceived of himself as a populist, a poet capable of speaking for the people even when his work remained obscure. As he says in "Populist," a poem that might be the credo of *Primitive*,

> I dreamed myself of their people, I am of their people,
> I thought they watched me that I watched them
> that they
>
> watched the sun and the clouds for the cities
> are no longer mine   image   images
>
> of existence   (or song
>
> of myself?)
>
> (*P*, p. 20)

Oppen's search for appropriate images always drives him between the self and the world, a dialectic on which he has become dependent for the tensions that give form to his work.

We are left, finally, with the title of Oppen's latest book, for the poetic process with which he has been engaged seems anything but primitive. The poem "Primitive" (*CP*, p. 115) from *This in Which* may provide a slight clue. It describes a woman in a jungle hut waking out of nightmare, crying out in terror and waking her husband and child as well. Around the hut lie all the common objects of the family's daily life. The self wakes and cries out in the midst of what is most familiar; it is the most immediate and frightening encounter of self and world. *Primitive* too records that sudden awakening, as the basics of Oppen's world—his language, his poetic tradition, and the matter of his life—are seen in a new light. As an old man, Oppen dares to begin again.

---

8. Northrop Frye, *Anatomy of Criticism* (Princeton: Princeton Univ. Press, 1957), p. 106.

THEODORE ENSLIN

OF WHAT IS PRIME AND PRIMAL:
CONSIDERATIONS OF GEORGE OPPEN'S PRIMITIVE[1]

One of the great joys for which I count myself fortunate
since the early sixties when I began to read Oppen seriously, and
subsequently met him in New York, has been the constancy of the
consideration. It is certainly true that I rarely pass a day without
seriously thinking of both the man, and the poet, both parts of the
consumate craftsman. I do not wish to give the impression of a
religious ritual, but the extreme importance which I attach to his
work and his presence. There are a very·few influences which one
can wisely sustain lifelong, but I admit to Oppen's on me with no
reservations. It is not in my nature to follow slavishly after any
man, nor is *my* use of George Oppen's precepts necessarily always
what he has meant. It is more that there are things to be found in
that working which lie naturally, familiarly, to my hand. It is the
greeting and spark of recognition given between two people who
prize their own individuality—that each should, as Thoreau said
earlier, give a just report from his own country. And in this slim
book, coming after the publication of the *Collected Poems* several
years prior, is the essence of that report—refined and dynamized
to consumate proportions and power. When the *Collected Poems*
appeared many of us wondered whether there would be another
book. There seemed an air of finality, something rigorously
accurate in the title, as there is in the man's work itself. It is a
delight that, in this case, it was not so. The appearance of a new
collection by George Oppen is cause for celebration—a celebration
best had in the work itself. May there be occasion for that celebration many times more. His poems are always what we have known
all along, but which we may not have realized clearly heretofore,

1. This is a slightly expanded version of a review which appeared in *American Book
Review*, January, 1979.

either because we haven't known how, or didn't bother to look closely enough. This was true of *Discrete Series*, first published in 1934, and it is equally true of *Primitive*, forty-four years later. The proving of homely truths never grows thin or platitudinous with Oppen. It is what needs to be said of what needs to be considered —no more—no less. The clarity is absolute, that clarity which he has invoked by name in some poems, and the news that can be read equally well close up, or from afar off. In this new book the language is honed even sharper than in the earlier ones. The sound is as of a bell at sea—sometimes, as in the poem, "Disasters," awesome in its purity:

> of wars o western
> wind and storm
>
> of politics I am sick with a poet's
> vanity[2]

And finally, through such very spare means as these, there is an eloquence as magnificent as anything in our language. No need to be adorned, it is the body itself, which needs no clothes. (The use of "o western wind" is a good example of the evocation—the old mediaeval song and poem through countless changes and references to the particular of the summer prevailing wind on Penobscot Bay where Oppen has sailed for many years—*his* personal western wind.) But the fact that some may know, as I do from personal observation of the Bay, what its prevailing summer wind may be, is not necessary to a thorough understanding of this poem. Similarly, as unthinkable as it is that anyone concerned with *any* poetry does not know "O Western Wind" it would not matter for the utter clarity laid open before us. There is never a need for footnotes in Oppen's poetry.

It is a great mistake to say, as I have heard it from some who profess to admire his work, that Oppen has never undergone significant development since the early days. There is no mere stasis in such work as this, though the vision is clear and steady from the first of those things which have a permanent quality in themselves. From the outset, Oppen was sure of where he was going, and what the materials were which he would find indispensable along the way. I don't mean to imply that *everything* was known in 1934, but enough was there to dispense with a young man's often justifiable floundering. There is certainly a very clear evolution of the style from beginning to any given point—a deepening of concern, matched with a parallel deepening of the mastery of

---

2. George Oppen, *Primitive* (Santa Barbara : Black Sparrow, 1979), p. 11. Hereafter cited as *P*.

craft. The spare clarity of *Discrete Series*, for all of its excellence,
does not have the resonant power of the later poems—say from *Of
Being Numerous* on. These are master works in the original sense,
and that is not to be confused with the loose use of such a term in
our present world of advertizing. The concern has been as rigorous
for each word, each line, or mark of punctuation, as for an entire
poem. The title itself, *Primitive*, is exact—that meaning of the
word which goes back to prime, and has no condescending over-
tone. Oppen insists that we cleanse our associations as we come to
his work, and he is very right in doing this. Such poems give us
back our rightful language among many other things. In these later
poems he uses a difficult syntax, but one which is absolutely correct, dictated by his material, welded to the form of these admirable poems. He plays a dangerous game, particularly in the
marked repetition of words and phrases, but his craft is so sure
that it is a dazzling triumph each time, and no mere tour de force.
Perhaps it would not have been possible for him to do this with
such economy of means even as late as *Seascape: Needle's Eye*,
though back in *Discrete Series* it was implicit that he would
manage it one day. The technical virtuoso might make brilliant
momentary flashes. Oppen kindles a fire. There is a definite
summing up of history in these poems—George Oppen's personal
history, rich with images of sailing and the sea which he loves, but
it is also all of our histories as individuals and a race. There are
hints of other written records, and some that may never have been
written. We are sure that we have read or heard them elsewhere,
but we have not—not as he has given them to us. We have known
them far more clearly as promptings in our blood, promptings of
love, of indignation, fear and triumph, disgust and failure—and the
triumph of acceptance and leavetaking, too. They are all here, and
this is their book.

I cannot apologize for the use of many superlatives. When I
am confronted with such excellence, clothed, if at all, with
another man's honesty and humility, there is nothing to be done
but to accept and acknowledge the gift. I quote one of the poems
entire. It speaks better than I can of it:

The Natural

world *the fog*
coming up in the fields we learned those
rural words later we thought it was ocean the flood
of the ocean the light
of the world help me I am

of that people the grass
blades touch

and touch the small

distances the poem
begins

                       (*P*, p. 25)

THE TESTAMENT

George & Mary Oppen. Photograph 1981, by Richard Friedman.

DAVID McALEAVEY

A BIBLIOGRAPHY OF DISCUSSIONS OF
GEORGE OPPEN'S WORK:
REVIEWS, ARTICLES, ESSAYS, AND BOOKS

Editor's Note: David McAleavey's comprehensive bibliography of the works of George Oppen appeared in the special issue of *Paideuma* devoted to Oppen. We here offer the second half of McAleavey's bibliography: a comprehensive listing of discussions of Oppen's work. This bibliography is arranged alphabetically by author. It is followed by an "Annotated Chronological Bibliography of Discussions of George Oppen's Work," which I have prepared in co-operation with my research assistant, Julie Courant. Most but not all of the items listed by David McAleavey are described in some detail in the "Annotated Chronological Bibliography." The reference numbers following most items in the McAleavey bibliography indicate where the item in question appears in the "Annotated Chronological Bibliography." Items that are not followed by a reference number are not included in the "Annotated Chronological Bibliography." [BH]

Author's Note: This list includes newspaper reviews, which are indicated as such by an asterisk preceding the item. Many reviews either have no title, or have a title which does not indicate which book is under consideration, or deal with the work of several poets; in such cases, the book of Oppen's being reviewed is indicated in brackets. Page numbers, where listed, generally refer only to pages on which Oppen's work is discussed. Items here are listed alphabetically by author or, in the case of anonymous reviews, alphabetically by title of publication. If an author has published more than one discussion of Oppen's work, the items are arranged chronologically under that author's name. [DM]

List of Abbreviations

A—*Alpine*. Mount Horeb, Wisconsin: Perishible Press, 1969.
CPF—*Collected Poems*. London: Fulcrum Press, 1972.
CP—*Collected Poems*. New York: New Directions, 1975.
DS—*Discrete Series*. New York: Objectivist Press, 1934; reprinted
 Cleveland, Ohio: Mother/Asphodel, 1966.
M—*The Materials*. New York: New Directions, 1962.
OBN—*Of Being Numerous*. New York: New Directions, 1968.
P—*Primitive*. Santa Barbara: Black Sparrow Press, 1978.
SNE—*Seascape: Needle's Eye*. Fremont, Michigan: Sumac Press,
 1972.
TW—*This in Which*. New York: New Directions, 1965.

† † † † †

Anon. [rev. OBN]. *Choice*, Feb. 1969.

Anon. [rev. SNE]. *Choice*, July-Aug. 1973, p. 209.

*Anon. [rev. TW]. *Fresno Bee*, 21 Nov. 1965.

*Anon. [rev. CP]. *Long Beach Press Telegram & Independent*,
 13 Nov., 1975.

Anon. [rev. DS]. *The Nation*, 18 July 1934. 5

*Anon. (?). [rev. OBN]. *N. Y. Free Press Critique*, 27 June 1968.

*Anon. (?). [rev. CP]. *Soho Weekly News*, 22 Jan. 1976, p. 24 (?).

*Anon. [rev. TW]. *Wilson's Library Bulletin*, Jan. 1966, p. 452.

Anon. [rev. CP]. *Wilson Quarterly*, Winter 1977, p. 146.

Allen, Dick, "Of Exhibitionist Poetry, Redwoods, and the Fluid
 Narrative Dramatic" [rev. TW]. *Antioch Review*, 26, 2
 (Summer 1966), pp. 273-5. 28

Almon, Bert. [rev. CP]. *New Orleans Review*, 5, 4 (1978 (?)),
 pp. 371-3. 85

Altieri, Charles. "The Objectivist Tradition." *Chicago Review*, 30, 3 (Winter 1979), pp. 5-22. [Discusses Oppen's work throughout.] 87

Andrews, Bruce. "Surface Explanation." *Ironwood*, 5, pp. 43-9 64

*Andrews, Lyman. [rev. CPF]. *London Times*, 15 July (?).

Auster, Paul. "Private I, Public Eye" [rev. CP]. *Bookletter*, 3, 11 (31 Jan. 1977), pp. 12-3 83

————, ————. "A Few Words in Praise of George Oppen." *Paideuma* 10, 1 (Spring, 1981), pp. 49-52 91

*"C. A. B." "A 'New Country' Is Explored in Verse" [rev. TW]. *Buffalo Evening Sun*, 5 Mar. 1966.

Benet, William Rose. "The Phoenix Nest" [regular column; rev. DS]. *The Saturday Review of Literature*, 10, 36 (24 Mar. 1934), p. 580 1

*Booth, Martin. "Gods, roots, and poetic violences" [rev. CP]. *London Tribune*, 26 Mar. 1976 78

Bowering, George. "George Oppen." *Unmuzzled Ox*, 2, 3 (1974), pp. 67-8 61

*Bronder, Howard George. [rev. CP]. *Valley News Dispatch*, 17 Dec. 1976.

Bronk, William. [rev. OBN]. *Elizabeth*, 14 (Nov. 1969), pp. 25-7 39

Cambon, Glauco. "Two Poets of New York" [rev. M]. *Poetry*, 102, 4 (July 1963), pp. 267-8 20

Carruth, Hayden. [rev. M]. *The Nation*, 10 Nov. 1962, p. 312 8

*Carver, Mabel MacDonald. [rev. M]. *The Villager*, 11 Oct. 1962 7

Connaroe, Joel O. [rev. TW]. *Shenandoah*, Summer 1967, pp. 84-91 33

Corman, Cid. "Together" [rev. CP]. *Parnassus*, Spring-Summer 1976, pp. 83-95 81

————, ——. "The Experience of Poetry." *Paideuma*, 10, 1 (Spring, 1981), pp. 99-103 92

Corning, Howard M. [rev. M] *Voices*, May-August 1963, p. 40 19

Crawford, John. "An Essay on George Oppen" [rev. SNE]. *New: Canadian and American Poetry*, 25, 6 (1975), pp. 131-40.

Cuddihy, Michael. "George Oppen: A Loved and Native Rock" *Paideuma*, 10, 1 (Spring 1981), pp. 25-6 93

Davie, Donald. "Notes on George Oppen's *Seascape: Needle's Eye*." *Grosseteste Review*, 6, 1-4 (1973), pp. 233-9 54

*DeLancey, Rose Mary. "Poet Oppen's Collection 'Exciting' " [rev. TW]. *Ft. Wayne News Sentinel* (Indiana), 5 Feb. 1966.

Dembo, L. S. "The Existential World of George Oppen." *Iowa Review*, 3, 1 (Winter 1972), pp. 64-91 44

————, ——. "Individuality and Numerosity." *The Nation*, 24 Nov. 1969, pp. 574-6 38

*Deutsch, Babette. [rev. DS]. *N. Y. Herald Tribune Books*, 1 Apr. 1934, sec. VII, p. 16 2

Dickey, William. [rev. TW]. *Hudson Review*, Spring 1966, p. 146 27

Dunn, Douglas. "Poetry Chronicle—Mechanics of Misery" [rev. CPF]. *Encounter*, Aug. 1973, pp. 79-80 47

DuPlessis, Rachel Blau. "George Oppen: 'What do we believe to live with?' " *Ironwood*, 5, pp. 62-77 65

————, ——————. "Oppen and Pound." *Paideuma* 10,1 (Spring 1981), pp. 59-83 94

Ehrenpreis, Irvin. "The State of Poetry" [rev. CP]. *New York Review of Books*, 22 Jan. 1976, pp. 3-4 76

Enslin, Theodore, "if it fails." *Ironwood*, 5, pp. 59-61 61

————, —————. [rev. TW]. *Elizabeth*, 9 (Mar. 1966), pp. 16-8 26

————, —————. "The Third Path" [rev. TW]. *Poetry*, Aug. 1966, pp. 339-41 29

————, —————. [rev. P]. *American Book Review*, Mar-Apr. 1979, pp. 6-7 86

Fauchereau, Serge. "Poésie Objectiviste." *Les Lettres Nouvelles*, pp. 124-40. Reprinted with minor revisions in *Lecture de la Poésie Américaine*. Paris: Edition de Minuit, 1968, pp. 125-40 31

————————, ————, *Poètes Américains.* Paris: Atelier de Création, 1969.

————————, ————. "Poetry in America: Objectivism." Tr. from the French by Richard Lebovitz. *Ironwood*, 6. Translation of "Poésie Objectiviste," as cited above.

————————, ————. "3 Oppen Letters with a Note." *Ironwood*, 5, pp. 78-85 67

Fauchereau, Serge, with Jacques Roubaud and Charles Dobzynski. "Une littérature méconnue" [conversation about Objectivism, in French]. *Europe: Revue Littéraire Mensuelle*, June-July 1977.

Finkelstein, Norman M. "Political Commitment and Poetic Subjectification," *Contemporary Literature*, 22, 1 (Winter, 1981), pp. 24-41 104

Galassi, Jonathan. [rev. CP]. *Poetry*, Dec. 1976 79

Gerber, Dan. "Of Fathers." *Paideuma*, 10, 1 (Spring 1981), pp. 149-51 95

Goldblatt, Eli. "Notes on Some Matters at Hand." *Paper Air*, 2, 2 (1979), pp. 59-61 89

Grigson, Geoffrey. [rev. DS]. *New Verse*, June 1934, pp. 20-2 3

Guli, Francesca. [rev. TW]. *Virginia Quarterly Review*, Winter 1966, p. xvi. Also printed in *Spirit*, July 1966, p. 85 24

Hamburger, Michael. [rev. CPF]. *Agenda*, 11, 2-3 (1973), pp. 92-95 57

Harris, K. G. [rev. CP]. *Library Journal*, 1 Mar. 1976, p. 721 77

Heller, Michael. [rev. OBN]. *Caterpillar*, 6 (Jan. 1969), pp. 136-7 35

——, ———. "Discrete Series." *Sumac*, 3, 2 (Winter 1971), pp. 156-7 43

——, ———. [rev. SNE]. *American Poetry Review*, 4, 2 (March/April, 1975), pp. 1-4 75

*——, ———. "Poems and a Companion" [rev. P]. *N. Y. Times Book Review*, (?).

——, ———. Typescript article ms., "The Objectivists: Some Discrete Speculations," 13 pp. [Apparently unpublished?]

——, ———. "For George Oppen." *Paideuma* 10,1 (Spring 1981), pp. 143-47 96

Hewitt, Geof. "George Oppen." In R. Murphy *et al.* (eds.), *Contemporary Poets of the English Language*. Chicago: St. James Press, 1970, pp. 822-4 41

Homberger, Eric. *The Art of the Real: Poetry in England and America since 1939*. London: Dent, 1977, pp. 102, 116, 180, 203-4 84

——, ——. "Luminous Moral Sense" [rev. CPF]. *London Times Higher Education Supplement*, 14 Sept. 1973 . . . 49

Hunt, Chris. "George Oppen: *Collected Poems*." *Perfect Bound* (England), 1976 (?), pp. 74-8.

Hunting, Constance. " 'At Least Not Nowhere': George Oppen as Maine Poet." *Paideuma*, 10, 1 (Spring 1981), pp. 53-8 97

Ignatow, David. "Poet of the City" [rev. OBN]. *New Leader*, July 1968, pp. 20-1 34

"C. J. K." [rev. P]. *Booklist*, 15 Sept. 1979 (?).

"K. J. K." [rev. M]. *Thin Line*, Fall, 1962.

Katz, Bill. [rev. TW]. *Library Journal*.

——, ——. [rev. SNE]. *Library Journal*, 1 Sept. 1973, p. 2446 48

*Kay, Jane Holtz. "Disenchanted Poets" [rev. M] in "The Bookshelf" [regular column]. [newspaper from Quincy, Mass.].

Kenner, Hugh. *A Homemade World: The American Modernist Writers*. N. Y.: Knopf, 1975, pp. 163-71 & pp. 183-8 ... 69

——, ——. [Excerpts from the above.] *Grosseteste Review*, 6, 1-4 (1973), pp. 230-2.

——, ——. [rev. CP]. *N. Y. Times Book Review*, 19 Oct. 1975, p. 5 72

——, ——. *The Pound Era*. Berkeley: Univ. of California Press, 1971, pp. 387, 404-5 42

Kimbrell, Allen. "*Of Being Numerous* by George Oppen." *The Mysterious Barricades*, 4 (Winter 1976), pp. 97-100 80

Korges, James. "James Dickey and Other Good Poets" [rev. M]. *Minnesota Review*, Summer 1963, pp. 474-5 21

Lake, Paul. "George Oppen's *Primitive*." *Occident* (U. C. Berkeley), 100, 1 (Spring 1980), pp. 49-52 90

Lanham, Richard. "Poetic and Anti-Poetic Imagery" [rev. M]. *Commonweal*, 16 Nov. 1962, p. 180 9

Levertov, Denise. "Poetry: Pure and Complex." [rev. M]. *The New Leader*, 18 Feb. 1963, pp. 26-7 13

Lieberman, A. Laurance. [rev. OBN]. *Poetry*, Apr. 1969, p. 47 36

*Linenthal, Mark. [rev. M]. *S. F. Chronicle—This World Magazine*, 10 Mar. 1963, p. 33 14

————, ——. "An Appreciation." *Paideuma*, 10, 1 (Spring 1981), pp. 37-8 98

Marcus, Adrienne. [rev. CP]. *Northeast Rising Sun*, 2, 10 (?), 1977 (?).

Marshall, Jack. [rev. CP]. *San Francisco Review of Books*.

McAleavey, David. *If to Know Is Noble: The Poetry of George Oppen* [Ph.D. dissertation, Cornell University]. Ann Arbor Microfilms, Inc., 1975 63

————, ——. "Unrolling Universe: A Reading of Oppen's *This in Which*." *Paideuma*, 10, 1 (Spring 1981), pp. 105-28 99

McBride, John. [rev. SNE]. *Invisible City*, 8, April 1973 . . . 46

McDonough, Robert E. [rev. CP]. *Newsletter: Poets League of Greater Cleveland*, Aug. 1977, p. 4.

McGrath, Thomas. [rev. M]. *National Guardian*, 28 Mar. 1963 15

McKinney, Irene. "Objects and Solitude." *The Trellis Supplement*, Summer 1974, p. 9 60

*Meredith, William. [rev. M]. *N. Y. Herald Tribune*, 7 April 1963, p. 39 16

Merton, Thomas. *Conjectures of a Guilty Bystander*. Garden City, N. Y.: Doubleday, 1966, pp. 318-20 30

Morse, Samuel French. "Poetry 1962: A Partial View" [rev. M]. *Wisconsin Studies in Contemporary Literature*, 4, 3 (Autumn 1963), pp. 374-5 22

*Mueller, Lisel. "Poetry Chronicle: New Collections and First Appearances" [rev. TW]. *Chicago Daily News*, 19 Feb. 1966, *Panorama* section, p. 8 25

Navero, William. [rev. CP]. *The Buffalo Spectrum*, 10 Dec. 1976, pp. 24-5.

*Nixon, Sally. "Oppen Poetry: 'Nearly Total Originality' " [rev. CP]. *Salisbury, N. C. Post*, 21 Apr. 1977.

O'Brian, Geoffrey. [rev. OBN]. *Stony Brook*, 3-4 (1969), pp. 387-9 37

*Oliphant, Dave. "Dust Jacket" [regular column by Sue Watkins; rev. TW]. *Austin American-Statesman*, 23 Jan. 1966, pp. 17 ff.

Oliveros, A. "La poesía de George Oppen" [rev. CPF]. *Poesía: Revista de Poesía y Teoria Poética* (Venezuela), 15, Nov.-Dec. 1973, 3, 3, pp. 46-8 57

*Oppenheimer, Joel. "Support Your Local Poet" [rev. CP]. *Village Voice*, 22 Dec. 1975, p. 46 74

Perlberg, Mark. [rev. SNE]. *Poetry*, June 1975, p. 172 71

Pevear, Richard. "Poetry and Worldlessness" [rev. CP]. *Hudson Review*, 29, 2 (Summer 1976), pp. 317-20 82

Plumly, Stanley. [rev. SNE]. *Ohio Review*, 14, 2 (Winter 1973), p. 104 52

Pound, Ezra. "Preface." In George Oppen, *Discrete Series*. New York: Objectivist Press, 1934.

Powell, Donald. " 'At the Time of the Rogue's First Flood'—A Life, Together." *Paideuma*, 10, 1 (Spring 1981), pp. 141-2 100

Power, Kevin. *Una Poetica Activa: La poesía norteamericana 1910-1975*. Tr. into Spanish by A. Carrasco *et al*. Madrid: Editoria Nacional, 1978. [A chapter on Oppen, pp. 73-90.]

*Powers, Dennis. [rev. M]. *Oakland Tribune*, 2 Nov. 1962.

Rakosi, Carl. "A Note on George Oppen." *Ironwood*, 5, p. 19. Reprinted from *Grosseteste Review*, 6, 1-4, (1973), p. 247.

———, ———. "A Note on George Oppen." *Grosseteste Review*, 6, 1-4 (1973), p. 247 56

*———, ———. [rev. SNE]. *Minneapolis Tribune*, 15 Apr. 1973 45

*———, ———. [rev. CP]. *Minneapolis Tribune*, 9 Nov. 1975 .. 73

———, ———. "Two Notes and a Poem for George Oppen." *Paideuma*, 10, 1 (Spring 1981), pp. 14-6. Reprinted in large part from *Grosseteste Review* and *Ironwood*.

Rasula, Jed. [rev. CP]. *BooksWest*, June 1977, p. 40.

Reznikoff, Charles. "A Memoir." *Ironwood* 5, p. 29.

Rothenberg, Jerome. "George Oppen" [preface to *Discrete Series*]. *Revolution of the Word* (New York: Seabury, 1974), pp. 181-1 62

Rudolph, Anthony. *European Judaism* (London), Winter 1973-4 53

"D. N. S." [rev. TW]. *Lillabulero*, Spring 1967 32

Schneider, Duane. [rev. OBN]. *Library Journal*, 15 Jan. 1968.

*Shapiro, Harvey. [rev. M]. *N. Y. Times Book Review*, 18 Nov. 1962, p. 40 10

Sherman, Bill. "Concerns and Language" [rev. CP]. [Published in Britain.]

Silliman, Ron. "Third Phase Objectivism." *Paideuma*, 10, 1 (Spring 1981), pp. 85-89 101

*Simpson, Louis. "Poetry in the Sixties—Long Live Blake! Down with Donne!" [rev. OBN]. *N. Y. Times Book Review*, 28 Dec. 1969, p. 18 40

Sorrentino, Gilbert. "Poetry Chronicle" [rev. M]. *Kulchur*, 3, 9 (Spring 1963), pp. 74-5 17

━━━━, ━━━━. "George Oppen: Smallness of Cause." *Paideuma*, 10, 1 (Spring 1981), pp. 23-4 102

*Starr, William W. "New Poets: From Good to Very Good" [rev. CP]. *Columbia, S. C. State*, 29 Feb. 1976.

Stepanchev, Stephen. [rev. M]. *Shenandoah*, Spring 1963, pp. 58-65 18

*Sullivan-Daly, Tess. "New Poetry Anthology" [rev. CP]. *Worcester Sunday Telegram*, 18 Jan. 1976.

Taggart, John. "Deep Jewel: George Oppen's *Seascape: Needle's Eye*." *Occurrence* 3 (1975), pp. 26-36 70

━━━━, ━━━━. *Intending a Solid Object: A Study of Objectivist Poetics* [Ph.D. dissertation, Syracuse University]. Ann Arbor Microfilms, Inc. (1974) 59

━━━━, ━━━━. "The New Primitive" [rev. P]. *Chicago Review*, 30, 3 (Winter 1979), pp. 148-51 88

Tomlinson, Charles. "An Introductory Note on the Poetry of George Oppen." *Grosseteste Review*, 6, 1-4 (1973), pp. 240-6. Reprinted in *Ironwood*, 5 55

━━━━, ━━━━. [rev M]. *New Mexico Quarterly*, Spring 1964, pp. 108-10 23

━━━━, ━━━━. "Two Poets" [rev. M]. Carbon copy of this review in the Oppens' possession, attributed publication to *Texas Review*. No date or other information.

van der Hallen, Marijke. "De 'Objectieve' Dichters." *Standaard du Letteren* (Belgium), 30 Dec. 1977.

━━━━, ━━━━. Introduction to *George Oppen Gedichten* (thesis, May 1977), pp. i-ii.

Wakoski, Diane. "The True Art of Simplicity." *Ironwood* 5, pp. 31-4 68

Waldrop, Bernard. "George Oppen" [rev. M]. *Burning Deck*,
1, (Fall 1962), p. 51 11

Weil, James L. "The Long & the Short of It" [rev. M]. *Elizabeth*,
?, pp. 14-5 12

Weinberger, Eliot. "A Little Heap for George Oppen." *Paideuma*,
10, 1 (Spring 1981), pp. 131-6 103

*Wertheim, Bill. "The Neglected George Oppen." *New York Herald*, 28 April 1972.

Williams, William Carlos. "The New Poetical Economy" [rev.
DS]. *Poetry*, 44, 4 (July 1934), pp. 220-5 4

———, ———. *The Autobiography of William Carlos Williams*. (New York: New Directions, 1951), pp. 264-5 . . 6

*Wolfe, Ann F. [rev. TW]. *Columbus, Ohio Dispatch*, 3 July 1966.

Wright, Martin. "George Oppen Collected." *Prospice* (England)
1 (Nov. 1973), pp. 66-8 50

Zweig, Paul. "Making and Unmaking" [rev. OBN]. *Partisan Review*, 2 (1973), pp. 273-6 58

BURTON HATLEN and JULIE COURANT

ANNOTATED CHRONOLOGICAL BIBLIOGRAPHY
OF DISCUSSIONS OF GEORGE OPPEN'S WORK:
REVIEWS, ARTICLES, ESSAYS, AND BOOKS

Editor's Note: The following annotated bibliography has been modelled on the extended annotated bibliographies in *Louis Zukofsky: Man and Poet* and *Basil Bunting: Man and Poet.* Our annotated bibliography, in imitation of the bibliographies which C. F. Terrell prepared for these earlier volumes, aspires to include all significant works on Oppen published to date. David McAleavey's bibliography, printed above, enormously simplified our efforts. He prepared his bibliography with the co-operation of the Oppens themselves, and it includes many items published in hard-to-trace, often short-lived journals. Except for casual newspaper reviews, we tried to hunt down every item in his bibliography; and we found almost all of them. We also added two or three important items which he had missed. Of course, it is likely that a few important items have slipped by all of us: i.e., George and Mary Oppen, David McAleavey, Julie Courant, and me. But this bibliography is as complete as we could make it, at this time.

The items in this annotated bibliography are arranged as far as possible in order of publication. Items with vague dates (Spring 1965) generally follow items from the same general period but with more specific dates (March 27, 1965). But an item dated Spring 1965 would precede an item dated (say) 16 June 1965. Items with *extremely* general dates (for example, an annual dated simply 1965) will generally appear at the end of the items for the year in question. In all of these respects, this bibliography again follows the model established by the earlier volumes in this series.

Julie Courant, formerly my research assistant, and now business manager of *Paideuma*, and herself a fine poet, did most of the leg-work for this bibliography. She first hunted down references, filled out inter-library loan requests, and prepared bibliography cards. She then wrote annotations for about two-thirds of the items in the bibliography. I reviewed all of her annotations, and I revised some of them. I then wrote the annotations for the remaining pieces, including most of the more extended pieces—for example, the essays of Dembo, Tomlinson, Taggart. This bibliography is thus in the fullest sense a joint effort, and I would like to express my deepest thanks to David McAleavey, who laid the foundations, and to Julie Courant, who erected the rafters. Of course, any errors or omissions remain my responsibility. [B.H.]

† † † † †

1. Benet, William Rose. "The Phoenix Nest." *The Saturday Review of Literature*, 10, No. 36 (24 March 1934), p. 580.

> Mr. Benet's brief review of *Discrete Series* attempts to be neither analytical nor kind. "Mr. Oppen's offering exhibits that extreme parsimony of words that is taken today to imply infinite profundity. I don't believe it implies anything of the kind. His writing is like listening to a man with an impediment in his speech."

2. Deutsch, Babette. Rev. of *Discrete Series*, by George Oppen. *N. Y. Herald Tribune Books*, 1 April 1934, Sec. VII, p. 16.

> Deutsch describes *Discrete Series* as "a pleasingly brief sequence . . . parts of which are reminiscent of Dr. Williams." Deutsch also notes that "the good twentieth-century emphasis on and pre-occupation with the agony and fantasia of transportation are set forth by Mr. Oppen with a preciseness that is all too rare in contemporary verse."

3. Grigson, Geoffrey. Rev. of *Discrete Series*, by George Oppen. *New Verse*, June 1934, pp. 20-22.

> In this brief, hostile review, Grigson describes *Discrete Series* as a series of "anti-poems" born not of a "poetic womb," but "an isolated, dried-up bladder."

4. Williams, William Carlos. "The New Poetical Economy." *Poetry*, 44, No. 4 (July 1934), pp. 220-25.

> This historically important essay is reprinted in this volume, pp. 267-70.

5. Anon., Rev. of *Discrete Series*, by George Oppen. *The Nation*, 18 July 1934, p. 84.

> This brief but remarkably perceptive anonymous review deserves to be quoted in full:

Mr. Oppen is an Objectivist, a descendent of the Imagists. Like William Carlos Williams he pictures boldly and allows the reader to relate the pictures given as separate images within a single poem. He differs from Mr. Williams, however, in that almost every poem describes an actual movement of objects. Either the images are those seen from a train or from some vehicle in which the poet is placed, or are actually in motion themselves. Sometimes Mr. Oppen presents, as it were, a level or plane of movement, images seen from a certain angle. He draws his images from modern industrial life. He presents them in much the same manner as the impressionist painter might. His work, however, has the fault which is characteristic of this whole school of poets. The images are not fused with the emotion. They merely objectify it.

6. Williams, William Carlos. *The Autobiography of William Carlos Williams*. New York: New Directions, 1951, pp. 264-5.

    Williams mentions Oppen's name twice in *The Autobiography* but does not comment on his work. First, Oppen is mentioned as being present at the inauguration of the "Objectivist theory of the poem" and, second, as having supplied money for the establishment of the Objectivist Press.

7. Carver, Mabel MacDonald. "Three Poets at the Gotham Book Mart," *The Villager*, 11 Oct. 1962, p. 7.

    Carver, in this review of *The Materials*, places Oppen's work "definitely in the modern vein." She quotes comments by William Carlos Williams and Ezra Pound on Oppen's work, as well as the poem "Chartres" in its entirety, noting that "punctuationless lines *can* have a subtle meaning. These do. . . ."

8. Carruth, Hayden. Rev. of *The Materials*, by George Oppen. *The Nation*, 10 Nov. 1962, p. 312.

    This review of *The Materials* deems Oppen's poems weak. "They try to have more meaning than they themselves say, but the meanings are surfaced, swimming like bits of tinsel in a pool." Carruth does, however, "recommend his book, especially for those who love engines and tools for their own sake, i.e., not as cultural devices. Oppen has a fine mechanic's sense."

9. Lanham, Richard. "Poetic and Anti-Poetic Imagery." *Commonweal*, 16 Nov. 1962, p. 180.

    Lanham describes the style of *The Materials* as "a mixture of 'anti-poetic' images and choppy rhythms, smoothing out in a form that is seemingly a string of syllogisms, but is actually a series of associations faultlessly joined together." Lanham finds in Oppen's work a powerful sense of "awe," strong "metaphysical concerns," and "an enviable lyric sense."

10. Shapiro, Harvey. Rev. of *The Materials*, by George Oppen. *N. Y. Times Book Review*, 18 Nov. 1962, p. 40.

> Noting Oppen's appearance in *An Objectivists' Anthology* in 1932, Shapiro quotes Zukofsky from the appendix of that book: "Writing occurs which is the detail, not mirage, of seeing and thinking with the things as they exist and of directing them along a line of melody." Zukofsky is describing "the kind of writing he admired, with special reference to Reznikoff's work," but Shapiro finds that Oppen's poems in *The Materials* also fit the description. "For all their solid heft . . . these are immensely sophisticated pieces, and their shock is finally metaphysical."

11. Waldrop, Bernard. "George Oppen." *Burning Deck*, 1 (Fall 1962), p. 51.

> Lamenting the fact that he has never seen a copy of *Discrete Series*, Waldrop calls for it to be reprinted immediately if it is of the same quality as *The Materials*. Dubbing Oppen a "materialist poet," he describes Oppen's poetry as "an attempt to realize matter, perhaps to identify with it" but with "no rambling catalogs of things, no ranting that he is part of the whole universe. . . ."

12. Weil, James L. "The Long and Short of It." *Elizabeth*, ?, (1962?), pp. 14-5.

> Weil sees Oppen as an "anti-urban" poet—indeed a pastoral poet concerned with nature, *not* as a "Wordsworthian temple" but rather as "sacred simply in that it is the place where wonderful things like love and song occur." But Oppen's pastoral is distinctively modern, Weil suggests, in that it takes as its subject "heartburn as well as heartache, the stomach along with the soul." But "because the poems of George Oppen, Robert Creeley, and Theokritos begin at the base with the base, they come down to the purest and rise with the noblest," and thus for Weil Oppen takes his place among the greatest of the pastoral poets.

13. Levertov, Denise. "Poetry: Pure and Complex." *The New Leader*, 18 Feb. 1963, pp. 26-7.

> Reviewing *The Materials*, Levertov states that Oppen "does not imitate Williams; but he is plainly indebted to him, which is closer to being a virtue than a vice." She classifies some of Oppen's poems as "affirmative," namely "Product," "California," and, "in its wry way," "Pedestrian," which she quotes in the review. She finds the more typical category of Oppen's poems "those . . . that rise up with an effort out of inner conflict, coming to no facile resolution but pulling the conflict with them into the cruel daylight." Levertov sees a "pervasive frustration" in his poems "as if at times the poet threw up his hands helpless before the demands of the material." She is quick to say she does not mean Oppen lacks craftsmanship, but that

"his craft is involved in a desperate struggle with the intricacies of his sense of life. His poems are essentially of process, not tasteful art-objects. . . ." Levertov closes her review by noting that Oppen's poems "at times . . . have a powerful grip," and quotes "Survival: Infantry" as an example of that grip.

14. Linenthal, Mark. Rev. of *The Materials*, by George Oppen. *S. F. Chronicle—This World Magazine*, 10 March 1963, p. 33.

> Oppen's *The Materials* is briefly compared to Reznikoff's *By the Waters of Manhatten* in this review, and is found to be "more spare, drier or cooler, more sophisticated: his fine surfaces more quietly suggestive." A quote from "Product" is offered as an example of Oppen's "leaner esthetic."

15. McGrath, Thomas. "A Roundup of Recent Poetry." *National Guardian*, 28 March 1963, p. 10.

> McGrath has high praises for *The Materials*: "perfect in its own way . . . it's style . . . purer than that of most of Williams' brand of non-functional rhetoric—the curious elisions, portentous and meaningless repetitions, the phoney precision of three verbs where one (the right one) is all that is needed." And McGrath offers only a hint of criticism: "There are poems which one might have risked more—and not much risk either for a poet who can see in the slums, in a woman, 'the instep naked to the wooden floor' a symbol of 'The city's/Secret warmth.' "

16. Meredith, William. Rev. of *The Materials*, by George Oppen. *N. Y. Herald Tribune*, 7 April 1963, p. 39.

> This review of *The Materials* says little more than that the book "contains some of the most craftsmanlike free verse that has been published in a long time."

17. Sorrentino, Gilbert. "Poetry Chronicle." *Kulchur*, 3 (Spring 1963), pp. 69-82.

> Sorrentino devotes one paragraph of this omnibus review to *The Materials*, which he finds a "remarkable achievement in clarity and precision." Oppen's poetry, Sorrentino notes, grows out of a desire for a world "where love might grow," an absolute fidelity to the immediate experience, and a "reverence for words."

18. Stepanchev, Stephen. "Eight Poets." *Shenandoah*, Spring 1963, pp. 58-65.

> Stepanchev devotes one paragraph of this omnibus review to Oppen's *The Materials*. He senses a "lack of passion and personal

involvement" in Oppen's poetry but praises his determination "to
assimilate the machine to poetry, to make it part of our emotional
climate."

19. Corning, Howard M. "In the Course of Recognition." *Voices*,
May-August 1963, p. 40.

> A short, positive, but less than enthusiastic review of *The Materials*.
> Corning finds in Oppen's poems "an adroit and effective shifting of
> stresses that bespeak the practiced craftsman. "In certain poems,
> however, the treatment is too spare and the reader is offered intima-
> tions where realities are solely needed."

20. Cambon, Glauco. "Two Poets of New York." *Poetry*, 102, 4
(July 1963), pp. 267-8.

> Discussing both *The Materials* and Charles Reznikoff's *By the Waters
> of Manhattan*, Cambon speaks of the two poets as "imaginatively
> committed to New York," and finds that "in spite of Oppen's more
> limited range . . . he makes me breathe more amply." He justifies
> as follows his preference for Oppen as a poet of New York: "All of
> us modern city dwellers . . . are exiles . . . and Oppen succeeds in
> expressing precisely this shared predicament with the resources of a
> searching control that lends apocalyptic finality to common speech."
> Cambon illustrates his comments with quotes from "Tourist's Eye,"
> "Population," and "Myself I Sing."

21. Korges, James. "James Dickey and Other Good Poets."
Minnesota Review, Summer 1963, pp. 474-5.

> Korges' reaction to *The Materials* in this 16-book salad review is
> brief and sarcastic: "George Oppen's *The Materials* has received
> Important Blurbs from Important People [WCW & EP]. . . .Oppen
> is a craftsman. My only difficulty is that I cannot figure out which
> craft he is craftsman *of*. . . ." So . . . "for all the rumble of Impor-
> tant Blurbists, the book seems to me exactly what its title says:
> 'the materials' for poems yet unwritten."

22. Morse, Samuel French. "Poetry 1962: A Partial View."
Wisconsin Studies in Contemporary Literature, 4, 3 (Autumn
1963), pp. 374-5.

> This review of *The Materials*, as do most, mentions Oppen's "debt to
> Williams," decides that "Oppen shares with Williams some character-
> istic habits of mind and observation," but also argues that "influence
> and originality are far more complicated matters than those raised
> by critics, including Pound. Oppen is, beyond all question, a poet
> who practices what he knows. . . .His stripped excellence is a rarity."

23. Tomlinson, Charles. Rev. of *The Materials*, by George Oppen. *New Mexico Quarterly*, Spring 1964, pp. 108-10.

> This important review essay makes clear the affinities between Oppen and Tomlinson. Tomlinson here establishes a clear demarcation between Oppen and Williams (Oppen is "a far more 'intellectual' poet than Williams") and places Oppen with Zukofsky as two of the most important (but in 1964 still almost entirely unrecognized) presences in the American poetic tradition. Tomlinson finds in *The Materials* a continuity from *Discrete Series*, in the poet's acute awareness of "the coexistence or qualification of human and non-human." Tomlinson also notes Oppen's admiration for the "sense of workmanship" displayed by, for example, the boatbuilder of New England, and he suggests that this idea of workmanship brings "to the fore . . . that dialectic . . . of flesh against 'the materials' " which is Oppen's central theme.

24. Guli, Grancesca. Rev. of *This In Which*, by George Oppen. *Virginia Quarterly Review*, 42 (Winter 1966), p. xvi.

> This four sentence review emphasizes Oppen's "suspicious" sense of the "unreliability" of words and concludes that "his hostility to words which contain music or stir feelings dooms his poetry to a sameness, a flatness, a prosaic quality."

25. Mueller, Lisel. "Poetry Chronicle: New Collections and First Appearances." *Chicago Daily News*, 19 Feb. 1966, p. 8.

> In her brief review of *This In Which*, Mueller says Oppen "works language hard . . . cutting away embellishment and discarding vagueness." She sees his poems as "consisting of a series of concise declarative statements, or parts of statements which . . . frequently miss coalescing into the shape of meaning." She quarrels with Oppen and all Objectivist poets who contend that "this represents ordinary speech—if, indeed, ordinary speech is a virtue in poetry." But she has no quarrel with those who praise Oppen for the "firmness and precision of his constructions."

26. Enslin, Theodore. Rev. of *This In Which*, by George Oppen. *Elizabeth*, 9, (March 1966), pp. 16-8.

> Enslin salutes the publication of *This In Which* as "an event," because Oppen "says more, and structures what he says better, than a great many of his contemporaries with bulging shelves." Enslin briefly recounts the history of the Objectivist movement, and makes a pungent comparison of Oppen to "the pundits of the New Criticism." But in the end Enslin returns to Oppen's work itself, which he admires for the poet's willingness to "take a stance, one that continues." This quality in Oppen, Enslin notes, gives his work "qualities of endurance. It breathes and is healthy."

27. Dickey, William. Rev. of *This In Which*, by George Oppen. *Hudson Review*, Spring 1966, p. 146.

> Dickey is convinced in his review of *This In Which* by "the sense of immediate pleasure" in a passage from the poem "Psalm," but asserts that the same passage "argues that the poet is not required to convince the reader of the validity of his observation or his vision, but is required only to *assert* that such a validity exists." In Oppen's poetry, Dickey says, this "assertion of immediacy" becomes "the excuse for a number of deficiencies." Dickey expresses dissatisfaction with the lack of "supported argument" in Oppen's work. Oppen, says Dickey, "asserts things as if they were relationships, as if their slightest juxtaposition necessarily conveys meaning." Dickey obviously wants from poetry something more than an accidental collision of objects. Obviously too, Dickey cannot understand why Oppen gives us objects rather than ideas *about* objects. Yet despite this lack of sympathy, Dickey has seen and described some important features of Oppen's poetic method.

28. Allen, Dick. "Of Exhibitionist Poetry, Redwoods, and the Fluid Narrative Dramatic." *Antioch Review*, 26, 2 (Summer 1966), pp. 273-5.

> In this brief review of *This In Which*, Allen praises Oppen's "mature wisdom" and his concern with "strict honesty." He quotes "The Gesture" in its entirety and paraphrases the question Oppen poses in that poem: "How can the poet communicate a realization of the concrete object *as object* without drawing the reader's attention to *the way* in which he communicates?" He quotes "Carpenter's Boat" as an example of Oppen's "exploration of reality, of a natural way of seeing and expressing." Praising "A Narrative" as "one of the best longer poems I have read in years," Allen notes in this poem also Oppen's concern "with society, with the fabric of our everyday life in America."

29. Enslin, Theodore. "The Third Path." *Poetry*, August 1966, pp. 339-41.

> In his second review of *This In Which*, Enslin chooses to emphasize Oppen's ability "to talk about anything with which he comes in contact, because he doesn't allow any contact to be unimportant to him." Oppen, says Enslin, "is one poet who is at home in the world," no less at home in Maine than New York, no less at home in the realm of "ideas" than in the "inner climate of the poet himself." "If I feel at ease in this way about Oppen's work," Enslin adds, "I imply the smaller technical excellence. He couldn't write as he does unless he brought the same care to the making of poems as he does to the life behind the poems."

30. Merton, Thomas. *Conjectures of a Guilty Bystander*. (Garden City, N.Y.: Doubleday, 1966), pp. 318-20.

Merton devotes the concluding pages of this book to Oppen, whom
he presents as an example of a poet who knows "that the world
[Merton is using this term in an explicitly theological sense, as
denoting everything that stands over against God] lies." "Yet the
poet," Merton goes on, "knows another and more real world, the
world . . . of life. The world of life is itself manifest in words, but is
not a world of words." Merton quotes Oppen's "Sara in Her Father's
Arms" as an instance of the poet's ability to "listen to life itself in
its humility, frailty, silence, tenacity."

31. Fauchereau, Serge. "Poésie Objectiviste." *Les Lettres Nou-
     velles*, May 1967, pp. 124-40.

This extended essay seeks to explain Objectivism to a French audience. In the process, Fauchereau mentions several of Oppen's poems;
indeed, he treats *Discrete Series* as the archetypal Objectivist text.
Fauchereau sees the Objectivists as the true American equivalent of
the Auden group in England, in that both groups of poets sought
to respond to the social issues of the 1930s. But the Objectivists
have received less public recognition than Auden and his friends
because they were not content to respond to these issues on a
merely intellectual level; instead they also sought new poetic forms—
forms which some readers still find startling and offensive. Fauchereau quotes at length from the letters which George Oppen wrote to
him (the letters printed in *Ironwood* 5) to explain the difference
between Imagism and Objectivism. In Oppen's words ". . . the
strength of Imagism [is] its demand that one actually *look*. Its
strength, in the poem, that the world stops, but lights up. That
lucence, that emotional clarity, the objectivists wanted, and by that
they are related to Imagism. But not the falsity of ingenuity, of the
posed tableau, in which the poet also, by implication, poses." Building on Oppen's comment, Fauchereau sees the "return to the object"
as the essence of Objectivism: "The objectivists returned to the
object, a chest full of tools, a rock. [Fauchereau is here alluding to
two images in Oppen's 'Myself I Sing.'] Williams had rehabilitated
the object, but he had found no followers. Marianne Moore loved
objects, especially if they were strange; she described them with precision but her poems remained intellectual games, exercises on a
trapeze. The Objectivist poem did not so much seek to describe as
to create a momentary pause in which the object could reveal itself,
or give itself to our eyes." But, Fauchereau adds, the Objectivist
poet "does not see only objects, he also sees men, all the while
refusing to look egoistically at his own reflection in a mirror. Social
reality is no less present in the poems of the Objectivists than in the
vibrant and self-congratulatory poems of those poets of the 1930s
who called themselves 'neo-humanists' or 'Marxists.' " Fauchereau
further proposes that Objectivism is not only a uniquely American
movement but also "the first literary movement that deliberately
defined itself as American." (The Imagist movement, he points out,
was launched from London, and saw itself as a cosmopolitan movement.) The Objectivist movement, says Fauchereau, effectively
ended in 1940. After this point, "one can no longer speak of Objectivism as a movement, but must instead speak of 'Objectivisms and

Objectivists.' '' Yet he sees the re-discovery of the Objectivists in the 1960s as one of the most important literary developments of that epoch, and he argues throughout the essay that the Objectivists were the chief link in the chain that joins "the trinity Pound-Williams-Cummings" to "Olson and the Black Mountain Group."

32. D. N. S., Rev. of *This In Which*, by George Oppen. *Lillabu-lero*, Spring 1967.

> This anonymous review of *This In Which* lauds Oppen's poetry as "honorable and honest . . . the honesty becomes evident when he wrestles his dilemmas out and into the light of his poems, unresolved." The review also notes Oppen's facility with images: "They are alive, presented rather than spoken about." Oppen's "unique mark" is declared to be his use of juxtaposition.
>   While the reviewer has high praises for Oppen, emphasizing his "gift with images" and his "honesty," she/he does take Oppen to task for his use of the double negative, and the questionable unity of his long poem.

33. Connaroe, Joel O. Rev. of *This In Which*, by George Oppen. *Shenandoah*, Summer 1967, pp. 84-91.

> Connaroe devotes two pages of this essay to *This In Which*. He confesses that "a few of the poems, written in a sort of shorthand, remain incomprehensible. The spring is sometimes wound too far, and the sought for compression results, instead, in confusion." He also criticizes Oppen for being "at times . . . dominated by Williams" and cites "Night Scene" as a poem in which one is "at a loss to know which of the two men is speaking." He does however mention the poems "Philai te kou philai," "Boy's Room," "Bahamas," and "The Forms of Love" as worthy of praise.

34. Ignatow, David. "Poet of the City." *New Leader*, July 1968, pp. 20-1.

> In this long review article, Ignatow develops an extended comparison between *Of Being Numerous* and Williams' *Paterson*. Ignatow sees Williams as seeking a resolution to the impersonal "flux of city life" in "the symbol of traditional esthetic content"—specifically, the "sexual, life-enhancing" Unicorn of Book Five of *Paterson*. Oppen, Ignatow contends, refuses such a resolution. Instead he is determined "to remain exposed to the city." Rather than retreating into the esthetic symbol, Oppen attempts to "rescue the self through the consistent exercise of consciousness." Williams, Ignatow notes, "was able to associate empathetically with the men and women trapped in . . . the slums of Passaic," but "he felt himself to be ultimately independent of his environment." In Oppen's poetry, on the other hand, "all is held in tension, there being no choice for him, a man of the city." The result is "a civilized poem, a lone being, it's true, but . . . a comfort among the ashes. . . ." "The entire book," Ignatow

concludes, "is the work of a man who rests his faith in the mind as a value in itself on which the individual may depend." This commitment places Oppen "in the line of our best contemporary poets"— Ignatow mentions Stevens, Williams, Eliot, and Pound. But Ignatow also sees Oppen as "carrying the point a step beyond them in time, close to our very skin."

35. Heller, Michael. Rev. of *Of Being Numerous*, by George Oppen. *Caterpillar*, 6 January 1969, pp. 136-7.

Heller's response to *Of Being Numerous* is brief enough to be quoted in full:

My God. How rare and impressive this book is. The method: no lies, no evasions, no esthetics, no appeals. Feeling, complexity, richness all stemming from that source. The cadences falling where they do out of dark necessity without indulgence. The collateral possibilities of the poems' development: social, political, philosophical surfaces—flaring in, channeling the reader to see that most unreasonable of situations, the dumdum bullet of

" . . . the

real

That we confront"

A lurch at madness, the madness of purely understanding and *purely* lacking answers so that the world, existence, poem pivot on the word 'curious,' that tenacious redemptive act of wanting to know, of willingness to

"Imagine a man in the ditch
The wheels of the overturned wreck
Still spinning—

I don't mean he despairs, I mean if he does not
He sees in the manner of poetry"

36. Lieberman, A. Laurance. Rev. of *Of Being Numerous*, by George Oppen. *Poetry*, April 1969, p. 47.

Lieberman feels that *Of Being Numerous* marks a "traditional stopgap" in Oppen's work: "most of Oppen's rigorous economizing—his spareness of phrase—has given way to a slackening of measure. Evidently the long poem is not Oppen's forte. The burden of a protracted structure seems to drain intensity out of his line, and to divert his journalistic eye from the momentous—the telling—details."

37. O'Brien, Geoffrey. Rev. of *Of Being Numerous*, by George Oppen. *Stony Brook*, 3/4 (1969), pp. 387-9.

O'Brien sees Oppen's poetry as finding its "working area" in "that narrow margin where art is usually prepared to admit its impotence, the moment of real things in movement, and of humans making contact with them." O'Brien sees Oppen as moving beyond Imagism, which sought to make language a reflection of things, to a new sense of words as "objects through which meanings drift, to which in varying degrees they adhere. And the words on the page have the same qualities—discreteness—impenetrable clarity—as things. But they are not like things, they are things." Nevertheless, O'Brien also recognizes that "words also describe concepts." In the case specifically of *Of Being Numerous*, the concept at issue is a particularly thorny one: "humanity." But Oppen doesn't make the mistake of telling us what this concept means. Rather he makes his poem, says O'Brien, an "investigation" of the central question—i.e. in Oppen's words, "whether we can deal with humanity as something which actually does exist." "In all 40 sections," O'Brien points out, "there is no answer but that implied by the repetition of the question, and behind it the 'act of faith' by which a reality is accepted."

38. Dembo, L. S. "Individuality and Numerosity." *The Nation*, 24 November 1969, pp. 574-6.

Dembo here discusses Oppen's life and his general poetic position for several paragraphs, before turning specifically to *Of Being Numerous*. Dembo sees Oppen as essentially a "phenomenological" poet. "Poetry . . . became for Oppen the language of faith in the material world and the means for expressing its ultimate mystery," Dembo says. He adds:

> The noun is the central part of speech in Oppen's universe, since it signifies the existence of an object but provides no knowledge about it:
>
>> There are words that mean nothing
>> But there is something to mean.
>> Not a declaration which is truth
>> But a thing
>> Which is.
>
> That reality—as epitomized, for example, by the islands in the polar mist of "Narrative"—can inspire the poet with dread and the sense of *Néant*, as well as with joy and the sense of Being, points up the profound ambivalence in Oppen's view of the world. The "life of the mind," which Oppen believes to be the only life for humanity, coexists with *Angst*, boredom and despair. Yet underlying these opposing responses is the idea that reality in all its manifestations must be respected as truth. Nontruth is represented by the invented ethic, detached from actual feeling, or in objects by the hollow decorations of an affluent civilization.

Turning specifically to *Of Being Numerous*, Dembo finds in the title poem

> a crisis of faith in which Oppen posits an idea of humanity but cannot consistently believe in the metaphysic that will transform the infinite series of single lives into continuity and community.
>
>> the metaphysic
>> On which rest
>> The boundaries
>> Of our distances.

> Generations succeed one another, Oppen implies, only to be lost in "the great mineral silence . . . a process/Completing itself."

Dembo also comments on "Route," which reflects, he says, "a profound determinism. . . .It has a vision of love, but love understood as a biological phenomenon." In his conclusion, Dembo celebrates Oppen as an example of "existential man . . . whose integrity compels him to face down an impersonal universe and whose lucidity keeps him from despair." Oppen, Dembo also asserts, "has realized the full potentiality of his objectivist allegiance: he has become a poet of the first order."

39. Bronk, William. *Elizabeth*, 14 (Nov. 1969), pp. 25-7.

Bronk, in this review, carefully traces out the lines and contours of *Of Being Numerous*:

> No doubt we are insular even to the extent that as the intensity of our seeing increases, so does the channel between us seem to widen so that our distance apart increases. And yet part of what one means is to be found in the things we live among and in our multiplicity. . . .

In Oppen's poetry, Bronk finds "an insistence on the external world which he finds impenetrable as matter." Oppen's poetry, Bronk also notes, "is made of the external object without much explanation but with clarity which seems to him the most beautiful thing in the world."

40. Simpson, Louis. "Poetry in the Sixties—Long Live Blake! Down with Donne!" *N. Y. Times Book Review*, 28 Dec. 1969, p. 18.

Simpson here briefly discusses Oppen's book in the course of a lengthy meditation on some differences between the noisy, activist poetry of the 1960s and the tame, academic poetry of the 1950s:

> Oppen shows how Pound's "Cantos" can be used as a basis from which to develop. Oppen's language has been stripped clean of references to things outside the poem itself. Yet, as in Pound,
>
>> The context is history
>> Moving toward the light of the conscious
>
> Reading Oppen I am aware of all that has been excluded by a very discriminating mind in order to arrive at significant life. The mind, moving toward clarity, sheds those matters that are, as Gatsby said, "just personal." As it begins to know itself, the mind moves, and thought is felt as movement, along the line. We experience the life of the mind in its physical reality, the movement of verse.

41. Hewitt, Geof. "George Oppen." In R. Murphy, *et al.* (eds.), *Contemporary Poets of the English Language*. (Chicago: St. James Press, 1970), pp. 822-4.

Hewitt finds Oppen "one of the best and one of the worst of poets. The vantage from which he writes is high: the poetry of George Oppen declaims, defines, and finally, establishes for us a series of dicta by George Oppen." If Oppen's goal is clarity, Hewitt argues, then he "must tackle seemingly insoluble problems if his work is to distinguish itself." Hewitt is also bothered by what he calls "Oppen's out" from these problems, which he defines as an attempt at "clarification of everything," and he complains that "no indication of humility and a great many self-assured statements can strain the wary reader's belief." Another of Oppen's practices which irks Hewitt is his use of abstraction and double negatives, and his "bothersome detachment." What Hewitt will grant is that "Oppen is attempting a poetry far more difficult than most poets will dare, and the finest moments of his work raise questions (rather than answers) that will haunt every reader."

42. Kenner, Hugh, *The Pound Era* (Berkeley: Univ. of California Press, 1971), p. 387 and pp. 404-5.

> Kenner mentions Oppen's association with Pound, and he briefly discusses Oppen's work in a chapter titled "Syntax in Rutherford," as a poet who—along with Zukofsky, Williams, Reznikoff, Rakosi, and Bunting—has clearly grasped a powerful poetic principle: that the word is "not a focus for sentiment" but rather "an element in the economy of a sentence."

43. Heller, Michael. Rev. of *Discrete Series*, by George Oppen. *Sumac*, 3, 2 (Winter 1971), pp. 156-7.

> This review of the re-issue of *Discrete Series* broadens into a discussion of Oppen's work in general. Oppen is, says Heller, determined "to see the world (plainly). But the eye is that of the phenomenologist, which knows, to quote Merleau-Ponty: 'The decisive moment in perception: the upsurge of a *true* and *accurate* world.' " Nor is this, Heller adds, merely "a case of getting a 'fresh start' on things, that oldest saw of a bankrupt avant-gardist. The eye, courageously, plods along acknowledging its historical load." In Oppen's work Heller finds an abiding commitment: "the poet whose only area of control ends at the beginning of sight confronts and honors his obsession."

44. Dembo, L. S. "The Existential World of George Oppen." *Iowa Review*, 3, 1 (Winter 1972), pp. 64-91.

> Dembo here expands his useful 1969 review of *Of Being Numerous* into a full-dress attempt to "place" Oppen. The title suggests the focus of the essay. Taking his cue from Oppen's Heidegger and Maritain epigraphs, Dembo sees Oppen as an exponent of existential phenomenology: "Oppen's reasoning is phenomenological: since consciousness is consciousness of an object, rigorous investigation of one's consciousness provides knowledge about the object." Dembo

traces Oppen's "rigorous investigation of [his] own consciousness" through each of his books, from *Discrete Series* through *Of Being Numerous*. The seven page introductory section focuses on *Discrete Series*, which Dembo sees as composed of a series of discrete observations:

> For all its limitations, . . . this kind of observation is the most empirical and the most "sincere"; it represents without mitigation the "actual experience" of a poet who is committed to his eyes and refuses to fabricate an emotion or to "construct a meaning" that is fanciful. The poet perceives reality from a rocking boat or a moving train—sometimes a cause of despair, sometimes a cause of joy, but always a fact of life to a man of integrity.

The sum total of these observations is, says Dembo, boredom: "For Oppen, the attempt to acquire knowledge about 'what is/really going on' can only end in ennui, for nothing is going on that is reducible to meaning. Aesthetic joy or intellectual depression are the two basic responses to bare reality."

In the later books, says Dembo, "the 'empiricism' of *Discrete Series* reaches social and cosmic dimensions. Dembo gives ten pages to *The Materials*, explicating in some detail "Return," "Blood from a Stone," "Resort," "Myself I Sing," "Vulcan," and "Image of the Engine," while commenting more briefly on several other poems. Dembo's discussion of the "existential" implications of "Blood from a Stone" will serve as an example of his critical method. In this poem, he says, "Mother Nature"

> is dead, man is "deserted" and has only himself to ease his loneliness in the world. The Sequoia, one might argue, is a form of life that exists totally "in the singular" and, perhaps, "lone in a lone universe . . . suffers time/Like stones in sun" ("Birthplace: New Rochelle"). "Men do not," and it is in their children that they seek fulfillment. Or, it would be better to say, Oppen seeks fulfillment in his own child. . . .
>> Outside of this kind of experience, life is perhaps limited to "remote/Mechanics, endurance." And the perpetual renovation of the city, with its destruction of the pasts of individual men, suggests that even endurance, if it is to be associated with continuity rather than mere durability, is almost impossible.

In *The Materials* Dembo finds some brief, affirmative moments. But while a figure like Petra in "The Return" seems to represent the impulse toward community and family, the eros that makes human beings more than objects," nevertheless, "this impulse is constantly negated," for to Oppen "community and even family are no more than conceptions that men require for survival." In *This In Which*, Dembo finds a persistent emphasis on poetry as "the language of faith in the material world and the means for expressing its ultimate mystery." False art, it follows, falsifies the truth of the world. True art gives us instead reality: "Reality is what is and what has happened: 'the relation of the sun and earth' beyond the circle of the visible, the 'sea in the morning,' and the 'hills brightening.' It is also history and the social and psychological condition of men." And it is this reality that Oppen's poetry itself offers us.

The five pages that Dembo devotes to *Of Being Numerous*
parallel in part his 1969 *Nation* essay. Again Dembo emphasizes
Oppen's refusal to find a refuge either in a specious "individualism"
or an equally specious "community": "The Singular Man had the
power of seeing intensely, but not of communicating; the shipwreck
of the singular is really the failure of the poet to fulfill himself outside the community. On the other hand, there is a question as to
whether any community actually existed."

In his concluding paragraph, Dembo sums up as follows
Oppen's basic intellectual position:

> In a world of overwhelming numerosity of persons, things, and
> days the poet seeks a "limited, limiting clarity" (#1). In its
> ultimate sense, the shipwreck of the singular is the failure to
> realize the finite and to achieve true Clarity. "The mind creates
> the finite" (#11) and clarity is part of the emotion that causes
> to see, but, as we have been told in "Of Being Numerous," the
> power of the mind "is nothing/And does nothing" against "The
> fatal rock/Which is the world." "We want to defend/Limitation/
> And do not know how" ("Of Being Numerous," #26). On the
> other hand, if a man does not despair, "he sees in the manner of
> poetry" ("Route," #8). Perceptual joy as well as conceptual
> boredom is possible, and "the lyric valuable" is obtainable. But
> perhaps even the lyric valuable will not be sufficient if Reality
> deprives men of the love necessary for sanity and they are faced
> with "Cataclysm . . . cataclysm of the plains, jungles, the cities."
> "Route," as well as Oppen's vision in general, ends in an appre-
> hension of the "void eternally generative," of the space that is
> vivaparous in the time of the missile ("Time of the Missile"),
> those
>
> things at the limits of reason, nothing at the limits
>   of dream, the dream
> merely ends, by this we know it is the real
>
> That we confront

45. Rakosi, Carl. "Can you see it?" *Minneapolis Tribune*, 15 April, 1973.

Rakosi likes Oppen, respects him. "You could get the flavor of
Oppen's poetry if you sat down with him some night at his kitchen
table in his flat in San Francisco and just talked. . . .Oppen is a tough
old bird. . . .Oppen has a great eye, precise and irreducible. If you've
never seen what he sees, it is because you haven't sat still long enough
and looked as hard. . . ."

As for Oppen's *Seascape: Needle's Eye*, Rakosi quotes from
"A Morality Play: Preface" and simply says, "see for yourself."

46. McBride, John. Rev. of *Seascape: Needle's Eye*, by George Oppen. *Invisible City*, 8 (April 1973), p. 8.

McBride sees *Seascape: Needle's Eye* as "writing of a new impulse."
The dialectic of the poet's voice "that at once ties to, and tears him
from, the world"—a dialectic that was hinted at in *Discrete Series*—
is given fuller expression in *Seascape*. "*Seascape* goes beyond, including, the early virtues of clarity and definition." McBride finds in

Seascape a new control of prosody: "the distinct advance of these poems is flexible firm lines, linked end to end without confusion." Beyond a few comments such as these, however, this review consists largely of extended quotations from Oppen's book.

47. Dunn, Douglas. "Poetry Chronicle—Mechanics of Misery." *Encounter*, August 1973, pp. 79-80.

Dunn summarizes the history and the basic tenets of Objectivism, and then declares that all "-isms" bore him. But he likes Oppen's poetry, finding in it a "plain, sleek and original dispensing of ordinary words." Dunn also notes in Oppen a determination to (quoting Sartre here) treat words "as things and not as signs"—an enterprise that Dunn connects with Existentialism and Marxism. In Oppen's case the end result is a "poetry virtually uncomplicated by self," but pervaded by a "human concern." But Dunn also (paradoxically!) sees the "absence of personal crisis" in Oppen's poems as a "luxury." Dunn suspects that there may be something a little dishonest, and perhaps something dangerously dogmatic, in a poetry that substitutes the "We" for the "I." Despite these cavils, however, Dunn concludes by labelling Oppen's poetry "important."

48. Katz, Bill. Rev. of *Seascape: Needle's Eye*, by George Oppen. *Library Journal*, 1 Sept. 1973, p. 2446.

This mini-review offers brief praises for *Seascape: Needle's Eye*: "Perhaps no living poet is better at the sparse, direct description of what it means to truly investigate the human condition in all too human surroundings."

49. Homberger, Eric. "Luminous Moral Sense." *London Times Higher Education Supplement*, 14 Sept. 1973.

Briefly tracing Oppen's career from the publication of the British edition of the *Collected Poems*, Homberger describes Oppen as "a complex poet, though he is only rarely obscure." Homberger salutes Oppen's motive of clarity, "the clarity of a thing seen, and known, by a profoundly moral sensibility," but notes that Oppen is a humanist, not a moralist, a man who recognizes that "our basic humanity makes it possible for us to live . . . that imagination is not, in itself, of greater value than life." Oppen is a poet who "refuses the temptations of dogmatism and moral outrage."

Though Oppen himself rather than his *Collected Poems* is the focus of Homberger's attention, the last line of this review announces that "his *Collected Poems* is a remarkable book."

50. Wright, Martin. "George Oppen Collected." *Prospice*, 1 (Nov. 1973), pp. 66-8.

Wright, in reviewing the British edition of the *Collected Poems*, would like an explanation for the five poems left out of *Discrete*

Series, the epigraph and six poems omitted from *The Materials,* the epigraph and five poems omitted from *This In Which,* and the lack of any clear relationship between *Seascape: Needle's Eye* and the section called "Of the Needle's Eye 1968-1969" in the *Collected.* While he does have a quarrel with Fulcrum for their claim to have brought "together [Oppen's] lifetime's work," Wright does not quarrel with the quality of Oppen's work: "His stripped rhetoric allows him a gentle clarity of both sight and insight." Wright does not want "to suggest that Oppen is a philosophic writer as such," but, noting Oppen's use of epigraphs from Maritain and Heidegger, Wright says that "Oppen believes . . . that conceptual knowledge is at worst inadequate, at best misleading, in describing his relation to reality. His poetry insists that physical reality is mysterious and must be apprehended sensuously not rationally."

51. Oliveros, A. "La poesia de George Oppen." *Poesia: Revista de Poesia y Teoria Poética* (Venezuela), 15 (Nov.-Dec. 1973), pp. 46-8.

> Oliveros briefly summarizes Oppen's entire career, and then offers a succinct description of Oppen's poetic method:
>
> > In all the texts the constant formal preoccupation is noticeable: a different form, of extreme verbal economy, where the "contexture" of which Ransom speaks (details and independent attributes which enrich the argument) scarcely exists. The words shape a complex and perfect equilibrium in which the use of adjectives is greatly reduced. The text becomes a kind of linguistic transcription of the object.

52. Plumly, Stanley. Rev. of *Seascape: Needle's Eye,* by George Oppen. *Ohio Review,* 14, 2 (Winter 1973), p. 104.

> "If *Of Being Numerous* was notable for its concreteness," Plumly declares, then *"Seascape: Needle's Eye* . . . is memorable for its symbolic logic." Quoting from "A Mortality Play: Preface," Plumly finds that "the central location of the image is far more ontological than physical—the emotion, to paraphrase Eliot, having become thought." He declares "Some San Francisco Poems" the best of *Seascape:* "a poetry of sequences, attachments, juxtapositions . . . wide on the page, implicative, persuasive. . . ."

53. Rudolph, Anthony. "George Oppen." *European Judaism* (Winter 1973-4), p. 37.

> This short biographical note precedes a printing of "The Book of Job and a draft of a poem in Praise of the Paths of Living." According to Rudolph, "An attentive reading of his work, which includes some of the finest love poems of the century, reveals the involvement with his European and Jewish roots."

54. Davie, Donald. "Notes on George Oppen's *Seascape: Needle's Eye." Grosseteste Review,* 6, 1-4 (1973), pp. 233-9.

This important essay is reprinted in this volume, pp. 407-412.

55. Tomlinson, Charles. "An Introductory Note on the Poetry of George Oppen." *Grosseteste Review*, 6, 1-4 (1973), pp. 240-6.

> The first half of this essay reprints, with minor emendations, Tomlinson's review of *The Materials* (see no. 23 above). Tomlinson then appends a discussion of Oppen's later work:

>> Oppen's later work collected in *This In Which* (1965), *Of Being Numerous* (1968) and *Seascape: Needle's Eye* (1972) has gone on to develop, in its Heideggerian attachment to "the arduous path of appearances," a poetry of metaphysical statement. With their relatively slow pace—urged upon us also by a deliberate capitalisation of the first letter of each line—the later poems have a sobriety and gravity of utterance in keeping with the work of a wise middle age.

> And Tomlinson eloquently sums up the meaning of Oppen's career as a whole:

>> Style as an ethic—here is the continuity with that deliberate bareness of *Discrete Series*. And Oppen, the most human of poets, aware that the stylist (in his sense) is creating his own isolation—for who would not prefer gesture to style?—equates in *Of Being Numerous* poetry with lived life, with life seen in its full human measure—by the man whose refusal of gestures often means solitude.

> In his conclusion, Tomlinson sees Oppen as preserving and extending "Williams' concern for a democracy of language where the smallest units take on a substantial meaning."

56. Rakosi, Carl. "A Note on George Oppen." *Grosseteste Review*, 6, 1-4 (1973), p. 247.

> These brief notes affirm Rakosi's personal admiration for George Oppen. The same notes have also been printed in *Ironwood* 5; in *Paideuma* 10, 1; and in two issues of the *Minneapolis Tribune*: 15 April 1973, and 9 Nov. 1975.

57. Hamburger, Michael. Rev. of *Collected Poems*, by George Oppen. *Agenda*, 11, 2-3 (1973), pp. 92-5.

> This essay has recently been included in a collection of Hamburger's essays, and it is also reprinted in this volume, pp. 413-5.

58. Zweig, Paul. "Making and Unmaking." *Partisan Review*, 2 (1973), pp. 273-6.

> Zweig focusses on the long poem "Of Being Numerous," in this (decidedly belated) review of the volume *Of Being Numerous*. This poem is, Zweig says, a "meditation on the city." Zweig speaks of Kierkegaard and Whitman as defining "the limits within which the poem's meditations probe and develop . . . the two representing opposite illuminations: one the illumination of loneliness, what

Oppen calls 'the bright light of shipwreck,' and the other the illumination of community, the sunlit oneness of buildings." Zweig also focuses on the character of Crusoe: "Crusoe, for Oppen is the perceiver and the poet who knows that strong experience requires separateness, that seeing isolates. . . ." In the end, Zweig judges "Of Being Numerous" as "one of the most important single poems to be written in years."

59. Taggart, John Paul. "Intending a Solid Object: A Study of Objectivist Poetics." Diss. Syracuse University 1974.

Taggart's dissertation elucidates not so much the poetics of Objectivism as the poetics of Louis Zukofsky. Yet Zukofsky was Oppen's chief teacher, and thus Taggart's dissertation should be consulted by serious students of Oppen's work. Taggart also at times mentions Oppen in passing (for example, on pages 105 and 125), and on pages 162 to 164 he offers a useful explication of Oppen's "Carpenter's Boat," from *This In Which*.

60. McKinney, Irene. "Objects and Solitude." *The Trellis Supplement*, Summer 1974, p. 9.

McKinney here reprints a section of "Of Being Numerous," as an example of "the poetry of objects." Her introductory comments praise the "poetry of objects" as a way to "re-establish the vital links between [the self] and the world." But, referring specifically to Rilke, she also expresses concern that a devotion to "objects" may entail an abnormal "solitude." What all this has to do with Oppen isn't very clear.

61. Bowering, George. "George Oppen." *Unmuzzled Ox*, 2, 3 (1974), pp. 67-8.

Bowering's highly personal prose-poem tribute to Oppen, found under the "MISC." heading of this magazine, begins "He stood & said his poems & I sat & I cried in front of him. I sat on the chair & it was solid there." The rest of the story goes something like this: one evening Bowering had a good cry as he listened to George Oppen read poems, placing his "human words . . . one by one on the table." And somehow all this becomes a fine meal for Bowering: "He will not ask you to cry he will ask you to listen. You listen & it is plain as a table on which he places them one by one, a plate you may eat from a fork with which you may lift a piece of meat."

62. Rothenberg, Jerome (ed.). *Revolution of the World: A New Gathering of American Avant Garde Poetry 1914-1945*. (New York: Seabury, 1974), pp. 181-9.

Rothenberg here provides a two paragraph biographical note as introduction to a reproduction of the complete *Discrete Series*. "The work shows . . . a remarkable continuity of attentions—a concern with structure . . . & with the process that informs that structure (the poem as 'a test of truth. . .').'"

63. McAleavey, David. "If to Know is Noble: The Poetry of George Oppen." Diss. Cornell University 1975.

McAleavey's dissertation remains an essential resource for every student of Oppen's work. The introduction places Oppen's work first within the context of the *avant garde*, with its paradoxical struggle to create *tradition* out of the constantly re-initiated search for the *new*, and then (somewhat hesitantly) within the context of Objectivism. The introduction concludes with a brief characterization of Oppen's poetry as built out of a "dialectical" interplay of oppositions.

McAleavey's first chapter begins by reconstructing the aesthetic situation in which Oppen first came to poetry, through an intensive analysis of the book in which Oppen first discovered the "new" American poetry: Conrad Aiken's 1922 anthology, *Modern American Poetry*. In the last half of the chapter, McAleavey examines poems from *An "Objectivist's" Anthology*, the theoretic statements of Zukofsky, and some comments by Rexroth, in an attempt to define the poetic principle that guided the Objectivist movement.

In Chapter Two, McAleavey turns to *Discrete Series*, which he sees as a deliberate effort to confront the two spectres that haunt our century: boredom and sentimentality. Oppen attempts (this, says McAleavey, is the burden of the first poem in *Discrete Series*) to make of boredom a way of knowing the world; and he attempts to avoid sentimentality through a rigorous avoidance of abstraction. In *Discrete Series*, says McAleavey, Oppen made some progress in establishing for himself a useable poetic. But in this book Oppen also "fails somehow as a poet, since he does not locate in poetry sufficient value to keep him writing."

The third chapter of this dissertation focuses on *The Materials*. The opening paragraph sums up the argument of this chapter.

> His first book after long silence, [*The Materials*] documents the presence of hope (in poetry, in history, in humanity) sufficient to inspire him. In part as I shall show this hope is based on a re-assertion of the early Objectivist faith that the world can be directly grasped and man feel himself at home in it. The dynamic of the book, however, and here I am not dealing sequentially with the poems as they are printed, involves a rejection of several approaches to reciprocity or communality as being unrealistic or involving a projection of self *into* the world. The resolution offered in this book is an affirmation of the imagination's ability to put an end to this drifting of consciousness from faith in to doubt of reciprocity. The imagination, Oppen argues, can temporarily enter the present moment, in which experience exists by an acceptance of the bounds and demands of the "material" world. One question Oppen asks throughout, and in later books as well as this, is how to reach a level of reality which is more than merely arbitrary; and yet, attaining the present moment, even temporarily, does not necessarily mean that absolute value has been reached. *The Materials* is the book in which Oppen learns to reject several false solutions and in the process comes to face new formulations of his search for value.

McAleavey's fourth chapter, a discussion of *This In Which*, has been published, in much revised form, in the Oppen issue of *Paideuma* (see item 99 in this bibliography). And much of the material from his fifth chapter, on *Of Being Numerous*, appears in this volume, pp. 381-404. Therefore I shall not summarize these chapters here. The sixth and last chapter seeks, primarily through an examination of Oppen's later work, to define the basic principles of Oppen's prosody:

> In Oppen's newest work we meet a crafted style which uses the form of the letters, the words, the writing on the page to indicate manipulations of sound, pace, cadence, etc. (the oral-aural forms). Form marks form. Furthermore, style and context reinforce each other and form itself seems to create meaning.

McAleavey also finds similar formal principles at work, less ostentatiously, in Oppen's earlier poems, and the chapter as a whole demonstrates that Oppen's poetic ear is at least as finely tuned as those of his masters, Pound and Zukofsky.

64. Andrews, Bruce. "Surface Explanation." *Ironwood*, 5 (1975), pp. 43-9.

Rather than offering us a ratiocinative "explanation" of Oppen's poetry, Andrews remains at the surface of the Oppen text. He gives us a series of prose poems, each of which consists of a collage composed of some phrases from Oppen, interspersed with phrases (*not* sentences) by Andrews himself. Here is a sample:

> Silences filling up everywhere with rumination. The pleasure of carpentering. "That stops . . . We cannot live on that." Synchrony. Look. "Thru the glass" placed end to end with a gesture of a refusal of mortality (or that which is right before us), as references bleed into what comes next and the literal has disfigured the memory. So there is "I want to ask you if you remember. . . When we were happy!" Fallen dancers. "Outside, and so beautiful." Go, there, on the page, with all your eyes.

65. DuPlessis, Rachel Blau. "George Oppen: 'What Do We Believe to Live With?' " *Ironwood*, 5 (1975), pp. 62-77.

DuPlessis is a long-time friend of George and Mary Oppen and a careful reader of George's poetry. Her *Ironwood* essay remains (along perhaps with Dembo's *Iowa Review* article and Taggart's *Occurrence* article) one of the fullest and most valuable early (I would date as early anything before the *Paideuma* special issue) exegeses of Oppen's poetry. The essay begins with some passages from letters written by Oppen to DuPlessis. One such passage offers a powerful summation of Oppen's poetic position:

> There are certain things, appearances, around which the understanding gather[s]. They hold the meanings which make it possible to live, they are one's sense of reality and the possibility of meaning. They are there, in the mind, always. One can sit down anytime and sink into them—can work at them, they come into the mind, they fill the mind—anytime. One tries to pierce them——

> The process by which sometimes a line appears, I cannot trace. It happens. Given a line, one has a place to stand, and goes further—
>
> It is impossible to make a mistake without knowing it, impossible not to know that one has just smashed something—. Unearned words are, in that context, simply ridiculous—. tho it is possible to be carried astray little by little, to find oneself, quite simply, trying to deceive people, to be 'making a poem.' One can always go back, the thing is there and doesn't alter. One's awareness of the world, one's concern with existence— they were not already in words—And the poem is NOT built out of words, one cannot make a poem by sticking words into it, it is the poem which makes the words and contains their meaning. One cannot reach out for *roses* and *elephants* and *essences* and put them in the poem————the ground under the elephant, the air around him, one would have to know very precisely one's distance from the elephant or step deliberately too close, close enough to frighten oneself.
>
> When the man writing is frightened by a word, he may have started.

Building on these quotations from his letters, DuPlessis defines Oppen as a poet "deliberately devoid of certainty and absolutes," a "philosophic poet who distrusts a total intellectual system," yet paradoxically also a poet who "will not reject belief, or stop thinking about belief." As a consequence, "his poetry constantly expresses dilemma—in the original sense of that word: di-lemma or two propositions":

> In his poetry, there is thus an overwhelming sense of oppositions, along with a far more muted sense of a conclusion to any of these opposing issues, unless, as is also possible, one takes the "conclusion" or "resolution" to be no more and no less than the person himself: the man who stands holding those ideas.

DuPlessis traces this interplay of oppositions and this ("muted") search for resolution through each of Oppen's books from *Discrete Series* through *Seascape: Needle's Eye*. In *Discrete Series* the oppositions develop as

> another person or set of people, or objects, intersects with the poet, who attempts to state many of the things that occur to him and the other from both points of view simultaneously. This perspectivism occurs because what is empirically true for the soda jerk, or for the loved one, or for the Hopperesque movie house must be accounted for, as well as what is true for the poet about them.

At some points in *The Materials* and *This In Which*, DuPlessis finds patterns of opposition set up within individual poems ("Philai te kou philai") or between pairs of poems, sometimes poems on facing pages—for example "Chartres" and "The Crowded Countries of The Bomb" in *The Materials*.

However, DuPlessis gives her fullest attention to *Of Being Numerous*, in which she finds two inter-related patterns of opposition:

> The poem "Of Being Numerous" [is] the location of four major propositions, with each pair in a constant internal dialogue. Both dilemmas deal with finding a source of value: one offers a highly

attenuated hope in the people, perhaps the "children" of a
future generation, despite the social atomism and political violence that characterize our time. The other offers hope in the
knowledge of the world which, for Oppen, takes shape as wonder, while resolutely facing the counter-proposition that the
world may baffle the mind. In both pairs of dilemmas, the poet
searches for meaning while simultaneously discussing its negation—respectively the meaninglessness of "numerosity" and the
impossibility of meaning. Hence the impression the poem gives
is a warmth of search and speculation and a stoical paralysis at
the same time.

In her conclusion, DuPlessis notes that

There is an aspect of Oppen which wants to move beyond the
structure of alternatives and the thematic concern for propositions and their negation. He tries to do this . . . by asking what
the *basic* element is which provides some kind of value. He
decides that this basic thing is the natural world itself, whose
presence sometimes allows the poet to voice a belief in something beyond alternatives.

DuPlessis quotes "Psalm" as an example of Oppen's faith in the
natural world, and she then suggests that in Oppen's later work this
movement beyond dialectic toward ontology comes to fruition:

The most memorable fictive landscapes and actions of Oppen's
recent poetry are born from the desire to move beyond the
struggle with alternatives. Having argued, posited, and negated,
he will simply turn his back and move away from the necessity
for this struggle into a beautiful, stark landscape of awe, almost
devoid of man-made objects and certainly empty of a mass of
people.

So, it would seem, this most poignant of our philosophic poets has
come home at last, to an empty but luminous world of pure
presence.

66. Enslin, Theodore. "if it fails." *Ironwood* 5 (1975), pp. 59-61.

Enslin here salutes Oppen as "a conscience of our times, no less a
poetic conscience than a moral one." Reading Oppen, says Enslin,

is like one of those rare days when a man steps outside, and finds
that the sun and air, and he himself are in such agreement that
it is impossible to say where the tips of the fingers end, and the
air around them begins.

To this eloquent metaphor, Enslin appends a no less eloquent anecdote:

Another time, when we were both listening to an open reading
of student poetry—not as gruesome an experience as that can be,
and often is, there was a vague feeling of uneasiness, which I
think many of us shared. George put his finger on it: "They
don't like themselves enough." Oppen lives the life in his poems,
and he lives it well. That is where the poems come from.

67. Fauchereau, Serge. "3 Oppen Letters with a Note." *Ironwood* 5 (1975), pp. 78-85.

At the suggestion of Laughlin, Fauchereau wrote to Oppen asking for information on the history of Objectivism. This request elicited a series of valuable letters. The first letter includes some biographical information and an illuminating paragraph on "truth" in poetry:

> I think it is still true that the weakest work even of the best of the young poets occurs where the poet attempts to drive his mind in *pursuit* of emotion for its own sake, in pursuit of excitement in the conviction that all that is not excitement is insincere.. I would hold that the mere autonomy of the mind or the emotions is mendacity, that all that is not truth or the effort to achieve truth is adulteration. I believe that a poem, if it is indeed poetry, is always revelatory; it is perhaps the inability even to imagine the possibility of a new conception which has created the all-but infinite reduplication of confusion on the order of "a poem must not mean, but *be*."

The first letter concludes with some comments on the history of Objectivism:

> The Objectivists were rather wiped out, weren't they? by the generation of the Academics. The Academics having by now disappeared without a trace, we seem rather to have been stumbled on by the young poets who must have wondered what if anything could have been going on between themselves, that is, between their appearance and Pound, Williams, Eliot and Stevens, who are at least three generations before them.

† † † † † † † † †

> And, as to continuity: it remains my opinion that Reznikoff, Rakosi, Zukofsky, Bunting of Briggflats are the most considerable poets of my own generation.

Fauchereau, encouraged by Oppen, decided to translate some of Oppen's poems into French, and he then sent drafts of these translations to Oppen. Oppen's second letter is largely given over to comments on these draft translations. Oppen recognizes the difficulty which his poems pose to a translator:

> I do indeed know that my poems are difficult to translate. The line sense, the line breaks, and the syntax are intended to control the order of disclosure upon which the poem depends—And the tone, the intention, is often conveyed of course, by the prosody. I had often reflected that the poems might hardly be translatable —I think your translations an excellent job.

Oppen then goes on to propose alternative phrasings for some passages in the translations.

In the third letter Oppen comments at length on the relationship of Objectivism to Imagism and on the distinctively "American" ambience of Objectivism:

> We could say—surely *I* would say—The image for the sake of the poet, not for the sake of the reader. The image as a test of sincerity, as against (tho I may quote inaccurately here): "The sun rose like a red-faced farmer leaning over a fence," which last is a "picture" intended for the delectation of the reader who may be imagined to admire the quaintness and ingenuity of the poet, but

can scarcely have been a part of the poet's attempt to find himself in the world—unless perhaps to find himself as a charming
conversationalist. That quotation, of course, does not represent
the best of Imagism: the weakness of Imagism has been this
affectation and feminine self-love, the strength of Imagism its
demand that one actually *look*. Its strength, in the poem, that
the world stops, but lights up. That lucence, that emotional
clarity, the objectivists wanted, and by that they are related to
Imagism. But not the falsity of ingenuity, of the posed tableau,
in which the poet also, by implication, poses. The image as a
factor of a realistic art, a realist art in that the poem is concerned
with a fact which it did not create.
   As you well say, an American movement. American—when
written by Americans—as a consequence of the definition of
poetry as "ineluctably the direction of historic and personal particulars." (Zukofsky) These distinctions might well justify sub-
suming Bunting under Objectivism—a categorizing to which I am
quite sure he would agree, tho I believe it is quite true that none
of the poets who have regarded themselves to any degree as
Objectivists have resembled each other in their surfaces, their
manner, their lives or in their ultimate concerns as men. I believe
it to be rather sharply distinguished from most of the movements which have had their centers in Paris by this fact.

The Fauchereau letters are (along with the Dembo interview, "The
Mind's Own Place," and the letters quoted by Rachel Blau DuPlessis
in her *Ironwood* article) an essential resource for anyone seeking to
understand Oppen's poetic principles. These samples of Oppen's
letters also serve to whet the appetite for the forth-coming volume
of collected letters by Oppen, which Rachel Blau DuPlessis and Eliot
Weinberger are currently editing.

68. Wakoski, Diane. "The True Art of Simplicity." *Ironwood* 5
     (1975), pp. 31-4.

Wakoski's essay centers on "Route," which she sees as typical of
Oppen's work, in two ways. First, "the gestures of 'Route' are prose
gestures. Yet the effect is poetry. To me, that indicates the uniqueness of a master's voice. He can speak commonly, yet the effect is
uncommon." Second, "Route" "is an existential poem, one acknowledging the relativity principle both in history and in human drama,
and [using] it to try to understand, to see, as it is the poet's function to see." Wakoski adds some broader generalizations:

> Oppen really does embrace a kind of wisdom that can only show
> us that complexity is equal to simplicity. His poetry is neither
> understated or overstated. He has that rare art of saying, simply,
> what he thinks, feels, sees, means, in just a few words. Oppen, at
> his best, makes us see how many Victorian cobwebs are still
> wrapped around both our thinking processes and the language
> which expresses them.

† † † † † † † † †

> George Oppen is a 20th century philosopher who has rejected
> the artifice of 20th century philosophy—its language. He speaks
> of unities, of being, of beginnings, ends, life death and I suppose
> the metaphor we all use today—that poetry is life and that the

poet's vision is what lifts him from the limitations of death—that is, despair.

69. Kenner, Hugh. *A Homemade World: The American Modernist Writers*. (New York: Knopf, 1975), pp. 163-71 & pp. 183-8.

Kenner's book on 20th century American writers includes a chapter on the Objectivists, whom he sees as inheriting and extending the tradition of modernism.

> The Objectivists seem to have been born mature, not to say middle-aged. The quality of their very youthful work is that of men who have inherited a formed tradition: the tradition over the cradle of which, less than twenty years previously, Ezra Pound had hoped to have Henry James, O.M., speak a few sponsoring words.
>
> The work [of the Objectivists] frequently led into systems of small words. "The little words that I like so much," said Oppen, "like 'tree,' 'hill,' and so on, are I suppose just as much a taxonomy as the more elaborate words." This is important; it avoids Hemingway's implication that the small words have a more intrinsic honesty. It is cognate to Mallarmé's famous realization that nothing is producible of which we can say that "flower" is the name. . . .That the word, not anything the word is tied to, is the only substantiality to be discovered in a poem gave Mallarmé ecstatic shivers; to command words' potencies was to oversee magic; to let them take the initiative was to set in motion glitterings "like a trail of fire upon precious stones." Oppen prefers to note that whatever words may be, men cannot survive without them.

Kenner comments specifically on the opening poem of *Discrete Series* ("Often young men affect to be quietly bitter, but not with so geometric a refusal to raise the voice") and on "Psalm":

> —A poem as bare as the street the sheriff walks, past the tied horses, past the bar, past the bank: the street that so nearly does not exist at all, indistinguishable from the wild plain but for board fronts that define it: boards the afternoon wind makes as if to level, and that shelter a few human rites maintained by common agreement, always evanescent. Like the Western camera, the Objectivist poet is the geometer of minima.

Kenner also meditates briefly on the echoes that resonate around the phrase "the edge of a nation" from *Seascape*; he comments at some length on "Song, The Wind of Downhill"; and he ends by suggesting that the Objectivists moved beyond Pound in one way at least:

> . . .*No Myths* might be the Objectivist motto.
> No Myths. It is here that Pound, the all-father, is left behind, and Williams, the Muse's obstetrician, looks as though he'd erred somewhat in his *Paterson* period. For Myths stand between facts and words. They are like "plots" and "statements" and even, lord help us, "messages": units of perception detachable from the language.

70. Taggart, John. "Deep Jewel: George Oppen's *Seascape: Needle's Eye*." *Occurrence* 3 (1975), pp. 26-36.

"These poems . . . possess a surpassing density, a co-ordinate density of syntax surface and of undistracted reflection." So begins Taggart's meditation on *Seascape: Needle's Eye*, and the essay as it proceeds builds systematically on this idea of "density." Taggart contrasts Oppen's "density" to earlier forms of density: the elaborate systems of analogies created by 17th century poets like Marvell, the arid cross-word puzzles of modern would-be imitators of 17th century poetry (Empson, Tate), and the ego-centered density of Pound's *Cantos*.

> My suggestion has been that Oppen's density is somehow distinct, and therefore particularly valuable, from the metaphysical play upon received ideas and from Pound's self-ideogramic method. To be sure, he is much closer to Pound than to Marvell. I think this is because Oppen has chosen to stand fast to the conception of image as center, foundation, and base for composition. Which, if not Pound's original notion, is surely his emphasis. Oppen's task as a poet sympathetic with this emphasis has been to avoid flat out duplication, to turn it to his own use. What he, along with Zukofsky and Williams in their different ways, has successfully attempted is "to construct a method of thought from the imagist technique of poetry—from the imagist intensity of vision."

Oppen's "technique," then, is not new. But Oppen adapts these techniques to a new purpose. To Taggart, the purpose itself is simple: Oppen wants *"to think actively in his poetry"* (Taggart's italics).

> Is this not the true goal, beyond the superficial release from closed metrical writing, of Olson's composition by field, of Duncan's desire that the poem contain all the "incidentals" of its composition process? For if we cannot do this, no matter how fine the style, nothing will be done; poetry will lapse, as it has lapsed with a Swinburne, with a Robert Bridges, with each gentleman's present day equivalents, from its high heuristic function to pinching the cheeks of a perennially debased "beauty."

What distinguishes Oppen from his immediate predecessors is, then, not his technique but "the quality of his mind." And the mind that most resembles Oppen's, Taggart suggests, is that of William Blake. The two share a willingness to "say absolutely anything." They differ, however, in Oppen's refusal to create a synthetic mythic universe. "By his refusal to make such a synthetic construction, Oppen is placed at the disadvantage of continually refinding his 'subject' in each new poem." The refusal to create a mythic system also makes Oppen (unlike Blake, who "has all the answers") a "tragic" poet. In *Seascape: Needle's Eye*, Oppen is, as always, "beginning again," says Taggart. And the poems in this book represent a new departure for Oppen in at least one important respect. In the earlier books ellipses serve to remind us that "something has been left out—that for all his sincerity he is still involved with artifice." But "the ellipse becomes a literal space gap in the *Seascape* poems":

> Where there once were ellipses, gaps of white space, "silence," now exist. Does this mean anything? I think it does: a further move toward the substantive, the atomization of facts' totality now laid down like the giant stones of Macchu Picchu, no mortar

between them, only a few verbs of being remaining here and there. Poets as opposed as Frost and Pound are agreed that the sentence is a form of power. When you alter syntax out of recognizable subject-verb-object orders, you run the risk of losing that torque-torsion energy transfer that Fenollosa long ago perceived as grammar's replication of the whole physics of nature.

†††††††††

The advantage of a near verbless poetry is solidity. And the snare of the poem become solid object is that it may actually become just that, an object—voiceless box—stuck in the three dimensional statue space of unvisited public parks. What saves Oppen from this objectivist trap is, again, his mind, his voice as his mind's agent, insistent to state the truth.

†††††††††

There is another factor which prevents Oppen's poetry from turning into so much verbal masonry: the reader. If you are to read him at all, it must be done actively, yourself involved in the statement's gradual composition: otherwise, it can make no sense. This involvement means that the reader necessarily contributes to the poem's final density.

These comments seem as illuminating as anything yet written on Oppen's later work. All in all, Taggart's article must be ranked as one of the most useful essays on Oppen published to date.

71. Perlberg, Mark. "Shorthand." *Poetry*, June 1975, p. 172.

Perlberg has trouble with *Seascape: Needle's Eye*. "So involved is George Oppen's book with a kind of gnomic reticence, that it moves toward silence. . . .With the exception of a few brief, vivid passages, these highly condensed, elliptical poems remain a private shorthand that rarely leaves the page."

72. Kenner, Hugh. "Collected Poems." *New York Times Book Review*, 19 Oct. 1975, p. 5.

Kenner salutes the publication of *Collected Poems*. After briefly reviewing Oppen's career, Kenner offers some general comments on the poetry. In particular he emphasizes Oppen's sense of craft: "As the wood acquires its meaning from the craftsman . . . so the poem, according to Oppen, isn't the sum of virtuous words but is what confers upon the words their virtue (Who'd care about the word 'nightingale' save for Keats?)." Kenner also emphasizes the "clean-cut silences" of Oppen: "Nothing better characterizes Oppen than this wariness about language itself, this distrust of inherent fluency."

73. Rakosi, Carl. Rev. of *Collected Poems*, by George Oppen. *Minneapolis Tribune*, 9 Nov. 1975.

Quoting extensively from his own earlier review of *Seascape: Needle's Eye*, Rakosi is still intrigued with Oppen the man. *Collected Poems* makes clear for Rakosi Oppen's "extraordinary integration of his personality, its inner and outer consistency," as well as the "intense, unremitting condensation" in Oppen's poems. Rakosi again emphasizes Oppen's "precise and irreducible" eye, his "honesty," and the fact that he is "always deeply serious in the existential sense; and never ingratiating." Rakosi quotes "A Narrative," taking liberties with Oppen's punctuation and spacing, as well as #29 from "Of Being Numerous."

74. Oppenheimer, Joel. "Support Your Local Poet." *Village Voice*, 22 Dec. 1975, p. 46.

Oppenheimer is here recommending volumes of poetry fine enough for "gifting." Oppen's *Collected Poems* is included in the "bumper crop of good books," but Oppen receives only a sentence or two of attention: he is offered us as "master craftsman . . . [who's] got a profound sense of the place and function of the poet in this country. . . ."

75. Heller, Michael. Rev. of *Seascape: Needle's Eye*, by George Oppen. *American Poetry Review*, 4, 2 (March/April, 1975), pp. 1-4.

This extended essay on *Seascape: Needle's Eye* is reprinted in this volume, pp. 417-28.

76. Ehrenpreis, Irvin. "The State of Poetry." *New York Review of Books*, 22 Jan. 1976, pp. 3-4.

In reviewing *Collected Poems*, Ehrenpreis first summarizes Oppen's general methods and motives. Oppen's "discreteness," plain language, and "constant re-employment of his own phrases" are discussed as supportive of "the main drama of Oppen's work, which is the effort of the mind to reach clarity of vision. . . .Honesty, clarity, illumination, are his *desiderata*." Ehrenpreis, finally, criticizes Oppen for his "sparseness." "The elliptical character of his style barely distinguishes it from the cryptic. . . .I wonder whether by resisting the lure of abundance he has not been left with a style that is pinched and thin."

77. Harris, Katheryn Gibbs. Rev. of *Collected Poems*, by George Oppen. *Library Journal*, 1 March 1976, p. 721.

A single paragraph acknowledgement of the publication of *Collected Poems*: Oppen's "distinctive voice is slender, contains great leaps and stretches of mind, and is shown in this collection to be entirely worthwhile as poem."

78. Booth, Martin. "Gods, Roots, and Poetic Violences." *London Tribune*, 22 March 1976, p. 7.

> In Booth's opinion, *Collected Poems* "establishes Oppen, one feels, as the longest-lasting and best of his 'objectivist' school of poetry." Booth has little room in the scant 2 paragraphs of his review to speak of Oppen's poetry in anything but general terms: "His poetry seeks to provide a link between the obvious and the emotive, and language is the link." And Booth acknowledges "the massive influence Oppen and William Carlos Williams have had upon modern verse."

79. Galassi, Jonathan. Rev. of *Collected Poems*, by George Oppen. *Poetry*, Dec. 1976, pp. 164-8.

> In this review of *Collected Poems*, Galassi describes Oppen's lines as moving "in fits and starts; they are slowly accrued 'discrete series' of phrases, chains of associations which aim directly, often painfully, at an identifiable point." He continues, "The lesson, the articulation of a meaning, is what matters. Words, imperfect and sometimes untrustworthy, are only the means to this end." Galassi describes Oppen's tone as "openly, even severely didactic," but he also finds there "pure word-pictures." Further, he finds Oppen's work, his "fragmentary approach, his moral certitude, his conception of the poet's task" to resonate "more and more profoundly the longer we spend with it."

80. Kimbrell, Allen. *"Of Being Numerous by George Oppen." The Mysterious Barricades*, 4 (Winter 1976), pp. 97-100.

> In a dense, intense, elliptical prose, Kimbrell nominates Oppen as the only true heir of Pound. Pound, says Kimbrell, engaged in a "surgery of transplants":
>
> > His assault on the duration of tradition, a critical battle in the war of modernism, had as its program the simultaneity of all authentic culture, the recovery of that tradition as anti-tradition, the mechanical reproduction of literature. Though he sought to remake the ideologies of past discourse, to reconverse, as if drama was greater than life, his poems relived the past with the objects of sense transcendent, the brackets of use-value shattered.
>
> But Zukofsky and Williams, seduced by the "latent necrophilia" of the "cult of tradition," or by the "eunuch-like logic of the positivists" and "the Wittgenstein fetish for predicates," retreated from Pound's radical position. Thus,
>
> > Only Oppen, of all of them, has survived the purge, the banishment of history to the classroom, the stasis of form which is death, the anomaly of the artless mystic, the critic as seer.
>
> Kimbrell associates Oppen with Weston and Hopper: artists who "refuse to defraud the senses," whose fidelity to what is *there* "allows no evasions." Oppen firmly refuses to predicate a "humanity"

that he cannot verify on his senses: "the meaning 'of being nume-rous' . . . still [lies] in the darkness beyond." Yet "Oppen's great art, his long, blue voyage, abides, evidence that the light men read by was never extinguished." In "Of Being Numerous," Oppen tells the nurse who attends the dying man, "You are the last/Who will know him." But, says Kimbrell, "that 'You are the last/Who will know him . . .' the poetry itself denies." And Kimbrell's essay concludes with a resounding ecomium:

> But from the pantheon of poets we know as great, already reced-ing into myth, or worse, tradition, Oppen almost alone survives the distance. His poems, somehow, are truly coeval with the con-tent of our consciousness today and affirm at their root of lan-guage the meaning whose absence consumes them.

81. Corman, Cid. "Together." *Parnassus*, Spring-Summer 1976, pp. 83-95.

Corman doesn't see much use in talking *about* Oppen's poetry. Instead he wants to tell the reader to "Look, Look, Look" at the poetry itself. His essay is therefore largely given over to long quota-tions from Oppen's poems. Corman intersperses among the quota-tions some quotable aphorisms. Here are a few of these:

> Oppen has a transparent faith—an active confidence—a loyalty to—his word—which is—as he realizes—ours too. "I was thinking about a justification of human life, eventually, in what I call the life of the mind." He joins Stevens at this point. But where Stevens—in his own version of the romantic—improvises and brings off remarkable cadenzas—Oppen prefers to try to see closer to find his leverage—as metaphysical Archimedes—towards spiritual community.

††††††††††

> Oppen often repeats words—not for mere effect ever—but as if he were literally discovering the sense in them and he were startled by it.

And of the disrupted syntax of "Birthplace," Corman says,

> Nevermind—O academic grammarian—the syntax that demands one's remaking. It is precisely there we enter and share feeling.

82. Pevear, Richard. "Poetry and Worldlessness." *Hudson Review*, 29, 2 (Summer 1976), pp. 317-20.

Pevear here devotes four closely-argued pages to Oppen. Pevear rejects the idea that Oppen's is an "empirical" poetics, "based on the primacy of sight, of seeing." Even in the much discussed "Psalm," Pevear finds "nothing *seen*." Rather, "Psalm"

> is a poem about words, and its real effort is to name not the deer but *that in which* they "startle, and stare out," which is not the forest or the night or nature herself, which cannot be perceived phenomenally but can be realized only by the human mind, and

then only through the mediation of words. The expérience is felt as a kind of seeing, but the perception is of what is most fugitive and fleeting; "alien" and "strange" are the words Oppen associates with it.

Rather than affirming the primacy of the visual, Oppen's poetry instead seeks, says Pevear, to accomplish

one of the beginning tasks of poetry: the holding open of the common world, the place of humanity. He is a civic poet, as Solon was a civic poet; but without a *polis*, and that is the modern aspect of his work.

† † † † † † † † †

The profound and unexpected originality of Oppen's poetry lies in its construing of the relationships between perception ("virtue of the mind") and the opening of a public realm, a *polis*, a place for humanity, in which humanity transcends mass isolation. For, contrary to the views of most politicians, and perhaps most political thinkers, the public thing is not grounded in opinion, in consensus, in theory, in state power or institutions, but in "the right construction of what-is." Those words are a paraphrase from Hölderlin, who also wrote: "Poets, even the spiritual ones, must be worldly." A poet's work belongs to the world, but before that it is an opening up of the common, of what-is for humanity. Before it is speech, poetry is a space prepared for speech . . . Works of that kind do not only belong to the world, they enact the "worlding" of the world.

In the last pages of his discussion, Pevear shows how "Chartres," "Of Being Numerous," and "Eros" enact the " 'worlding' of the world" and reveal to us that "both the singular and the numerous are negations of the common, the political, open space constituted by a plurality of singular acts."

83.   Auster, Paul. "Private I, Public Eye." *Bookletter*, 3, 11 (31 Jan. 1977), pp. 12-3.

Paul Auster opens his review of *Collected Poems* with praise: "George Oppen is a simple poet. In some sense, to read his work is to be forced to learn it . . . one is hardly prepared for the nakedness of Oppen's language—for a syntax that seems to derive its logic as much from the silences around the words as from the words themselves." From his admiration of Oppen's language, Auster turns with equal admiration to Oppen's philosophy: "His work begins at a point beyond the certainty of absolutes, beyond any prearranged or inherited system of values, and attempts to move toward some common ground of belief. . . .The locus is always the natural world, and the process is one that originates in the perception of objects beyond ourselves, in the primal act of seeing." Auster is particularly interested in the "act of seeing" and its implications for Oppen, the "public poet," "for his concern is less with event than with feeling, with concern itself and the obligation to see 'That which one cannot/Not see.' But *seeing* in his poetry is not simply a physical act; it implies a moral commitment as well. And the moment one posits

the necessity of seeing the world . . . of entering it—one must be prepared to take one's stand among other men. As a consequence,
speech belongs to the realm of ethics. Oppen's awareness of this consequence gives his work a luster of maturity that few lyric poets
achieve."

84. Homberger, Eric. *The Art of the Real: Poetry in England
    and America since 1939.* (London: Dent, 1977), p. 102,
    p. 116, p. 180, pp. 203-4.

> Homberger mentions Oppen as a poet who "came in from the cold"
> in the 1950s and as an associate of Williams and of Tomlinson. He
> also suggests that in some fashion *Discrete Series* looks forward to
> later examples of the serial poem, such as Berryman's *Dream Song*
> and Lowell's *Notebook.*

85. Almon, Bert. Rev. of *Collected Poems*, by George Oppen.
    New Orleans Review, 5, 4 (1978), pp. 371-3.

> The review yokes together an odd couple: Oppen and Robert Penn
> Warren. Almon reviews Oppen's career and exposes a preference for
> the later poems over *Discrete Series*, because in these later poems,
> although "he still wants circumstances to speak for themselves,"
> nevertheless he now "often enters the poems as a questioning or
> evaluative voice." Almon praises Oppen's "critique of American
> life," but he complains of a certain "stylistic monotony" in Oppen's
> work, which also seems to him ridden with "frequent echoes of
> Williams." "Most of [Oppen's] themes can be found readily in
> Williams' *Paterson* or the work of other Objectivists," says Almon,
> and in his conclusion he makes clear his preference for Warren over
> Oppen.

86. Enslin, Theodore. "Of What is Prime and Primal: Considera-
    tions of George Oppen's *Primitive.*" *American Book Review*,
    March-April 1979, pp. 6-7.

> Enslin's essay on *Primitive* is reprinted, with some revision, in this
> volume, pp. 445-8.

87. Altieri, Charles. "The Objectivist Tradition." *Chicago Review*,
    30, 3 (Winter 1979), pp. 5-22.

> Altieri here mentions Oppen by name only in passing. Yet this
> essay is important to an understanding of Oppen's work because
> Altieri here extends to the Objectivists his influential theory (for
> examples of this influence, cf. the essay in this volume by DuPlessis,
> as well as my essay on *The Materials*) that we can distinguish two
> distinct traditions in 20th century American poetry. In *Enlarging
> the Temple* (Lewisburg: Bucknell Univ. Press, 1979) Altieri called
> these traditions "immanentist" and "symbolist." But in this essay

he changes his key terms, and speaks instead of "symbolist" and "objectivist" styles. But the content of these two categories remains the same:

> [Symbolist styles] stress in various ways the mind's powers to interpret concrete events or to use the event to inquire into the nature or grounds of interpretive energies, while objectivist strategies aim to "compose" a distinct perceptual field which brings "the rays from an object to a focus." Where objectivist poets seek an artifact presenting the modality of things seen or felt as immediate structure of relations, symbolist poets typically strive to see beyond the seeing by rendering in their work a process of mediating upon what the immediate relations in perception reflect.

(Compare Altieri's early definitions of "symbolist" and "immanentist" poetic methods, as quoted in my essay in this volume, pp. 325-57.) Altieri's new terminology has one important consequence: it implicitly recognizes that Reznikoff, Zukofsky, and Oppen are the true heirs of Pound and the chief link between Pound and the Black Mountain poets, within what I would call the "alternative tradition" in 20th century American poetry.

88. Taggart, John. "The New Primitive." *Chicago Review*, 30, 3 (Winter 1979), pp. 148-51.

Taggart begins by defining the precise inflection of "primitive," as Oppen uses the word in the title of his most recent book: "Not primitive as unskilled in the use of tools, but the *new* primitive: one who would put aside tools and the skills acquired over a lifetime to come upon the universe as if for the first time, who would come to language and the writing of poems as if for the first time." Taggart then proposes that the book centers on two kinds of light: the "light within the commonplace things of the external world," and "the light within the conscious self, the mind, or within poetry as an event or construction of language, which is understood as an invention of the mind." The "internal" light, by itself, can be dangerous: language may "pervert what is to be seen and acted upon," and the internal light can lull us "into a false beatific slumber." Thus in *Primitive* Oppen seeks to bring these two kinds of light together. In the poems collected in this volume, we usually

> begin with . . . literal things found in the external world and proceed through the act of discovery involved with these things to come upon images that build to poems yielding still more images, which culminate in a revelation of condition. This revealed condition, the results of vision and not sociology, implies the recognition of others and the connected need for action "in" that condition rather than in poetry.

89. Goldblatt, Eli. "Notes on Some Matters at Hand." *Paper Air*, 2, 3 (1979), pp. 59-61.

Goldblatt devotes a paragraph to the assertion that "two neglected intensities in George Oppen's poems are his political commitments and his determination to speak accepting a spiritual presence." The political commitment of the Oppens is demonstrated, Goldblatt implies, by the fact that they "joined the Party in the '30's because, as they have said, 'Simply, nobody else was doing anything about the situation for workers.' " The spiritual presence, although unnamed, is said to be "around and about" even though Oppen's poems "are never directly about politics or spirit."

90. Lake, Paul. "George Oppen's *Primitive.*" *Occident*, 100, 1 (Spring 1980), pp. 49-52.

Lake sees *Primitive* as marking a new stage in Oppen's pursuit of a language that is absolutely poetic. Here this quest leads Oppen to discard even the conventions of "orderly syntax and punctuation." Lake expresses some ambivalence about this poetic method. Lake admires some of the poems in *Primitive*:

> What results when the poetry is successful is a language whose rapid transitions allow perception to follow on the heel of perception, the reader not so much filling in the gaps with the logic of normal syntax as submitting himself to an alogical form of discourse with its own unexpected felicities and idiosyncratic grace.

However, he finds some of the poems intolerably obscure:

> Not surprisingly, however, this radically disjunctive style is not always successful, and frequently results in verse that is as cryptic and tantalizingly fragmentary as the barely discernible lines on a tattered palimpsest.

After his opening discussion of *Primitive*, Lake moves on to a more general assessment of Oppen's poetic position, in the attempt to trace to its source Oppen's "disjunctive" style. In his attempt to build upon the imagist method, Lake argues, Oppen was beguiled into "a serious misapprehension of the nature of language"—specifically,

> a static model of language in which poetic "terms" follow one another like beads on a string rather than being integrated into the larger, more dynamic patterns produced by verbal discourse. Oppen has, in effect, created a poetics of the noun.

This "poetics of the noun" is, Lake argues, privatistic: imagism (as Oppen himself said in a letter to Fauchereau) "for the sake of the poet, not for the sake of the reader." Yet there are, Lake points out, "apparent contradictions between the seemingly privatistic aesthetic underlying the poetry, and the poet's own political activism in the public realm." Lake states that this "apparent contradiction" is "resolved" if we see Oppen, not as a "Marxist in the European sense," but rather as a Populist. He therefore argues at length that the Oppens were drawn to the Communist Party not by an interest in the ramifications of Marxist theory but rather by a simple desire to do something about hunger and unemployment. That the Oppens' politics place them in a native American Populist tradition seems clear enough. Yet a "privatistic" aesthetic seems no less incompatible with a Populist politics than with a Marxist politics. The contradiction remains; and it is a real, not merely an "apparent" contradiction. On this point there seems to be a major gap in Lake's argument.

In his conclusion, however, Lake seems to reverse himself, and to recognize that perhaps the strength of Oppen's poetry arises precisely from his *refusal* to resolve the contradiction here at issue—i.e., from his determination to remain faithful to the rigors of his poetic method, while simultaneously refusing to write off "the people": "Whatever difficulties Oppen's poetry might offer, the fidelity of his verse both to his rather austere aesthetic and to the community it addresses is both rare and admirable." To which one can only say, Amen.

91. Auster, Paul. "A Few Words in Praise of George Oppen." *Paideuma*, 10, 1 (Spring 1981), pp. 49-52.

> Auster here condenses and revises his 1977 review of *Collected Poems* (see no. 83 above).

92. Corman, Cid. "The Experience of Poetry." *Paideuma*, 10, 1 (Spring 1981), pp. 99-103.

> Corman here meditates on three poems from *Primitive*: "A Political Poem," "Walking Who Knows," and "The Natural." In these poems Corman finds the "directness of an exploring sensibility." There is nothing to say *about* these poems, says Corman. "Like so much of Dr. Williams' poetry, [Oppen's poetry] mutes professors." Rather than "trying to analyze what is going on" in Oppen's poetry, our goal should be to "move with it":
>
> > George often tends to feint with his language; that is—as in the uses of "nothing" in this poem—expections fall into the trite, but only to alter it beyond triteness. Which forces us—if we stay with the words at all—to attend more acutely.

93. Cuddihy, Michael. "George Oppen: A Loved and Native Rock." *Paideuma*, 10, 1 (Spring 1981), pp. 25-6.

> Cuddihy comments briefly on Oppen's "extraordinary reticence," on the political dimension of his poetry, and on "the depth of his . . . feelings, his concern for people."

94. DuPlessis, Rachel Blau. "Oppen and Pound." *Paideuma*, 10, 1 (Spring 1981), pp. 59-83.

> A retitled and extensively revised version of this essay appears in this volume, pp. 123-48.

95. Gerber, Dan. "Of Fathers." *Paideuma*, 10, 1 (Spring 1981), pp. 149-51.

Gerber here places Oppen with Wordsworth, Hardy, Whitman, Rilke, and Sherwood Anderson in the gallery of Gerber's own poetic fathers. Gerber professes little interest in the "poetry of objects"; but Oppen, he contends, "has made the poem his object, an artifact which gives consciousness and breath" to the things of this world. Thereby, says Gerber, Oppen actually affirms, "with the Buddhists that all inanimate objects expound the *dharma* (the teachings) because they expound the mind that perceives them as well as the mind that created them."

96. Heller, Michael. "For George Oppen." *Paideuma*, 10, 1 (Spring 1981), pp. 143-7.

Heller offers a poem of his own, and then describes the chain of reflection that led him to discover Oppen's presence within the poem in question. He then moves to a celebration of "the kind of example which George set":

> He had made it clear through his work that the contemporary poet's major thrust involved an exposure of the received knowledge of one's time. This was the underlying thematic unity of his work, perhaps most clearly stated and developed in "Of Being Numerous" where George lays bare, possibly more clearly than in any other 20th century poem, the failed strands of *communitas*, of our so-called social ethic. And in the act of doing this, he had fulfilled the most ancient of poetic tasks, that of actually unifying the community. "Of Being Numerous" was a massive clearing of the air of bankrupt and sentimental talk of unity, and an opening up of the possibility of a community built on the acknowledgement of our own and each other's awareness of our aloneness.

97. Hunting, Constance. " 'At Least Not Nowhere': George Oppen as Maine Poet." *Paideuma*, 10, 1 (Spring 1981), pp. 53-8.

Hunting first comments on Oppen as "a traveler, a wanderer," responding to New York and San Francisco and Chartres. She then discusses his response to Maine in "Product," "Penobscot," "Ballad," and "Workman."

98. Linenthal, Mark. "An Appreciation." *Paideuma*, 10, 1 (Spring 1981), pp. 37-8.

Linenthal pays homage to Oppen first as teacher and mentor, and then as poet. Linenthal finds in Oppen's poetry "a unique combination of quick lightness of movement and an intensity of concentration":

> The lightness, I think, comes from the constant shift of attention between the word and what it points to, from a process both sceptical and assertive, from the sense of search, of words in motion, or words seeking their connections within and beyond the poem. The concentration or intensity of the poetry, its weight, comes from an abstemiousness, a plain speaking, a determination to say (and say only) what is so for him.

In his conclusion, Linenthal briefly notes the stultifying effects of the New Critical model of the "invulnerable" poem, grounded upon "a clear personal identity, a developed ego," and he proposes Oppen's work as an alternative model. The theories of the New Criticism, Linenthal says,

> made for a highly constructed kind of writing, a poetry of elaborately metaphorical statement to be decoded in the classroom. In time the developed ego upon which so much depended came to seem arbitrary and officious, determined to have its way and to prove itself right in all circumstances. Those of my generation who managed to find their way to the work of Oppen and some of the other Objectivists discovered a sudden freshness, a poetry of language rather than statement, a rendering of experience which keeps the process of rendering in view, authentic personal presence among the circumstances of its unfolding.

99. McAleavey, David. "Unrolling Universe: A Reading of Oppen's *This In Which*." *Paideuma*, 10, 1 (Spring 1981), pp. 105-28.

This essay, adapted from McAleavey's dissertation, explores at some length the modalities of the self/world relationship in *This In Which*. In *The Materials*, McAleavey contends, Oppen had proposed the possibility of a union between the self and the world, in an unmediated world of pure presence. In *This In Which*, McAleavey then suggests, Oppen's

> chief desire remains that of achieving an immediate, reciprocal relation with the world. The difference is that in the later book this desire is seen to be insatiable: Oppen feels he cannot reconcile self-consciousness with his desire for reciprocity with the world.
> Instead he examines the quandary he is in, the *this in which*, impartially, voicing his own dilemma as clearly as he can. Basically, Oppen is torn between two concerns. One is an examination of the self's attempts to confront and understand existence. The other involves a search for a causal explanation of consciousness, an historical, not an "existential" search. Both concerns are motivated by a wish for meaning, and Oppen lets them compete; both are defeated because Oppen can let neither be successful.
> This is what gives his work its authority and even its healing power: passionately contesting the rift between the world and what consciousness wants to know makes that rift less painful.

McAleavey then develops this general thesis through a meticulous examination of many individual poems in *This In Which*, including "Technologies," "Vertigo," "Eros," "Monument," "Giovanni's *Rape of the Sabine Women* at Wildenstein's," "Guest Room," "A Narrative," "The Mayan Ground," "The People, The People," "Rationality," "Penobscot," and "Philai te kou philai."

100. Powell, Donald. " 'At the Time of the Rogue's First Flood'— A Life, Together." *Paideuma*, 10, 1 (Spring 1981), pp. 141-2.

Powell here muses briefly upon the mystery at the center of Oppen's work: the mystery of his relationship with Mary.

101. Silliman, Ron. "Third Phase Objectivism." *Paideuma*, 10, 1 (Spring 1981), pp. 85-9.

> The revival of Objectivism in the 1960s was, Silliman argues, a pivotal moment in literary history. This period saw some important achievements by the major Objectivists. Zukofsky returned to *"A"* after an interval of almost a decade, and brought the work to completion; Bunting published *Briggflatts*; and Oppen wrote a body of verse that far exceeds in quantity all his previously published work. Silliman then proposes that Oppen's work from the 1960s differs not only in quantity but in kind from the poetry he had written during the first phase of the Objectivist movement. Specifically, in Oppen's later works he "has demonstrated himself to be a master in calling attention to *the importance of what the poem says*"—as opposed to what Williams, in his review of *Discrete Series*, had called the "poem as a mechanism." In shifting emphasis from the poem as mechanism to the poem as a means of communicating meaning, Oppen opened up what Silliman calls a " 'middle road' half-way between the New American writers and those academics who'd moved on their own toward a poetry founded on speech." Silliman suggests that Oppen's Objectivist past enabled him to show more traditional poets a better way to foreground "what the poem says." In this respect Oppen is a "bridge-poet" whose influence "restructures the entire field of American verse." Yet Silliman also seems to sense in Oppen's "third phase Objectivism" a retreat from the radicalism of "first phase Objectivism."

102. Sorrentino, Gilbert. "George Oppen: Smallness of Cause." *Paideuma*, 10, 1 (Spring 1981), pp. 23-4.

> Sorrentino here discusses the "exquisite," "almost 'depthless' " metaphor on which "From a Photograph" turns—the metaphor which defines the child as the "branch" from which the parents "fall."

103. Weinberger, Eliot. "A Little Heap for George Oppen." *Paideuma*, 10, 1 (Spring 1981), pp. 131-6.

> In a series of brief, eloquent notes, Weinberger comments on such topics as Oppen's New Rochelle roots, his wit, his political years, his experience as a soldier, his status as a "literary exile," his concern with walls, his eroticism, his use of pauses, and his insistence on writing out of his own experience. Weinberger rejects the notion that Oppen was an "Objectivist." And he ends his tribute with an extraordinary collage of phrases culled from Oppen's poems, all turning in some way on the words "small" or "little."

104. Finkelstein, Norman M. "Political Commitment and Poetic Subjectification: George Oppen's Test of Truth." *Contemporary Literature*, 22, 1 (Winter 1981), pp. 24-41.

> Oppen's poetry, Finkelstein argues, begins in an attempt to achieve a "loss of subjective consciousness in the diffusion of objective reality," but it never actually achieves this goal. And when the "object" perceived demands a moral response from the viewer, the limits of such a poetic method become apparent, as some of the poems in *Discrete Series* reveal. Thus when Oppen encountered a situation (Depression America) which demanded a moral and political response, his Objectivist method did not offer him a way to articulate such a response. So he gave up poetry instead. In short, "*Discrete Series* is the culmination and dissolution of extreme objectivist poetry, in which the moral impetus of the objectivist stance confronts the boundaries beyond which the aesthetic it demands cannot go."
>
> However, "When Oppen resumes his poetic career in the late fifties, a decidedly new note enters his work: the poems are imbued with a new sense of subjectivity." In some measure Oppen's new poetic procedure follows the example set by Williams, but "Oppen modifies Williams' poetics in order to establish a style of lyric poetry in which the object and the subject's reaction to the object totally interpenetrate, thus resolving the conflict he encountered at the outset of his career." The result is a poetry which gives powerful expression to "the unending conflict between desire and the insufficient or repressive social formations that desire must endure. . . ." Finkelstein traces the development of this conflict from *The Materials* through its culmination in *Of Being Numerous*, which centers on "the shipwreck/Of the singular":

>> The result of this "shipwreck" is actually the entrance into an ideological no man's land where the inadequacy and alienation of capitalist social relations are recognized, but a genuinely communistic vision remains problematic. Such a crisis of faith is oddly reminiscent of those experienced by the Victorian poets, such as Arnold in "Stanzas from the Grande Chartreuse" and Tennyson, who must move through a series of tortuous meditations in the lengthy *In Memoriam* before he achieves spiritual reconciliation. Oppen too must move in such a manner, and it is the cumulative power of the series poem that allows him to consider the many possibilities of the people's "numerosity" without entirely losing his faith to his omnipresent skepticism.

> To Finkelstein, Oppen's fusion of "politics, philosophy, and poetics" is "an achievement unmatched in contemporary verse"; and he salutes Oppen himself as a hero:

>> Oppen's struggle to achieve a sense of identity with the people is heroic, and such heroism is congruent with a poetic tradition in which the poet-hero's greatest act is the dissolution of the self into the greater selfhood of community.

> Yet he also admires Oppen for his willingness to leave this struggle unresolved:

In a sense, the dialectic remains unresolved, for the struggle constantly renews itself, as consciousness yearns for its object, and the people yearn for a way of life whose outlines, in the midst of change, can hardly be articulated. The hope of the future, the new generation, remains forever in question, but this recognition is itself a major advance, an implicit reconciliation of Oppen's political and poetic identities.

In the elliptical late poems, Oppen's openness, Finkelstein notes in conclusion, continues and expands. Behind these poems stand Pound "as an *eminence grise*," and in poems like "To the Poets: To Make Much of Life" Oppen "follows Pound and Williams into what has become a modernist tradition, the next realm of light that stands for the overwhelming strength of immediate experience." In such moments, Finkelstein adds "what seems to be the entire objectivist endeavor dissolves into the greater poetic tradition, as if a purely poetic reality could for once assert itself over Oppen's resolute grasp of tangible experience."

INDEX OF PEOPLE, TITLES, AND MOVEMENTS

Compiled by Cathleen Bauschatz and Paul Vatalaro

WORKS OF GEORGE OPPEN

BOOKS

POEMS

ESSAYS

LETTERS

INTERVIEWS